Direct Effect of WTO Agreements: Practices and Arguments

European University Studies
Europäische Hochschulschriften
Publications Universitaires Européennes

Series II
Law

Reihe II Série II
Rechtswissenschaft
Law

Vol./Bd. 5284

PETER LANG
Frankfurt am Main · Berlin · Bern · Bruxelles · New York · Oxford · Wien

Ching-Wen Hsueh

Direct Effect of WTO Agreements: Practices and Arguments

PETER LANG
Internationaler Verlag der Wissenschaften

Bibliographic Information published by the Deutsche Nationalbibliothek
The Deutsche Nationalbibliothek lists this publication in the Deutsche Nationalbibliografie; detailed bibliographic data is available in the internet at http://dnb.d-nb.de.

Zugl.: Köln, Univ., Diss., 2011

D 38
ISSN 0531-7312
ISBN 978-3-631-62227-8

www.peterlang.de

Preface

In winter semester 2011/2012, this book was adopted as doctoral dissertation by Faculty of Law, University of Cologne. First, I would like to thank my doctoral father, Professor Dr. Stephan Hobe, for his guidance and great supports to my dissertation as well as my studies in University of Cologne. Also, I would express my appreciations for the advice from Professor Dr. Bernhard Kempen, who served as the second examiner of my dissertation. Last but not the least, I would like to show my gratitude to Professor Dr. Chang-Fa Lo, the Honorable Justice of the Constitutional Court (Taiwan). If he hadn't lead me to the fields of international economic law, I would not have the chance to write this book.

Ching-Wen Hsueh, 25.10.2011

Table of Contents

Abbreviations

ADP	Anti-dumping Agreement
GATT	General Agreement on Tariffs and Trade
GATS	General Agreements on Trade in Services
GPA	Agreement on Government Procurement
DSU	Understanding on Rules and Procedures Governing the Settlement of Disputes
DSB	Dispute Settlement Body
EEC	Treaty Establishing the European Economic Community
ICJ	International Court of Justice
Marrakesh Agreement	Marrakesh Agreement Establishing the World Trade Organization
PCIJ	Permanent Court of International Justice
SCM	Agreements on Subsidies and Countervailing Measures
SG	Agreement on Safeguards
SPS	Agreement on the Application of Sanitary and Phytosanitary Measures
TBT	Agreement on Technical Barriers to Trade
TFEU	Treaty on the Functioning of the European Union
TRIM	Trade Policy Review Mechanism
TRIPS	Agreement on Trade-Related Aspects of Intellectual Property Rights

Introduction

0.1. Origin and Purposes of the Research

Paragraph 4 of the Article XVI of the Marrakesh Agreement Establishing the World Trade Organization (the Marrakesh Agreement) requires members to fulfill their obligations under the WTO agreements. It provides, "Each Member shall ensure the conformity of its laws, regulations and administrative procedures with its obligations as provided in the annexed Agreements."[1] Paragraph 4 does not mention whether to grant the WTO agreements direct effect. The panel in *US-Section 301 Trade Act* points out that the GATT/WTO institutions have not so far interpreted the GATT and other agreements under the WTO framework as legal orders producing direct effect.[2] However, this fact does not mean the question has been settled. The panel states, "[w]hether there are circumstances where obligations in any of the WTO agreements addressed to Members would create rights for individuals which national courts must protect, remains an open question, in particular in respect of obligations following the exhaustion of DSU procedures in a specific dispute."[3] The panel, in fact, is very careful about providing any definite opinion on the issue. In the case of *China-Intellectual Property Right*, China did not argue about the supremacy of the Bern convention, as incorporated by the TRIPS agreement. The panel thus cannot rule on the direct effect issue.[4] The panel nonetheless refers to the provisions incorporated in the TRIPS as having "possible direct effect."[5] The panel consistently leaves the door open for the direct effect of the WTO agreements at the international level. The issue still might surface anytime in the future.

There are three reasons why the consideration of the direct effect of the WTO agreements is significant. First, direct effect is concerned with the separation of

1 The World Trade Organization, the Legal Text, Results of The Uruguay Round of Multilateral Negotiations, 13 (1999).

2 Panel Report, United States – Sections 301-310 of the Trade Act of 1974 (US-Section 301 Trade Act), WT/DS152/R, footnote 661 (Jan. 27, 2000)

3 *Id.*

4 Panel Report on China -Measures Affecting the Protection and Enforcement of Intellectual Property Rights (China-Intellectual Property Right), para. 7.70,WT/DS362/R (Mar. 20, 2009).

5 *Id.*

powers, specifically with the extent of involvement of the judicial branch of the member state in enforcing its obligations.[6] If the national courts are kept distant from the enforcement of the obligations, then the legislative and executive branches – especially the executive branch – would have overwhelming power over the trade-related affairs and this might in turn eventually compromise the balance of power envisioned by the writers of the constitutions of the member states.[7] Second, the effectiveness of the WTO agreements depends more and more on the cooperation of national courts. Several WTO agreements have circumvented the legislative branch and set forth specific rules that the executive branches of the members must respect.[8] That is especially the case when the WTO wants to secure the imported goods from arbitrary or unfair trade sanctions.[9] The national courts obviously can supervise the actions of their own governments better than the international tribunals. This phenomenon also has been confirmed by provisions that require the member states to provide judicial reviews on certain governmental actions and on the issues relating to the interests of individuals.[10] Third, direct effect relates to legal protection for individuals who engage in international trade. The provisions of the WTO agreements directly affect the rights of the individual.[11] Individuals do not have any access to the protection of the WTO agreements. Only governments may take measures under the WTO framework against a member who breaches its obligation to grant the aforementioned protections. However, the governments must consider the overall interests of the state, not the interests of any particular individual, in deciding whether to take measures.[12] Direct effect could grant greater protection for the interests of individuals.

This research primarily aims to give an answer to the debate of whether the direct effect of the WTO agreements should be granted. The subordinated and interre-

6 See Thomas Cottier, The Challenge of the WTO Law: Collected Essays 323 (2006).

7 Concerns about little involvement of the courts in the enforcement of the WTO obligations, see John Jackson et al, Legal Problems Of International Economic Relations: Cases, Materials And Text on The National and International Regulation of Transnational Economic Relations 110 (4th ed.,2002)

8 See Sabino Cassese, *Shrimps, Turtles and Procedure: Global Standards for National Administrations* 6-17 (New York University School of Law, Institute for International Law and Justice Working Paper No. 2004/4, 2004), available at SSRN: http://ssrn.com/abstract=692761.

9 *E.g.*, Agreement on Anti-dumping (AD), Articles 5.3, 5.5,6.; Agreement on Subsidies and countervailing Measures (SCM), Articles 11 and 12

10 *E.g.*, Agreement on Trade-Related Aspects of Intellectual Property Rights (TRIPS), Articles 41-49.

11 See Steve Charnovitz, *The WTO and the Rights of the individual*, (2001) March/April Intereconomics 98.

12 Petros C. Mavroidis, Tomas Cottier, William J. Davey, Eleanor M. Fox, Norio Komuro and Douglas E. Rosenthal, Is the WTO Dispute Settlement Mechanism Responsive to the Needs of the Traders? Would a System of Direct Action by Private Parties Yield Better Results, 32 (2) JOURNAL OF WORLD TRADE 147, 148 (1998).

lated aims are (1) to clarify the positions of major members and reasons thereof, (2) to search grounds for granting the direct effect of WTO agreements, and (3) to identify the difficulties for granting the direct effect of WTO agreements.

0.2. Definition of Direct Effect

Various terms refer to the effect of international law, particularly domestic legal systems. The terms "direct effect," "direct application," and "self-executing" are most commonly used. These terms, however, are often used inconsistently.[13] Jackson applies the term "direct application" to the issue of "to what extent the treaty norms are treated directly as norms of domestic law ('statute-like law') without a further act of transformation."[14] Jackson goes on to clarify that "the term 'direct application' will not be limited to situations in which private parties can sue on the basis of the treaty norm, but will also cover situations in which governments, or different levels of government, might utilize the treaty norm as part of domestic jurisprudence."[15] The term "self-executing" means, as Aust suggested, "A treaty may, without legislation, become part of the domestic law once it had been concluded in accordance with constitution and has entered into force for the state."[16] Recently, the term "direct effect" has become prevalent in the field. The term "direct effect" is derived from European Union (EU) law and became a common phrase in international economic law, although this concept in EU law is unclear.[17] Jacobs describes "direct effect" as the situation where a treaty provision can be invoked in domestic courts.[18] Cottier illustrated the concept as "a private person in a state (or Union, respectively) may base a claim in, and be granted relief from, the domestic courts of that state against another private person or the state on the basis of the state's obligations under an international treaty."[19]

13 Francis G. Jacobs, *Introduction* in THE EFFECT OF TREATIES IN DOMESTIC LAW i, xxvii (Francis G. Jacobs & Shelley Roberts ed., 1987).

14 John Jackson, *Status of Treaties in Domestic Legal Systems: A policy Analysis*, 86 AMERICAN JOURNAL OF INTERNATIONAL LAW 310, 310 (1992).

15 Jackson also explains that the term "direct application" referred is different from that used in the EC jurisprudence, *id*, at note 1.

16 Anthony Aust, Modern Treaty Law and Practice, 146 (2002).

17 For the various definitions of direct effect, see PAUL CRAIG & GRÁINNE DE BÚRCA, EU LAW: TEXT, CASES, AND MATERIALS, 269-271 (3rd ed. 2008).

18 *Supra* note 13, at xxiii-xxiv.

19 Thomas Cottier & Krista Nadakavukaren Schefer, *The Relationship Between World Trade Organization Law, National and Regional Law*, 1 JOURNAL OF INTERNATIONAL ECONOMY LAW 83, 91 (1991).

The terms “self-executing”, “direct application”, and “direct effect” seem to refer to similar concepts, but simply use different words. “Direct application” and “self-executing” are almost identical,[20] except that “self-executing” was used originally by the U.S. courts and classified as doctrine of national law.[21] Still, as Jackson suggests, a distinction between “direct application” and “direct effect” could be made. Jackson uses the term “invocability” to “indicate the question whether *even though* a rule of an international agreement is directly applied, a particular party can rely on this rule as ‘law’.”[22] In this regard, the term “direct effect” covers the concepts of “direct application” and “invocability.”

For the purposes of this paper, the term “direct effect” will refer to an effect of an international agreement enabling an individual to raise a claim before a national court based on the provisions of that agreement.

0.3. Legal Background

“WTO agreements” refers to the agreements embodying the results of the Uruguay Round negotiations. They comprise the Marrakesh Agreements and its annexes. The Marrakesh Agreement serves as a “roof” for all the other agreements in the annexes.[23] The material rules are set by multilateral and plurilateral agreements. The plurilateral agreements (Agreement on Government Procurement [GPA] and Agreement on Trade in Civil Aircraft) are binding only on the signatories, while the multilateral agreements are binding on all the member states. The multilateral agreements include agreements on trade in goods,[24] the General Agreements on

20 *Supra* note 14.

21 Thomas Buergenthal, Self-Executing and Non-Self-Executing Treaties in National and International Law, 235 RECUEIL DES COURS 303,322 (1992).

22 John Jackson, *United States* in THE EFFECT OF TREATIES IN DOMESTIC LAW 141,157 (Francis G. Jacobs & Shelley Roberts,1987); Other author, like Thomas Cottier, does not distinguish between “direct effect” and “self-executing“, see *supra* note 14.

23 Structure of the WTO Agreements, see Götz J. Göttsche, *Die WTO als Rechtordnung und Institution* in WTO-RECHT 101,103 (Meinhard Hilf & Stefan Oeter eds, 2010); Werner Meng, *Das Vertragsystem der Welthandelsorganisation* in DIE EUROPÄISCHE GEMEINSCHAFT IN DER WELTHANDELSORGANISATION 63, 66 (Peter-Christian Müller-Graff eds.,1999); WTO, UNDERSTANDING THE WTO, 23-24 (4th ed.,2008)

24 Annex 1 A to Marrakesh Agreement:
General Agreement on Tariffs and Trade 1994
Understanding on the Interpretation of Article II: 1 (b) of the General Agreement on Tariffs and Trade 1994.
Understanding on the Interpretation of Article XVII of the General Agreement on Tariffs and Trade 1994.

Trade in Services (the GATS),[25] and the Agreement on Trade-Related Aspects of Intellectual Property Rights (TRIPS).[26][27] These multilateral agreements are the three pillars for the material rules of the WTO system.[28] Understanding on Rules and Procedures Governing the Settlement of Disputes (the DSU)[29] was drafted to preserve the material rules of the WTO.[30] The Trade Policy Review Mechanism (TRIM)[31] also aims at adherence by the member states to the rules mentioned above.[32]

The material rules of the WTO are concerned not only with market access and tariff reduction, but also with various trade-related issues (e.g., exchange

---

Understandings on Balance-of-Payments Provisions of the General Agreement on Tariffs and Trade 1994.
Understanding on the Interpretation of Article XXIV of the General Agreement on Tariffs and Trade 1994.
Understanding in Respect of Waivers of obligations under the General Agreement on Tariffs and Trade 1994.
Understanding on the Interpretation of Article XXVIII of the General Agreement on Tariffs and Trade 1994.
Marrakesh Protocol to the General Agreement on Tariffs and Trade 1994.
Agreement on Agriculture.
Agreement on the Application of Sanitary and Phytosanitary Measures
Agreement on Textiles and Clothing.
Agreement on Technical Barriers to Trade.
Agreement on Trade-Related Investment Measures.
Agreement on Implementation of Article VI of the General Agreement on Tariffs and Trade 1994.
Agreement on Implementation of Article VII of the General Agreement on Tariffs and Trade 1994.
Agreement on Preshipment Inspection.
Agreement on Rules of Origin.
Agreement on Import Licensing Procedure.
Agreement on Subsidies and countervailing Measures.
Agreement on Safeguards.

25 Annex 1 B to Marrakesh Agreement: General Agreement on Trade in Services.

26 Annex 1C to Marrakesh Agreement: Agreement on Trade-Related Aspects of Intellectual Property Rights.

27 The plurilateral agreements are annexed to the Marrakesh agreement. However, according to paragraph 3 of the Article II of the Marrakesh Agreement, they are not the part of the WTO agreements. The plurilateral agreements, i.e. the Government Procurement Agreement and the Agreement on Trade in Civil Aircraft, apply to the relations among the members signing them.

28 See Göttsche, *supra* note 23; Marc Beise, Die Welthandelsorganisation (WTO): Funktion, Status, Organisation 105 ff. (2000).

29 Annex 2: Dispute Settlement Understanding.

30 See DSU 3.2

31 Annex 3: Trade Policy Review Mechanism.

32 Article A of the TRIM

control, sanitary and phytosanitary measures, and movement of personnel). Additionally, the material rules of the WTO established anti-dumping provisions and regulations of subsidies to deter member states from manipulating domestic and international markets. Furthermore, the WTO allows non-trade concerns, like environmental impact and human rights, to play a role in international trade[33] and therefore prevent "market failures" (i.e., a race to the bottom).[34]

Direct effect of WTO agreements is often discussed in the context of the enforcement.[35] The material rules of WTO agreements are enforced under the DSU procedure. According to Article 23.1 of the DSU, members are obliged to use the dispute settlement system as the only way to enforce their rights under the WTO agreements. Unilateral enforcement of WTO rights and obligations is strictly forbidden.[36] The primary contents of the WTO enforcement structure include mainly violation complaints[37] and implementation of the rulings of the DSB. Only when a violation is found may the winning complainants take measures (e.g., compensation or retaliation) to encourage the losing respondents to conform to the WTO law. Article 3.7 of the DSU clearly defines the general scheme of the implementations of DSB rulings. The ultimate goal of the mechanism is to secure the withdrawal of the WTO-inconsistent measures. Prompt compliance with rulings of the panel or the Appellate Body is always preferable. Although Article 23.1 of the DSU states that prompt compliance is essential, the deadline is a bit flexible. If immediate compliance is not practical, Article 21.3 outlines

---

33 General exceptions under GATT XX provide member countries general justifications for limiting the trade on environmental, labor, or other non-trade grounds. Further discussions about the non-trade issues in WTO, see generally INTERNATIONAL TRADE AND HUMAN RIGHTS: FOUNDATIONS AND CONCEPTUAL ISSUES (Frederick M. Abbott et al. eds, 2006); GEORGE A. BERMANN & PETROS C. MAVROIDIS, TRADE AND HUMAN HEALTH AND SAFETY (2006); GERD WINTER, MULTILEVEL GOVERNANCE OF GLOBAL ENVIRONMENTAL CHANGE: PERSPECTIVES FROM SCIENCE, SOCIOLOGY AND THE LAW (2006); ERNST-ULRICH PETERSMANN, INTERNATIONAL AND EUROPEAN TRADE AND ENVIRONMENTAL LAW AFTER THE URUGUAY ROUND (1995); Ernst-Ulrich Petersmann, *Human Rights and the Law of the World Trade Organization*, 37 JOURNAL OF WORLD TRADE 241-281 (2003); John Howard Jackson, *World Trade Rules and Environmental Policies: Congruence Or Conflict?*, 49 (4) WASHINGTON AND LEE LAW REVIEW 1227-1278 (1992).

34 Ernst-Ulrich Petersmann, *Rights and Duties of States and Rights and Duties of Their Citizens in* RECHT ZWISCHEN UMBRUCH UND BEWAHRUNG 1087,1091-92 (Ulrich Beyerlin et al.eds.,1995).

35 E.g. Petros C. Mavroidis, Tomas Cottier, William J. Davey, Eleanor M. Fox, Norio Komuro and Douglas E. Rosenthal, Is the WTO Dispute Settlement Mechanism Responsive to the Needs of the Traders? Would a System of Direct Action by Private Parties Yield Better Results, 32 (2) JOURNAL OF WORLD TRADE 147 (1998); Joel P. Trachtman, Bananas Direct Effect and Compliance, 10 (4) EUROPEAN JOURNAL OF INTERNATIONAL LAW 655 (1990).

36 *Supra* note 2, at par. 7.43.

37 The non-violation complains are not subject to Articles 21 and 22. Since there are no infringements to be bought into conformity, they are not the concerns of this research.

three ways to determine a reasonable period for implementations. The reasonable period is decided by the DSB according to the time proposed by the member states concerned, by the agreement of the member states concerned, or by the arbitrators.[38]

If the WTO-inconsistent measure cannot be brought into conformity within the reasonable time, the complaining member states may request compensation, which is both temporary and voluntary, pending the withdrawal of the measures at issue.[39] The last instrument of the enforcement is retaliation (i.e., suspension of concessions or obligations under the WTO agreements). By the authorization of the DSB, the complaining member state can suspend their concessions or obligations *vis-à-vis* the respondent member states. Article 22.6 describes this procedure. The members may resort to the compliance panel provided in Article 21.5 to decide whether the recommendations and rulings are in compliance. The complaining member state could directly request the authorization for retaliation; however, the reality is that the member states prefer to solve disagreements on the "measure taken to comply with the rulings" and its consistence with the WTO law in the first place.[40] It should be noted that neither the compensation nor the retaliation is a substitute for correcting the WTO-inconsistent measure. They are merely temporary measures to induce the respondent member state to comply.

Observers agree that the members are willing to obey the DSB rulings and the dispute settlement system is in good shape.[41] The statistics also show the dispute settlement system deserves to be described (as the former Director General Mike Moore of the WTO frequently does) as the "crown jewel"[42] of the multilateral

---

38 See DSU 21.3 (a)- (c).

39 See DSU 22.2.

40 For the analysis of the applications of 21.5 and 22.6, see generally Brendan Mcgivern, *Implementation of Panel and Appellate Body Rulings: An overview*, *in* KEY ISSUES IN WTO DISPUTE SETTLEMENT: THE FIRST TEN YEARS 98 (Rufus Yerxa & Bruce Wilson eds., 2005); JOHN JACKSON ET AL, LEGAL PROBLEMS OF INTERNATIONAL ECONOMIC RELATIONS: CASES, MATERIALS AND TEXT ON THE NATIONAL AND INTERNATIONAL REGULATION OF TRANSNATIONAL ECONOMIC RELATIONS 305 (4th ed.,2002); MITSUO MATSUSHITA ET AL., THE WORLD TRADE ORGANIZATION: LAW, PRACTICE, AND POLICY 108-119 (2006); Yuka Fukunaga, *Securing Compliance Through the WTO Dispute Settlement System: Implementation of DSB Recommendations*, 9 (2) JOURNAL OF INTERNATIONAL ECONOMIC LAW 383 (2006); Yoki Suzuki, *Sequencing and Compliance* in REFORM AND DEVELOPMENT OF THE WTO DISPUTE SETTLEMENT SYSTEM 367 (Dencho Georgiev & Kim van der Borght eds., 2006).

41 John H. Jackson, Sovereignty, The WTO And The Changing Fundamentals Of International Law, 134-37 (2006)

42 James Bacchus, Inside the World Trade Organization, 8 (Columbia Business School Discussion Paper No. 18, April 2002), http://www2.gsb.columbia.edu/apec/APECStudyCenter,ColumbiaUniversity/Discussion_Papers.html.

trading system.[43] However, the DSU has its limits in terms of the enforcement of WTO agreements.[44] First, it cannot provide timely relief for the infringement of WTO agreements. The procedures are time consuming. If one includes in the calculation the procedures of the compliance panel and authorizations for retaliation, then the whole procedures normally would last more than two years.[45] Furthermore, according to the wording of Article 21.5, the complainant may resort to the compliance panel whenever it doubts the existence of the complying measure. There are no limitations on how many times that Article 21.5 claims can be brought. It is likely that the first adjustment of the measure will still fail to comply with the first Article 21.5 ruling. Without a mutually-satisfying solution, the procedure may never end. This is exactly the problem in the case of *EC-Bananas III*.[46] This case was brought in 1995 and has been ongoing for 14 years.[47] Second, the enforcement mechanism cannot properly redress the damages incurred in the past, or the damages suffered by individuals or by a specific group of people.[48] The remedies are "prospective" in application.[49] The starting time for calculating damage is the end of the reasonable implementation period.[50] Besides, the retaliation is only temporary and must cease once the WTO-inconsistent measure is removed. Moreover, those injured by these measures might not even benefit from the retaliation, because the cross-agreement retaliations and cross-sector retaliations are allowed. The foregoing analysis reveals that the enforcement mechanism is rather meaningless to the provisions, which require prompt relief or provide protections for specific private parties.

---

43 See Bruce Wilson, Compliance by WTO Members with Adverse WTO Dispute Settlement Rulings, the Record to Date, 10 (2) Journal of International Economic Law 397 (2007).

44 There is also empirical study showing that the enforcement mechanism does not work well. See Marc L. Busch & Eric Reinhardt, *Testing International Trade Law: Empirical Studies of GATT/WTO Dispute Settlement* in THE POLITICAL ECONOMY OF INTERNATIONAL TRADE LAW 457, 462-474 (Daniel L.M. Kennedy & James D. Southwick eds., 2002).

45 WorldTradeLaw.net, Average Implementation Time Periods (in Months), http://www.worldtradelaw.net/dsc/database/implementaverage.asp; WorldTradeLaw.net, Timing of Referral, Composition, Issuance and Circulation of WTO Article 21.5 Panel Reports, http://www.worldtradelaw.net/dsc/database/paneltiming1.asp (last visited Jan. 12, 2011).

46 Appellate Body Report, *European Communities – Regime for the Importation, Sale and Distribution of Bananas*, WT/DS27/AB/R (Sep. 9, 1997).

47 The Appellate Body issued the second Article 21.5 report on 26 November 2008.

48 See Marco Bronckers & Naboth van den Broek, *Financial Compensations in the WTO: Improving Remedies, in WTO Dispute Settlement*, in REFORM AND DEVELOPMENT OF THE WTO DISPUTE SETTLEMENT SYSTEM 43, 48-49 (Dencho Georgiev & Kim van der Borght eds., 2006).

49 See Article 21.5 Panel Report, Australia -Subsidies Provided to Producers and Exporters of Automotive Leather (Australia -Automotive Leather II), paras.6.13, 6.31, 6.32, WT/DS126/RW (Jan.21, 2000).

50 Article 22.6 Arbitration Report, European Communities- Measures Concerning Meat and Meat Products (Hormones), para. 38, WT/DS26/ARB (July 12, 1999)

0.4. Starting Point for the Analysis: The Effect of International Agreements in Domestic Legal Systems

WTO agreements are part of the public international law system. The rules and principles of public international law are also applicable in the WTO context. The direct effect of WTO agreements raises an old and controversial issue of public international law: namely, the relation between international and domestic law. The theories and practices in this regard are the foundations for the discussions on the topic at hand.

The theories of monism and dualism explain the relationship of international and domestic law. The two schools of thought became the bases for discussion of the domestic effect of the international agreements.[51] Dualism assumes that international law and domestic law are different and separate legal systems. They are essentially different in terms of the subjects, the sources, and the contents of the rules.[52] Individuals are the subjects of domestic law, while international law takes states as its subjects. The sources of domestic law are parliamentary statutes and legal norms, which are formed within a domestic legal system. The sources of international law mainly are the law-making treaties and customs growing up in the international context. As regards the contents of the rules, domestic law governs the relationships among individuals, and the relationships between a state and its individuals, whereas international law regulates the relationships between states. It follows logically that international law is not a part of domestic law and not binding upon domestic courts. International law must be transformed into domestic law in order to be applied by domestic authorities.[53]

All the monists stress the common nature of international and national law, and perceive them to constitute a unitary legal system. However, there are divergent views, as represented by both Lauterpacht and Kelsen, on the basis for monism.[54] Lauterpacht observed that the primary function of international and domestic law

---

51 See generally Alfred Verdrross & Bruno Simma, Universelles Völkerrecht: Theorie Und Praxis 53-58 (3 rd. ed.1984);International Law: Cases And Materials, 20-40 (Lori Fisler Damrosch et al. eds., 4th ed.,2001); Ian Brownlie, Principles of Public International Law 31-35 (7th ed., 2008); Philip Kunig, *Völkerrecht und staatliches Recht* in VÖLKERRECHT 75, 90-96 (Wolfgang Graf Vitzthum ed, 5th ed., 2010); Stephan Hobe, Einführung in Das Völkerrecht, 231-235 (9th ed., 2008).

52 See Heinrich Triepel, Völkerrecht und Landesrecht 7-10 (Photo. Reprint 1955) (1899); Lassa Oppenheim, International Law: A Treatise 25 (Ronald F. Roxburgh ed., 3rd ed., 1920)

53 Oppenheim, *id*, at 26.

54 See Brownlie *supra* note 51, at 32; MALCOLM N. SHAW, INTERNATIONAL LAW 132 (6th ed., 2008)

is the preservation of the well-being of individuals. He advocated the supremacy of international law, by holding that international law is the best vehicle for human rights protection and the basis for the legal existence of states.[55] Kelsen's view of monism rested on his theory about the concept of the law. He defined the law as an order, which prescribes certain behavior and provides coercive acts as sanctions for acting inconsistently with that behavior.[56] In this sense, international law and domestic law are no different from each other, except that international law is a relatively decentralized, coercive order. International law is implemented by domestic law, not transformed into domestic law. [57] Also, he postulated two sets of valid norms must be comprehended as part of one harmonious and hierarchical system.[58]In his thoughts, international law determines the territorial, personal, and temporal spheres of domestic law, and it, therefore, is a higher norm.[59] The primacy of international law does not imply that a norm of domestic law is annulled for being inconsistent with international law. That would be only in the case that international law so requires.[60]

With few exceptions (e.g., the EU law), international laws do not address the effect of international agreements in domestic legal systems. International laws traditionally do not specify the method that states should take to implement an international agreement. The only imperative is the foundational principle *pacta sunt servanda*, as stated in Article 26 of Vienna Convention of Law on Treaties (VCLT).[61] The parties to international agreements are obliged to perform those agreements in good faith. Nevertheless, it is possible that an international agreement *per se* may provide for direct effect. In other words, it is a problem of international law, not exclusively of domestic law.[62]

In practice, most international agreements left the issue to the domestic legal systems. Most states take a more dualist approach.[63] In this context, it is conceivable that the member states would tend to refuse the direct effect of WTO agreements. However, as mentioned at the outset, the issue is not settled under the WTO legal framework. The panel implied that certain provisions of WTO agreements still could be construed as requiring the direct effect.

---

55 *Id*, see Lauterpacht, international law 149 (1950)

56 See Hans Kelsen, Principles of International Law 6 (1952)

57 See *id*, at 353,401.

58 See *id*, at 424.

59 See *id*, at 411.

60 See *id*, at 426.

61 SIR IAN SINCLAIR, THE VIENNA CONVENTION ON THE LAW OF TREATIES, 83 (2nd ed.,1984)

62 See Arnold Koller, Die unmittelbare Anwendbarkeit völkerrechtlich Verträge und des EWG-Vertrages im innerstaatlichen Bereich 119-21 (1971); see also Jackson, supra note 22, at 158.

63 See Shaw, *supra* note 54, at 139ff.; International Law: Cases and Materials 154 ff. (Louis Henkin et al. eds., 3rd ed., 1993)

0.5. Direct effect of the EU Treaty

The EU Treaty[64] is the one of few international agreements construed to grant direct effect. What is noteworthy is that the primary law of the EU has never explicitly recognized its direct effect. Furthermore, the parties to the Treaty of Rome did not expect or want to accept the direct effect of the EU law.[65] As shown in the famous case of *van Gend & Loos*,[66] the governments of the Netherlands, Belgium, and Germany opposed direct effect. Back then, the European Economic Community had six members. In other words, half of the Community expressly refused the idea of direct effect. It was the European Court of Justice (the ECJ) that established the direct effect of the EU law. Experience under EU law (although not necessarily comparable to WTO law) has shown that direct effect of an international agreement is not merely theoretical, but may occur in fact under certain conditions.

The direct effect of the EU Treaty was brought up in the *van Gend & Loos* case. A Dutch haulage company, van Gend & Loos, had imported a chemical substance from Germany into the Netherlands. Because the Dutch changed the tariff classification, the imported goods were subject to a higher duty. In response, van Gend & Loos raised a claim based upon Article 12 of the EEC (TFEU Article 30) before the national tribunal. The tribunal referred to the ECJ for a preliminary ruling provided in Article 177 of the EEC (TFEU Article 267).

The ECJ justified the direct effect doctrine by two strands of reasoning. The first was that, at the outset, the ECJ emphasized the Community's special legal nature. The ECJ found the EEC Treaty was more than an international agreement, which merely creates mutual obligations between the member states. By doing that, the EU law could circumvent the presumption (held by Holland, Germany, and Belgium) that the parties to international agreements have discretion on how to implement the international agreements in national legal systems.[67]

---

64 The EU Treaty refers generally to the treaties founding the European Communities and the European Union, including Treaty of Rome, Single European Act, Treaty of European Union, Treaty of Amsterdam, Treaty of Nice, and Treaty of Lisabon.

65 See Karen J. Alter, Establishing the Supremacy of European Law: The Making of Rule of Law in Europe 11-16 (2001).

66 Case 26/62, *NV Algemene Transport-en Expeditie Onderneming van Gend & Loos v. Neth. Inland Revenue Admin.*, 1963 E.C.R. 1, 1963

67 See *supra* note 66, at 7-8; see also Franz C.Mayer, *Van Gend en Loos: The Foundation of a Community of Law*, in THE PAST AND FUTURE OF EU LAW: THE CLASSICS OF EU LAW REVISITED ON THE 50TH ANNIVERSARY OF THE ROME TREATY 16, 19-20 (Miguel Poiares Maduro & Loïc Azoulai eds, 2010).

The ECJ observed,

> [T]he community constitutes a new legal order of international law for the benefit of which the states have limited their sovereign rights, albeit within limited fields, and the subjects of which comprise not only member states but also their nationals. Independently of the legislation of Member States, Community law therefore not only imposes obligations on individuals but is also intended to confer upon them rights which become part of their legal heritages.[68]

To support such a view, the ECJ resorted to the following provisions and institutional structure set by the EEC Treaty: (a) the preamble refers not only to the governments, but also to the peoples; (b) there are institutions that exercise their own sovereignty rights affecting members as well as their citizens; (c) the individuals participate in the function of the Community through the intermediary of the European Parliament and the Economic and Social Committee; and; (d) the objective of the preliminary rulings under Article 177 of EEC (TFEU Article 267) is to secure the uniform interpretations of the Treaty by national courts. According to the ECJ, these provisions have confirmed that the members have acknowledged that their nationals may invoke the Community Law before national courts. [69]

In fact, the EEC Treaty did not provide obvious textual support for direct effect. None of the provisions mentioned by the ECJ directly addressed the effect of the Treaty. Although the preliminary rulings under Article 177 of the EEC (TFEU Article 267) indicate that national courts might consider applying the Treaty, this does not lead necessarily to the conclusion that EEC treaty in general should be directly effective. The national courts might apply the treaty only indirectly, such as when using it as guidance for interpreting the domestic laws in a way to avoid conflicts between the national and community law. Furthermore, the national courts' interpretations of the Treaty were arguably inconsistent with the intention of the signatories.[70] Moreover, their constitutions did not provide legal bases for their national courts to annul or not to apply domestic laws that infringe Community laws.[71] It is hard to believe that member states were about to change their constitutions as they signed the EEC Treaty. Lacking textual support from the EEC Treaty,

---

68 *Supra* note 66, at 12.

69 See *id.*

70 See Karl Römer, Opinion of the Advocate General, Case 26/62, *NV Algemene Transport-en Expeditie Onderneming van Gend & Loos v. Neth. Inland Revenue Admin.*, 1963 E.C.R. 19, 24, 1963.

71 See Wilhelm Wengler, *Europäischer Gerichtshof, 5. 2. 1963 –Rechtssache 26/62: Unmittelbare, individuelle Rechte begründende Wirkung des Art. 12; Auslegung des Art. 177; neue Rechtsordnung des Völkerrecht*, 1963 Neue juristische Wochenschrift 1751,1752 (1963).

direct effect was better justified under the objective of the Treaty, or the visions of what the Community law should be. According to the ECJ, the objective of the EEC Treaty is "to establish the common market, the function of which is of direct concern of the interested parties in the Community."[72] In the view of the ECJ, the Community should not be a forum exclusively for the member states; far from it, the Community has called for the participation of every individual. Individuals should be liable for the obligations and entitled to the rights for that purpose. This is an idea drawn from the perception of the constitutional system of Community law.[73]

The second strand of reasoning is related to the effectiveness of the guarantees under the EU Treaty. This part of the rulings revealed a significant rationale for the direct effect: the *effet utile* ("the principle of effectiveness") argument.[74] The ECJ stressed that direct effect would enhance the effectiveness of the EEC treaty. They were worried about the effectiveness of Article 12, if an infringement can only be brought by the member states in the procedures under Articles 169 and 170 of EEC (TFEU Articles 258 and 259). This is especially the case when these procedures were set in place after the implementation of national measures infringing the EU law.[75] Besides, the individuals' vigilance to protect their rights may also serve as additional surveillance for the compliance of members.[76] The ECJ apparently held direct effect as an enforcement mechanism initiated by individuals, which could supplement the shortcomings of the public enforcement mechanism under Articles 169 and 170 of EEC (TFEU Articles 258 and 259).[77] Later, in the case of *Simmental II*, the ECJ further established a general rule that the courts of the member states also have to enforce the Community law for the effectiveness of the Treaty.[78]

Two arguments to support direct effect could be deduced from the rulings of the ECJ. First, individuals are recognized to have rights under the Community law, which the national courts must protect. Second, the effects and the goals of the Community law would be seriously derogated, if direct effect were denied.

---

72 *Supra* note 66, at 12.

73 See Pierre Pescatore, *The Doctrine of Direct Effect: An Infant Disease of Community*, 8 EUROPEAN LAW REVIEW 155,158 (1983).

74 See Craig & Búrca, *supra* note 17, at 275; see also Ian Loveland, Constitution Law, Administrative Law and Human Rights: A Critical Introduction 428 (4th ed., 2006); Sibylle Seyr, DER "EFFET UTILE" IN DER RECHTSPRECHUNG DES EuGH 126 (2008).

75 See *supra* note 66, at 13.

76 *Id.*

77 See Paul P. Craig, Once upon a Time in the West: Direct Effect and the Federation of the ECC Law, 12 OXFORD JOURNAL OF LEGAL STUDIES 454, 456-457 (1992).

78 See Rudolf Streinz, Der "effet utile" in der Rechtsprechung des Gerichtshofs der Europäischen Gemeinschaft, in Festschrift für Ulrich Everling 1491, 1499 (Ole Due et al., 1995); C 106/77, *Amministrazione delle Finanze dello Stato v Simmenthal SpA.*, paras 19-20,1978 E.C.R. 629.

These arguments may have application for other international agreements (*inter alia* the WTO agreements), because they are not based solely on the *a priori* nature of Community law, but have their roots in public international law.[79] The *effet utile*, upon which the second argument was based, is a well-accepted rule for interpretation of international agreements.[80] Besides, using protection of individuals as a ground for direct effect is not strange to public international law. In the case of *Danzig*, the Permanent Court of International Justice (PICJ) was asked to give an advisory opinion on whether an individual could enforce an international agreement before a national court. The opinion implied that individuals could rely on the provision of the international agreement at issue, if it creates rights and obligations for them.[81] There is one slight difference between the methods that the PCIJ and the ECJ each took to reach its conclusion. The PCIJ focused on the intention of contracting parties, which is shown in the contents and in the manner the agreement applied. On the other hand, the ECJ cared more about the objective of the EC Treaty. The key point is that there should be a ground upon which to construe the international agreement so as to create rights or obligations of individuals.

0.6. The Challenging Procedure and the Direct Effect of WTO Agreements

There is a concept akin to direct effect in the Government Procurement Agreement (GPA). The GPA provides that individuals can challenge an infringement of the GPA before national courts or an impartial and independent review body. This is called "challenging procedure." At first glance, the challenge procedure

---

79 See Mayer, *supra* note 67, at 20; see also Jan A. Winter, Direct Applicability and Direct Effect: Two Distinct and Different Concepts in Community Law, 9 COMMON MARKET LAW REVIEW 433,429 (1972).

80 Permanent Court of International Justice (PCIJ) and International Court of Justice (ICJ) have adopted the principle of the effectiveness in several cases. See *e.g.* Free Zones of Upper Savoy and District of Gex, 1929 P.C.I.J. (ser. A) No.22, at 13 (Aug. 19); Corfic Channel case, 1949 I.C.J. 4, 23 (Apr.9); Interpretation of Peace Treaties, 1950 I.C.J. 65, 77 (Mar.30); Interpretation of Peace Treaties (second phase), 1950 I.C.J.221, 229 (July 18). See WOLFGANG PÜHS, DER VOLLZUG VON GEMEINSCHAFTSRECHT: FORMEN UND GRENZEN EINES EFFEKTIVEN GEMEINSCHAFTSRECHTSVOLLZUGS UND ÜBERLEGUNGEN ZU SEINER EFFEKTUIERUNG, 82 (1997).

81 The PICJ did not presume individual can not rely on the international agreement at issue. It directly addressed the conditions for that international agreement to be applied in the legal relation between the administration and the individuals. See Jurisdiction of the Courts of Danzig, Advisory Opinion, paras 26, 37,1928 P.C.I.J. (ser. B) No. 15 (Mar. 3)

seems to suggest that the GPA shall be directly effective.[82] The text and the subsequent developments indicate, however, that the challenge procedure only requires the national courts to participate in the enforcement of the GPA. Article XX: 2 of the GPA reads, "Each Party shall provide non-discriminatory, timely, transparent and effective procedures enabling *suppliers* to challenge *alleged breaches of the Agreement* arising in the context of procurements in which they have, or have had, an interest"[83] (emphasis added). Nothing in Article XX explicitly demands the signatories to allow individuals to raise a claim based on the GPA. This provision can also be construed as a procedural obligation, which requires the timely and effective legal relief for individuals in the domestic system. Signatories may fulfill this obligation merely by establishing a review system compatible with Article XX of the GPA. Courts or review bodies still can make their findings based on domestic laws implementing the GPA, but not on the GPA itself.[84] Furthermore, such a reading is consistent with the provisionally agreed text of Agreement on Government Procurement (hereinafter "the revised GPA text").[85] The revised GPA text serves as the basis for accession negotiations with countries wanting to join the GPA, although it has not yet been made effective.[86] Article XVIII of the revised GPA text illustrates the challenge procedure under Article XX of the GPA. Article XVIII: 1 provides the following:

> Each Party shall provide a timely, effective, transparent, and non-discriminatory administrative or judicial review procedure through which a supplier may challenge: (a) a breach of the Agreement; *or (*b) where the supplier *does not have a right* to challenge *directly* a breach of the Agreement under the domestic law of a Party, a failure to comply with a Party's measures implementing this Agreement (emphasis added).[87]

---

82 See THOMAS COTTIER, THE CHALLENGE OF THE WTO LAW: COLLECTED ESSAYS, 315 (2006); see also Dorthe Dahlgaard Dingel, *Direct Effect of the Government Procurement Agreement*, 5 PUBLIC PROCUREMENT LAW REVIEW 245,254 (1996).

83 GPA XX:2, available at http://www.wto.org/english/docs_e/legal_e/gpr-94_02_e.htm#articleXX (last visited Jan. 10, 2011)

84 See Isabel Dendauw, *New WTO Agreement on Government Procurement: Analysis of the Framework for Bid Challenge Procedures and the Question of Direct Effect*,18 (3) Journal of Energy & Natural Resources Law 254, 265-266 (2000); Mavoidis & Zdouc, Legal Means to Protect Private Parties' Interest in the WTO,1 JOURNAL OF INTERNATIONAL ECONOMIC LAW 407, 413 (1998).

85 GPA/W297, Dec. 11, 2006, available at http://docsonline.wto.org/DDFDocuments/t/PLURI/GPA/W297.doc. (last visited Jan. 10, 2011).

86 See brief interaction of the re-negotiation of the Agreement on Government Procurement, http://www.wto.org/english/tratop_e/gproc_e/negotiations_e.htm (last visited Jan. 10,2011)

87 *Supra* note 85.

The drafters differentiate between claims about the infringement of the GPA and claims about the domestic measures implementing the GPA. The former obviously means direct effect of the GPA. The term "or" suggests that signatories still may choose whether direct effect should be granted. In other words, the challenging procedure may include, but does not require, direct effect of the GPA.

Considering the revised GPA text, direct effect is just one of the options to fulfill a general obligation of national courts to implement the GPA. The rationale for the challenging procedure is nevertheless essential to meaningful discussion of direct effect, for it is acknowledged for the first time in the WTO framework that national courts should intervene in the implementation of the international agreements at issue. The challenging procedure is provided because the obligations of the GPA cannot be enforced properly under the DSU.[88] In a government procurement procedure, the measure at issue usually relates only to a single event: the opportunity to bid. All the actions and damages happened in the past. However, all the countermeasures in the DSU could only affect the ongoing infringement and only decrease the future damages, which occur after the expiration of the reasonable periods for rectifying WTO-inconsistent measures.[89] In the case involving the government procurements, when the panel or the Appellate Body makes the findings and the recommendations, no measure is left to be brought into conformity. The DSB rulings alone do not constitute a sufficient remedy and would not provide a sufficient deterrent.[90] National courts are believed to be able to solve the problem of obtaining effective redress in respect of complaints about specific procurements.[91]

0.7. Structure of the Research

In the introduction, the author briefed the concepts and background relevant to the discussion of direct effect of WTO agreements. The question of whether direct effect of WTO agreements should be granted will be explored from the empirical and normative aspects. The WTO grants member states discretion in implementing their obligations under WTO agreements. The practice of the members is therefore a useful starting point. In the first part, the author described views and concerns of the four members: United States, European Union, China, and Taiwan. The positions of the U.S. and the EU will be analyzed in chapter 1,

---

88 See Dendauw, *supra* note 84, at 255-256.

89 See 0.3. *supra.*

90 See panel Report, Norway-Procurement of Toll Collection Equipment for the City of Trondheim, para. 4.22, BSID 40S/319 (May 13,1992).

91 *Id*, para. 4.27.

and analyses of the positions of China and Taiwan will be presented in chapter 2. In these chapters, the author will attempt to explain the reasons for their respective positions. In the second part, the focus will be on the substantial grounds for and against direct effect. In the first chapter of the second part, the literature on direct effect will be presented in detail and reviewed. In the second chapter of the second part, the author will identify the key elements extracted from the practices of the member states and the literature that touch upon direct effect of WTO agreements. Also, the author will make an assessment on the issue. According to the previous analysis, the author will provide a conclusion on whether or not to grant direct effect of the WTO agreements.

Part I:
Empirical Analysis-Practices of the Member States

Chapter 1: Positions of the United States and the European Union

The empirical analysis starts with two of the most important members in the west: the US and the EU. Both the US and the EU are members of the GATT and the WTO. It would also be meaningful to contrast the positions and the reasoning in the GATT period and that in the WTO epoch. Such a comparison would reveal these members' intentions more clearly.

1.1. The Laws and Practices in the United States

The law concerning the effect and the application of the international agreements in the domestic legal system of the United States is remarkably complicated. The United States' legal system is a mixture of dualism and monism; thus, the effect of the treaty should be decided case by case.[92] Another reason for the complexity is the different types of international agreements under the US constitutional principles.[93] In general, the effect of international agreements in the US legal system, including the WTO, concerns mostly the balance of power among the executive, legislative, and judicial branches.

1.1.1. The Domestic Legal Status of International Agreements in General

In this section, the intention is not to clarify each question concerning the application and the effect of an international agreement in the US legal system. Rather, the questions that facilitate the understanding of the US position on the GATT/WTO will be addressed briefly.

92 Jackson *supra* note 22, at 141.

93 *Id.*

1.1.1.1. Treaty and Executive Agreements

The US Constitution established only one type of international agreement, which is referred to as a "Treaty." Article II, Section 2, clause 2 reads: "He (the President) shall have power, by and with the advice and consent of the Senate, to make Treaties, provided two thirds of the Senators present concur" (note added).[94] Accordingly, the President may ratify an international agreement if the Senate gives its advice and consent with a two-thirds vote. Although not expressively provided for in the Constitution, there are alternative ways, called "executive agreements," for the US to enter into international agreement. Even in the early days of the United States, the Congress authorized the executive branch to negotiate and conclude agreements with foreign governments.[95] The Supreme Court also has recognized such a practice.[96]

The executive agreements can be sorted into four categories: (1) Congressional previously authorized executive agreement; (2) Congressional subsequently approved executive agreement; (3) Presidential executive agreement; and (4) treaty-authorized executive agreement.[97] The consent of the Congress is required for the agreements under the first two categories. The difference lies in whether the Congress has the chance to review the provisions of the international agreement concerned. The agreements fall into first category if the President is authorized to directly ratify a future international agreement that has not been reviewed by Congress. The second type of executive agreement is the type that must be submitted to the Congress for approval after the President concluded the negotiation. Presidential executive agreements are based on the sole constitutional authority of the President and congressional participation is not required. The last type of agreements refers to cases wherein a fully approved and ratified agreement allows the parties to solve certain lacuna or to develop certain applications by a later agreement. These later agreements can be considered "subordinate" agreements.[98] [99] These procedures are the ways provided under the domestic legal system for the United States to enter into international agreements. They are also the channels for international agreements to be recognized by the United States as her international obligation. If an international agreement cannot be qualified as treaty or executive agreement, it cannot be binding under the domestic legal system.

---

94 U.S. CONST. art. II, §2, S. Doc. No 105-11 (1997)

95 See The Congressional Research Service, Library of Congress, CONSTITUTION OF UNITED STATES OF AMERICA: ANALYSIS AND INTERPRETATION, S. Doc, No. 108-17, at 517-518 (2004).

96 Jackson, *supra* note 22, at 142

97 Jackson, *supra* note 22, at 143

98 *Id*, at 144

99 Examples , see *supra note* 95, at 520-521

Whether the presidential executive agreements could become the "law of the land" [100] (i.e., statute-like law) was a matter of concern. The effect of Presidential executive agreements in this regard is questionable because Congress does not participate in Treaty making. Participation of the legislative branch is lacking; therefore, these agreements do not meet the political requirements that a domestic law should have. The Supreme Court, however, consistently sees the executive agreements as no different as the "Treaties" under Article II. [101] The executive agreements are almost identical in terms of the effect in the domestic legal system, except for a few occasions.[102] For instance, the Presidential executive agreements do not supersede statute, whether the statute was passed before or after the executive agreement.[103] Such a distinction indicates that the balance of treaty-making power between the executive branch and legislative branch is crucial for the domestic effect of international agreements.

1.1.1.2. Self-executing and the Hierarchy of the Norms

Article VI, Section 2 briefly addresses the effect of an international agreement in domestic law, which says: "This Constitution, and the Laws of the United States which shall be made in pursuance thereof; and all Treaties made, or which shall be made, under the Authority of the United States, shall be the supreme law of the land." [104] At first glance, one might believe that international agreements, at least the "Treaties" in Article II, could be directly applied in the United States. The Supreme Court has further clarified this provision and established conditions for such an effect. Chief Justice Marshall's opinion in the case of *Foster v. Neilson*[105] regarding the domestic law effect of the treaty still leads the way. Marshall noted that a treaty is in nature a contract between two nations and not a legislative act. He then stated the following:

> In the United States, a different principle is established. Our constitution declares a treaty to be the law of the land. It is, consequently, to be regarded in courts of justice as equivalent to an act of the legislature, whenever it oper-

100 See United States v. One Bag of Paradise Feathers, 256 F. 301, 306 (2d Cir. 26, 1919); Green H. Hackworth, 5 DIGEST OF INTERNATIONAL LAW 426 (1944).

101 See United States v. Belmont, 301 U.S. 324 (1937); United States v. Pink, 315 U.S. 203 (1942); American Insurance Association v. Garamendi, 539 U.S. 396 (2003).

102 *Supra* note 98. Hekin, on the contrary, observes certain executive agreements are inferior to federal law, See LOUIS HENKIN, FOREIGN AFFAIRS AND THE UNITED STATES CONSTITUTION, 226-229 (2nd ed.,1996.

103 Restatement of Law, Third, the Foreign Relations of the United States, §§142-144 (1987).

104 Supra note 94.

105 27 U.S.253 (1829).

ates of itself without the aid of any legislative provision. But when the terms of the stipulation import a contract, when either of the parties engages to perform a particular act, the treaty addresses itself to the political, not to the judicial department; and the legislature must execute the contract before it can become a rule for the Court.[106]

Accordingly, the agreements are self-executing if they can operate by themselves without any implementing legislation. In the case of *Foster v. Neilson*, the Supreme Court did not address situations where the implementing legislations are not required. The courts use various factors to appraise the issue.[107] No universal criteria fit every case.[108] Nonetheless, these cases provide some direction. For instance, the content of the provision should be akin to the domestic law. The *Head Money* case mentioned whether any provisions of international agreements confer certain rights upon the individuals. Such provisions "partake of the nature of municipal law, and which are capable of enforcement as between private parties in the courts of the country."[109] Another consideration is pertinent to the delegated powers. Some kinds of obligations might never be self-executing because the Constitution reserves powers to the Congress.[110] For example, the courts have stated that obligations of international agreements intending to define a crime would not be self-executing.[111]

Whenever a certain provision of an international agreement is self-executing, it would be "law of the land as an act of the Congress."[112] Accordingly, its status in the domestic legal hierarchy is the same as a statute. Article VI, Section 2 explicitly states that the "Treaties" are superior to the state law. In terms of the effect in the domestic legal system, the courts do not distinguish in most of the cases the executive agreements from the Treaty. The executive agreements also are superior to state law. Nevertheless all international agreements (Treaty and

---

106 *Id*, at 314.

107 *E.g.* Head Money Cases, 112 U.S. 580; Fuji v. States, 38 Cal. 2d. 718 (1952); Roca v. Thompson, 23 U.S. 332 (1912); Factor v. Laubenheimer, 290 U.S. 276 (1932); Arizona v. California, 373 U.S. 546 (1963).

108 See Charles W. Stotter, Self-Executing Treaties and Human Rights Provisions of United Nations Charter: a Separation of Powers Problem, 25 BUFFALO LAW REVIEW 773,779 (1976); see also Jackson, supra note 22, at 151.

109 Head Money Cases (Edye and Another v. Robertson, Collector – Cunard Steamship Company v. Robertson), 112 U.S. 580,598 (1884).

110 See *supra note* 95, at 499; see also LOUIS HENKIN, FOREIGN AFFAIRS AND THE UNITED STATES CONSTITUTION, 198-200 (2nd ed.,1996);Carlos Manuel Vázquez, *The Four Doctrines of Self-Executing Treaties*, 89 AMERICAN JOURNAL OF INTERNATIONAL LAW 695,722-23 (1995).

111 *E.g. the Over the Top,* 5 F 2d. 838,845 (D. Conn.1925).

112 Supra note 109.

executive agreements) are inferior to the Constitution. The Supreme Court ruled in *Reid v. Covert* that "no agreements with a foreign nation can confer power on Congress or any other branch of government, which is free from the restraints of the Constitution."[113] In case of inconsistency between a provision of an international agreement and a statute, whichever is executed at the later date will prevail.[114] In other words, a statute may repeal an international agreement and *vice versa.*

In cases where international agreements are given effect as a statute, the courts determine its meaning as a matter of federal law.[115] The decisions of international tribunals interpreting international agreements are not binding on the courts.[116] The courts would rather give more weight to the views of the department of government in charge of negotiating and enforcing the international agreements.[117]

1.1.1.3. International Agreements as Guidance for Interpreting Domestic Law

Non–self-executing agreements still might influence domestic courts, while they apply and interpret certain provisions of domestic law. The courts acknowledge that they would construe the statute so that it does not conflict with international law or with an international agreement of the United States.[118] In other words, the international agreements provide guidance for interpreting federal statutes. Their status of serving as guidance for interpreting federal statutes is called the indirect effect of international agreements.[119] In *Murray v. Schooner Charming Betsy* (hereafter *Charming Betsy*),[120] the Supreme Court mentioned for the first time that the international agreements could be a guide for interpreting federal statute.

113 Reid v. Covert, 354 U.S. 1, 16 (1957)

114 See Head Money Cases, 112 U.S. 580,599 (1884);see also Cook v. United States, 288 U.S.102 (1933).

115 Sanchez-Llamas v. Oregon, 548 U.S. 331, 349 (2006)

116 *Id*, at 354

117 Kolovrat v. Oregon, 366 U.S. 187, 194 (1961); Sanchez-Llamas v. Oregon, 548 U.S. 331,354 (2006).

118 See generally Restatement of Law, Third, The Foreign Relations of The United States § 114 (1987).

119 The concept of indirect effect originates in the EC law. It is a principle compelling national courts to interpret 'so far as possible' national legislation in accordance with EC directives. Barceló uses the term "indirect effect" to describe the effect of the international agreement on interpreting the ambiguous federal statutes, see John J. Barceló ,*Status of the WTO Rules in the US Law*, 5-6 (Cornell Legal Studies Research Paper No. 06-004, Mar.03, 2006), <http://ssrn.com/abstract=887757>; see also JOHN J. JACKSON, LEGAL PROBLEMS OF INTERNATIONAL ECONOMIC RELATIONS: CASES, MATERIALS AND TEXT ON THE NATIONAL AND INTERNATIONAL REGULATION OF TRANSNATIONAL ECONOMIC RELATIONS, 244 (4th ed., 2002).

120 Murray v. Schooner Charming Betsy, 6 U.S. (2 Cranch) 64 (1804).

Chief Justice Marshall observed that an "act of Congress ought never to be construed to violate the law of nations if any other possible construction remains."[121]

Although *Charming Betsy* has been followed since it was decided,[122] its application might be affected by the rulings in *Chevron USA. Inc. v. Natural Res. Def. Council Inc.* (hereafter *Chevron*).[123] The Supreme Court in the *Chevron* case sidestepped addressing the issue whether the courts should interpret statutes to avoid conflicting with international agreements. Rather, *Chevron* concerns the discretion an administrative agency may have in interpreting statutes. In this case, it was found that a court should respect an administrative agency's interpretation of statutes (as long as the interpretation is reasonable). In *Chevron*, the court took a two-step review. At first, the court reviewed whether Congress has expressed its intention unambiguously. If so, the courts and the agency must follow such an intention. If the statute is silent or ambiguous regarding the specific issue, the court then proceeded to review whether the agency's answer is based on a permissible construction of the statute.[124] Because an administrative agency is empowered to administer statutes, the Court held it can form the policy and rules to fill the gap left implicitly or explicitly by Congress. In such a case, a court may not substitute its own construction of a statutory provision for a reasonable interpretation made by an agency.[125] In some cases, the agency's interpretation of a statute might be inconsistent with certain US international obligations. In this sense, the *Chevron* doctrines conflict with the decision made in *Charming Betsy*. The Court has resorted to the *Chevron* doctrine to sustain the agency's interpretation of trade remedy statutes, even if it is inconsistent with WTO agreements.[126] The *Chevron* doctrine is certainly crucial to the question whether an international agreement could serve as interpretative guidance. It is also noteworthy that the courts tend to refrain from reviewing administrative actions concerning foreign affairs. The Supreme Court acknowledges that certain administrative decisions pertinent to foreign affairs are in nature political – not judicial. Such decisions are exclusively delegated by the Constitution to the political department of the government (i.e., executive and legislative branches). Such decisions involve large elements of prediction. They are and should be undertaken only by those directly responsible to the people whose welfare they

121 *Id*, at 118.

122 Most recently cited in Spector v. Norwegian Cruise Line Ltd., 545 U.S. 119 (2005)

123 Chevron U.S.A. Inc. v. Natural Res. Def. Council Inc., 467U.S. 837 (1984).

124 *Supra note* 123, at 843.

125 *Id*, at 843-44.

126 *E.g.* Timken Co. v. U.S., 354 F. 3d 1334 (Fed. Cir. 2004).

help or hurt.[127] In international trade cases, the courts also acknowledge their limited role of review and the broad discretion the executive branch may have.[128]

The influence of non-executing agreements over state law is more significant than influence over the statute. Mere existence of international agreements may indicate federal preemption of a matter at issue.[129] The courts reiterate that the power over foreign affairs belongs exclusively to the federal government and such power is not shared with the states.[130] The states may not take actions inconsistent with the federal government. In *United States v. Pink*, the Supreme Court ruled, "If state action could defeat or alter our foreign policy, serious consequences might ensue. The nation as a whole would be held to answer if a State creates difficulties with a foreign power."[131] In *Hines v. Davidowitz*, the Supreme Court held federal power in the field affecting foreign relations should remain entirely free from local interference.[132] The Court of Appeals of Second District in *Bethlehem Steel Corporation v. Board of Commissioners* cited *Hines v. Davidowitz* and further developed its reasoning. The Court of Appeal held if state legislation is permitted to operate simultaneously in the field of foreign affairs the relations between governments would likely be endangered. The foreign trade is conferred to national concern, not state regulation. The interference of the state can only impede (not foster) national trade policies.[133] In other words, the state should act consistently with international agreements accepted by the United States, even if they are not necessarily laws of the United States. The federal government, not the state, may decide how to implement international agreements. The federal government also decides whether to comply with its obligations under international agreements.

1.1.1.4. Summary

The legal status of international agreements in US domestic law is summarized as follows. The authorization for the President to accept an international agreement

---

127 Chicago & South Airlines Inc. v. Waterman S.S. Corp., 333 U.S. 103, 111 (1948).

128 *E.g.* Maple Leaf Fish Co. v. United States,762 F. 2d 86, 89 (Fed. Cir.1985); Suramericana de Aleaciones Laminadas v. United States, 966 F.2d 660 (1992).

129 Jackson, *supra* note 22, at 102.

130 See United States v. Belmont, 301 U.S. 324 (1937); Hines v. Davidowitz, 312 U.S. 52 (1941); United States v. Pink, 315 U.S. 203 (1942); Crosby v. National Foreign Council, 530 U.S. 363 (2000); Bethlem Steel Corporation v. Board of Commissioners, 276 Cal. App. 2d. 80 (1969); National Foreign Council v. Nations, 181 F.3d 38 (1st Cir. 1999).

131 United States v. Pink, at 232.

132 See Hines v. Davidowitz, at 63.

133 See Bethlehem Steel Corporation v. Board of Commissioners , 276 Cal. App. 2d 221, 80 Cal. Rptr. 800,803 (1969).

also provides the legal basis for that international agreement to be recognized by the United States as her international obligations. Not all of the international obligations are part of US domestic law. Only those obligations that meet the requirements of self-executing are part of domestic law. Where conflict exists between federal law and provisions of international agreements, the one of the later date prevails. A self-executing provision is superior to state law, whether prior or subsequent. Non–self-executing provisions still could be guidelines for interpreting federal law. The states ought to act consistent with international agreements, even if they are not self-executing.

The effect of international agreements in the US legal system is complicated and varies from case to case. The key is to allocate powers among branches of federal government as well as allocating powers between federal and state governments.

1.1.2. The Legal Status of the GATT 1947 in Domestic Law

GATT is supposed to be a provisional agreement and incorporated into the framework of the International Trade Organization (ITO).[134] While the ITO ultimately was never created, the GATT gradually filled the gap. The GATT was not (and was not intended to be) submitted to Congress because it was supposed to be only provisional. The ITO agreement should have been the agreement reviewed by the Congress.[135] The GATT is an Executive Agreement not explicitly approved by the Congress. For the purpose of this section, several questions will be explored. First, is GATT a valid international agreement under the US law? Second, is GATT a part of domestic law? If so, what is the status of GATT in the hierarchy of norms in domestic law? If not, what are the influences the GATT may have over the domestic legal system? These questions are extremely difficult to answer because the GATT contains sets of agreements. Moreover, the domestic authorization for GATT was unclear. Jackson and Hudec have written extensive articles about these issues.[136] It is inevitable to base the following discussion on their thorough research because no meaningful conclusions could otherwise be found.

---

134 History of the origin of the GATT, see Matsushita, *supra* note 40, at 2-3; see also SIMON LESTER ET AL., WORLD TRADE LAW, TEXT, MATERIALS AND COMMENTARY, 66-69 (2008).

135 John Jackson, The Jurisprudence of GATT and The WTO, 210 (2000)

136 John Jackson, The General Agreement on Tariffs and Trade in the United States Domestic Law, 66 Michigan law review 249 (1967); Robert E. Hudec, The Legal Status of GATT in the Domestic Law of the United States in THE EUROPEAN COMMUNITY AND THE GATT 187 (Meinhard Hilf et al. eds., 1986).

1.1.2.1. *Provisions of the GATT 1947 as International Obligations under Domestic Law*

Article I, Section 8 of the Constitution delegates to the Congress the power to regulate "the commerce with foreign nations.[137] One Court of Appeals held the Congressional power in this regard is superior to the President's more general power of "foreign affairs."[138] This ruling is consistent with the intention of Congress. Since 1934, the Congress has enacted a series of trade acts, which delegate the President to negotiate and enter into trade agreements.[139] The GATT includes two distinct sets of agreements. The original 1947 text and the subsequent amendments are the first set. In addition, separate side agreements, the "codes," were negotiated in the Tokyo Round. Different statutes delegate the President the authority to accept the GATT 1947 and the Tokyo Round agreements.

a) The GATT 1947

The United States entered into the GATT by ratifying the Protocol of Provisional Application (hereafter the PPA),[140] not the GATT 1947 itself. The President relied on the authorization provided for in Section 350 of Reciprocal Trade Agreements Act of 1934,[141] which was further amended and extended in 1945. The President (with such authorization) may enter into foreign trade agreements. To implement the trade agreement, the President is authorized to proclaim the modification of existing duties or other import restrictions. For that purpose, he or she is similarly authorized to proclaim additional import restrictions, as well as continuing existing customs and treating articles covered by the trade agreement.[142] The content of GATT is more than an agreement of tariff concessions. It is therefore arguable that Section 350 (a) could really provide an explicit authorization for the President. Jackson had undertaken a detailed examination to establish the statutory validity of the adherence to GATT 1947. He raised several arguments to support this observation. First, the term "trade agreement" under Section 350 (a) can be logically construed to cover the provisions of the GATT

---

137 *Supra* note 94.

138 United States v. Guy W. Capps Inc., 240 F. 2d 655 (4th Cir. 1953).The case was appealed to the Supreme Court. The Supreme Court did not rule on this question discussed by Court of Appeals. See 348 U.S. 296 (1954).

139 See generally, Jackson, *supra* note 119, at 78-90.

140 U.N. Econ & Soc. Council, Protocol of Provisional Application of the General Agreement on Tariffs and Trade, E/PC/T/214.ADD.2 REV.1 (Jan 1, 1940).

141 Reciprocal Trade Agreements Act of 1934, Pub. L. No. 73-316, 48 Sat. 943 (1934)

142 See 59 Stat. 410,411 (1945).

1947.[143] Second, the legislative history indicates that the Congress did deliberate the subject matters like those in the GATT 1947.[144] Third, the Congress accepted previous trade agreements with provisions like those in GATT 1947.[145] Fourth, the Congress never took any action to explicitly disapprove the GATT 1947. For instance, the Congress carefully stated that the extension of the Trade Acts "shall not be construed to determine or indicate the approval or disapproval by the Congress of the Executive Agreement known as General Agreement on Tariffs and Trade."[146] On the contrary the Congress gradually acknowledged the existence of the GATT 1947 as a legitimate executive agreement.[147] Last but not least, the courts have made decisions or opinions that necessarily imply the validity of the GATT 1947 under US law.[148] In practice, the courts usually would not explain whether the GATT 1947 has been recognized as international obligations of the United States. Rather, they would simply cite or mention the provisions of the GATT 1947. It is not surprising that the courts would not analyze the question; as Hudec observed, materials relevant to that question are complex and even incomplete.[149]

It is fair to say the GATT was not explicitly recognized or rejected by the Congress, at least in 1947. Nonetheless, the executive branch still might resort to the President's inherent power to justify the adherence to the GATT. In 1988, the Congress finally acknowledged the existence of GATT 1947. The Omnibus Trade and Competitiveness Act of 1988 contains several provisions that explicitly refer to the GATT.[150]

b) Tokyo Round Agreements

Both the Congress and the executive branch have learned from the confusing situation surrounding the GATT 1947. The authorizations for the Tokyo Round agreements are relatively straightforward. The Trade Act of 1974 authorized the

---

143 See Jackson, *supra note* 136, at 261-262.

144 *Id*, at 262-264.

145 *Id*, at 264-265, Appendix A to the article.

146 See Trade Agreements Extension Act of 1951,65 Stat. 72,75 (1951); Trade Agreement Extension Act of 1953, 67 Stat. 472,472 (1953); Trade Agreement Extension Act of 1955, 69 Stat. 162,163 (1955); Trade Agreement Extension Act of 1958, 72 Stat. 673,689.

147 *Supra note* 136, at 265-269.

148 *Id*, at 269-270.

149 See Hudec, *supra note* 136, at 199.

150 See section 1101 (b) of Omnibus Trade and Competitiveness Act of 1988, Pub. L. No. 100-418., 102 Stat. 1121.

President to negotiate the Tokyo Round agreements.[151] One of the major goals of the Tokyo Round is to regulate the non-tariff trade barriers (hereafter the NTB).[152] The NTB agreements were more politically controversial than the reciprocal agreements on tariff concessions. The Congress was fully informed about the negotiations and had reviewed the agreements.[153] The Tokyo Round negotiations were concluded in 1979. The Trade Agreement Act of 1979 provided the authorization for accepting these agreements.[154] For these trade agreements to be accepted, the President must submit the final trade agreement, including text, notifications of changes, and annexes.[155] The President, abiding by the reciprocal doctrine, has discretion regarding whether to accept certain Tokyo Round agreements.[156] The explicit authorization provided in the Act of 1979 removes any legal uncertainty regarding the validity of the Tokyo Round Agreements.

1.1.2.2. The Effect of the GATT

a) The GATT 1947

i. GATT as A Non–self-executing Agreement

Jackson and Hudec both accepted that the provisions of the GATT 1947 are not self-executing.[157] Considering the intention of the Congress and the texts of relevant statutes and the agreements, such observation is quite convincing.[158] Section 350 (a) of the Reciprocal Trade Agreement Act stated the President is authorized: "from time to time (1) to enter into trade agreements… (2) To *proclaim* such modifications of existing duties and other import restrictions, or such additional import restrictions… , as are required or appropriate to *carry out* any foreign trade agreement that the President has enter into hereunder"[159] (Emphasis added).

---

151 See John Jackson et. al., Implementing the Tokyo Round: Legal Aspects of Changing International Economic Rules, 80 (2) MICHIGAN LAW REVIEW 267, 349 (1982).

152 Brief introduction of Tokyo Round, see http://www.wto.org/english/thewto_e/whatis_e/tif_e/fact4_e.htm#tr (last visited Jan. 10, 2011)

153 See Jackson, *supra* note 119, at 82.

154 Section 2 (c), Trade Agreement Act of 1979, Pub. L. No. 96-36, 93 Stat. 148 (1979).

155 Section 2 (b), paragraph 1, 93 Stat. 147 (1979).

156 *Id*, Section 2 (b), paragraph 3.

157 See Hudec, *supra note* 136, at 210; also Jackson, *supra* note 136,288-289.

158 But see Ronald A. Brand, *The Status of General Agreement on Tariff and Trade in the United States Domestic Law*, 26 STANFORD JOURNAL OF INTERNATIONAL LAW 479,505-506 (1989-1990).

159 Supra note 142.

These provisions indicate the trade agreement is not part of domestic law. Otherwise, there would be no need to make proclamation to carry out the agreements. Certainly this provision can be read to allow the GATT 1947 to be self-executive, if the proclamation is construed as a mere announcement or symbolic act, which enables the public to notice the agreement and has no legal effect. However, such a reading does not fit in the context of this provision. The provision clearly stated the duties may change by the proclamations.[160] The proclamation is treated as an act of domestic law-making, through which the President may implement the obligations under the trade agreements.[161] This view is also confirmed by the intention of the Congress as shown in the legislative history. The 1934 House Report stated that the President is delegated the power to fix tariffs and to enter into trade agreements.[162] The Congress seems to consider the power to enter into agreements and power to proclaim in Section 350 (a) as separate and different. At the time of the extension of the Act, the Senate Report further clarified "Under the Trade Agreement Act, changes in our tariff rates are made ... by the President's proclamation under the authority of the Trade Agreement Act. Changes in the tariff rates are not made by the agreement, *per se.*"[163] The Congress would not contemplate that the GATT 1947 was self-executing.

Furthermore, neither did the drafters of the GATT 1947 intend to make it self-executing. Certain provisions of the GATT are formed in a way as though they were able to be directly applied as domestic law.[164] However, it is noteworthy that the GATT 1947 itself was never literally accepted. Instead, the Protocol of Provisional Application became effective. Paragraphs 2 and 3 of the PPA both stated that governments "shall make effective such provisional application of the General Agreement."[165] Accordingly, the governments are required only to implement the GATT. The evidence in the negotiation history, found by Jackson, indicated the drafters did not intend a self-executing effect.[166]

In short, the provisions and rules of the GATT 1947 became part of US domestic law by virtue of the proclamation under Section 350. The PPA is not self-executing, nor is the GATT 1947. This way of implementing the GATT 1947 gives the political branch more flexibility while it conducts foreign trade affairs.

---

160 See Jackson, *supra note* 136,282-283.

161 See Hudec, *supra note* 136, at 197.

162 HR Rep. No. 1000, 73 rd Cong. 2nd Sess., 11 (1934).

163 S Rep. No.258, 78th Cong. 1st Sess.47,48 (1943).

164 *E.g.* GATT 1947 Article III: 2, or GATT 1947 Article IV:3. available at http://www.wto.org/english/docs_e/legal_e/gatt47_01_e.htm (last visited Jan. 10, 2011).

165 *Supra* note 140, at 2.

166 Jackson, *supra note* 136,285-286.

The President may selectively implement provisions under the GATT, even if it might contrast with US obligations.

Since the United States accepted the GATT, many cases have involved matters pertinent to the GATT. Some among them address the domestic legal status of the GATT.[167] In *United States v. Yoshida International, Inc.*, the Court of Customs and Patent Appeals rejected the arguments relied upon the GATT. The importer, who bought zippers from Japan, challenged the validity of the Presidential proclamation imposing an import duty of 10 percent, which is one of several emergency measures relating to a balance of payment crisis. The Court reversed the decision of the US Customs Court in favor of the importer. In its footnote, the Court clearly opposed the idea that the GATT could have effect in the domestic legal system. It acknowledged the surcharge was inconsistent with the GATT. However, the Court dismissed the importer's argument because the Congress never ratified the GATT.[168] The Court could have easily justified the surcharge by virtue of the exception provisions under GATT XX or GATT XXI, but it made a faulty explanation instead. This also indicated that the Court was either unfamiliar with the GATT provisions or reluctant to apply them (even indirectly).

It is notable that the Court of Custom and Patent Appeals did apply the provision of the GATT in an earlier case, *United States v. Star Industries, Inc.*[169] The case involved the validity of Presidential Proclamation which withdraws previous tariff concessions. Pursuant to Article 252 (c) of the Trade Expansion Act of 1962, the President was authorized to withdraw tariff concessions via proclamation. This proclamation was challenged for withdrawing the concession on a most-favored nation basis (i.e., such concessions were not withdrawn only as to a particular party but to all parties). Firstly, the Court analyzed and interpreted Article XXVIII of GATT and found that the most-favored nation treatment was required thereby.[170] The Court went on to consider whether the statue allowed the President to deviate from that obligation. In light of the legislative history of the statute at issue, the US international obligations must be considered. The proclamation was affirmed valid. In this case, the Court applied the GATT because the statute at issue required due regards for US international obligations to be taken.[171] Furthermore, Article XXVIII:3 of GATT has been explicitly incor-

167 E.g., Holm & Co. v. Hardin, 449 F. 2d 1009 (D.C. Cir. 1971);Calnetics Corp. v. Volkswagen of America Inc., 532 F. 2d 674 (9th Cir.), cert. denied, 429 U.S. 940 (1976); United States v. Yoshida International ,Inc., 526 F. 2d 560 (C.C.P.A. 1975);Zenith Radio Corp. v. United States, 437 U.S. 443 (1978); Japan Lines Ltd v. County of Los Angeles , 441 U.S. 434 (1979).

168 526 F. 2d 560, 575 (C.C.P.A. 1975).

169 59 C.C.P.A. 159; 462 F.2d 557 (1972).

170 *Id*, at 164-165.

171 See *id* , at 165.

porated into the proclamation. The Court did not recognize the provision of the GATT *per ser* as self-executing.

The Supreme Court has made two decisions concerning the GATT. In *Zenith Radio Corp. v. United States*, an American manufacturer asserted that the executive branch had erred in interpretation of subsidies. The manufacturer alleged that the commodity taxes of exported products were refunded in Japan and the remission ought to constitute a subsidy. The administration thinks otherwise. The government did not argue that the provision of the GATT was superior to the statute.[172] The Supreme Court, nonetheless, held that such longstanding administrative construction of subsidies has been incorporated into the widely accepted GATT. This administrative construction became, via incorporation into the GATT, the general understanding of subsidy, on which the foreign tax system and the expectations of private parties were based. Considering these reliance interests, the Supreme Court affirmed the administrative interpretation of the statute. [173] In this case, the Court did not apply the provision of the GATT or recognize its legal status in domestic law. Merely, the Court used the GATT provision as evidence establishing that the governmental and private reliance were consistent with the government's interpretation of US countervailing duty law. Another case involving an argument based on the GATT was *Japan Line. LTD et al. v. County of Los Angeles et al.* The Japanese shipping companies, which were based in Japan, protested against the property taxes on their shipping containers. One of their arguments was that the tax violated GATT III.[174]The Court found such an argument was deemed "frivolous" because the GATT III prohibited discriminative measures against foreign products, and because the property was imposed equally to domestic and foreign products. [175] The Court did not deny the existence of the GATT; moreover, it made its own interpretation of the GATT provision. Still, the provisions of the GATT in both cases were not actually considered as law in the domestic legal system.

The cases mentioned previously are only a few pieces of the puzzle, which might give clues to the position of the courts on this issue. The courts often give few lines or briefly address the issue in the footnote. In most cases, the reasoning concerned is relatively short and insufficient.[176] At least one thing is clear; the courts do not find the provisions of the GATT self-executing. Such view is in line with the intentions of the Congress and the drafters of the GATT. At almost

172 37 U.S. 443, footnote 13.

173 *Id.*, at 457.

174 441 U.S. 434,439, footnote 4.

175 *Id.*

176 See Hudec, *supra note* 136, at 218.

every end of the GATT period, the Court of International Trade stated that provisions of GATT became part of US law via the executive order (i.e., the proclamation, pursuant to Congressional delegation of power to the President).[177] In other words, the GATT are not-self executing.

ii. Relationship to Federal and State Law

Because the GATT is not self-executing, there would be no need to consider the possible conflict between the GATT and federal law. The issue would be whether the obligations under the GATT incorporated into the Presidential proclamation overturns the existing statutes conflicting therewith. Two distinguished scholars, Hudec and Jackson, have explored such issues but came to different conclusions. Hudec observed that the provisions of the GATT incorporated into the proclamation are inferior to existing federal law.[178] Jackson concluded the opposite.[179] To review the issue, one should first turn to Section 350 (a) of the Reciprocal Trade Agreement Act, which authorized the proclamation. Subsection (2) of Section 350 (a) reads, "To proclaim such modification of existing duties and import restrictions."[180] Hudec based his observation on the idea that the Congress may authorize the President to negotiate international agreements without necessarily giving him authority to make new federal law in each and every field of that agreement.[181]

Hudec thinks Subsection (2) of Section 350 (a) was intended to cover typical provisions of trade agreement (i.e., the immediate, product-specific commitments). In the GATT context, that would be tariff concessions. Most of these terms in trade agreement involve changes to federal law. The President is therefore granted additional proclaiming power to make these terms effective. Hudec's observation about the proclamation would be perfectly true in cases where the President does not have competence to change *any* federal law. The "import restrictions" under Section 350 (a) could be a statute. In this sense, Subsection 2 of Section 350 (a) did authorize the President to change certain federal laws. It would be hard to presume the Congress would differentiate the effect of the proclamation and other Congressional statute without saying so.[182] Moreover, considering the President has inherent power over foreign affairs, more materials are needed to support the argument that the proclamation is inferior. The opinions of the courts could have provided more support for

177 Footwear Distributors and Retailers of America v. United States, 18 C.I.T. 391,410; 852 F. Supp 1078 (Ct. Int'l Trade 1994).
178 *Id*, at 208 and 210.
179 Jackson *supra note* 136, 293.
180 Supra note 141.
181 See Hudec, *supra note* 136, 209.
182 Jackson *supra note* 136, 293.

such an argument if they gave more explanations for their positions in favor of the federal law. The courts often disposed of the arguments based on the provisions of the GATT. They either denied that provisions of GATT are binding[183] or they held the supremacy of federal law.[184] The *American Express Co. v. United States* is one of these typical cases. The court clearly stated, "GATT is a trade agreement, which if conflicts with a law of Congress, must yield to the later."[185] Unfortunately, the court gave no more guidance, except for this statement. In the *Public Citizen v. Office of United States Trade Representative*, the court recognized that the federal statute prevailed over the GATT.[186] The court reasoned that the GATT and its subsequent modifications are not Senate-ratified treaties, and they therefore do not have the status of statutory law. This case was brought in 1992. The reasoning in this case was still curt, although the GATT through proclamation has been applied for decades.

This issue was partially solved because the PPA contained a grandfather clause. Paragraph 1 of PPA, subparagraph (b) required the government to apply "Part II of that Agreement to the fullest extent not inconsistent with existing legislation."[187] Many crucial and controversial provisions, *inter alia* trade remedies, were listed in Part II of the GATT. The grandfather clause would significantly protect the pre-1947 legislations and decrease the possibility of conflicts between the federal law and the GATT obligations incorporated into the proclamations. The courts still must solve the conflicts between existing legislations and other obligations listed in Part I and III (e.g., the most-favored nation treatment and the tariff concessions) incorporated into the proclamation. The courts have ruled these obligations are inferior to existing legislations, although they did not give convincing reasoning.

Both the supremacy clause (Article VI, Section 2 of the Constitution) and the foreign commerce clause (Article I, Section 8, Clause 3 of the Constitution) support the argument that provisions of the GATT, which were incorporated into proclamation, supersede conflicting state law. In light of the opinions given by the Supreme Court, the states cannot act inconsistent with the obligations of the GATT, even if they are not self-executing.[188] Supreme Courts of certain states have recognized the GATT had a treaty status and therefore was superior to the

---

183 *E.g.* United States v. Yoshida International, Inc, 526 F. 2d 560 (C.C.P.A. 1975); Select Tire Salvage Co. v. United States, 386 F.2d 1008 (Ct. Claims,1967).

184 E.g. Select Tier Salvage Co. v. United States, 386 F.2d 1008 (Ct. Claims,1967); American Express Co. v. United States, 332 F. Supp.191 (Cust. Ct. 1971), affirmed, 472 F. 2d 1050 (C.C.P.A. 1973).

185 *Id*, at 201.

186 804 F. Supp. 385,388 (1992).

187 Supra note 140.

188 Decisions of the Supreme Court on the influence of an international obligation over the state law, see Part I, section 1.1.1.3 supra.

state law.[189] The Supreme Court has never ruled on this issue, but its position can be deduced from *Japan Line LTD et al. v. County of Los Angeles et al.* In this case, the Supreme Court once again confirmed that the states cannot interfere in foreign trade affairs, which is a power that belongs to Congress. The Court found that California's tax at issue prevented the federal government from "speaking in one voice" in international trade. Furthermore, the state tax subjected the United States to retaliation by foreign government, so the nation as a whole would suffer.[190] Following this reasoning, the obligations under the GATT should be superior to state law. Otherwise, the United States as a whole would face the countermeasures under GATT due to a GATT-inconsistent measure taken by single state. It is also noteworthy that the GATT noticed local governments were possibly non-compliant. Article XXIV: 12 of the GATT requires the governments take "reasonable measures" available to ensure the observance of the provisions of the GATT by the local government.[191] This provision, nevertheless, should not be construed as exempting the local government from the obligations under the GATT.[192] To comply with this provision, it is preferable to recognize the supremacy of the GATT over the state law.

b) Tokyo Round Agreements

The Congress has made its intention clear for the effect of Tokyo Round Agreements. The Trade Agreement Act of 1979 unambiguously stated the effect of these agreements and their relation to the federal law. Section 3, Subsections (b) and (c) provide for how the Tokyo Round Agreements should be implemented.[193] These provisions have shown that these agreements cannot be self-executing. Moreover, Subsection (f) of Section 3 states these agreements shall not be construed as creating "private right of action or remedy for which provision is not explicitly made under this Act or under the Laws of United States."[194] In this light, these agreements would never fill the requirements of self-executing agreements. The Statement of Administrative Action accompanied with the Trade Agreement

---

189 *E.g.* Territory of Hawaii v. Ho, 41 Haw. 565,568 (1957); K.S.B. Technical Sales Corp. v. North Jersey Water Supply Comm'n, 75 N.J. 272,279, 381 A. 2d 774 (1977), appeal dismissed, 435 U.S. 982 (1978).

190 See *supra note* 174, at 452-453.

191 See http://www.wto.org/english/docs_e/legal_e/gatt47_02_e.htm#articleXXIV (last visited Jan. 11, 2011).

192 The ambiguity of this provision and the arguments thereto, see Jackson, *supra* note 136, at 302-311.

193 93 Stat. 148-150 (1979).

194 *Id*, at 150.

Act states unequivocally that "[T]he Trade Agreements negotiated are not self-executing and accordingly do not have independent effect under U.S. law."[195]

The relation between the Tokyo Round Agreements and federal law appears in Subsection (a) of Section 3, which reads: "No Provision of any trade agreement approved by the Congress under Section 2 (a), nor the application of any such provision to any person or circumstance, which is in conflict with any statute of the United States shall be given effect under the laws of the United States."[196] Pursuant to this subsection, the provisions of the Tokyo Round Agreements are inferior to federal law. However, the Trade Agreement Act remained silent on the relation between these agreements and state law. The previously mentioned considerations under the GATT 1947 context are similarly true for the Tokyo Round Agreements. In addition, Tokyo Round Agreements have provisions similar to Article XXIV: 12 of the GATT.[197] The state law should be inferior to the provisions of these agreements.

In summary, the provisions of the GATT and its subsequent agreements are not self-executing. The provisions of GATT 1947 and Tokyo Round Agreements can be part of US law, only if they are implemented by the President or the Congress. The federal law would always prevail with the provision of these agreements, whether it is prior or later than these agreements. And state law should yield to the obligations under these agreements.

1.1.3. The Legal Status of the WTO Agreements in Domestic Law

The legal status of the GATT in the US legal system is extremely complicated because the Congress said too little about these agreements. Nor did the courts help to solve the puzzle with intensive reasoning. The United States did not repeat this somehow confusing episode in the GATT period. Instead, the legal status of the WTO agreements were discussed and written in black and white. Nonetheless, the implementing legislation is consistent with the practice in the GATT period. The Uruguay Round negotiation was launched in 1986 and formally concluded at the final ministerial meeting at Marrakesh on April 15, 1994. Many ambitious agendas have been completed, including revision of the Tokyo Round Codes, new rules for non-tariff barriers, and rules for intellectual property rights. The Uruguay Round negotiation took a "single package" approach and established an entire

195 U.S. House of Representatives, Trade Agreements Act of 1979: Statements of Administrative Action, H.R. Doc. No. 153 pt.2, 96th Cong., 1st Sess. (1979).

196 93 Stat. 148 (1979).

197 *E.g.* Agreement on Technical Barrier to Trade (Standards Code), Article 6.

new treaty for members to join. Two institutional important structures were also established. Firstly, the WTO Agreement provides for a formal international trade organization charter and structure. Second, the DSU has fixed some defects in the dispute settlement mechanism under the GATT 1947, especially the "blocking" problem. These new developments would make negotiators struggle with the concerns of losing "sovereignty."[198] The Uruguay Round package is incredibly far-reaching and imposes constraints on members. The United States thus took months to complete the domestic constitutional procedures; various aspects were extensively debated.[199] The domestic legal status of the WTO agreements is an issue closely related to the debates concerning sovereignty. The Uruguay Round Agreement Act (hereafter the URAA) concluded the debates of sovereignty, as well as the legal status of the WTO agreements. The URAA and its legislative history would clarify the grounds for the US position on the effect of the WTO agreements in the domestic law.

1.1.3.1. Uruguay Round Implementing Legislation

The Omnibus Trade and Competitiveness Act of 1988 regulates the acceptance and the implementation of the trade agreements. Section 1102 and Section 1103 provide the "fast-track" procedure, which was applied to the Uruguay Round Agreements (i.e., the WTO agreements). The President may change the tariff barrier by proclamation.[200] The Congress acknowledges using the fast-track procedure to implement the non-tariff barriers. At least 120 days before entering into the non-tariff trade agreement, the President shall consult the Congress about matters regarding how to implement such agreements.[201] After signing the agreement, the President must submit the implementing Bill along with a statement of administrative action, which explains how the President would administer the implementing legislation.[202] The implementing Bill may also be passed under the fast-track procedure. Under such procedure, the Bill can only be ap-

---

198 See John H. Jackson, The Great 1994 Sovereignty Debate: United States Acceptance and Implementation of the Uruguay Round Results, 36 COLUMBIA JOURNAL OF TRANSNATIONAL LAW 157, 167 (1997).

199 *Id.*

200 See Omnibus Trade and Competitiveness Act of 1988, section 1102 (a), Pub. L. No. 103-49, 102 Stat. 1126 (1992), amended by An Act: To provide authority for the President to enter into trade agreements to conclude the Uruguay Round of multilateral trade negotiations under the auspices of the General Agreement on Tariffs and Trade, to extend tariff proclamation authority to carry out such agreements and to apply congressional "fast track" procedures to a bill implementing such agreements, Pub L. No. 103-49,107 Stat. 239 (1993).

201 An Act amending the Omnibus Trade and Competitiveness Act of 1988, Pub L. No. 103-49,107 Stat. 239 (1993)

202 See section 1103 (a), 102 Stat. 1128-1129 (1992)

proved or rejected as a whole and cannot be amended. The Committees must discharge the Bill within a certain number of days, so that they cannot bottle up the process. Each House must vote within a certain number of days, and the debates in both Houses are not unlimited.[203] The Uruguay Round Agreement Act was introduced in September and adopted in December 1994.

a) *The Uruguay Round Agreements Act and the Statement of Administrative Action*

The URAA[204] is the major implementing legislation of the WTO agreements. The Statement of Administrative Action (hereafter the SAA),[205] accompanied by the submission of the URAA, was approved by the Congress. The URAA and the SAA established the legal status of the WTO agreement in US domestic law. In other words, they regulate the extent to which the United States must act in line with the WTO agreements. Besides describing the implementing bill and administrative actions, the SAA also provides reasons why such a bill and actions are suitable to carry out the WTO agreements. These considerations would be thus more clearly expressed in the SAA than in the URAA. The URAA states the SAA is an authoritative expression by the United States in any judicial proceeding concerning interpretation or application of the URAA and the WTO agreements.[206] The URAA is often read in conjunction with those interpretations.

The URAA itself implies that the WTO agreements are not self-executing. This bill is intended to bring the US law into compliance with her obligations under the WTO agreements by amending WTO-inconsistent laws or by creating new provisions of law.[207] Furthermore, the Congress has precluded a private party from bringing a suit against the federal and state government based on the provisions of the WTO agreements. Neither shall a private party defend a case under these provisions. [208] Accordingly, the WTO agreements are not part of US law. Section 102 of the URAA describes the relationship of the WTO agreements to federal and state law.

---

203 See section 1103 (b)-(e), 102 Stat. 1129-1132 (1992).

204 Uruguay Round Agreement Act, Pub. L. No.103-465, 1994 HR 5110.

205 Statement of Administrative Action, H.R. Rep. No. 316, 103RD Cong., 2ND Sess. 1994 U.S.C.C.A.N. 4040.

206 URAA, section 102 (d), 19 USC 3512 (d).

207 See SAA, 1994 U.S.C.C.A.N. 4050.

208 URAA, section 102 (c) (1), 19 USC 3512 (c) (1).

i. Relationship to Federal Law

Pursuant to the Section 102 (a) (1), the WTO agreements or the applications of these provisions, which are inconsistent with US laws, shall not have effect. The "effect" means the binding force of these agreements on the United States in the domestic legal system.[209] This provision does not imply the United States would not intend to comply with these agreements. The SAA explains it does not prevent the administration from acting consistently with these agreements, where the terms of the statutes permit. Instead, Section 102 (a) (1) reveals the Congress' intention that all the changes in federal statutes, which are necessary to implement these agreements, should be specifically enacted. The Congress will not create an overall preemption of the federal statutes.[210] It is therefore conceivable that the Congress intends to have more opportunities to supervise the future implementation of US obligations under the WTO agreements, and to ensure that no existing federal statutes other than those addressed by the URAA are affected. A similar intention is shown in Section 102 (a) (2), which requires the URAA not to be construed to amend laws of the United States. The Congress would like not only to control the potential effect of the WTO agreements; it would also like to limit the potential effect of the URAA itself.

ii. Relationship to State Law

In the GATT period, the provisions of the GATT prevail over the conflicting state laws. On the contrary, the URAA respects the autonomy of states in many ways. First, it does not perceive the provisions of the WTO agreements as necessarily superior to the state laws. No state law or its application could be declared invalid in that it is inconsistent with the WTO agreements, unless the federal government

---

209 URAA, section 102 (a) (1), 19 USC 3512 (a) (1).

210 In the passages relating to the relationship to federal law , U.S.C.C.A.N. 4050, the SAA reads: Section 102 establishes the relationship between the Uruguay Round agreements and US law. The implementing bill, including the authority granted to federal agencies to promulgate implementing regulations, is intended to bring US law fully into compliance with US obligations under those agreements. The bill accomplishes that objective with respect to federal legislation by amending existing federal statutes that would otherwise be inconsistent with the agreements and, in certain instances, by creating entirely new provisions of law .... Section 102 (a) (1) clarifies that no provision of a Uruguay Round agreement will be given effect under domestic law if it is inconsistent with federal law, including provisions of federal law enacted or amended by the bill. Section 102 (a) (1) will not prevent implementation of federal statutes consistently with the Uruguay Round agreements, where permissible under the terms of such statutes. Rather, the section reflects the Congressional view that necessary changes in federal statutes should be specifically enacted rather than provided for in a blanket preemption of federal statutes by those agreements.

brings a suit for that purpose.[211] The Congress has retained actions challenging the invalidity of state laws exclusively for the federal government. Such intention is provided in sweeping language in Section 102 (c) (2) as well as in the SAA.[212] These suits brought by the private parties are not appropriate means for ensuring the state compliance because these suits would interfere with the President's conduct of foreign trade affairs and with suitable resolutions under the DSU.[213] The SAA states "the nature of the federal-state relation in implementing the Uruguay Round agreements are likely to be entirely cooperative in nature."[214] The legal challenge brought by the federal government is intended to be the secondary mean to ensure the state compliance.[215] It is preferable to seek state compliance with WTO agreements on a voluntary basis.

The consultation process in Section 102 (b) (1) is another example in favor of the autonomy of the state. The President shall consult with the states, via the intergovernmental policy advisory committees on trade, to make the state laws and practices conform to the WTO agreements.[216] The United States Trade Representative (Trade Representative) will designate a "WTO Coordinator for State Matters" in the Office of United States Trade Representative (hereafter the USTR). The coordinator serves as a connection between the states and the Trade Represen-

---

211 URAA, section 102 (b) (2) (A), 19 USC 3512 (b) (2) (A).

212 URAA, section 102 (c) (2), 19 USC 3512 (c) (2) provides:

It is the intention of the Congress through paragraph (1) to occupy the field with respect to any cause of action or defense under or in connection with any of the Uruguay Round Agreements, including by precluding any person other than the United States from bringing any action against any State or political subdivision thereof or raising any defense to the application of State law under or in connection with any of the Uruguay Round Agreements–

(A) on the basis of a judgment obtained by the United States in an action brought under any such agreement; or (B) on any other basis

In the passages relating to private law suits, 1994 U.S.C.C.A.N. 4054, the SAA provides:

Moreover, as section 102 (c) (2) makes clear, through its approval and implementation of the Uruguay Round agreements Congress will have "occupied the field" with respect to any cause of action or defense that seeks, directly or indirectly, the private enforcement of those agreements. That means that private parties may not bring suit or raise defenses:

directly under those agreements;

on the basis of a successful judgment against a state in a suit brought by the Attorney General under the agreements; or

on any other basis, including Congress' Commerce Clause authority.

213 See 1994 U.S.C.C.A.N. 4054.

214 1994 U.S.C.C.A.N. 4055.

215 In the passages relating to Section 102 (b) (2), 1994 U.S.C.C.A.N. 4054, the SAA provides:

[T]he authority conferred on the United States under this paragraph is intended to be used only as a "last resort", in the unlikely event that efforts to achieve consistency through the cooperative approach discussed above have not succeeded.

216 URAA, section 102 (b) (1) (A), 19 USC 3512 (b) (1) (A).

tative. The coordinator transmits information and advice from the states concerning WTO- related matters that directly affect the states. The Trade Representative also informs the states about the ongoing basis of these matters.[217] The federal government would consider information and advice submitted by the states in formulating the US positions regarding these matters affecting the states.[218]

The federal government will even more closely cooperate with states in cases where other members argue consistency of state law with the WTO agreements under the DSU procedures. The state concerned is informed and kept involved in development of the positions of the United States at each stage of dispute settlement proceedings. The Trade Representative shall notify the state concerning the current stage of the proceedings in a timely manner. The state is consulted throughout the consultation period, panel procedure, Appellate Body procedure, compliance panel, and other proceedings. All the submissions and documents related to these proceedings are available to the state concerned. That state may advise and assist the Trade Representative in preparing factual information and arguments. It also may attend the panel and Appellate Body hearings. In the event the state measures are found under the DSU to be inconsistent with the WTO agreements, the Trade Representative will work with the state to settle the dispute with other members. The federal government would not necessarily seek to invalidate the state law or to require the state to change that law. [219] If the federal government does seek to invalidate a WTO-inconsistent state law in federal court, the panel and the Appellate Body reports with regard to that state law cannot be introduced to the court. Instead, the court should consider the matter *de neno*.[220]

iii. Implementation of DSB Rulings

The Congress seems to have some concerns about the DSU proceedings. The URAA provides several rules for conducting the dispute settlement procedures, which make the procedure more transparent and open to the Congress as well as to the public.[221] On the other hand, the effect of the DSB rulings in the domestic legal system is limited. The DSB rulings are not self-executing and not even necessarily implemented. For instance, the Trade Representative shall consult with the appropriate Congressional committee whether the United States would implement an adverse panel report.[222] The implementation process is compli-

217 URAA, section 102 (b) (1) (B), 19 USC 3512 (b) (1) (B), and SAA, 1994 U.S.C.C.A.N. 4051.
218 URAA, section 102 (b) (1) (B), 19 USC 3512 (b) (1) (B), and SAA, 1994 U.S.C.C.A.N. 4052.
219 URAA, section 102 (b) (1) (B), 19 USC 3512 (b) (1) (B), and SAA, 1994 U.S.C.C.A.N. 4053.
220 URAA, section 102 (b) (2) (B), 19 USC 3512 (b) (2) (B), and SAA , 1994 U.S.C.C.A.N. 4054.
221 URAA, section 123 (d), (e), (f), 19 USC 3533 (d), (e), (f) and section 127, 19 USC 3537.
222 URAA, section 123 (f) (3).

cated. The statute law and administrative regulations apply different implementing procedures. If a statute is found to violate the US obligations under the WTO agreements, only the Congress may change the statute. In addition, the SAA indicates that the executive branch would not use the fast-track procedure to modify the statute.[223] If the administrative regulations or practices are found to violate the US obligations, they cannot be modified until certain requirements fulfilled. The Trade Representative must consult with the concerned Congressional committees, seek advice from private sector, and submit a report to the Congressional committees concerned. Also, the relevant department or agency should provide an opportunity for the public to comment on the proposed modification.[224] The modified regulation may be effective until 60 days after the consultations with the Congressional committees begin.[225] During that period, the Committee on Ways and Means of the House of Representatives and the Committee on Finance of the Senate may vote their approval or disapproval of proposed modifications. These votes, however, are not binding.[226]

If the regulations and the practices concerned are made by the International Trade Commission (hereafter the ITC), the previously mentioned procedures do not apply.[227] The Trade Representative may request the ITC to issue an advisory report on whether the ITC would be permitted under the US law to bring its regulation and practice in conformity with the DSB rulings concerning trade remedies (i.e., anti-dumping, safeguards, and countervailing duties).[228] If the ITC finds the compliance to be possible, the Trade Representative shall consult with the Congressional committees concerning the matter and may require the ITC to issue this affirmative report. Before this affirmative report is implemented, the Trade Representative shall consult with the relevant congressional committees.[229] Similar procedures apply to the determinations of Department of Commerce about countervailing and antidumping duties.[230]

---

223 In 1994 U.S.C.C.A.N 4050, SAA reads:

> Accordingly, at this time it is the expectation of the Administration that no changes in existing federal law, rules, regulations, or orders other than those specifically indicated in the implementing bill and this Statement will be required to implement the new international obligations that will be assumed by the United States under the Uruguay Round agreements. Should it prove otherwise, the Administration would need to seek new legislation from Congress or, if a change in regulation is required, follow normal agency procedures for amending regulations.

224 URAA, section 123 (g) (1), 19 USC 3533 (g) (1).

225 URAA, section 123 (g) (2), 19 USC 3533 (g) (2).

226 URAA, section 123 (g) (3), 19 USC 3533 (g) (3).

227 URAA, section 123 (g) (4), 19 USC 3533 (g) (4).

228 URAA, section 129 (a) (1), 19 USC 3538 (a) (1).

229 URAA, section 129 (a) (3), (4), (5), 19 USC 3538 (a) (3), (4), (5).

230 URAA, section 129 (b), 19 USC 3538 (b).

In general, the United States chooses a more flexible approach to implement its obligations under the WTO agreements. The United States agrees to modify the existing law to conform with the WTO agreement to the extent that the United States considers appropriate. No decisions of the DSB in this regard are binding for the United States. Also, the domestic courts cannot overrule the US law with provisions of the WTO agreements. These provisions are not self-executing and not necessarily superior to state laws. Only the political branch, the executive and the Congress, may decide whether and to what extent to fulfill its obligations under WTO agreements. There would be no general legal mandate to ensure the full WTO compliance by federal government or the states.[231]

b) Sovereignty Concerns in the Legislation

The Congress has never addressed the issues of the GATT's legal status in domestic law because the GATT 1947 was never formally submitted to the Congress. In the Uruguay Round, the Congress has access to the negotiations conducted by the President and has the final say on the domestic legal status of the WTO agreements. Before accepting the URAA, the Congress and the Senate have conducted various debates and held many hearings, wherein the participants argue for and against the WTO agreements. The legislative history is significant for exploring the grounds for the previously mentioned provisions of the URAA. In reviewing the legislative history, the sovereignty issue was prominent in considering the domestic legal status of WTO agreements.[232] The developments brought by the WTO, such as the rules for non-tariff barriers and the decision-making process, raise concerns that the US sovereignty would be severely impeded. The Trade Representative clearly states that the Congress retains the authority to change the US law; the WTO would in no means affect such an

231 See David W. Leebron, *Implementation of the Uruguay Round Results in the United States* in IMPLEMENTING THE URUGUAY ROUND 175, 234 (John H. Jackson & Alan O. Skyes eds., 1997).

232 See generally URUGUAY ROUND AGREEMENTS: A LEGISLATIVE HISTORY OF PUBLIC LAW NO. 103-465 (Bernard D. Reams Jr. & John S. Schultz eds. , 1995).The sovereignty concern was raised in various committees. The following hearings focused more specifically on this concern. See *World Trade Organization: Hearing before the Committee on Ways and Means in the House of Representatives*, 103d Cong., 2d Sess., (1994); *GATT Implementing Legislation: Hearing on S. 2467 Before the Committee on Commerce, Science, and Transportation in the Senate*, 103d Cong., 2d Sess., (1994); *Results of the Uruguay Round Trade Negotiations Hearings Before the Committee on Finance in the Senate*, 103d Cong., 2d Sess., (1994);*The World Trade Organization and the U.S. Sovereignty: Hearings Before the Senate Committee on Foreign Rations*, 103rd. Cong. (1994).

authority.[233] In other words, the WTO agreements are not self-executing and the US sovereignty is therefore intact.

The concept of "sovereignty" is ambiguous, so the general objection that sovereignty would be impeded is also unclear. When the objections are further examined for underlying reasons, the impacts of the WTO agreements on the US legal system become clear. In the context of the Uruguay Round debates, sovereignty normally refers to the questions about the allocation of power (i.e., the power of decision-making).[234] Some would define the "sovereignty" in this context as law-making authority.[235] Both concepts concern the government's decision-making power.

i. Excessive Constraints on Domestic Decision Making Power

Opponents to the WTO agreements are concerned that decision-making power will shift from Washington, DC to Geneva, Switzerland. These opponents perceive the WTO as a system of international governance with legislative, executive, and judicial powers.[236] The arguments focus on four aspects. Firstly, it is criticized that the United States does not have weighted voting or a veto in the WTO decision-making process. Opponents to the WTO agreements believe the United States should have more decision-making influence, considering the US financial contribution to the WTO budget as well as it importance in world trade. In general, all the decisions in the WTO are made by consensus. If consensus cannot be generated, the decision shall be made by voting; each nation has one vote.[237] For instance, the WTO allows changes by a majority vote of the members.[238] There are similar provisions in relation to adopting a formal interpretation (Marrakesh Agreement, Article IX: 2), waivers (Marrakesh Agreement, Article IX: 3 and 4), and to changing the DSU ((Marrakesh Agreement, Article IX: 8). The rule of "one nation, one vote" in conjunction with the majority vote process causes

233 World Trade Organization: Hearing before the Committee on Ways and Means in the House of Representatives, 103d Cong., 2d Sess., 13 (1994) (statement of Michael Kantor, U.S. Trade Representative).

234 See Jackson, *supra note* 198, at 159

235 See Letter from Professor Anne-Marie Slaughter, Harvard Law School, to Senator Ernest F. Hollings 5 (October 18, 1994) reprinted in *GATT Implementing Legislation: Hearings on S. 2467 Before the Senate Committee on Commerce, Science and Transportation*, 103d Cong., 2d Sess. 286-290 (1994).

236 See GATT Implementing Legislation: Hearings on S. 2467 Before the Senate Committee. on Commerce, Science and Transportation, 103d Cong., 2d Sess., 351 (1994) (statement of Ralph Nader, Consumer Advocate, Public Citizen).

237 See Marrakesh Agreement Establishing the World Trade Organization, Articles IX:1 and X:1.

238 *Id*, Article X:4 and Article X:5.

concern that the United States might have to undertake international obligations, which it would not intend to accept.

Secondly, the dispute settlement procedure is criticized for lacking the procedural safeguards, which the federal and state judicial systems usually have.[239] The economic disinterest of panellists is not required. There is no conflict of interest standard to guarantee the impartiality of the panel. Besides, the proceedings are not open to the public. All submissions, briefs, and materials, which are required to be open in the US courts, are kept confidential. Furthermore, outsiders, including those that might have substantial interests on the disputes, may not present before the panel or the Appellate Body. These problems would be made more critical by the enhanced power to adopt and enforce the panel/Appellate Body reports.[240] The United States cannot reject an adverse panel or Appellate Body report because it would be *de facto* automatically adopted by the DSB. Moreover, the countermeasures authorized by the DSB would also make the United States think twice before it totally ignores the adverse reports. In short, the WTO enhances the binding force of the DSB determinations and thus makes the determinations more similar to rulings made by the courts. However, it does not simultaneously establish procedural requirements like those the domestic courts ought to follow.

Thirdly, concerns exist that the impact of the substantial rules, *inter alia* rules for the non-tariff barriers, would be so significant to limit the United States to make its own law. The opponents contended that Article XVI: 4 of the Marrakesh Agreement clearly imposed a stringent and inflexible obligation on the members to ensure their laws and practices in line with the WTO agreements.[241] To support such a view, the opponents compared the current provision with the draft text of the Marrakesh Agreement. The draft text merely requires members to "endeavour to take all necessary steps," whereas the current provisions state "members shall ensure the conformity." They also cited the Congressional Research Services (hereafter the CRS) legal memo on domestic law effect of the draft text of WTO provisions for Trade Representative Jill Long. The CRS concluded that a party would no longer control whether to change the GATT-inconsistent policy or

---

239 See Prepared Statement of Ralph Nader, GATT Implementing Legislation: Hearings on S. 2467 Before the Senate Committee. on Commerce, Science and Transportation, 103d Cong., 2d Sess., 360 (1994).

240 *Id.*

241 *Id*, see also *GATT Implementing Legislation: Hearings on S. 2467 Before the Senate Committee. on Commerce, Science and Transportation*. 103d Cong., 2d Sess., 292-93 (1994) (statement of Laurence Tribe, Professor of Harvard University Law School); Prepared Statement of Lori Wallach, *Implications of General Agreement on Tariff and Trade: Hearing Before the Committee on Labor and Human Resources in the Senate*, 103d Cong., 2d Sess.65-106 (1994).

law.[242] Even the weaker formula could have such a strong effect, let alone the more stringent wording in Article XVI: 4. The WTO agreements cover a broad range of issues, and the substantial rules are thus believed to significantly alter the US domestic laws. Among the changes necessary to conform to the WTO agreements, those concerns with Section 301 were perhaps the most important political bellwether of the sovereignty considerations.[243] Section 301 would be inevitably subject to Article 23 of the DSU, which limits unilateral trade retaliations. For the opponents, Section 301 is also a handy tool to defend the domestic policy against the possible trade retaliation, which specifically aims at such policy. In particular, certain state laws, even if upheld by the Supreme Court, might be vulnerable to the challenge based on the WTO agreements. These state laws might even be the bargain chips that the federal government can use in dealing with other countries.[244]

Furthermore, the provisions of the WTO agreements in the field of food and product standards raise deep concerns that the US consumer, environmental, and labour policies would be undermined. The health, labour, safety, and environmental measures would be jeopardized in the following ways. Firstly, the United States may not necessarily set its own level of protection. Pursuant to the TBT agreement and SPS agreement, members had better base standards of public health, safety, and environment on relevant international standards.[245] A higher level of protection to public health, safety, or environment would be the exceptional case.[246]The international standards are generally developed with extensive industry input and without public oversight or participation. Thus, they are often weaker than the US standards.[247] These provisions in fact require the United States to follow such downward harmonization. In addition, the assessments of the risk to these goals are required to use solely scientific evidence.[248] Indeed science plays a valuable role in forming the protection level to human, animal, or plant life or health. The final decision is nonetheless political. Ultimately, the Congress or the state legislature decides how much risk the society will face. The Congress certainly may make a political decision to allow zero risk of a particular

242 See Wallach, *id*, also Nader, *supra note* 239.

243 See Jackson *supra note* 198, at 181.

244 See GATT Implementing Legislation: Hearings on S. 2467 Before the Senate Committee on Commerce, Science and Transportation, 103d Cong., 2d Sess., 330-332 (1994) (Tribe's answer to Senate Stevens' question).

245 See SPS 3.1 and 3.2; TBT 2.4 and 5.4.

246 See SPS 3.3 and 5; TBT 2.4.

247 See Wallach, supra note 241.

248 See SPS 5.1 and 5.2.

hazard.[249] Also, the TBT agreement provides an exhaustive list of legitimate objects.[250] Other important objects, like animal welfare or child labor, are excluded from the consideration of standards and regulations of goods. Even in promoting the WTO-allowable goals, the means the United States may use are limited to less trade-restrictive means.[251] The United States would also be required to accept imports that do not meet its standards so long as they meet other countries' standard equivalent.[252] The determination of equivalent would be done under a subjective comparison of different standards without clear guidelines for the factors that must be considered. This could circumvent US law.[253]

Fourthly, the WTO agreement could create a chilling effect on the Congress, even when the Congress proposes laws that appear irrelevant to the trade barriers. For example, Congressman Dingell issued a proposal for a telecommunications law. The proposal set forth a 60% domestic content requirement. Shortly after the Congressional report to his committee, the Trade Representative wrote him a letter indicating it would be inconsistent with GATT.[254] Ironically, the USTR took this letter as an example to show that the United States is not required to change laws.[255] The United States may certainly have laws inconsistent with the WTO agreements, if the United States will compensate for this inconsistency. The Trade Representative wrote to the Congressman that the proposal would be inconsistent with the GATT and would lead to retaliations, which would hurt US telecommunication exports worth approximately $10 billion.[256] In other words, the letter from the Trade Representative tagged the price for a WTO-inconsistent proposal. The potential cost would make the Congress constantly worry about these far-reaching international agreements when they propose laws.

ii. Derogation of Federalism and Democracy

At the domestic level, the opponents are also concerned that the decision-making power would be over concentrated in the federal government, more specifically the executive branch. Thus state sovereignty would be in jeopardy; in particular, the states play major roles in establishing food safety standards, which are subject to

---

249 See Wallach, supra note 241.

250 TBT 2.4.

251 See SPS 5.6 and TBT 2.3.

252 See SPS 4 and TBT 2.7.

253 See Wallach, supra note 241.

254 See Nader, *supra note* 239

255 See Implications of General Agreement on Tariff and Trade: Hearing Before the Committee on Labor and Human Resources in the Senate, 103d Cong., 2d Sess., 24 (1994) (statement of Ira Shapiro, General Counsel, United States Trade Representative).

256 *Id.*

the TBT agreement and SPS agreement. A state does not have a standing before the panel or the Appellate Body. When a state law is challenged under DSU procedure, the state must depend on the degree of sympathy the federal executive branch has for that state law.[257] Furthermore, the USTR would be involved in the DSU procedure as well as implementing affairs in the United States. Therefore, the executive branch is forced into an institutional conflict of interest. Once the challenged state law is found WTO-inconsistent, the USTR would face an awkward situation where they must argue both for the state law in international forum and argue against it before domestic courts. They would tend to use arguments based on the DSB decisions, even if the decision itself does not bind the US courts.[258] If the US finally decides to revise its WTO-inconsistent law, the USTR will have incentive to trade away state laws rather than federal laws. The USTR cannot promise the foreign countries that the federal law will be changed without the consent of the Congress. They may, however, bring legal actions on their own to change the contested state law on the ground of inconsistency with the WTO agreements. It would be easier for the USTR to deliver a promise to change state law. As a result, the state law would become particularly convenient bargain chips in international disputes.[259]

The fast-track procedure triggers concern that the decision-making power of the WTO-relevant issues would significantly shift from the legislative branch to the executive branch. Such a procedure would undermine the Constitution's structural safeguards, which are designed to protect states, citizens, and each branch of the federal government from aggrandizement of power by those who temporarily hold public office. Even when the aggrandizement seems wise as a matter of policy, these safeguards should not be abandoned.[260] For some, it is not necessarily constitutionally impermissible to impose certain limits on the sovereignty – either the state sovereignty or the nation as a whole. Such an imposition would be unconstitutional or unwise only if the safeguards of Article II, Section 2 of the Constitution (Treaty Clause) are not followed.[261] The Treaty-making process is an alternative legislative process, which is carried out in conjunction with foreign countries.[262] The process involves delegation and subsequent constraint on US sovereignty under international law. The Senate is accountable for people

257 See Prepared Statement of Laurence Tribe, GATT Implementing Legislation: Hearings on S. 2467 Before the Senate Committee on Commerce, Science and Transportation, 103d Cong., 2d Sess., 305 (1994).

258 See id.

259 See *id.*

260 See *id.*

261 See *id*; Slaughter, *supra note* 235.

262 See Slaughter, *supra note* 235.

as a whole and equal representation of states. The framers set forth the Treaty Clause to ensure that the interest of the people and the states would not be unduly bargained away. Indeed, the Constitution acknowledges that not all of international agreements qualify as a treaty. Only those that have significant constraints on sovereignty of the nation and /or the states will follow the Treaty Clause. Considering the degree, scope, and duration of the constraints on the sovereignty, the WTO agreements shall be subject to the Treaty Clause.[263]

The arguments against the URAA illustrate the extent to which WTO might interfere with the US domestic law and the consequences of that interference. However, everyone does not share their reading of the WTO agreements.[264] The USTR stated none of these concerns will materialize because the WTO agreements in fact would not affect the US sovereignty. Moreover, the provisions of WTO agreements are not self-executing.[265] The provisions of URAA and the SAA suggest that the executive branch may circumvent the sovereignty problem by disregarding the US obligations under the WTO agreements in necessary cases. However, such provisions would severely threaten the efficacy of the international legal system regulating the world trade, which the US has fought for decades to strengthen. This would also encourage other members to take their obligations under the WTO agreements similarly slightly.[266]

1.1.3.2. The Indirect Effect of the WTO Agreements

Although WTO agreements are not self-executing, they still might serve as guidance for interpreting domestic laws. It is acknowledged under the *Charming Betsy* doctrine that the US law shall not be construed to conflict with its international obligations.[267] The international agreements operate as a controlling source for interpreting domestic law. Scholars refer to such influence over interpretation of domestic law as indirect effect.[268] The WTO agreements, under the US consti-

---

263 See *id.*

264 Arguments supporting URAA, see Prepared Statement of John H. Jackson, *The World Trade Organization and U.S. Sovereignty: Hearing before the Committee on Foreign Relation in the Senate*, 103d Cong., 2d Sess., 195-204 (1994); Testimony of Clair Reade, American Bar Association, *GATT Implementing Legislation: Hearings on S. 2467 Before the Senate Committee on Commerce, Science and Transportation, 103d Cong., 2d Sess.*, (Oct. 18, 1994).

265 See Kantor, *supra note* 233; see also *The World Trade Organization and U.S. Sovereignty: Hearing before the Committee on Foreign Relation in the Senate*, 103d Cong., 2d Sess., (1994) (statement of Rufus Yerxa, Ambassador, Deputy United States Trade Representative) (LEXIS, Congressional, Federal Document Clearing House Congressional Testimony).

266 See Slaughter, *supra note* 235

267 See Part I, section 1.1.1.3 *supra*

268 See John J. Barceló, The Paradox of Excluding WTO Direct and Indirect Effect in the U.S. Law, 21 Tulane European & Civil Law Forum 147, 150 (2006); JOHN JACKSON ET. AL. LEGAL

tutional practice, can and should have indirect effect on US courts and officials.[269] However, the URAA seems to impose an obstacle to the indirect effect of the WTO agreements.[270] Section 102 (c) (1) prohibits individuals from bringing or defending a case under any provision of the WTO agreements. The SAA further clarifies that individuals via litigation cannot require the administrative agencies to exercise discretionary authority in conformity with the WTO agreements.[271] Rather, the administrative agencies in legal suits may, but not have to, argue their actions in conformity with the WTO agreements.[272] The Department of Commerce, for instance, does not have to exercise its discretionary authority to interpret the anti-dumping statute in light of the Antidumping Agreement.[273]

It is noteworthy that the URAA and the SAA do not explicitly exclude their indirect effect. The courts still could clarify the question whether the WTO agreements have indirect effect. To this end, the court should address two questions. The first question is whether Section 102 (c) of URAA totally bars individuals from litigating the WTO-inconsistent measures of government. The second question is to what extent the administrative agencies may have discretion to interpret ambiguous statutes.

a) Admissibility of the Cases

Several cases explicitly address these issues. Especially in the field of trade remedy, the courts are constantly requested to review the legality of agencies' interpreta-

---

PROBLEMS OF INTERNATIONAL ECONOMIC RELATIONS: CASES, MATERIALS AND TEXT ON THE NATIONAL AND INTERNATIONAL REGULATION OF TRANSNATIONAL ECONOMIC RELATIONS, 244 (4th ed., 2002).

269 *Id*, Jackson et al.

270 Arwel Davies, Connecting or Compartmentalizing the WTO and United States Legal Systems? The Role Of The Charming Betsy Canon, 10 (1) JOURNAL OF INTERNATIONAL ECONOMIC LAW 117, 130-132 (2007).

271 In 1994 U.S.C.C.A.N 4055, SAA reads:
[T]he provision also precludes a private right of action attempting to require, preclude, or modify federal or state action on grounds such as an allegation that the government is required to exercise discretionary authority or general "public interest" authority under other provisions of law in conformity with the Uruguay Round agreements.

272 *Id*, the SAA further states:
The prohibition of a private right of action based on the Uruguay Round agreements, or on Congressional approval of those agreements in section 101 (a), does not preclude any agency of government from considering, or entertaining argument on, whether its action or proposed action is consistent with the Uruguay Round agreements, although any change in agency action would have to be authorized by domestic law.

273 See Barceló, supra note 268, at 162.

tions.[274] In *Timken Co. v. U.S.*, a private company, Koyo Seiko, argued in an appeal that the Commerce's statutory interpretation was unreasonable in light of the Appellate Body's interpretation of the Antidumping Agreement.[275] The government contended that pursuant to Section 102 (c) of URAA prohibits the Koyo Seiko from bringing this case. The Court of Appeal agreed with Court of International Trade to give a narrow construction to this section. In their view, Section 102 (c) merely bars claims directly against the government on the ground that the Commerce acted inconsistent with the URAA. This case is based on the assumption that the US law would be interpreted to avoid a conflict with international obligations. The court is therefore not prevented from addressing the appeal.[276]

In *Corus I*, the Court of International Trade (hereafter the CIT) faced a similar situation. The *Corus Staal BV* in light of the *Charming Betsy* doctrine argued for the indirect effect of the Antidumping Agreement, while the Commerce defended by virtue of the URAA. The CIT did not address this issue, but directly went on the analysis of the provisions of the Antidumping Agreement.[277] Several courts also have directly reviewed the substantial issues without addressing the admissibility of the cases, when agencies' interpretations of US law are challenged on the ground of the conflict with WTO agreements.[278] Considering these cases, claims indirectly based on the WTO agreements are not subject to limitation on private remedy under Section 102 (c).

b) Administrative Agencies' Discretion on Interpreting Ambiguous Statutes

Individuals may challenge agencies' interpretations and applications of US laws inconsistent with US obligations under the WTO agreements. However, this does not necessarily mean that such interpretations should be vacated. Both the *Charming Betsy* doctrine and the *Chevron* doctrine apply to cases concerning the

---

274 *E.g.* Caterpillar, Inc. v. United States, 941 F. Supp. 1241 (Ct. Int'l Trade, 1996); Hyundai Elecs. Co., Ltd. v. United States, 53 F. Supp. 2d 1334 (Ct. Int'l Trade, 1999); Corus Staal BV v. Dep't of Commerce (Corus I), 259 F. Supp. 2d. 1253 (Ct. Int'l Trade, 2003); Timken Co. v. U.S., 354 F. 3d 1334 (Fed. Cir. 2004); Allegheny Ludlum Corp. v. United States, 367 F. 3d 1339 (2004); Koyo Seiko Co. v. United States, 551 F.3d 1286 (Fed. Cir 2008); Searing Indus. v. United States, SLIP OP. 2009-129 (Ct. Int'l Trade, 2009).

275 354 F. 3d 1334, 1339.

276 See 354 F. 3d 1334, 1341.

277 See 259 F. Supp. 2d. 1253,1262 (Ct. Int'l Trade 2003).

278 *E.g.* Hyundai Elecs. Co., Ltd. v. United States, 53 F. Supp. 2d 1334 (Ct. Int'l Trade, 1999); George E. Warren Corp. v. United States EPA, 159 F. 3d 616 (1998); NSK Ltd. v. United States, 510 F. 3d 1375 (2007); Koyo Seiko Co. v. United States, 551 F.3d 1286 (2008); SKF USA Inc. v. United States, 611 F. Supp. 2d 1351 (Ct. Int'l Trade 2009); Searing Indus. v. United States, SLIP OP. 2009-129 (Ct. Int'l Trade 2009).

administrative agencies' interpretations of implementing legislations.[279] The *Chevron* doctrine favors the administrative agencies' discretion on statutory interpretation, while the *Charming Betsy* doctrine supports the argument supporting the indirect effect of the WTO agreements. The courts should respect agencies' interpretations of ambiguous statutes, unless such interpretations are unreasonable. If the indirect effect of the WTO agreements is actually granted, the courts would further confine agencies' discretion and deem the WTO-inconsistent interpretations as unreasonable.

In a series of cases, courts gradually form a clear position on whether to acknowledge the indirect effect of the WTO agreement. Dozens of cases relate to this issue, but only a few leading cases are addressed here. Most of the cases concern the "Zeroing" practice. "Zeroing" is a method the administrative agencies used to assess the dumping margin of the products under the anti-dumping investigations and the administrative reviews. The Commerce would assign a price exceeding the normal value of a zero dumping margin. Such methodology makes the price over the normal price unable to offset the margin caused by prices below the normal value.

In *Corus Staal BV v. United States (Corus I)*, the court applied the *Chevron* doctrine to determine whether to sustain the Commerce's interpretation of the anti-dumping duties statute. The court found the anti-dumping duties statute itself is ambiguous and then further made its own reading of the Antidumping Agreement. According to the court's reading, the zeroing practice appears to comply with the Antidumping Agreement, since the Antidumping Agreement does not expressively prohibit such practice.[280] The court rejected Corus' argument that the Appellate Body found zeroing inconsistent with the Antidumping Agreement in *EC-Bed Linen.*[281] The DSB decision in *Bed Linen* cannot be the basis for striking Commerce's methodology because the DSB decisions are not binding upon the Commerce or the court. Furthermore, the court found that the concept of *stare decisis* does not apply to WTO rulings. The DSB decisions seem to have limited precedential value and are binding only upon the parties involved in that particular dispute. They are neither binding upon other members, nor upon the future panels.[282] In addition, the court presumed that the Congress did not intend to prohibit zeroing practice. Zeroing is a long-standing practice that Congress is probably familiar with. The Congress could have prohibited the practice in the WTO implementing legislations, if it so chose. The court con-

279 See Part I, section 1.1.1.3 *supra.*

280 See 259 F. Supp. 2d. 1253,1263.

281 European Communities-Antidumping Duties on Imports of Cotton-Type Bed Linen from India (EC-Bed Linen), WT/DS141/AB/R (Mar. 1, 2001).

282 See Corus Staal BV v. United States , 259 F. Supp. 2d. 1253,1264 (Ct. Int'l Trade 2003).

cluded to defer to Commerce's interpretation when it faced an ambiguous statute and international agreement.[283]

The *Chevron* doctrine was again applied in *Timken Co. v. U.S.* The court also found that the anti-dumping statute does not explicitly exclude the zeroing methodology, and the Commerce may have discretion on interpretation.[284] Even if the *EC-Bed Linen* case should be considered, the Commerce's zeroing practice would still be reasonable. It is not sufficiently persuasive to the court that the reasonableness of the Commerce's practice is determined by the *EC-Bed Linen* alone. The Commerce's long-standing and consistent interpretation is entitled considerable weight.[285] Besides, the court distinguished the current case over the *EC-Bed Linen.* The *EC-Bed Linen* did not involve the United States and dealt with an anti-dumping investigation, whereas the current case addresses administrative review of anti-dumping.[286] The court implied the interpretations in the *EC-Bed Linen* may not properly suit the current case due to these distinctions.

In the previous cases, the courts did not explicitly give priority to Commerce's interpretation when this interpretation allegedly conflicted with the US international obligation. Rather, the courts construed the US obligation under the Antidumping Agreement by themselves and found the zeroing practice consistent with those obligations. They also circumvented the *EC-Bed Linen* decision by claiming circumstances in the decision were different from the case before them, or by claiming the decision is not generally binding on all other members not involved in the dispute. Nonetheless, the Court of Appeal in *Corus I* did give the Commerce substantial deference in its administration of the statute because the foreign policy includes a dumping determination.[287] The court would not attempt to carry the duties that fall within the exclusive province of the political branches. The court stressed it will not overturn Commerce's zeroing practice based on the ruling by the WTO, "unless and until such ruling has been adopted pursuant to the specified statutory scheme."[288]

In 2006 and 2007, the WTO Appellate Body issued two decisions in which it found that Commerce's zeroing practice is inconsistent with Antidumping Agreement.[289] These decisions, the *US-Zeroing (EC) and US-Zeroing (Japan)*, could

---

283 *Id.*

284 See 354 F. 3d 1334, 1341.

285 See *id*, at 1344.

286 *Id.*

287 Corus Staal BV v. United States, 259 F. Supp. 2d. 1253,1264 (Ct. Int'l Trade 2003).

288 *Id.*

289 Appellate Body Report, United States-Laws, Regulations and Methodology for Calculating Dumping Margins (US-Zeroing (EC)), WT/DS294/AB/R (Apr. 18, 2006); Appellate Body Report, United States-Measures Relating to Zeroing and Sunset Reviews (US-Zeroing (Japan)), WT/DS322/AB/R (Jan. 9, 2007).

be the death knell to the Commerce's zeroing practice. The courts may no longer deny the fact that Commerce's zeroing practice is inconsistent with US international obligations. The *US-Zeroing* decisions give the courts no choice but to directly answer the question whether the Commerce's discretion on statutory interpretation should be aligned with US international obligation under the Anti-dumping Agreement. Due to these new developments, in *CorusII* the importer asked the court to remand this case so that Commerce could reconsider the final results of the second administrative review of the anti-dumping order in light of the *US-Zeroing (EC)*. In spite of finding the use of zeroing in anti-dumping investigations was inconsistent with the US obligations under the Anti-Dumping Agreement, the Appellate Body upheld the use of zeroing in administrative reviews. Commerce intended thus only to discontinue the zeroing practice in investigation.[290] Commerce also made clear that the new policy would apply prospectively. Following the ruling in *Corus I*, the court accorded the Commerce substantial deference in its administration of the antidumping statute.[291]

In *NSK Ltd. v. United States*, several companies (the NSK, NTN, and Koyo Seiko) also sought the Court of Appeal to remand the case to the Commerce to allow its agency to implement the *US-Zeroing (EC)* decision. The Commerce opposed such a remand. The court followed the *Corus I* and found that it would not overturn the zeroing practice on the ground of *US-Zeroing (EC)* until and unless such ruling has been adopted pursuant to the specific statutory scheme.[292] This court similarly agreed the Commerce could have the final decision on discontinuing the zeroing practice. In the present case, the manner in which the DSB decision would be implemented by the Commerce was far from clear. The remand might afford these companies more time to wait for the Commerce to implement the DSB decision. However, the Commerce has stated that it would continue the zeroing practice in administrative review such as this one. The remand would not result in the outcome the NSK and others expected. Accordingly, the court refused to remand the case. Consistent with *Corus I* and the *NSK Ltd. v. United States*, the Court of Appeal again refused to remand the matter to the Commerce in *Koyo Seiko Co. v. United States (the Koyo III)*. The court stated, "The determination whether, when, and how to comply with the WTO's decision on 'zeroing', involves delicate and subtle political judgments that are within the authority of the Executive and not the Judicial Branch."[293]

Following the Court of Appeals' precedent, the Court of International Trade unconditionally supports the new Commerce policy on the zeroing in recent

290 Corus Staal BV v. United States, 502 F.3d 1370. 1373 (Fed. Cir. 2007).
291 See *id*, at 1375.
292 510 F.3d 1375, 1380 (Fed. Cir. 2007).
293 551 F.3d 1286,1291 (2008).

cases.[294] The Commerce determined to continue the zeroing practice in administrative review. As the Court of International Trade has observed, the Court of Appeal's precedent entirely precludes the court from requiring Commerce to change this zeroing practice.[295] This is because such practice is the determination made under the URAA Section 123. The Congress has clearly entrusted the implementation of the adverse DSB decision to the executive branch.

In general, the courts still stand for the Commerce's discretion. The courts refrain from reviewing the administrative agencies' statutory interpretation, even indirectly, by virtue of the WTO agreements or the Appellate Body's interpretation. The interpretive role of WTO agreements is not significant. By virtue of the *Charming Betsy* doctrine, the courts do agree in a few cases that the administrative interpretation should be in line with US obligations under the WTO agreement.[296] However, none of them has ever overturned the administrative interpretation on the ground of *Charming Betsy* doctrine. In *Allegheny Ludlum Corp. v. United States*, the Court of Appeal firstly applied the *Chevron* doctrine and found the administrative interpretation reasonable. Then, the court cited an Appellate Body report to support this judgment. The court used the *Charming Betsy* doctrine to support an interpretation consistent with the determination of the Appellate Body. In doing so, the court stated that the *Charming Betsy* doctrine is only a "guide" and the Appellate Body report is nonetheless not binding.[297] The Court of Appeal took a similar approach in *George E. Warren Corp. v. United States EPA*.[298] In *Hyundai Elec. Co., Ltd. v. United States*, the Court of International Trade placed more weight on US international obligation than it usually does. The court stated the WTO report (though itself not binding) was a sound reasoning of the panel or the Appellate Body and may inform the court's decision. In absence of express language to the contrary, the statute should not be construed to conflict with provisions of WTO agreements.[299] These statements do not mean that the court would mainly depend on the *Charming Betsy* doctrine to make its decision. The standard of review was, nonetheless, the *Chevron* doctrine.[300] Furthermore, this court was prudent to upset administrative agencies' regulatory authorities under the *Charming Betsy* doctrine. The

---

294 Fujian Lianfu Forestry Co., Ltd. v. United States, 638 F. Supp. 2d 1325 (Ct. Int'l Trade, 2009); JTEKT Corp. v. United States, SLIP OP. 2009-147 (Ct. Int'l Trade, 2009); Searing Indus. v. United States, SLIP OP. 2009-129 (Ct. Int'l Trade, 2009).

295 See JTEKT Corp. v. United States, SLIP OP. 2009-147 (Ct. Int'l Trade, 2009).

296 George E. Warren Corp. v. Environmental Protection. Agency, 159 F.3d 616, 624 (D.C. Cir. 1998); Hyundai Elecs. Co., Ltd. v. United States, 53. F. Supp. 2d 1334 (Ct. Int'l Trade 1999); Allegheny Ludlum Corp. v. United States, 367 F. 3d 1339 ((Fed. Cir. 2004).

297 367 F. 3d 1339,1348.

298 See 159 F. 3d 616, 624.

299 See 53. F. Supp. 2d 1334,1343-44.

300 *Id*, at 1338.

court would not consider this doctrine unless there was a "conflict between an international obligation and Commerce's interpretation."[301] In the end, the reasoning of the Appellate Body report still was not accepted; the court made its own interpretation of the Antidumping Agreement. In fact, the *Charming Betsy* doctrine is only a secondary consideration in these cases. The courts use it as an additional support for the determination in favor of the administrative agencies' interpretations. It would be hard to infer that these courts have accepted the indirect effect of the WTO agreement. Rather, the cases concerning the zeroing practice truly reflect the dominant opinions of the courts. They would be reluctant to give the WTO agreements effects of any kind in the US legal system.

Considering the URAA and the SAA, such reluctance is not surprising. The premise of the *Charming Betsy* doctrine is the Congress would not intend to violate US international obligations. And such a premise seems not to exist in the WTO context. Sections 102, 123, and 129 of the URAA and their legislative histories show that the Congress does not necessary plan to comply with the US obligations under the WTO agreements. The executive branch is entrusted with the determination of whether to change certain measures, which the Appellate Body or the panel finds to be WTO inconsistent. The Trade Representative has made clear that the WTO agreements cannot affect the US sovereignty because the Congress can disregard the US obligations. The courts certainly could not and would not admit that the URAA implies the Congress intention of non-compliance. However, what they can do is to declare the political branch's excusive authority over the implementation and to sustain the administrative agencies' interpretation as much as possible.

1.1.4. Conclusion

In general, the effect of international agreements in the US legal system is complicated and varies from case to case. The key is the allocation of powers among branches of federal government and the allocation between federal and state governments. An international agreement could greatly influence the domestic legal system, if the Congress so wishes. In the GATT period, the Congress did not clearly address the effect of the GATT 1947 in the domestic legal system. In absence of Congress' explicit statement, it became complicated to determine the effect of the GATT. The courts should fill the gap the Congress left behind. Although the courts did not provide sufficient reasoning, few things are certain: The provisions of the GATT 1947 and its subsequent agreements are not directly

301 *Id*, at 1345.

effective. They can be part of US law only if they are implemented by the President or the Congress. The federal law would always prevail with the provision implementing these agreements, whether it is before or after these agreements. State law should yield to the obligations under these agreements, although the GATT 1947 and its subsequent agreements do not have direct effect.

The Congress avoided the puzzling situation in the GATT 1947 period by passing the implementing legislation, the URAA. The URAA is consistent with practices of the GATT 1947, except that the URAA and SAA further confined the effect of the provisions of the WTO agreements. The provisions of the WTO agreements are not directly effective. Furthermore, the URAA itself would yield, whenever it conflicts with other statutes. In this light, the influence of the WTO agreements would significantly decrease. Pursuant to the URAA, the WTO agreements would not prevail over state laws in cases of conflict. Congress intended to block the provisions of the WTO agreements from the US legal system for sovereignty concerns. Several reasons underlie the sovereignty concerns. Firstly, it is criticized that WTO agreements impose excessive constraints on domestic decision making. Secondly, the states' autonomy would be degraded.

The Congress entrusts the executive branch with implementing the WTO agreement as well as the adverse panel/Appellate Body reports. The courts are inclined not to interfere in the administrative authorities in this regard. They also deny the indirect effect of the WTO agreements. Accordingly, implementing the WTO law within the US legal system depends on the Executive Branch's willingness to conform its interpretation of ambiguous statutes to WTO requirements.

The provisions of URAA and the SAA suggest that the executive branch may circumvent the sovereignty problem by disregarding the US obligations under the WTO agreements. There seems to be a paradox. On one hand, the US advocates for a strong international legal system regulating world trade. On the other hand, the Congress insisted that the US legal system would not be directly or indirectly bound by the WTO agreements. As the largest economy in the world, such an inconsistent attitude severely threatens the efficacy of the world trade laws. This would also encourage other members to view their obligations under the WTO agreements similarly slightly.

1.2. The Laws and Practices in the European Union

The Treaty of Lisbon entered into force on 1 December 2009. It amends the Treaty on European Union (hereafter the TEU) and the Treaty establishing the European Community (hereafter the EC). The EC has been renamed as Treaty on the Functioning of the European Union (hereafter the TFEU). The Treaty of Lisbon reforms the structure of the European Union and significantly influences the development of the European integration.[302] The European Union will replace the European Community pursuant to paragraph 3 of Article 1 of the Treaty on European Union (the EU Treaty).[303] In the meantime, decades of the practices of the European Community mostly remain valid. To fit the legal context under which the actions or the judgments were made, the original provisions are used in the following sections. For the same reason, the terms "European Economic Community" and "European Community" are used in the relevant context. The numeration of Articles under the EU Treaty and the TFEU is provided in parentheses.

1.2.1. The Legal Status of International Agreements in General

The European Union is an international organization, although not a traditional one. Member states confer the Union the competence to exercise their external powers on certain matters.[304] The Union may conclude international agreements with third-party states and other international organizations. The standard procedure for negotiating and concluding international agreements is provided in Article 218 of TFEU (ex Article 300 EC). The Union negotiator, nominated by the Commission or by the High Representative of Union for Foreign Affairs and Security Policy, conducts the negotiation of international agreements. In light of paragraph 4 of Article 218 of TFEU, the Council may supervise the negotiations. In consultation with the European Parliament or with their consent, the Council, as proposed by the negotiator, concludes the international agreements. There are other ways to conclude an international agreement. For instance, Article 207 of TFEU (ex Article 133 EC) established negotiation and conclusion of international agreement concerning common commercial policy.

The effect of international agreements is briefly addressed in paragraph 2 of Article 216 of TFEU (ex paragraph 7 of Article 300 EC): "Agreements concluded by the Union are binding upon the institutions of the Union and on its Member States." However, the EC did not address the effect of the international

---

302 Introduction of the new developments under the Treaty of Lisbon, see generally STEPHAN HOBE, EUROPARECHT, 287-296 (4th ed., 2009).

303 Consolidated versions of the Treaty on European Union and the Treaty on the Functioning of the European Union. 2008/C 115/01, available at http://eur-lex.europa.eu/en/treaties/index.htm (last visited Jan. 21, 2010).

304 *E.g.* TFEU Articles 207,217. The external competence of the EC, see generally, Paul Craig & Gráinne de Búrca, *supra* note 17, 127 ff; THE GENERAL LAW OF EC EXTERNAL RELATIONS, 115 ff (Alan Dashwood & Christophe Hillioneds, 2000);Stephan Hobe & Patrick Müller-Sartori, *Rechtsfragen der Einbindung der EG/EU in das Völkerrecht*, JURISTISCHE SCHULUNG 2002 8.

agreement within the Community, nor does the TFEU address the effect in the Union law context. The European Court of Justice (hereafter the ECJ) filled the gap and developed principles by virtue of "the interpretation and application of the Treaties" provided under the EC Article 220, paragraph 1.[305] Article 220 of the EC was repealed, but such provision reappears in paragraph 1 of Article 19 of the EU Treaty. The ECJ judgments are therefore the major basis for analyzing the effect of the WTO agreements. In some cases, the ECJ simply applies international agreements without addressing the direct effect issue.[306] In certain cases, however, the question of direct effect was raised.

1.2.1.1. The Relationship to the Community Law

The ECJ provided a detailed analysis of the relationship between the international agreements and the Community law in *International Fruit Company*.[307] In that case, a Dutch court referred the following questions to the ECJ: Does the ECJ, by virtue of Article 177 of EEC (TFEU Article 267), have the power to decide whether actions taken by the Community are consistent with international law? If so, are the EEC regulations at issue invalid because they are inconsistent with the GATT 1947? The ECJ ruled that the wording of Article 177 of EEC (TFEU Article 267) implies no limit on the reasons for which the validity of acts might be contested. Therefore, the ECJ may have power to decide such matters.[308] The ECJ did not provide substantial grounds for this interpretation of Article 177 of EEC. The Advocate General (hereafter, the AG) resorted to the purpose of Article 177 to define the scope of ECJ's competence. The AG pointed out that the conflict between Community law and international agreements binding on the Community indeed might not be brought before the ECJ. The solutions to such conflict are found in international law. In the context of the preliminary ruling, however, the situation is totally different. The preliminary ruling is set to ensure the uniformity of interpretation of Community law. Such a system is quite

305 See Paul Craig & Gráinne de Búrca, *supra* note 17, at 97.

306 *E.g.* Case 126/83, STS Consorzio per Sistemi di Telecomunicazione via Satellite SpA v Commission of the European Communities. – Second Lomé Convention, 1984 ECR 2769; Case 218/83, Les Rapides Savoyards Sàrl and others v Directeur Général des Douanes et Droits Indirects, 1984 ECR 3105; general survey on the cases in which international agreements were involved, Pescatore, *Die Rechtsprechung des Europäischen Gerichtshofs zur innergemeinschaftlichen Wirkung völkerrechtlicher Abkommen*, in VÖLKERRECHT ALS RECHTSORDNUNG INTERNATIONALE GERICHTSBARKEIT MENSCHENRECHTE – FESTSCHRIFT FÜR HERMANN MOSLER 661 (Rudolf Bernhardt et al. eds, 1983).

307 Jointed Cases 21-24/72, International Fruit Company N.V. and Others v. Produktschap voor Groenten en Fruit, 1972 ECR 121, 1972.

308 *Id*, paras. 4-5.

important in cases involving Community regulations, such as this one, because these regulations are obligatory in all their elements and directly applicable in member states.[309] In other words, the ECJ may have broad competence of preliminary ruling, whenever the uniform interpretation is required.

Regarding the second question, the ECJ described two conditions under which a provision of international agreement affects the validity of the Community law with which it is inconsistent. Firstly, the Community is bound by such provision. Secondly, this provision should create the rights for those who are subject to the Community's jurisdiction. To this end, one should view the spirit, the structure, and the terms of the international agreement.[310] The ECJ eventually determined the GATT 1947 failed to fulfill the second condition.

International Fruit Company is the starting point for analyzing the legal status of international agreements in the Community. It not only recognized the direct effect of international agreements and the conditions for such effect. This judgment also sheds some light on the ECJ's understanding of "the law is observed" in Article 164 of EEC (EU Treaty Article 19, para. 1). The ECJ held a relatively broad view of laws to be observed to include pertinent international agreements binding on the Community.[311] This judgment also implied the status of international agreements in the hierarchy of norms. The ECJ considers international agreements as "any rules relating to its (the Treaty) application" (TFEU Article 263). The ECJ reviewed the validity of regulations by virtue of such rules relating to Treaty application, in this case the international agreements, if certain criteria are fulfilled. In doing so, the ECJ implies international agreements should be inferior to the primary community law but superior to the secondary community law.[312]

The *International Fruit Company* is still followed. In the *Commission v. Germany,* the ECJ further clarified the influence of international agreements on secondary law. The ECJ stated "the primacy of international agreements concluded by the Community over provisions of secondary Community legislation means that such provisions must, so far as is possible, be interpreted in a manner that is consistent with those agreements."[313] In recent cases, the ECJ inferred from paragraph 7 of Article 300 of EC (TFEU Article 216) that international

309 *Id.* Opinion of the AG.

310 *Supra note* 307. paras. 7, 8. 20.

311 Judge Pierre Pescatore, *Treaty-Making by European Communities* in THE EFFECT OF TREATIES IN DOMESTIC LAW 171,182 (Francis G. Jacobs & Shelley Roberts eds., 1987).

312 *Id* See Karl Meesen, *The Application of Rules of Public International Law within Community Law*, 13 COMMON MARKET LAW REVIEW 485, 500 (1976); STEPHAN HOBE, EUROPARECHT, 104 (5 th ed., 2010).

313 Case C-61/94, Commission v. Federal Republic of Germany, para. 52, 1996 ECR 3989.

agreements concluded by the Community are superior to secondary Community legislations.[314] A secondary legislation would be illicit if it is incompatible with these international agreements.[315]

1.2.1.2. The Relationship to the Domestic Law of Members

In certain cases, the ECJ are requested to address the compatibility of members' domestic law with international agreements binding on the Community. Conditions established by the ECJ are consistent with those in the cases concerning the compatibility of the Community law with international agreements. These cases also further indicate factors that the ECJ would consider in assessing the direct effect of international agreements.

In *Haegman*, the ECJ was requested to interpret certain provisions of the Agreement, which created an association between the European Economic Community and Greece. The Agreement was concluded by the Council and therefore an act of the Community.[316] In light of Article 177 of EEC (TFEU Article 267), the ECJ held it has jurisdiction to interpret this agreement. It stated, "The provisions of the agreement, from the coming into force thereof, form an integral part of Community law."[317] Such a statement might infer that international agreements concluded by the Community could have certain key characteristics of the Community law. In particular, the international agreements could have direct effect in the Community and the member states. Nonetheless, the direct effect issue was not addressed in this case.

In *Bresciani*, the ECJ was asked whether certain provisions of the Yaounde Convention have direct effect. These provisions were concluded between the EEC and African States associated with the Community. This judgment provides some concrete conditions for the direct effect of international agreements. The ECJ held "regard must be simultaneously paid to the spirit, the general scheme and the wording of the convention and of the provision concerned."[318] A provision could have direct effect if the obligations undertaken by the Community should

---

314 *E.g.* Case C-311/04, Algemene Scheeps Agentuur Dordrecht BV v. Inspecteur der Belastingdienst – Douanedistrict Rotterdam, 2006 ECR 609;Jointed Cases C-402 & 415/05, Yassin Abdullah Kadi and Al Barakaat International Foundation v. Council of the European Union and Commission of the European Communities, 2008 ECR 6351; Case C-308/06, The Queen on the application of International Association of Independent Tanker Owners (Intertanko) and Others v. Secretary of State for Transport, para. 43, 2008 ECR I-04057.

315 Supra note 312.

316 Case 181/73, *R. & V. Haegeman v Belgian State*, paras. 2-4, 1974 ECR. 449.

317 *Id*, para. 5.

318 Case 87/75, 1976, Conceria Daniele Bresciani v Amministrazione Italiana delle Finanze, para. 16, 1976 ECR 129.

be specific and not subject to any implied or express reservation on the part of Community.[319] In this case, the obligations undertaken under this convention is non-reciprocal. The ECJ found this imbalance is inherent in the special nature of the convention and not necessarily exclude its direct effect. Furthermore, the convention refers to provisions of the EEC and the Community undertook precisely the same obligations to these associated states as to the member states.[320] The provision at issue was therefore found directly effective.

In *Pabst*, a German court requested a preliminary ruling on whether Article 95 of EEC (TFEU Article 110) and Article 53, paragraph 1 of the agreement establishing an association between the European Economic Community and Greece have direct effect. The ECJ firstly found Article 95 of EEC (TFEU Article 110) directly effective. Then, the ECJ found paragraph 1 of Article 53 of the association agreement has direct effect. To reach such conclusion, the ECJ relied largely on its similarity to the language and function of Article 95 of EEC (TFEU Article 110). The ECJ also stressed the provision at issue was set to prepare for Greece to enter into the Community and to adjust gradually to the requirements of Community law.[321] In addition, the ECJ gave certain instructions on how precise a provision should be. The provision should contain a clear and precise obligation, which is not subject (in its implementation or effects) to the adoption of any subsequent measure.[322]

The ECJ made several significant statements in *Kupferberg*. The free trade agreement between the EEC and Portugal was involved. The ECJ was required to answer whether the non-discrimination provision in the FTA is directly applicable. The ECJ sustained similar criteria in the previous cases. The stipulation should be unconditional and sufficiently specific to have direct effect. It should be assessed in light of the object, the purpose and the context of the agreement.[323] Furthermore, the ECJ clarified the reasons why the international agreement could have direct effect. These reasons were not clearly provided in the previous cases. The ECJ firstly cited the *Haegman* case and explained how the provisions of international agreement form an integral part of Community law. Pursuant to paragraph 7 of Article 228 of EEC (Paragraph 2 of Article 216 of TFEU), the ECJ held that international agreements concluded by the Community are binding on Community as well as the member states. Thus, the Community and member

---

319 *Id*, para. 25.

320 *Id.*

321 See Case 17/81, Pabst & Richarz KG v Hauptzollamt Oldenburg. Pabst & Richarz KG v Hauptzollamt Oldenburg, paras. 24, 26, 1982 ECR 1331.

322 *Id,* para. 27.

323 Case 04/81, Hauptzollamt (Chief Tax Office) Mainz v. C. A. Kupferberg & Cie KG A.A., para. 23, 1982 ECR 3641.

states are all responsible for implementing the provisions of the agreements. The necessary implementing measures are either taken by the Community or the member states respectively, according to their competence. In doing so, the member states fulfill not only their obligation to the parties to that agreement. Most importantly, their obligation to the Community is also fulfilled.[324] Such an observation is reasonable because the member states under the Treaty have conferred part of their external competence to the Community. The Community is assumed responsible for the due performance of the agreement in the Community as a whole. Therefore, the member states must assist the Community in implementing the agreement. Accordingly, the provisions of international agreements possess characteristics of Community law.

It is noteworthy that the ECJ did not infer the direct effect of an international agreement in the Community from the special character of Community law. Instead, it resorted to the general rules of international law. The ECJ indicated the Community institutions are free to negotiate the effect of an international agreement in the internal legal systems of the contracting parties. If the question is not settled in that agreement, the ECJ is responsible to settle the question in the same way as any other question of interpretation concerning implementation of that agreement in the Community.[325] In accordance with the general rules of international law, each contracting party may determine appropriate legal means to implement its obligations in its legal system, unless "the agreement, interpreted in the light of its object and purpose, itself specifies those means."[326] Courts of one contracting party might construe a certain provision of the agreement as directly effective; however, the courts of another party might rule precisely otherwise. The ECJ noticed such an inconsistency, but held this inconsistency alone would not mean that the agreement was in absence of reciprocity in implementation.[327]

While the ECJ provided grounds for direct effect of international agreements in *Kupferberg*, it explained the basis for its jurisdiction over such matters in *SPI and SAMI.* The case involved only the measures of member states. In this case, it was questioned whether the ECJ may still have jurisdiction under Article 177 of EEC (TFEU Article 267) in cases where no community measures were involved.[328] The ECJ reiterated the provisions of international agreements should be uniformly applied throughout the community. Any difference in interpretation and application would not only jeopardize the unity of commercial policy, but

324 *Id*, paras. 11-13.

325 *Id*, see para. 17.

326 *Id*, para. 18.

327 *Id.*

328 Joined Cases C-267/81, 268/81 and 269/81,1981,Amministrazione delle Finanze dello Stato v Società Petrolifera Italiana SpA (SPI) and SpA Michelin Italiana (SAMI), 1983 E.C.R. 801, para. 11.

also create the distortion in trade within the Community.[329] It made no difference whether this inconsistency is attributed to the member state or to the Community. To ensure the uniform interpretation and application of international agreements, the ECJ certainly has jurisdiction to assess the compatibility of member states' measures with the commitments the Community made.

Although the results of the ECJ's assessments vary, the standards for reviewing the issue are established. In sum, the ECJ consistently holds it has jurisdiction over the issue of whether the provisions of international agreements are binding on the Community. It also acknowledges the direct effect of a provision of international agreements if the provision is unconditional and sufficiently specific in light of the spirit, the structure, and the terms of international agreement. In the recent cases, the ECJ attributed direct effect to association agreements as well as to partnership and cooperation agreements.[330] In recent years, the ECJ seems to be quite open toward the direct effect of international agreements.[331]

1.2.1.3. Grounds for Direct Effect of International Agreements: Uniform Application and Protection for Individual Rights

The reasoning in the *International Fruit Company* case represents the ECJ's standard procedure of analyzing the direct effect of an international agreement. The ECJ firstly determines whether an international agreement is binding on the Community. Once this binding force is affirmed, the ECJ applies the conditions for direct effect. However, the ECJ has not clearly elaborated the substantial grounds for the direct effect of international agreements.

It is generally agreed that merely the binding force of international agreements cannot lead to the application of direct effect. The ECJ in *Haegman* filled the gap by stating that the international agreement concluded by the Community is part of Community law. It seems reasonable to state that international agreements should be enforceable by the individuals as any piece of Community law.[332] However, such inference is not compelling because a norm may be part

329 *Id*, para. 15.

330 E.g. Case C-257/99, The Queen v Secretary of State for the Home Department, ex parte Julius Barkoci and Marcel Malik, 2001 ECR 6557; Case C-268/99 *Aldona Malgorzata Jany and Others v Staatssecretaris van Justitie*, 2001 ECR 8615; Case C-63/99; Case C-253/99, The Queen v Secretary of State for the Home Department, ex parte Eleanora Ivanova Kondova, 2001 ECR 6427; Case C-265/03, Igor Simutenkov v Ministerio de Educación y Cultura and Real Federación Española de Fútbol, 2005 ECR 2579.

331 Christine Kaddous, *Effects of International Agreements in the EU Legal Order* in EU FOREIGN RELATIONS LAW: CONSTITUTIONAL FUNDAMENTALS 291,311 (2008).

332 Ernst-Ulrich Petersmann, *Application of GATT by the Court of Justice of the EC*, Common Market Law Review 20,397,435 (1983).

of Community law without direct effect.[333] Such inference would be more logical if international agreements, as integrated part of Community law, share grounds for direct effect similar to those for Community law itself.

The ECJ justified the direct effect of the Community law by virtue of the Community's special legal nature. The EEC Treaty is more than an international agreement that merely creates mutual obligations between the member states. The object of the EEC Treaty is to establish a common market; the function of this market is of direct concern to interested parties in the Community.[334] From this perspective, international agreements are more likely capable of being directly effective, if they are closely tied to the Community or more integrated to the common market. The ECJ seems to adopt such an approach in *Pabst* case and the *Bresciani* case.[335] In *Bresciani*, the agreement at issue institutionalizes the arrangements favoring the former colonies and the related member states, while the association agreement in *Pabst* was meant to prepare a non-member state to join the Community. The AG in the *Kupferberg* held a similar opinion. One of the AG's arguments against the direct effect of the Free Trade Agreement between Portugal and EEC is that this agreement has more limited object and content than the association agreement. In addition, the wording of the provision at issue is considerably different from its corresponding provisions of the EEC Treaty.[336]

In *Kupferberg* case, however, the ECJ dispels the notion that direct effect of an international agreement is based on the type of agreement involved.[337] Notwithstanding the fact that the EEC treaty and the FTA pursue different objectives, the ECJ still applied criteria for determining the effects of provisions of a purely Community origin.[338] Their difference in structure does not stop the ECJ from doing so either. In other words, this international agreement would not necessarily have any Community law nature except that it must be concluded by the Community. If that is true, what is the connection between the "international agreements as an integrated part of community law" and direct effect of international agreements in the Community legal system? As the ECJ stated, the member

---

333 See Jacques H.J. Bourgeois, *Effects of International Agreements in European Community Law: Are Dice Cast?*, 82 Michigan Law Review 1250,1260 (1984).

334 See Case C-26/62, *NV Algemene Transport-en Expeditie Onderneming van Gend & Loos v. Neth. Inland Revenue Admin.*, 1963 E.C.R. 1, 1963.

335 See R. Brand, *Direct Effect for International Economic Law in the United States and the European Union*, 17 Northwestern Journal of International Law and Business 556, 587 (1997).

336 *Supra note* 323, opinion of the AG.

337 Supra note 335, at 588; see also Maria Victoria Liavero, The Possible Direct Effect of the Provision s on Competition in the EEC Free Trade Agreements in the Light of the Kupferberg Decision, 11 Legal Issues of European Integration 83, 91 (1983).

338 *Supra note* 323, see paras. 23 and 30.

states are imposed simultaneously an obligation of implementation to the Community and the other non-member contracting parties, once the Community concludes a certain international agreement. The international agreement becomes part of Community law via members' obligations of implementation to the Community. This obligation secures the Community's external competence.

Uniform and effective application of the international agreement is therefore necessary to reach this end. If the laws originated purely in the Community are seen as internal Community laws, international agreements could be seen as external Community laws that originate outside the Community. The direct effect is proven to be the major tool to ensure that internal Community laws will be applied in a uniform and effective way.[339] It would presumably be more significant in applying the international agreement as an external Community law; the Commission might have less incentive to bring a case under TFEU Articles 258 and 259 for breaches of external Community law.[340]

The need for uniform application of external community law alone would not allow introducing direct effect of international agreement in the Community legal system. The direct effect mainly stands for protecting individual rights in a specific case. Uniform observance of the Community law would rather be the task of Commission, as provided for in TFEU Articles 258 and 259.[341] The procedures raised by individuals could *de facto* share such a task in cases where the Commission is reluctant to bring a case. However, their contribution to applying Community external law in a uniform and effective way is nonetheless a side benefit. The ECJ has recognized the differences in the object and effects between the proceedings by individuals and the procedure under Articles 169 and 170 of EEC (TFEU Articles 258 and 259). The ECJ stated, "proceedings by an individual are intended to protect individual rights in a specific case, whilst intervention by the community authorities has as its object the general and uniform observance of community law."[342] The ECJ would not consider the direct effect of an international agreement, if it does not recognize individual rights provided in this agreement should be protected in the first place. This observation is also consistent with ECJ's willingness to consider international instruments, which protects individual rights or human rights, within the framework of Community law.[343]

339 See *supra note* 333, at 1272.

340 See *supra note* 333, at 1273.

341 *Supra* note 36.

342 Case C-28/67, Firma Molkerei-Zentrale Westfalen/Lippe GmbH v. Hauptzollamt Paderborn, 1968 E.C.R. 143, 153.

343 See e.g. Case C-4/73, J. Nold, Kohlen- und Baustoffgroßhandlung v Commission of the European Communities, 1974 E.C.R. 491, para. 13; Jointed Case C-s C-402 & 415/05, *Yassin Abdullah*

1.2.2. The Legal Status of the GATT 1947 and the WTO Agreements

Following a well-established practice, the ECJ performs a two-prong assessment in determining the effect of GATT 1947 within the Community legal system. Firstly, the ECJ will determine whether the international agreement is binding on the Community. If so, a provision must be unconditional and sufficiently specific in light of the spirit, the structure, and the terms of international agreement.

1.2.2.1. Participation of the Community in the GATT and the WTO

The EEC never formally joined the GATT. Instead, the member states were contracting parties to the GATT. Belgium, France, Netherlands and Luxembourg acceded to the GATT in 1947, [344]whereas Italy and Germany did so in 1950 and 1951, respectively.[345] Other member states joined the GATT within two decades, which was prior to their accession to the Community. [346] The Six[347] requested a waiver for certain obligations of GATT 1947 to fulfil their obligations under the Treaty establishing the European Coal and Steel Community (hereafter the ECSC Treaty). The High Authority of the ECSC could participate in the consultations under the GATT and should act in accordance with the obligations undertaken by the member states.[348] Furthermore, any institution of the ECSC may not require the member states to act inconsistent to their obligations under the GATT. Whenever doubt exists about the consistency of actions of the Community with the obligations of the GATT, the Contracting Parties' recommendations, findings, or decisions regarding that question are as binding.[349] Accordingly, the EC High Authority participated in the subsequent negotiation as negotiator on behalf of the member states in the field of coal and steel products. In addition, the tariff concession made by the ECSC was listed in a separate schedule of

---

Kadi and Al Barakaat International Foundation v. Council of the European Union and Commission of the European Communities, 2008 ECR 6351, para. 283.

344 Second Session of the Preparatory Committee of the United Nations Conference on Trade and Employment: ITO Preparatory Committee Final Meeting and Signing of Final Act and of Protocol of Provisional Application, PRESS RELEASE NO.479, 1947.

345 Signature of various protocols. Addendum: Annecy Protocol of Terms of Accession, GATT/CP/40/ADD. 14, 1050; Signatures of the Torquay Final Act and Annexed Documents. Addendum, GATT/CP/112/ADD. 3, 1951.

346 See http://www.wto.org/english/theWTO_e/gattmem_e.htm (last visited Jan. 30, 2010).

347 The six funding members of the European Communities, including Belgium, France, Germany, Italy, Luxembourg and Netherlands.

348 Report of Working party 4 on the European Coal and Steel Community, G/35, Nov. 7, 1952, 8.

349 See *id*, at 9.

concession and was no longer incorporated into the national schedule of its members.[350] Although the ECSC did not officially accede to the GATT 1947, it participated in the GATT and was bound by the GATT 1947 as well.

Before the Treaty of Rome became effective, pursuant to GATT XXIV: 7, the Contracting Parties had to examine whether the Treaty fits the requirements for the regional trade agreement provided for in GATT XXIV: 5. The Contracting Parties could make recommendations to the parties of the Treaty, if it held these requirements had failed. The Treaty should not enter into force, unless the parties make modifications according to these recommendations. By examining the Treaty of Rome, the Contracting Parties made a somewhat ambiguous conclusion. The examination was not officially completed because there would be no sufficient information at that time. On the other hand, the rights of the parties of the Treaty were not prejudiced; the other contracting parties of the GATT still might challenge the measures taken by the Six regarding the implementation of the Treaty in light of GATT XXIV.[351] The EEC has never formally joined the GATT and its legal status was not addressed as clearly as that of the ECSC. Nonetheless, the EEC's membership in the GATT was gradually secured during the subsequent practices. In the Tokyo Round, the EEC formally substituted its member states; participation of individual member states was no longer required.[352]

According to the EEC Treaty, the EEC is also bound by the GATT 1947. According to Article 234 of the EEC (TFEU Article 351), the rights and obligations deriving from international agreements that are concluded between member states and third-party states before its accession to the EEC are not affected by the Treaty. The EEC overtook several competences of the member states, but did not generally succeed to their sovereignty. By virtue of functional succession,[353] the EEC undertook member states' obligations under the GATT 1947.[354]

Contrary to the pragmatic participation in the GATT, the EC prepared for the new round of trade negotiations from the very beginning. In fact, the preparation started before the negotiations were formally launched. In 1985 the Council declared the Community's commitment for launching new negotiations.[355] The

350 See Ernst-Ulrich Petersmann, *The EEC as a GATT Member-Legal Conflict between GATT Law and European Community Law* in THE EUROPEAN COMMUNITY AND THE GATT, 23, 34 (Meinhard Hilf et al. eds., 1986).

351 Summary Record of The Nineteenth Meeting, SR 13/19, 202, Dec. 2, 1958.

352 See *supra note* 350, at 39.

353 Christian Tomuschat in KOMMENTAR ZUM EU/EG-VERTRAG, Vol.5, Art. 210 para. 52, (Groeben et. al. eds, 5 th ed., 1997).

354 Robert Uerpmann, *International Law as an Element of European Constitutional Law: International Supplementary Constitutions*, Jean Monnet Working Paper 9/03,32, available at http://centers.law.nyu.edu/jeanmonnet/papers/03/030901.html (last visited Jan. 31, 2010).

355 Bull. EC 3-1985, para. 2.2.12.

Commission submitted a communication to the Council on its approach to the negotiations.[356] Along with the approach to negotiations, the expectation of the trade partner and other relevant issues were addressed in the communication. In a meeting in June, the Council agreed with the Commission's general approach to further negotiations.[357] By virtue of Council's approval to the Commission's overall approach, the Commission may play an active role in negotiation for the aims, the method, and the subjects of the new round of trade negotiations.[358] In the minister meeting in Punta del Este, Uruguay, the members of the GATT officially decided to launch the Uruguay Round negotiations.[359]

The Commission submitted the ministerial declaration for approval and requested permission to start the negotiation. In the EC, the major debate about the Uruguay Round did not focus on whether the Community and the member states should join the new agreements. Instead, the Commission argued with the Council and the member states about the competence of the Community. The Council eventually approved the declaration and avoided the competence issue at the time. In the council meeting approving the declaration, it was stated that the "decision did not prejudge the question of the competence of the Community or the member states on particular issues."[360] Meanwhile, the Council and the member states agreed with the Commission would be the sole negotiator on behalf of Community and the member states "in order to ensure the maximum consistency in the conduct of the negotiation."[361] The member states and their political leaders still had many opportunities to discuss the negotiations with non-member countries. According to paragraph 3 of Article 113 of EEC (TFEU Article 207), the Commission should work closely with a special Council committee for trade policy (i.e., the so-called 113 Committee). This Committee included officials of the member states and kept the member states updated about the negotiations. It also provided a way for the member states to express their positions on issues that were being negotiated.[362]

---

356 Communication from the Commission to the Council: Overall Approach: New Round of Trade Negotiations in Defense of Open Multilateral Trade, SEC (86) 840 final.

357 Bull. EC 6-1986, point. 2.2.2.

358 *Id*, point 2.2.3.

359 Punta del Este Ministerial Declaration,20 Sep. 1986, available at http://www.sice.oas.org/trade/Punta_e.asp (last visited 27 Feb., 2010).

360 Opinion 1/94, Competence of the Community to conclude international agreements concerning services and the protection of intellectual property, 1994 ECR 5267, para. 3.

361 *Id.*

362 Conducts of the Institutions of the EC during the Uruguay Round, see Peter L.H. Van den Bossche, The European Community and the Uruguay Round, in IMPLEMENTING THE URUGUAY ROUND 23,53 ff. (John H. Jackson & Alan O. Skyes ed., 1997).

The competence issue was raised again at the end of the Uruguay Round. The Commission requested the ECJ's opinion about whether the Community had the competence to conclude all of the WTO agreements, in particular the GATS and the TRIPS.[363] The ECJ found the Community has exclusive competence to conclude agreements on trade in goods, including the TBT and SPS. The Community and the member states jointly may conclude the GATS and TRIPS.[364] The ECJ also obligated the Commission and the member states to cooperate. When the subject matters fall within the competence shared by the Community and member states, the Community and member states should closely cooperate in negotiation as well as the conclusion and implementation of the agreements. This obligation flows from the requirement of unity in international representation of the Community.[365] Both the Community and the EC members signed the Final Act embodying the results of Uruguay Round of Multilateral Trade Negotiations. Article XI of the Marrakesh agreement explicitly stated the EC is an original member. The WTO agreements are concluded by Community and certainly binding on the Community.

1.2.2.2. The Assessments of the ECJ on the Effect of the GATT/WTO Agreements

In general, the ECJ's rulings concerning the legal status of the GATT are still applicable in the WTO epoch. Furthermore, the major scheme of the effect of the GATT/WTO agreements was drawn in the GATT 1947 period. Most of the significant judgements were made during that time; moreover, the ECJ did not alter its position after the entry into force of the WTO agreements.

a) Denial of Direct Effect of the GATT 1947

In the early cases, the ECJ applied the GATT 1947 only to the relationship between member states and third-party countries. In *Commission v. Italy*, the ECJ distinguished the international agreements concluded between the member states and third-party countries from those between the member states. Only those agreements concluded between member states and third-party countries are entitled to Article 234 of the EEC (TFEU Article 351), which relates to the maintenance of rights and obligations arising from prior agreements concluded with third countries. The GATT 1947 was concluded prior to the EEC Treaty; however, the relationship between member states is subject only to the EEC Treaty in matters governed by

363 *Supra* note 360 , para. 6.

364 *Supra* note 360, operative part.

365 *Supra note* 360, para. 108.

the Community.[366] In the *SIOT* case, the ECJ reached the same conclusion by virtue of Article XXIV: 8 of the GATT. The Community is a custom union under XXIV and therefore exempt from applying GATT to the relationship among member states.[367]

In cases involving the relationship between member states and third-party countries, the major concern is whether the GATT is unconditional and sufficiently specific – in light of the spirit, the structure, and the terms – to be directly effective. The ECJ decided the GATT is neither unconditional nor sufficiently specific. In *International Fruit Company*, the ECJ held that the GATT is not directly effective because its provisions are so flexible. The ECJ indicated several clauses lead to such findings. Firstly, the preamble shows that the GATT regime is based on the principle of negotiations seeking reciprocity and mutual advantages. Moreover, the GATT allows contracting parties to deviate from the GATT. The safeguard clause entitled the parties to suspend unilaterally their obligation or concession.[368] Furthermore, the ECJ noticed dispute settlement procedure implies the obligations are not necessarily followed. In cases of non-compliance to the GATT, the parties concerned shall seek a satisfactory adjustment via consultation. If the satisfactory adjustment is not found, the Contracting Parties shall make recommendations and may authorize suspension of the concessions or other obligations under the GATT. If the authorization for such suspension were granted and in fact occurred, the party subject to such suspension (i.e., the non-compliant party), is offered the option of denouncing the GATT 1947.[369] Meanwhile, the AG indicated the GATT 1947 was never ratified by the parliaments of the EEC member states. The GATT is applicable to the member states of the EEC by virtue of the Protocol of Provisional Application (the PPA), which is a "law of approbation" or "law of execution."[370] The PPA *per se* would not provide subjective rights capable of being meaningfully invoked before a jurisdiction. Moreover, the PPA states that the provisions of Part II of the GATT are binding insofar as these provisions are compatible with the existing legislations of the parties. Such a system does not correspond to the criteria of direct effect.[371]

---

366 Case C-10/61, Commission of the European Economic Community v. Italian Republic, 1962 ECR 1, Ground, Section II. B.

367 Case C-266/81, *Società Italiana per l'Oleodotto Transalpino (SIOT) v Ministero delle finanze, Ministero della marina mercantile, Circoscrizione doganale di Trieste and Ente autonomo del porto di Trieste*, 1983 ECR 731, para. 12.

368 *Supra* note 307, see para. 26.

369 *Supra* note 307, see para. 25.

370 *Supra* note 307, Opinion of the AG, Section II. B.

371 *Supra* note 307, Opinion of the AG.

The ruling in *International Fruit Company* is the cornerstone for the subsequent cases. The ECJ virtually repeated the rationale of the *International Fruit Company* in the *Schülter* case.[372] In the *SPI and SAMI* case, which involved the tariff protocols of the GATT, the ECJ first referred to the *International Fruit Company* case and concluded provisions of the GATT as not directly effective. As for the tariff protocols annexed to the GATT, the ECJ also rejects their direct effect; the general scheme of these tariff protocols cannot be effective without the custom tariff of the contracting parties as an intermediary.[373] In the *SIOT* case, the ECJ simply relied on the judgment of the *International Fruit Company* and denied the direct effect of the GATT. The ECJ also made clear that denial of the direct effect would not affect the Community's obligations to comply with the GATT.[374] In *Singer*, the ECJ found the tariff protocols not directly effective even without any further explanations.[375]

b) Rules of the GATT 1947 as Guidelines for Interpreting and Applying Community Law

In the previously-mentioned cases, the ECJ persistently refused to attribute the direct effect to the GATT 1947. There were cases in which the ECJ did not explicitly deny the applicability of the GATT by individuals. Instead, it construed the Community law as compatible with the GATT. In the *Dürbeck* case, for instance, the provisions of the GATT at issue could not question the validity of the Community measure – not because the GATT rules are not directly effective, but because the provision should not be interpreted as prohibiting the Community from reacting to serious disturbance.[376] In addition, the ECJ referred the legality of the Community measures to be confirmed by a special examination group of the GATT.[377] Some perceive the *Dürbeck* judgment as a silent move to change practices.[378] Others hold that the case merely shows the ECJ's avoidance

372 Case C-9/73, *Carl Schlüter v Hauptzollamt Lörrach*, 1973 ECR 1135, para. 29.

373 *Supra* note 328, para. 24.

374 *Supra* note 367, para. 28.

375 Jointed Cases C-290/81 and 291/81, *Compagnia Singer SpA and Geigy SpA v Amministrazione delle finanze dello Stato*, 1983 ECR 847, para. 7.

376 See Case C-112/80, *Firma Anton Dürbeck v Commission of the European Communities*, 1982 ECR 1251, paras. 44-45.

377 *Id*, at 46.

378 See Gehard Bebr, Agreements Concluded by the Community and Their Possible Direct Effect: From International Fruit Company to Kupferberg, 20 Common Market Law Review 35, 46 (1983); Pieere Pescatore, Die Rechtsprechung des Europäische Gerichtshofs zur innerstaatlichen Wirkung völkerrechtliche Abkommen in VÖLKERRECHT ALS RECHTSORDNUNG – INTERNATIO-

of the direct effect issue; in the alternative, the Court simply found an absence of conflict between the GATT and the Community's measures.[379]

A few years later, the ECJ adjusted the rules set by the previous judgments. The ECJ acknowledged that the provisions of the GATT are applicable in certain cases. This adjustment was first mentioned in *Fediol III*. The Seed Crushers' and Oil Processors' Federation (the "Fediol") sought the annulment of the Commission's Decision, which rejected its request for initiating an examination procedure in respect of illicit commercial practices of Argentina in light of Council Regulation No. 2641/84. Article 2, paragraph 1 of the Regulation defines the "illicit commercial practices" as international trade practice "incompatible with international law or with the generally accepted rules."[380] The *Fediol* raised several arguments. One of these arguments was that the practices of Argentina are contrary to certain provisions of the GATT 1947. Although the Court certainly noticed the direct effect of the GATT 1947 was denied in previous cases, it contrasted the *International Fruit Company* case with the present one. The ECJ noticed that the GATT provisions form part of the rules of international law to which Article 2 (1) of regulation 2641/84 refers.[381] In order to establish whether certain specific commercial practices should be considered incompatible with those rules, the ECJ would interpret and apply the rules of GATT to a given case. The ECJ stated, "[T]he GATT provisions have an independent meaning which, for the purpose of their application in specifics cases, is to be determined by way of interpretation."[382] Furthermore, the ECJ held the dispute settlement procedure under the Article XXIII of GATT 1947 is not "as such to preclude the interpretation by the Court." To support such a view, the ECJ referred to the *Kupferberg* case, in which a special institutional framework for consultation and negotiations on implementing international agreement is established "not in itself sufficient to exclude all judicial application of that agreement."[383] Finally, the ECJ noticed that the Regulation itself entitled the individuals to rely on the GATT 1947 to lodge a complaint to the Commission to establish the illicit nature of the commercial practices. Accordingly, these individuals should be similarly entitled to

---

NALE GERICHTSBARKEIT – MENSCHENRECHTE: *FESTSCHRIFT* FÜR HERMANN *MOSLER*, 667, 674 (RudolfBernhardtet al. eds, 1983).

379 Marc Maresceau, *The GATT in the Case C – Law of the European Court of Justice* in THE EUROPEAN COMMUNITY AND GATT, 107, 121 (Meinhard Hilf et al., 1986).

380 Case C-70/87, Federation de l'industrie de l'huilerie de la CEE (Fediol) v Commission of the European Communities. Common commercial policy, 1989 ECR 1781, para. 2.

381 *Id*, para. 19.

382 *Id*, para. 20.

383 *Id*, para. 21.

request the Court to review the legality of the Commission's decision applying the GATT 1947.[384]

In *Fediol III*, the ECJ did not overturn the rulings in the *International Fruit Company* and other similar cases. The provisions of the GATT 1947 are more like guidelines for interpreting and applying the Regulation at issue. Those provisions were applied not because they were directly effective, but because they formed an indispensable part of the application of the Regulation at issue. In Nakajima, the ECJ made a similar ruling. Nakajima, a Japanese manufacturer of typewriters and printers, sought to void Council Regulation No 3651/88. This regulation imposed an anti-dumping duty on printers that originated in Japan. Nakajima did not rely on the direct effect of the Anti-Dumping Code. In fact, it questioned the legality of the Regulation in light of Article 173 of EEC (TFEU Article 263), namely "the infringement of the Treaty or of any rule of law relating to its application."[385] The ECJ found the Anti-Dumping Code should not be directly effective because the Code was designed to interpret and to implement Article VI of the GATT 1947, which was denied having direct effect. The ECJ indicated the Regulation at issue was adopted to comply with the Community's obligations under the Anti-Dumping Code. Accordingly, the ECJ eventually interpreted and applied the Code in this case.[386]

The judgment in *Germany v. Council* occurred at the end of the GATT period and confirmed all of the leading cases, such as *International Fruit Company*, *Fediol III*, and *Nakajima*. It was the first case in which a member state, pursuant to Article 173 of EEC (TFEU Article 263), relied on the GATT 1947 to request annulment of a Council Regulation. To achieve a single market for bananas, the Regulation No. 404/93 provided for common organization of the bananas market. Germany argued that the regulation breached GATT rules.[387] The ECJ performed a two-step assessment. First, it repeated the rulings of the cases, in which the GATT provisions were found conditional and therefore not directly effective. Then, the ECJ considered whether it might review the legality of the Community act from the viewpoint of the GATT rules.[388] The Court would apply the GATT rules only if the Community intended to implement a particular obligation within

384 *Id*, para. 22.

385 Case C-69/89, Nakajima All Precision Co. Ltd v Council of the European Communities, 1991 ECR 2069, para. 1.

386 *Id*, paras. 30-31.

387 Case C-280/93, Federal Republic of Germany v Council of the European Union, 1994 ECR 4973, para. 26.

388 *Id.*, paras. 105-108.

the framework of the GATT, or if the Community's act expressly refers to specific provisions of the GATT.[389]

It is important to note that the case was brought by a member state, not by individuals. Germany maintained that the direct effect issue was not in fact involved and the rulings concerned should be irrelevant. The ECJ simply concluded the features of the GATT also preclude it from considering the provisions of the GATT in cases brought by the member states. The AG, on the contrary, provided a more detailed reply to the argument. The AG cited the notion in the *Kupferberg* that the parties to an international agreement may decide the effects of that agreement in their internal legal order. The AG observed that the contracting parties of the GATT did not intend to make such a decision. The effect of the GATT within the Community legal order is to be determined by the ECJ.[390] Were the provisions of the GATT deemed as "the rule of law" provided in Article 173 of EEC (TFEU Article 263), the Community institutions would have to respect these provisions. Such a decision would confine the possibilities for the Community institutions to safeguard the community's interest within the legal framework of the GATT.[391] In addition, the ECJ did not accept in general that the provisions of the GATT could be invoked in an application under Article 173 of the EEC (TFEU Article 263), although the applicant in *Nakajima* did bring a case based on this Article. The ECJ in that case found the GATT applicable because of the Community's intention to comply with the GATT. The AG maintained the reasons for excluding the direct effect of the GATT are of such a nature to prevent the GATT from being the legal basis for ECJ's review under Article 173 of EEC (TFEU Article 263).[392]

In summary, the ECJ cannot apply the provisions of the GATT, unless they are intermediated by a Community law that refers to a specific provision or shows the Community's intention to comply with the GATT. A general reference to the Community's international obligation would not be sufficient. When the ECJ does apply the GATT, the Community law is nevertheless the legal basis in each and every case. The provisions of the GATT are applied because the Community law inexplicitly or explicitly so requires.

---

389 *Id*, para. 111.

390 Opinion of the Advocate General, Case C-280/93, *Federal Republic of Germany v Council of the European Union*, 1994 ECR 4973, paras 126-129.

391 *Id*, para. 131.

392 *Id*, paras. 136-137.

c) *Reconfirming the Rulings Concerning the GATT 1947*

Although the WTO agreements made considerable modification to the GATT 1947 and its subsequent agreements, the ECJ still follow the cases in the GATT period. In *Portugal v. Council*, the Portuguese Government brought a case under Article 230 of EC (TFEU Article 263) for annulment of Council Decision 96/386/EC. This decision concluded the Memoranda of Understandings between the EU and Pakistan and India on arranging market access for textiles.[393] The Portuguese government contested the Decision breached GATT 1994, the Agreement on Textile and Clothing (hereafter the ATC) and the Agreement on Import Licensing Procedures (hereafter the LIC). The Council maintained that these provisions should not be directly effective and cannot be relied on.[394] In response to Council's contention, the Portuguese government argued the WTO agreements are significantly different from the GATT 1947. In particular, the dispute settlement procedure was radically altered. Moreover, Portuguese government contended the direct effect issue was not necessarily involved; the Decision concerned bilateral agreements between the community and third-party countries governing those matters in which WTO rules should apply.[395] The ECJ did not address Portugal's last argument; instead, it merely analyzed whether the WTO agreements have direct effect.

The ECJ interpreted the WTO agreements in light of their subject matters and purposes and found these agreements not directly effective. The WTO agreements actually did not determine the appropriate legal means of implementation within members' legal systems. The ECJ noticed the significant modifications of the GATT 1947. Nonetheless, the WTO agreements accord considerable importance to negotiations between the parties. For instance, Article 3.7 and Article 22 of the DSU provide negotiation for temporary compensations, when a WTO-inconsistent measure is not withdrawn in time. The judicial organs would deprive the legislative and executive organs from entering into negotiating this arrangement, if they are required to refrain from applying the WTO-inconsistent domestic law.[396] Besides, according to the preamble of the Marrakesh Agreement, the WTO agreements still are founded on the principle of negotiations to enter into reciprocal and mutually advantageous arrangements. The WTO agreements did not introduce certain asymmetry obligations or create special relations of integration with the Community. They are thus significantly different from international

393 Case C-149/96, Portuguese Republic v Council of the European Union, 1999 ECR 8395, para. 1.
394 *Id*, para. 29.
395 *Id*, para. 33.
396 *Id*, see paras. 36-40.

agreements with these features; ECJ found such agreements directly effective.[397] Furthermore, some of the Community's most important commercial partners do not agree that the WTO rules could be applied by their judicial organs. Lack of reciprocity in this regard may lead to inconsistent application of WTO rules.[398] If the ECJ accepted the direct effect of the WTO agreements, it would deprive the Community's legislative or executive organs of "scope for manoeuvre enjoyed by their counterparts in the community's trading parties."[399] Finally, the ECJ found such interpretation is also aligned with Decision 94/800, which concerns the conclusion of the WTO agreements.[400] The final sentence of the preamble of the Decision stated, "by its nature, the Agreement establishing the World Trade Organization, including the Annexes thereto, is not susceptible to being directly invoked in Community or Member State courts."[401]

While denying the direct effect of the WTO agreements, the ECJ acknowledged reviewing the Community's measures in light of the WTO rules in certain circumstances. Either the Community intends to implement a particular obligation under the WTO agreement or the Community measures expressly refer to the precise provisions of the WTO agreements.[402] The ECJ found the purpose of the Decision at issue was simply to approve the Memoranda of the Understanding. The Decision is not qualified for any of the circumstances in which WTO agreements might apply.[403]

The rationales in *Portugal v. Council* are in principle no different from *Germany v. Council*. The rulings concerning the GATT 1947 can still be applied. The ECJ held the modifications of the GATT 1947 did not change its position because the WTO agreements are still based on the similar principle of reciprocal negotiation.

---

397 *Id.*, para. 42.

398 *Id*, para. 45.

399 *Id*, para. 46.

400 *Id*, para. 48.

401 94/800/EC: Council Decision (of 22 December 1994) concerning the conclusion on behalf of the European Community, as regards matters within its competence, of the agreements reached in the Uruguay Round multilateral negotiations (1986-1994), Official Journal L 336, 1.

402 *Supra note* 393, para. 49.

403 *Id.*

d) Further Developments on the Issue of Direct Effect – Legal Status of Dispute Settlement Body Decision and Indirect Effect of the WTO Agreements

The ECJ has maintained the rulings in *Portugal v. Council.*[404] It has been settled that the WTO agreements do not have direct effect in the Community legal system. In recent cases, the ECJ explicitly rejected the contention that the decisions of the Dispute Settlement Body (DSB) should have bearing on the validity of the Community's measure. The DSB decisions concerning the banana disputes have found several Community measures inconsistent with its obligations under the WTO agreements. These decisions have resulted in litigation within the Community legal system; also, the effect of DSB decisions was finally brought before the ECJ.

In *Van Parys*, the ECJ was requested to provide a preliminary ruling on whether individuals may rely on the WTO agreements to challenge the validity of the Community's legislation where the DSB has found that legislation WTO-inconsistent.[405] The ECJ held the dispute settlement system accorded considerable importance to negotiations between the parties, even if the DSB has found WTO-inconsistent measures. The legislative and executive organs would be deprived of the possibility of negotiation, if the courts were stopped from applying WTO-inconsistent domestic rules.[406] In fact, the Community sought to reconcile its obligations under the WTO agreements with those in respect of ACP counties and with its common agricultural policy. The Community's efforts would be compromised if the Community Courts may review the legality of the Community's measures in accordance with the WTO rules.[407] The ECJ is also concerned about lack of reciprocity because the major trade partners of the

---

404 E.g. Case C-307/99, OGT Fruchthandelsgesellschaft mbH v. Hauptzollamt Hamburg, 2001 ECR 3159; Joined Case C-s 27/00 and C-122/00, *The Queen v Secretary of State for the Environment, Transport and the Regions, ex parte Omega Air Ltd (C-27/00) and Omega Air Ltd , Aero Engines Ireland Ltd and Omega Aviation Services Ltd v Irish Aviation Authority (C-122/00)*, 2002 ECR 2569; Case C-76/00 P, Petrotub SA and Republica SA v. Council and Commission , 2003 ECR 79; Case C-93/02 P, Biret International SA v. Council of the European Union, 2003 ECR 10497; Jointed Case C-s 120/06 P and C-121/06 P, Fabbrica italiana accumulatori motocarri Montecchio SpA (FIAMM) and Fabbrica italiana accumulatori motocarri Montecchio Technologies LLC (C-120/06 P), Giorgio Fedon & Figli SpA and Fedon America, Inc. (C-121/06 P) v Council of the European Union and Commission of the European Communities, 2008 ECR 6513.

405 Case C-377/02, Léon Van Parys NV v. Belgisch Interventie- en Restitutiebureau (BIRB),2005 ECR 1465, para. 37.

406 *Id*, see paras. 46-48.

407 *Id* , para. 50.

Community do not accord to the WTO agreement direct effect.[408] However, the ECJ would exceptionally review the Community's measures in light of the WTO rules on occasion, where the Community intends to comply with particular obligations under the WTO in its internal legal system. Accepting the DSB decision at issue did not mean the Community has such intention.[409]

FIAMM and Fedon is another case where the applicants tried to rely on the DSB decisions concerning banana disputes to challenge the Community's act. The FIAMM and the Fedon were companies subject to the countermeasures imposed by the US. These countermeasures were authorized by the DSB because the EC failed to withdraw its WTO-inconsistent measure. FIAMM and Fedon respectively brought a case and argued the Community had incurred non-contractual liability due to the unlawful conduct of its institutions. The Court of First Instance dismissed such requests and both FIAMM and Fedon appealed to the ECJ.[410] The appellants asserted the individuals should have the right to rely on the DSB decision itself to challenge the actions of Community institutions. The ECJ held it is not necessary to draw a distinction between the direct effect of the WTO rules imposing substantial obligations and direct effect of the DSB decision. When the ECJ refuses to accord direct effect to a WTO rule that the DSB found infringed by the Community, the Court has excluded the direct effect of the DSB decision itself as well.[411] The ECJ held the only objective of the DSB is to determine the legality of members' measures in light of their obligations under the WTO agreements.[412] The DSB decision cannot be fundamentally distinguished from the substantive rules that convey members' obligations. Furthermore, the DSB decision cannot confer more rights than the substantive rules. Article 3.2 of the DSU expressly requires that the recommendations or the rulings of the DSB decision cannot add or take away rights or obligations under the agreements concerned. The WTO agreements do not require the members to accord direct effect to these agreements; the Community, in light of Articles 21 and 22 of the DSU, still has discretion in implementing the DSB decision and certain scope for negotiation about the measures responding to the decision. Accordingly, the DSB decision cannot be directly effective.[413]

---

408 *Id*, para. 53.

409 *Id*, para. 41.

410 Fabbrica italiana accumulatori motocarri Montecchio SpA (FIAMM) and Fabbrica italiana accumulatori motocarri Montecchio Technologies LLC (C-120/06 P), Giorgio Fedon & Figli SpA and Fedon America, Inc. (C-121/06 P) v Council of the European Union and Commission of the European Communities, 2008 ECR 6513, paras 30-31.

411 *Id*, para. 127.

412 *Id*, para. 128.

413 *Id*, para. 131.

The ECJ constantly blocks any possibility of according direct effect to the WTO agreements. In the meantime, the Court also puts some weight on their impact on interpretation of the national rules, in particular the indirect effect of the WTO agreements. In *Hermès*, the district court of Amsterdam requested a preliminary ruling on interpretation of Article 50.6 of the TRIPS agreement.[414] Article 50.6 provides provisional measures for preventing infringement of intellectual property rights or preserving evidence of an alleged infringement. The ECJ ruled the national courts are required to apply national rules with regard to provisional measures "as far as possible, in light of the wording and the purpose of Article 50 of the TRIPS agreement."[415] In other words, the ECJ recognized the indirect effect of the TRIPS agreement. In the *Dior* case, the ECJ was asked in a preliminary ruling procedure whether Article 50, in particular Article 50.6, has direct effect.[416] The Court followed *Portugal v. Council* and found TRIPS agreement is not directly effective. The ECJ believed this finding actually did not help the national courts to solve their problems fully and further elaborated the guidelines for application of the TRIPS agreement. In the field in which TRIPS applies and the Community has legislated, the ECJ followed the judgment in *Hermès*. The national courts are required by virtue of Community law to apply the national rules as far as possible in light of the wording and the purpose of the TRIPS. If the Community has not yet legislated in this field, the protection of intellectual property rights does not fall within the scope of Community law. In such circumstances, the direct effect issue is determined solely by the member states.[417]

It seems clear that national courts should interpret national rules pertinent to intellectual property rights in line with the TRIPS.[418] Although the provisions of the TRIPS do not have direct effect, they are *per se* guidelines for interpreting national rules (i.e., having indirect effect). Such effect follows from the fact that the Community has undertaken obligations under the TRIPS. It should be noted that the Community legislation referred to in *Dior* is not a prerequisite for using TRIPS as guidelines for applying national rules. The Community legislation is merely the criterion for distribution of competence over the protection of intellectual property rights, which the Community shares with member states.

---

414 Case C-53/96, Hermès International (a partnership limited by shares) v FHT Marketing Choice BV, 1998 ECR 3603, para. 1.

415 *Id*, para. 28.

416 Case C- 300/98, Parfums Christian Dior SA v TUK Consultancy BV and Assco Gerüste GmbH and Rob van Dijk v Wilhelm Layher GmbH & Co. KG and Layher BV, 2000 ECR 11307, para. 27.

417 *Id*, see para. 45.

418 See also Case C-89/99, Schieving-Nijstad vof and Others v Robert Groeneveld, 2001 ECR 5851, para. 55; Case C-245/02, Anheuser-Busch Inc. V Budějovický Budvar, národní podnik, 2004 ECR 10989, para. 57.

In *Řízení Letového Provozu ČR, s. p. v Bundesamt für Finanzen*, the finance court of Cologne requested a preliminary ruling on whether "the third states" provided in the refund clause of Directive 79/1072/ EEC should be interpreted to include countries entitled to the MFN treatment of the GATS.[419] The ECJ simply followed the judgment of *Commission v. Germany*. In that case, whenever more than one possible interpretation of a secondary legislation is available, the ECJ preferred to interpret in a compatible way with international agreements concluded by the Community.[420] The primacy of international agreements over secondary community legislation requires the latter to be interpreted as much as possible in conformity with those agreements.[421] Such a finding does not mean that the ECJ changed its position on direct effect. The AG pointed out the question referred did not concern the possible direct effect of the MFN treatment under the GATS, but rather the interpretation of the directive.[422] To some extent, the GATS limited the interpretations of secondary legislation. This effect comes from the binding force of the GATS pursuant to paragraph 7 of Article 300 of the EC (TFEU Article 216).[423] The AG also noticed the ECJ took this approach in *Dior*.[424] In light of *Dior* and cases thereafter, the ECJ indeed recognized the indirect effect of the WTO agreements. In the latest case, the ECJ again held the ruling in *Dior* was also applicable in other agreements adopted in the context of the WTO.[425]

According to all of the previously mentioned cases, individuals absolutely cannot rely on the WTO rules to challenge the measures of Community as well as of member states. The WTO agreements are binding on the Community, but they are not the "rule of law" provided under Article 263 of TFEU. Nevertheless, the WTO agreements still could have indirect effect.

---

419 Case C-335/05, Řízení Letového Provozu ČR, s. p. v Bundesamt für Finanzen, 2007 ECR 4307, para. 14.

420 See Case C- C-61/94, *Commission v*. Federal Republic of *Germany*, 1996 ECR 3989, para. 52.

421 *Id*, see also Case C-311/04, Algemene Scheeps Agentuur Dordrecht BV v. Inspecteur der Belastingdienst – Douanedistrict Rotterdam, 2006 ECR 609, para. 25; Jointed Case C-477/05 and 488/05, Thomson Multimedia Sales Europe and Vestel France v Administration des douanes et droits indirects, 2007 ECR 2049, para. 30.

422 Opinion of the Advocate General, Case C-335/05, Řízení Letového Provozu ČR, s. p. v Bundesamt für Finanzen, 2007 ECR 4307, para. 53.

423 See *id*, paras. 54-55.

424 *Id*. para. 56

425 See Case C-260/08, *Bundesfinanzdirektion West v. HEKO Industrieerzeugnisse GmbH*, para. 22 (Dec. 10,2009), available at http://eur-lex.europa.eu/Notice.do?val=505283:cs&lang=en&list=507709:cs,505283:cs,&pos=2&page=1&nbl=2&pgs=10&hwords=c%20260-08~ (last visited Feb. 20, 2010)

1.2.2.3. *ECJ's Rationale Against Direct Effect of the WTO Agreements*

Generally speaking, the ECJ is quite open to the direct effect of international agreements. However, the ECJ tends to be extremely conservative regarding GATT/WTO agreements. There are certainly doubts about the reasons for distinguishing the GATT/WTO agreements from those agreements, which the ECJ found directly effective. The critics and supporters view the ECJ's rulings differently.[426] Generally speaking, the ECJ's rationales are not legally sustainable.

---

426 Comments on the rulings of the ECJ, see e.g. Gerhard Bebr, *Agreements Concluded By the Community and Their Possible Direct Effect: from International Fruit Company to Kupferberg*, 20 Common Market Law Review, 35 (1983); Maresceau, 'The GATT in the Case-Law of the European Court of Justice', in Meinhard Hilf, F.G. Jacobs and E.-H. Petersmann (eds.), The European Community and GATT (1986), 107; Bourgeois, Effects of International Agreements in European Community Law: Are Dice Cast?, 82 Michigan Law Review (1984) 1250; Ernst-Ulrich Petersmann, Application of GATT by the Court of Justice of the European Communities, 20 Common Market Law Review 397 (1983); Werner Meng, *Gedanken zur Frage unmittelbarer Anwendung von WTO-Recht in der EG*, in RECHT ZWISCHEN UMBRUCH UND BEWAHRUNG: FESTSCHRIFT FÜR RUDOLF BERNHARDT 1063 (Berlin et. al. 1995); Mora, 'Equilibrium: A Rediscovered Basis for the Court of Justice of the European Communities to Refuse Direct Effect to the Uruguay Round Agreements', 30 JWT (1996) 43; Ronald A. Brand, *Direct Effect of International Economic Law in the United States and European Union*, 17 Northwestern Journal of International Law and Business 556 (1996-1997);Ulrich Everling, Will Europe Slip on Bananas? The Bananas Judgment of the Court of Justice and National Courts, 33 Common Market Law review 401 (1996); K.EES JAN KUILWICK, THE EUROPEAN COURT OF JUSTICE AND THE GATT DILEMMA: PUBLIC VERSUS INDIVIDUAL RIGHTS (1996); Ernst Ulrich Petersmann, *Darf die EG das Völkerrecht ignorieren?*, Europäische Zeitschrift für Wirtschaftsrecht 1997, 325; Judson Osterhoudt Berkey, The European Court of Justice and Direct Effect for the GATT: A Question Worth Revisiting, 9 European Journal of International Law 626 (1998); Cottier, 'Dispute Settlement in the World Trade Organisation: Characteristics and Structural Implications for the European Union', 38 CMLRev (1998) 325, at 365-377; 1; and Mengozzi, Private International Law and the WTO Law, 292 RdC (2001) 263; Jacques H. J. Bourgeois, 'The European Court of Justice and the WTO: Problems and Challenges', in THE EU, THE WTO AND THE NAFTA 71 (J.H.H. Weiler ed., 2000); Steve Peers, *Fundamental Right or Political Whim? WTO Law and the European Court of Justice*' in THE EU AND THE WTO, LEGAL AND CONSTITUTIONAL ISSUES 112, 122 (Gráinne de Búrca & Joanne Scott eds., 2001); Naboth van den Broek, *Legal Persuasion, Political Realism, and Legitimacy: The European Court's Recent Treatment of The Effect of WTO Agreements in The EC Legal Order*, 4 (2) Journal of International Economic Law 411 (2001); Piet Eeckhout, *Judicial Enforcement of WTO Law in the European Union-Some Further Reflections*, 5 (1)Journal of International Economic Law 91 (2002); Geert A. Zonnekyn, *EC Liability for Non-Compliance of WTO Dispute Settlement Decisions-Are the Dice Cast?*, 7 (2) Journal of International Economic Law 483 (2004); PIET EECKHOUT, EXTERNAL RELATIONS OF THE EUROPEAN UNION: LEGAL AND CONSTITUTIONAL FOUNDATIONS (2004); Armin Von Bogdandy, *Constitutionalism in International Law: Comment on a Proposal from Germnay*, Harvard International Law Journal 223 (2006); Adrian Emch, *The European Court of Justice and WTO Dispute Settlement Rulings-End of the Flirt*, 7 (4) Journal of World Investment and Trade (2006); Fabrizio Di

The ECJ determines the effect of WTO agreements within the Community legal system in an approach that is identically applied to other international agreements. The ECJ made a two-prong assessment to find provisions of international agreement directly effective. The first prong is whether the international agreement is binding on the Community. Then the ECJ would consider whether the provision is unconditional and sufficiently specific in light of the spirit, the structure, and the terms of the international agreement. The ECJ unexceptionally found the WTO agreements failed in the second stage. Certain provisions of the WTO agreements are indeed quite specific and unconditional and could be capable of granting rights to individuals.[427] In most of the cases, however, the ECJ denied the direct effect of the WTO agreements because they think the system of the WTO agreements as a whole is not set to have direct effect. Whether any particular provision is unconditional and specific enough to have direct effect is therefore not the concern of the ECJ. The ECJ focused on the flexibility of the WTO agreements and emphasized the principle of reciprocity in the WTO context.

a) Flexibility of the GATT/WTO Agreements

The ECJ found the GATT 1947 was not directly effective due to its flexibility embodied in Articles XIX, XXII, and XXIII. Contracting parties may deviate from their obligations assumed under the GATT 1947. Although the WTO agreements modify the safeguard clause and the dispute settlement procedure, the ECJ found this flexibility unchanged. If direct effect of the WTO agreements were established, the legislative and the executive organs would be deprived of the negotiations provided in Article 22 of the DSU.

It is true that the GATT 1947, like most international agreements, sets forth obligations and exemptions from these obligations. However, the mere existence of exemption would not invalidate an obligation. The safeguard clauses enable contracting parties to exercise considerable flexibility to introduce measures for economic and political purposes. In the meantime, the contracting parties are required to impose such measures in a transparent way that is least harmful economically.[428] Articles XXII and XXIII resemble a self-help module of implemen-

---

Gianni and Renato Antonini, *DSB Decisions and Direct Effect of WTO Law; Should the EC Courts Be More Flexible When the Flexibility of the WTO System Has Come to an End?*, 40 (4) Journal of World Trade 777, 793 (2006); Antonis Antoniadis, *The European Union and WTO Law: a Nexus of Reactive, Coactive, and Proactive Approaches*, 6 (1) World Trade Review 45,55 (2007).

427 See Introduction *supra.*

428 See Ernst Ulrich Petersmann, *The EEC as a GATT Member* in THE EUROPEAN COMMUNITY AND THE GATT,23, 53 (Meinhard Hilf et al. eds., 1986).

tation of the GATT obligations. The consultations and negotiations provided in Articles XXII and XXIII do not mean that the obligations should not be observed. Nor would the compensation substitute for the obligations under the GATT framework. The real crisis of the dispute settlement procedures lies in the consensus requirement for adopting the panel reports, which ascertains an infringement of the GATT 1947. Without such definite determination, the contracting parties are totally free to claim no infringement at all and thus may have some room to escape their obligations. The ECJ did not challenge the flexibility of the GATT in this regard, but criticized the means of implementation. Compared to other international agreements, the means of implementation of the GATT 1947 are not really as flexible as the ECJ might think. In addition, the dispute settlement procedures are proven to be one of the most effective international legal instruments for maintaining rule of law in international trade; they also may exclude any "*exception non-adimpleti contractus.*"[429]

The flexibility argument appears more doubtful when the ECJ made a totally contrasting assessment on the Free Trade Agreement (the FTA) between the Portugal and the EEC in the *Kupferberg* case. The FTA includes safeguard clauses as well as a dispute settlement procedure. Pursuant to paragraph 3 (d) of Article 30 of the FTA, the contracting party may impose immediately "precautionary measures strictly necessary to remedy the situation, where exceptional circumstances requiring immediate action make prior examination impossible."[430] The contracting party may unilaterally launch safeguard measures and certainly may deviate from the obligations under the FTA. Regarding the dispute settlement procedure, the Jointed Committee is responsible for ensuring the proper implementation of the FTA. If a party failed to fulfill its obligation under the FTA, the Jointed Committee would examine the situation to seek a solution that works for both parties. The Committee is composed of the representatives of the Community and Portugal. Paragraph 2 of Article 33 requires the Committee to act by "mutual agreement." In this light, each party may block the Committee's action.[431] Considering all these provisions, the AG of *Kupferberg* questioned to what extent the obligations under the FTA were truly unconditional.[432] All these features of the FTA between Portugal and EEC are exactly the same as those criticized by the ECJ in cases concerning the GATT 1947. However, the ECJ in the *Kupferberg* case

429 *Id.*

430 Agreement between the European Economic Community and the Portuguese Republic, Official Journal L 301, 31/12/1972 P. 0165.

431 Gerhard Bebr, *Agreements Concluded by the Community and Their Possible Direct Effect: From International Fruit Company to Kupferberg*, 20 Common Market Law Review 35, 64 (1983)

432 See Opinion of Advocate General, Case C-104/81, *Hauptzollamt (Chief Tax Office) Mainz v. C. A. Kupferberg & Cie KG A.A.*, 1982 ECR 3641, p. 8.

found the safeguard clauses and the dispute settlement procedure conducted by the Joint Committee did not make the obligations flexible. The ECJ indicated "the mere fact that the contracting parties have established a special institutional framework for consultations and negotiations inter se in relation to the implementation of the agreement is not in itself sufficient to exclude all judicial application of that agreement."[433] The Court further clarified the existence of safeguard clauses does not affect the prohibition on tax discrimination, except in those specific situations provided for. The existence of the safeguard clauses was found "not sufficient in itself to affect the direct applicability which may attach to certain stipulations in the agreement."[434]

Even if the obligations under the GATT 1947 are as flexible as the ECJ might have seen, the safeguard clauses and the dispute settlement procedures are significantly improved in the WTO epoch. The SG agreement set forth detailed application for safeguard measures. One of the purposes of the SG agreement, as provided in the Preamble, is to "re-establish multilateral control over safeguards and eliminate measures that escape such control." Pursuant to Article 3 of the SG agreement, the member shall conduct an investigation and consult with interested parties before it applies safeguard measures. The competence authorities of the members must seek information on their own motion to fulfill their obligation to evaluate all relevant factors.[435] In addition, the competence authorities shall provide reasoned and adequate explanations for their findings.[436] Failure to conduct the investigation correctly would also mean the conditions for safeguard measures would fail.[437] The members may still unilaterally impose safeguard measures under the SG agreement. However, they cannot make such a decision arbitrarily. Moreover, the DSU further eliminates the flexibility of the WTO agreements. The DSU elaborates on procedural rules for settling disputes and makes up the flaws of the dispute settlement procedures under the GATT 1947. For instance, the negative consensus excludes the members from blocking the adoption of the panel reports. In light of Articles 21, 22, and 26, the DSU clearly establishes a preference for an obligation to perform the recommendations. The matter would always be

433 Case C-104/81, Hauptzollamt (Chief Tax Office) Mainz v. C. A. Kupferberg & Cie KG A.A., 1982 ECR 3641, para. 20.

434 *Id*, para. 21.

435 Appellate Body Report on United States – Definitive Safeguard Measures On Imports Of Wheat Gluten From The European Communities (US-Wheat Gluten), para. 54, WT/DS166/AB/R (Dec. 22, 2000).

436 Appellate *Body Report on* United States-Definite Safeguard Measures on Certain Steel Products (US-Steel Safeguards), para. 10.17, WT/DS248/AB/R, WT/DS249/AB/R, WT/DS251/AB/R, WT/DS252/AB/R, WT/DS253/AB/R, WT/DS254/AB/R, WT/DS258/AB/R, WT/DS259/AB/R (Nov. 11, 2003).

437 See *id.*

under surveillance until the DSB decisions are properly implemented.[438] The members actually are not given the choice to compensate or obey.

In summary, the members undertake more stringent and specific obligations under the WTO agreements. It would be unfair to say the WTO agreements are flexible in nature. The situation has already changed; the ECJ's reasoning in this regard would be obsolete.[439] The ECJ itself seems to notice the modifications of the dispute settlement procedures but emphasizes the possibilities for compensation – even temporary. However, the negotiations for temporary compensation alone do not prove the flexibility of the WTO agreements.

b) Principle of Reciprocity

Another reason against direct effect of the GATT 1947 is the principle of reciprocity. According to the Preamble of the GATT 1947, the ECJ found this agreement is "based on the principle of negotiations undertaken on a basis of "reciprocity and mutually advantageous."[440] Contrary to the long elaboration about the great flexibility of the GATT, the ECJ discussed the principle of reciprocity in only one sentence. The ECJ did not explain how the reciprocity consideration is relevant to the conclusion that the provisions of the GATT cannot have direct effect.[441] The principle of reciprocity may be applied in different stages of international agreements. It could be principle for the negotiations, the substantial provisions of international agreements, or for the implementation of the international agreements.[442] In the GATT period, the ECJ did not specify the kind of reciprocity upon which its decision is based.[443] In the WTO period, the ECJ referred to the reciprocity in implementation of the WTO agreements. The reciprocity consideration seems to be the major argument against direct effect because the WTO has significantly reduced the flexibility of the GATT 1947.

The ECJ did not explicitly explain why the reciprocity in implementation is required. The most likely passages in the judgment of *Portugal v. Council*, leading case for the direct effect, would be the following:

---

438 See John Jackson, The WTO Dispute Settlement Understanding-Misunderstandings on the nature of Legal Obligation, and 91 American Journal of International Law 60, 63.

439 See Giuseppe Tesauro, Opinion of Advocate General, Case C-53/96, *Hermès International (a partnership limited by shares) v FHT Marketing Choice BV*, 1998 ECR 3603, para 30.

440 *Supra note* 307, para. 21.

441 Petersmann, Application of GATT by the Court of Justice of the EC, Common Market Law Review 20, 397, 424 (1983).

442 Geert Wils, The Concept of Reciprocity of EEC Law: An Explanation into These Realms, 28 Common Market Law Review 245, 248 (1991).

443 *Supra* note 441.

lack of reciprocity in that regard on the part of the Community's trading partners, in relation to the WTO agreements which are based on 'reciprocal and mutually advantageous arrangements' and which must ipso facto be distinguished from agreements concluded by the Community, referred to in paragraph 42 of the present judgment, may lead to disuniform application of the WTO rules.[444]

The international agreements referenced in paragraph 42 of the judgment are agreements introducing a certain asymmetry of obligations, or creating special relations of integration with the Community, such as the FTA between EEC and Portugal. In light of this passage, the ECJ established the reciprocity in implementation by claiming the WTO agreements are based on reciprocal and mutually advantageous arrangements. Also, the ECJ linked the direct effect issue with the reciprocity in implementation.

Distinctions could be made between the reciprocity in negotiation for rights and obligations (which appears in most treaties and international agreements) and the reciprocity in implementation. Many treaties contain clauses requiring reciprocity in implementation, such as diplomatic privileges and immunities. However, there is no general principle of reciprocity in implementing international obligations. In particular, reciprocity in implementation is not applicable to multilateral agreements aiming at equality or non-discrimination.[445] These agreements move a step beyond the mere satisfaction of mutual interests of contracting parties toward establishing objective and universal rulings serving a general interest.[446] The ECJ presumed the GATT 1947 and the WTO agreements require reciprocity in implementation merely on one paragraph of their Preambles, both of which read "Being desirous of contributing to these objectives by entering into reciprocal and mutually advantageous arrangements directed to the substantial reduction of tariffs and other barriers to trade and to the elimination of discriminatory treatment in international trade relations." Such reasoning seems to be strained without further analyzing their contexts.

It is true that the GATT framework was based more on a balance of negotiated concessions and commitments – not a set of legal rules. In this light, a dispute settlement system would also deal with nullification or impairment of benefits caused by measures compatible with the GATT (the non-violation complaints). What is actionable is not so much the breach of obligations, but the

444 See *supra* note 393, para. 45.
445 See *supra* note 442, at 256.
446 *Id.*

upsetting of the negotiated balance of benefits.[447] Some observed the only sacred, inviolable aspect of the GATT was the overall balance of rights and obligations achieved via negotiations.[448] To maintain such a balance, the principle of reciprocity would play a central role in the negotiations for the GATT 1947 and implementing these rules. Nevertheless, it is not explicitly or implicitly provided in the GATT 1947 that the implementation of the GATT obligations is conditional. Each contracting party still may not unilaterally suspend its obligations under the GATT 1947, when another contracting party has breached the GATT rules. In other words, no contracting party may justify an infringement by asserting that equalization of the balance between the parties. It would be absurd to claim that the GATT 1947 requires reciprocity in implementation.

The reciprocity argument might be even more questionable in the WTO context. The text of the WTO agreements shows that the WTO is based more on a set of rules than a balance of negotiated concessions. The reciprocity in implementation is no way required under the WTO agreements. Firstly, the Preamble of the Marrakesh Agreements indicated the members wish "to develop an integrated, more viable and durable multilateral trading system" and to "*preserve* the basic principles and to further the objectives underlying this multilateral trading system" (emphasis added).[449] Secondly, the TRIPS agreement and SPS agreement set forth rules for minimum standards and minimum harmonization of members' measures. Although they would be part of members' assessment on the overall balance of their rights and obligations under the WTO, these provisions by themselves are remote from the balanced negotiated benefits. Thirdly, the WTO agreements include provisions on the concept of non-reciprocity, which provides more favorable treatments for developing countries. As indicated in the Preamble, members recognize "there is need for positive efforts designed to ensure that developing countries, and especially the least developed among them, secure a share in the growth in international trade." To this end, the Generalized Systems of Preference allows members to asymmetrically grant developing countries favorable treatments.[450] Developing countries are entitled to different and special treatments under several agreements (e.g., Part IV of the TRIPS[451] and

447 See Joost Pauwelyn, Enforcement and Countermeasures in the WTO: Rules are Rules – Toward a More Collective Approach, 94 (2) American Journal of International Law 335, 340 (2000).

448 Judith H. Bello, *The WTO Dispute Settlement Understanding: Less is More*, 90 American Journal of International Law 416, 417 (1996).

449 See Marrakesh Agreement Establishing the World Trade Organization, Preamble.

450 Differential and More Favourable Treatment Reciprocity and Fuller Participation of Developing Countries, Decision of 28 November 1979 (L/4903), available at *http://www.wto.org/english/docs_e/legal_e/enabling1979_e.htm* (last visited Mar. 3, 2010).

451 TRIPS, Articles 65-67.

Article 15 of the AD agreement). Lastly, most of the dispute settlement procedures have a rule-based nature. The panel and the Appellate Body may not deviate from rules set in the DSU while they review the disputes. The negative consensus provided in Articles 16.4 and 17.4 of the DSU can further ensure the rule-oriented resolution found by the panel and the Appellate Body. Although "temporary compensation" and "suspension of concessions or obligations" inherit the idea of bilateral balances of rights and obligations, they cannot substitute for withdrawal of illicit measures.[452] These countermeasures for non-compliance are viewed as incentives or catalysts for compliance. These provisions of the WTO agreements clearly are not set to ensure the balance of concessions.

Under this context, the phrase "entering into reciprocal and mutually advantageous arrangements" in the Preamble seems to describe generally the basic political and economic situations on which the WTO system should be based.[453] The Preamble actually would not support the ECJ's conclusion that the WTO agreements contain the calling for reciprocity in implementation. The ECJ's observation was based merely on one single paragraph of the Preamble and the Court overlooked the developments of the WTO agreements. Even if the ECJ's observation on the reciprocal feature of the WTO agreements is sustainable, it did not provide the linkage between the direct effect issue and reciprocity in implementation. The ECJ has found in *Kupferberg* that unilateral recognition of direct effect is not in itself alone to constitute absence of reciprocity in implementing an international agreement.[454] Although the members shall implement their international obligations in good faith, they may choose appropriate means for implementation. The reciprocity in implementation thus should focus on the outcome of implementation and not on the means for fulfilling or observing the international obligations.

The ECJ did maintain the ruling on the reciprocity in implementation in the *Kupferberg* case.[455] Still, it found the lack of such reciprocity would lead to "disuniform application of WTO rules." It should be noted that the principle of reciprocity actually did not require the parties of an international agreement to do exactly the same thing.[456] Their action must be equivalent, but not necessarily identical. The

---

452 *Supra* note 438.

453 See, Naboth van den Broek, Legal Persuasion, Political Realism, and Legitimacy: The European Court's Recent Treatment of The Effect of WTO Agreements in The EC Legal Order , 4 (2) Journal of International Economic Law ,411,430 (2001); but see Giuseppe Tesauro, supra note 439, at para. 34.

454 *Supra* note 323, para. 18.

455 *Supra* note 393, paras. 44.

456 See K.ees Jan Kuilwick, the European Court of justice and the GATT Dilemma: Public versus Individual Rights, 247-248 (1996)

"disuniform applications" are actually foreseen by the members and should not be the only criteria for assessing the reciprocity in implementation of WTO rules. The "disuniform applications" matters only if the means for implementation taken by other members cannot properly implement or ensure the observance of the WTO rules to the equivalent extent which the direct effect could reach. In other words, whether the granting of direct effect would substantially impair the balance of EC's rights and balance involves assessment on the implementing legislation and practice of other members.[457] No such assessments have ever made by the ECJ. The ECJ simply presumed the imbalance existed because the Community's major trade partners, United States and Japan, do not attribute direct effect to the WTO agreements. The ECJ stressed the executive and legislative organs of the Community would be deprived of "the scope for manoeuvre enjoyed by their counterparts in the Community's trading partners."[458] Such a finding shows that ECJ has concerns over the good faith of Community's trade partners on the application of the WTO rules. The ECJ implies that the trade partners might not only deny immediate judicial enforcement but also abstain from proper implementation of WTO obligations via legislative or executive acts.[459] To rebalance such disadvantages, the ECJ granted the Community organs "scope for manoeuvre," which might logically include non-compliance to the WTO rules.[460] What the ECJ required is not reciprocity in implementation, but reciprocity in "not to comply with the WTO rules." Such kind of reciprocity is contrary to the WTO rules and most importantly to Article 216 of TFEU, which explicitly states international agreements binding on the institutions of the Union and the member states.

c) Rationale behind the Scene: Discretion of Community's Political Organs

The direct effect to international agreements implies a certain amount of judicial control over the legislative and executive organs when foreign factors are involved. The political organs usually have more control over external affairs; these affairs are less subject to the judicial reviews. Yet, the ECJ may have competence to review the international agreements concluded by the community

457 See Jacques H. J. Bourgeois, *The European Court of Justice and The WTO: Problems and Challenges* in THE EU, THE WTO, AND THE NAFTA: TOWARDS A COMMON LAW OF INTERNATIONAL TRADE? 71, 119 (J.H.H. Weiler ed., 2000).

458 *Supra note* 393, paras. 46.

459 Stefan Griller, Judicial Enforcement of WTO Law in The European Union Annotation to Case C-149/96, Portugal v. Council, 3 (3) Journal of International Economic Law 441, 460 (2000).

460 See *id*, at 460-461; see also Petersmann's criticism toward the cases concerning GATT 1947, Ernst Ulrich Petersmann, *Darf die EG das Völkerrecht ignorieren?*, Europäische Zeitschrift für Wirtschaftsrecht 1997, 325, 327.

because they are an "integrated part of Community law." Nonetheless, these agreements did not lose their characteristics of international law. Whether the direct effect should be granted in a given case would depend on the specific features of the international agreement at issue.[461] These features are concluded from the provisions of the agreement at issue, which are formed by the political organs of the contracting parties. In assessing the direct effect, the ECJ would inevitably consider the political concerns and the discretions of the political organs, as shown in the provisions of that agreement. It is thus conceivable that the ECJ would respect the discretion of the political organs because of the "flexibility" and "reciprocity" of the WTO agreements.

The text of the WTO agreements, as illustrated previously, does not align with the ECJ's construction of those agreements. The ECJ's reasoning in this regard is not persuasive and reveals judicial self-restraint on the WTO-related issues. For instance, the ECJ would take positions corresponding to the view of Council expressed in the Preamble of the Decision 94/800, which is not binding on the ECJ on assessing the direct effect of WTO agreements.[462] Besides, according to the general rules established in *Nakajima* and *Fediol III*, the ECJ would apply the GATT/WTO rules, only if the political organs have decided to implement or comply with obligations of the EU. In cases that involve WTO-inconsistent measures found by the penal or the Appellate Body (e.g. the banana regime), the ECJ would also shield the political organs from any potential negative consequences under the Community law for not making the measure in conformity with the WTO rules.[463] Actually, any discretion the political organs may enjoy is significantly reduced after a reasonable compliance period has passed.[464] The ECJ, nevertheless, would not interfere in the actions of political organs even at this stage. In practice, the political organs do make good use of their discretion to reach mutually satisfactory arrangements, even beyond the

461 See Astrid Epiney, *Zur Stellung des Völkerrechts in der EU*, Europäische Zeitschrift für Wirtschaftsrecht 1999, 5, 6.

462 See Tesauro *supra note* 439, para. 24; Siegbert Alber, Opinion of Advocate General, Case C 93/02P, *Établissements Biret et Cie SA v Council of the European Union*, 2003 ECR 10497, paras. 98-99.

463 E.g. Case C-377/02, Léon Van Parys NV v. Belgisch Interventie – en Restitutiebureau (BIRB), 2005 ECR 1465; Fabbrica italiana accumulatori motocarri Montecchio SpA (FIAMM) and Fabbrica italiana accumulatori motocarri Montecchio Technologies LLC (C-120/06 P), Giorgio Fedon & Figli SpA and Fedon America, Inc. (C-121/06 P) v Council of the European Union and Commission of the European Communities, 2008 ECR 6513.

464 See Bourgeois, supra note 457, at 121; Fabrizio Di Gianni and Renato Antonini, DSB Decisions and Direct Effect of WTO Law; Should the EC Courts Be More Flexible When the Flexibility of the WTO System Has Come to an End?, 40 (4) Journal of World Trade 777, 793 (2006); Siegbert Alber, id, paras. 87-88.

limits of the DSU.[465] The political organs are almost free from the control of the courts in terms of implementing the Community's obligations under the WTO agreements. The ECJ requires only that the secondary legislation should be interpreted in line with the WTO rules as much as possible.

Without textual support in the WTO agreements, the ECJ still might find legal basis for such a broad discretion of the political organs under the Union legal framework. The misunderstanding about the WTO agreements stops the ECJ from going further in that direction. It should be made clear that the intent of the author is not to overturn ECJ's reasoning, but to reveal its intentions and concerns. The grounds against direct effect seem to be more about political reality because the legal reasoning is not persuasive. In reality, the direct effect of WTO rules certainly creates several consequences, which the ECJ might not want to bear. In particular, those discontented with the Union's measures probably resort to the ECJ instead of requiring their governments to bring cases before the DSB. The ECJ would become the principle forum where the Union's legislation would be challenged.[466] In addition, the ECJ's interpretations offer little guarantees that they actually are correct interpretations of WTO rules, which should be decided by the DSB.[467] Once the ECJ's interpretation explicitly conflicts with those interpretations made under the DSU, the Union faces a more difficult situation in terms of faithful implementation of its commitments.[468] Moreover, the trade partners of the Union would be reluctant to negotiate for a mutually satisfactory solution for the Union's alleged infringement of the WTO agreements, since the ECJ is expected to apply the WTO rules. The political organs of the Union certainly would have less bargaining chip. All of these considerations could be the reasons for refusal of direct effect. The ECJ focus only on the disproportion in terms of "scope for manoeuvre." What really worries the ECJ is the major trade partners would obtain huge commercial advantages from a unilateral direct effect of the WTO agreements.[469]

---

465 Arrangements deviate from the DSU, see Antonello Tancredi, *EC Practice in the WTO: How Wide is the "Scope for Manoeuvre"?*, European Journal of International Law 933,956-959 (2004).

466 Antonis Antoniadis, The European Union and WTO Law: a Nexus of Reactive, Coactive, and Proactive Approaches, 6 (1) World Trade Review 45, 55 (2007).

467 See Piet Eeckhout, *Judicial Enforcement of WTO Law in the European Union-Some Further Reflections*, 5 (1) JOURNAL OF INTERNATIONAL ECONOMIC LAW 91, 97 (2002).

468 See *id.*

469 Steve Peers, *Fundamental Right or Political Whim? WTO Law and the European Court of Justice*' in THE EU AND THE WTO, LEGAL AND CONSTITUTIONAL ISSUES 112, 122 (Gráinne de Búrca & Joanne Scott eds., 2001).

1.2.3. Conclusion

Paragraph 7 of Article 300 of the EC (TFEU Article 216 of TFEU) did not provide a clear answer to the legal status of the international agreements concluded by the Community. The ECJ by virtue of "the interpretation and application of the Treaties," which is provided in paragraph 1 of Article 220 of the EC (TEU Article 19), may have filled the gap and developed principles. The ECJ found the GATT 1947 and the WTO agreements not directly effective in the light of their spirit, structure, and terms. Since these agreements do not have direct effect, they cannot be the "rule of law" relating to Treaty's application provided in paragraph 2 of Article 230 of EC (TFEU Article 263). The ECJ would apply the GATT/WTO rules in exceptional cases, wherein the obligations under the GATT/WTO have been transposed to Community law or the Community intends to implement these obligations. In such cases, the WTO rules to some extent are incorporated into Community law and are not actually directly effective. Nevertheless, the binding force of international agreements provided in Paragraph 7 of Article 300 of the EC (TFEU Article 216 of TFEU) is not only descriptive in nature. The ECJ seems to acknowledge the indirect effect of WTO agreements in light of this provision.

The ECJ's major rationale against direct effect of the GATT/WTO agreements is to maintain the "scope for manoeuvre", because these agreements are flexible and reciprocal by nature. The GATT/WTO agreements do leave some room in response to difficulties of the members in implementation. However, this scope for manoeuvre is limited. Also, it does not mean that the obligation of implementation is negotiable. The ECJ grants the political organs of the Community more space than they should have under the GATT/WTO agreements. Accordingly, the acts of political organs would be less subject to the control of the ECJ. The relevant cases indicate the courts would interfere with the WTO-related issues only to a minimum extent. The ECJ implies that it would not tie the hands of the political organs in any sense; such organs must negotiate with the cunning trade partners of the Community. The ECJ places more weight on political concerns than legal ones.

1.3. Conclusion: Implementation of the WTO Rules as Policy Issue

Both the United States and the European Union deny the direct effect of WTO agreements out of political concerns. These political concerns are nonetheless different. The United States' refusal of the direct effect is based more on the concerns of sovereignty, far less on the legal reading of the WTO agreements.

For the United States (the Congress in particular), the WTO agreements seem to be a double-edged sword. On one hand, they can foster the access to the markets world wide. On the other hand, these agreements might interfere too much with domestic affairs. The United States was therefore cautious about losing its decision-making power and blocked, via URAA and the SAA, the WTO agreements from any legal effect, which an international agreement could have within the US legal system. The federal government is the only entity that may directly resort to the WTO agreements before a court. Except for such circumstances, the WTO agreements are totally isolated from the domestic law of the United States. The legislative history of the URAA has shown that policy concerns of the United States relate mainly to domestic legal issues (e.g., distribution of powers between the federal and state governments as well as between legislative and executive branches). The United States rarely considered the issue in the context of the WTO law or the positions of other members. In other words, the United States probably would not grant direct effect to the WTO rules if these domestic concerns cannot be solved. It would make no difference to the United States, even if other members or the WTO itself has switched to the position of pro direct effect.

In comparison to the United States, the European Union actually holds a more open attitude to the direct effect of WTO agreements. The European Union considers the direct effect issue more from an aspect of international law. It is settled that international agreements concluded by the Community/Union are an "integrated part of Community law" and may have direct effect under certain conditions, which are based on the text and structure of the international agreement at issue. The ECJ's assessments on the direct effect of WTO rules were focused on the legal readings of WTO agreements. Although the ECJ has refused their direct effect in general, these agreements may be applicable in some circumstances and serve as guidelines for interpreting Community/Union and national laws. The ECJ's findings imply that the provisions of the WTO agreements are not by nature incapable of having direct effect. Rather, the ECJ awaits the political organs making the final determination on a case-by-case basis. The ECJ highly respected the discretion of the political organs on implementing WTO rules. Such a broad discretion was given mainly because political organs of the major trade partners have similar discretion. It seems that the ECJ would not be the first one to accept direct effect of WTO rules. If the major trade partners of the Union favor the direct effect, the ECJ probably would have reconsidered. One thing is for sure: judicial institutions in the United States and the European Union would rarely apply, even indirectly, the WTO rules.

Chapter 2: Positions of China and Taiwan

In this chapter, the author turns to two members of the WTO in the east: China and Taiwan. China has been a member of the WTO since December 2001 and recently overtook Germany as the world's top exporter.[470] China's attitude toward the direct effect of the WTO agreements is important to other members. Taiwan, as a medium-sized economy, is a significant trade partner to the United States and European Union. Although Taiwan began the application for the GATT in 1990s, the support of several GATT signatories would be available only after China joined the GATT. Such a position has continued to be supported by most members since the WTO was established.[471] This informal agreement appears to have been made due to political concerns over potentially offending China.[472] Finally, in January 2002, a month after China's accession, Taiwan formally acceded to the WTO. China and Taiwan acceded to the WTO only a few years ago. Their practices concerning the direct effect of WTO rules are still young and might not be settled. At this stage, their views regarding the effect of international agreements in general appear to play some role in this issue.

2.1. Laws and Practices in China

It is noteworthy that the Constitution of China does not address the effect of international agreements within China's legal system.[473] The Constitution remains silent on this issue for historical reasons. China tended to follow the policy of the Soviet Union, whose Constitution did not address the legal status of international agreements. Also, the unequal treaties signed in the nineteenth century

470 See *WTO Says China is World Biggest Exporter*, UNITED PRESS INTERNATIONAL, Mar. 26, 2010.

471 See Wayne M. Morrison, *Taiwan's Accession to the WTO and Its Economic Relations with the United States and China*, CRS Report for Congress, 1-2 (2003), available at http://fpc.state.gov/documents/organization/23370.pdf (last visited Mar. 29, 2010).

472 *Id*, at footnote 1.

473 Constitution of Peoples' Republic of China, available at http://www.npc.gov.cn/englishnpc/Constitution/node_2825.htm (last visited Jan. 10, 2011).

make China hesitate to include such an issue in the Constitution.[474] China's position could be deduced only from various laws or administrative and judicial interpretations.

2.1.1. Domestic Legal Status of International Agreements in General

In this subsection, the author elaborates on the following questions: (1) whether or in what conditions international agreements would become part of laws of China and could be relied upon by individuals and (2) if these agreements are directly effective, what are their relations to other domestic laws?

2.1.1.1. International Agreements as Part of Domestic Law

The lack of clear instruction from the Constitution makes it difficult to find definite and general rules for whether the international agreements are directly effective. Several laws and regulations appear to acknowledge the direct effect of international agreements; however, other laws or regulations imply the opposite. Still, some observations and conclusions may be drawn.

a) Acceptance of Treaties and International Agreements

Although legal status of international agreements is not provided in the Constitution of China, the Constitution does establish requirements for accepting international agreements. The State Council has the power to conclude "treaties and agreements concluded with foreign states,"[475] while the Standing Committee of the National People's Congress (hereafter the NPC) is authorized to decide on the ratification of "treaties and important agreements concluded with foreign states."[476] The President, according to the decision of the Standing Committee of the National People's Congress, ratifies treaties and important international agreements.[477] In light of the wordings of paragraph 9 of Article 89 and paragraph 14 of Article 67 of the Constitution, not all treaties or international agreements appear to be subject to the decision of the Standing Committee of the NPC. The distribution of the powers between the Standing Committee and the

474 Liu Yuewei, Guo ji tiao yue zai zhong guo shi yong xi lun (Some New Thoughts on Application of Treaties), 2007 (2) Jurists Review 144, 145-146 (2007).

475 Article 89 (9) of the Constitution.

476 Article 67 (14) of the Constitution.

477 Article 81 of the Constitution.

State Council are provided in detail in the Law of the People's Republic of China on the Procedure of the Conclusion of Treaties.[478] The State Council negotiates all treaties and international agreements.[479] The State Council and the Standing Committee of NPC both may decide whether to accept treaties and international agreements. Treaties and international agreements listed in Paragraph 2 of Article 7 of the Law on the Procedures of the Conclusion of Treaties shall be subject to the acceptance of the Standing Committee of the NPC and ratification of the President. The acceptance of all the other treaties and international agreements shall be decided by the State Council.[480] The approval of State Council will constitute the acceptance of a treaty or an international agreement not subject to the ratification procedure. Treaties and international agreements are binding on China at international level, when these procedures are completed.

b) Laws and Regulations Addressing the Effect of International Agreements

The provisions mentioned above do not state the requirements for international agreements to be binding at the domestic level. It is generally agreed that the international agreement would be spontaneously binding at the domestic level (i.e., become part of domestic law) due to their acceptance.[481] However, there are disagreements about the effect of international agreements as part of domestic law. For some, the international agreements as part of domestic law should have an effect identical to that of pure domestic laws.[482] For others, international agreements may still need implementation legislations to be directly applied by the courts or administrative institutions.[483]

Both the terms "treaty" (条约) and "agreements concluded with foreign states" (外国缔结的协定) are referred to in the Constitution. However, neither the Constitution nor the Law of the People's Republic of China on the Procedure of the Conclusion of Treaties provides any distinctions between these terms. The term

---

478 Law of the People's Republic of China on the Procedure of the Conclusion of Treaties , (promulgated by the Standing Committee National People's Congress, Dec. 28, 1990, effective Dec. 28, 1990) available at http://law.npc.gov.cn:87/page/browseotherlaw.cbs?rid=en&bs=97568&anchor=0#go0.

479 Article 5 of Law of the People's Republic of China on the Procedure of the Conclusion of Treaties.

480 See Articles 11and 12 of Law of the People's Republic of China on the Procedure of the Conclusion of Treaties

481 See Guo ji fa (International law), 426 (Wang Tieyiai ed.,1995); Li Peihao, Tiao yue fa gei lun (Introduction ofLaw of Treaties), 384 (1987); see also the laws and regulations illustrated *infra*.

482 Jiang Guoqing, Guo ji fa yu guo ji tiao yue de ji ge wen ti (Few Issues Concerning International Law and International Treaties), 2000 (3) Wuai qiao xue yuan xue bao 8,17.

483 See Li Peihao, supra note 481, at 386; Chen Hanfong et al., *Guo ji tia yue yu guo nei fa de guan xi ji zhong guo de shi jian (*Relationship between treaties and domestic laws and the practices thereof in China), 2000 (2) TRIBUNE OF POLITICAL SCIENCE AND LAW 117,119 (2000).

"treaty" referred to in laws and regulations actually includes all international agreements concluded by China. The terms "treaty" and "international agreements" are used interchangeably in the official translations of Chinese laws and regulations.[484] In the following subsections, the author uses the term "international agreements" to refer to all the conventions, treaties, protocols, etc. concluded by China.

China uses different methods to implement its obligations under international agreements within the domestic legal system. Several laws and regulations clearly recognize the direct effect of international agreements. Sometimes, China also passes legislation to implement the international agreements.

i. Laws and Regulations Recognizing Direct Effect of International Agreements

From 1979 to March 2010, 83 laws and regulations have contained provisions that could be construed as granting international agreements direct effect.[485] These provisions could be sorted by their wording. The first group is provisions that establish priority of international agreements over the domestic law. For example, Article 142, paragraph 2 of General Principles of Civil Law of the People's Republic of China contains a typical expression:

> Where the provisions of an international treaty which the People's Republic of China has concluded or has acceded to differ from civil laws of the People's Republic of China, the provisions of the international treaty shall apply, with the exception of those articles to which the People's Republic of China has declared its reservation.[486]

Such a provision is found in dozens of laws[487] (e.g., Article 24 of Frontier Health and Quarantine Law,[488] Article 236 of Civil Procedure Law,[489] Article 72 of

484 Official translation of Chinese laws, available at http://law.npc.gov.cn:87 or Lexis Nexis China online: http://www.lexiscn.com/lnc/landing.php.

485 The list of laws and regulations issued between Dec 31, 1979 and Dec 9, 2004, see Wang Yong, Tiao yue zia zhong guo shi yong zh ji ben li lun wen ti yan jiu (Studies on the Basic Theory of Treaty Application in China), 112-118 (Apr. 2006) (unpublished Ph. D. dissertation, East China University of Political Science and Law, (on file with China Knowledge Integrated Database, at http://eng.cnki.net/grid2008/index.htm). From Jan 1, 2005 to Mar 31, 2010, five laws issued or amended contain provisions, which explicitly or implicitly acknowledge direct effect of international agreements.

486 http://www.lexiscn.com/law/content.php?lawid=469955.

487 *Supra* note 485.

488 Frontier Health and Quarantine Law of the People's Republic of China (promulgated by the Standing Committee National People's Congress, Dec. 2, 1986; revised Dec. 29, 2007), available at http://law.npc.gov.cn:87/page/browseotherlaw.cbs?rid=en&bs=97400&anchor=0#go0.

489 Civil Procedure Law of the People's Republic of China (promulgated by the Standing Committee National People's Congress, Apr. 9, 1991; revised on Oct. 28, 2007), available at http://law.npc.gov.cn:87/ page/browseotherlaw.cbs?rid=en&bs=97585&anchor=0#go0.

Administrative Litigation Law).[490] These provisions appear not to be unusual in the Chinese legal system.

The second group is the provisions about the application of international agreements in a given circumstance. Sometimes, the contents of international agreements are explicitly recognized as applicable under certain conditions. For instance, in Civil Procedure Law, manners of service in international agreements are applicable in cases wherein the party has no domicile in China.[491] Also, Article 4 of Individual Income Tax Law provides that "The following categories of individual income shall be exempted from individual income tax: ... (9) Income exempted from tax as stipulated in the international conventions to which the Chinese Government has acceded or in agreements it has signed."[492] A similar provision appears in Custom Law.[493] In several instances, international agreements may be applied along with other domestic laws. Article 27 of Crew Regulation requires the labor contract shall be abided by the laws and regulations as well as international agreements pertinent to their labor protection and social securities.[494] In addition, on some occasions international agreements would even be preferable. For instance, although the rules for inheritance involving foreign estates or foreigners have been addressed in paragraphs 1 and 2 of Article 36 of Law of Succession, paragraph 3 states that "Where treaties or agreements exist between the People's Republic of China and foreign countries, matters of inheritance shall be handled in accordance with such treaties or agreements."[495] In some cases, international agreements may be an available option. Patent Law contains such a provision. If a foreign applicant does not have a regular residence or place of business in China, "the application shall be handled under this Law in accordance with any agreement concluded between the country to which the applicant belongs and China, or any international treaty to which both countries are party, or on the basis of the principle of reciproc-

---

490 Administrative Litigation Law of the People's Republic of China (promulgated by the Standing Committee National People's Congress, Apr. 4, 1989, effectively Oct.1, 1990), available at http://www.lexiscn.com/law/content.php?lawid=535696.

491 *Id*, see Article 245 (1), Civil Procedure Law of the People's Republic of China.

492 Individual Income Tax Law of the People's Republic of China (promulgated by the Standing Committee National People's Congress , Dec 25, 1995, revised on Dec., 27, 2007) , available at http://law.npc.gov.cn:87/page/browseotherlaw.cbs?rid=en&bs=271230&anchor=0#go0.

493 Article 56 (6), Custom Law of the Republic of China (promulgated by the Standing Committee National People's Congress, Sep. 10, 1998, revised on July 8, 2000), available at http://law.npc.gov.cn:87/page/browseotherlaw.cbs?rid=en&bs=271230&anchor=0#go0.

494 Crew Regulation of the People's Republic of China (promulgated by the State Council, Apr. 14, 2007, effectively Sep. 1, 2007), available at http://www.gov.cn/flfg/2007-04/29/content_602810.htm.

495 Law of Succession of the People's Republic of China (promulgated by Standing Committee National People's Congress, April 10, 1985, effectively Oct. 1, 1985), available at http://law.npc.gov.cn:87/page/browseotherlaw.cbs?rid=en&bs=97364&anchor=0#go0.

ity."[496] All these provisions mentioned above clearly show that a large number of international agreements are laws applicable in the Chinese legal system.

The third group is provisions considering the international agreements as supplements to domestic laws. The international agreements apply when the domestic laws do not fully address the matters concerned. For example, Article 16 of Foreign Trade Law establishes the reasons for import and export restrictions on goods and technologies. The first ten paragraphs illustrate a detailed list of the reasons for trade restrictions; the very last paragraph further states that "other goods the import or export of which needs to be restricted or prohibited in accordance with the provisions of international treaties or agreements signed or acceded to by the People's Republic of China."[497] Such a method was taken again in Article 26, which regulates the trade in services.[498] Similarly, the Provisions of the People's Republic of China on the Use of Red Cross Signs clearly recognizes "the relevant provisions of Geneva Convention and its appended agreements shall apply, if there is anything concerning the protective use of red cross signs not covered in these Provisions."[499] These rules of international agreements could be applied only on limited occasions. However, they are applicable laws.

ii. Laws and Regulations Implementing the Rules of International Agreements

Besides those laws and regulations that explicitly and inexplicitly acknowledge the direct effect of international agreements, other laws and regulations implement the rules of international agreements. Such an implementation could occur before and after acceptance of international agreements.[500] In China, implementing international agreements does not necessarily mean that these agreements cannot be directly effective. The domestic laws and regulations still may contain provisions acknowledging the direct effect of those international agreements.[501] For example, Regulations of the People's Republic of China concerning Diplomatic Privileges and Immunities transformed the Vienna Convention on Diplomatic

496 Article 18, Patent Law of the People's Republic of China (promulgated by Standing Committee National People's Congress, Mar. 12, 1984, revised on Dec. 27, 2008), available at http://law.npc.gov.cn:87/page/browseotherlaw.cbs?rid=en&bs=98139&anchor=0#go0.

497 Article 16 (11), Foreign Trade Law of the People's Republic of China (promulgated by Standing Committee National People's Congress, May 12, 1994, revised on April 6, 2004), available at http://law.npc.gov.cn:87/page/browseotherlaw.cbs?rid=en&bs=194917&anchor=0#go0.

498 *Id.* Article 26 (6), Foreign Trade Law of the People's Republic of China.

499 Article 23, Provisions of the People's Republic of China on the Use of Red Cross Signs (promulgated by The State Council, Jan. 29, 1996, effectively Jan. 29, 1996), available at http://www.asianlii.org/cn/legis/cen/laws/potuorcs420/.

500 See Chen Hanfong et al., *supra* note 483, at 121.

501 *Id*, at 121.

Relations. In the meantime, Article 27 of the Regulation states the Convention and other pertinent international agreements have priority over the Regulation.[502]

Certain of laws and regulations purely implement rules of international agreements, but do not address their effects in the domestic legal system. The Regulations of the Origin of Imported/Exported Goods is one such regulation. The second sentence of Article 2, paragraph 2 reads: "Concrete measures will be formulated later, in accordance with the international treaties and agreements that the People's Republic of China has concluded and/or signed."[503] Also, Administrative Measures for Adopting the International Criteria states that these Administrative Measures were drafted in light of the relevant rules of WTO and of international standards organizations.[504] Without further clarification on the effect of international agreements, these laws and regulations appear to deny the direct effect of international agreements. The number of such laws and regulations is relatively insignificant. It is far less than laws and regulations recognizing direct effect of international agreements. These laws and regulations seem to be made randomly rather than intended to set a general rule for denial of direct effect.[505]

c) *Judicial Interpretations of the Effect of International Agreements in Domestic Legal System*

The Supreme People's Court (hereafter the Supreme Court), as the highest judicial organ, supervises the exercise of judicial powers by all the people's courts.[506] The Standing Committee of the NPC (not the courts) is entrusted with the interpretation of Constitution and laws.[507] To create uniform application of laws, the Standing Committee authorized the Supreme Court to interpret the application of laws and regulations in given cases.[508] To this end, the Supreme Court issues

502 Regulations of the People's Republic of China concerning Diplomatic Privileges and Immunities (promulgated by Standing Committee National People's Congress Sep. 5, 1986, effectively Sep. 5, 1986), available at http://www.lexiscn.com/law/content.php?lawid=146191 (last visited Apr. 3, 2010).

503 Regulations of the Origin of Imported/Exported Goods of the People's Republic of China (promulgated by The State Council on September 3, 2004, effectively Jan.1, 2005), available at http://www.lexiscn.com/law/content.php?lawid=228136.

504 Article 1, Administrative Measures for Adopting the International Criteria (promulgated by General Administration of Quality Supervision, Inspection and Quarantine of the People's Republic of China, Jan. 5, 2002, effectively Jan. 5,2002), available at http://www.lexiscn.com/law/content.php?provider_id=2&isEnglish=N&origin_id=38502&eng=0&keyword=&t_kw=.

505 See *id.* 485, at 128.

506 See *supra* note 473, Article 124 of Article 67 (14) of the Constitution.

507 See supra note 473, Article 67 (1) and (4) of the Constitution.

508 See Quan guo ren ming dai biao da hui Chang wu wei yuan hui guan yu jia qiang fa lu jie shi gong zuo de jue yi (Resolution of the Standing Committee of NPC on the Strengthening of Legal In-

general interpretations on laws or regulations applied in given cases or gives instructions and guidelines for how a specific law or regulation should be applied. The Supreme Court usually issues the "规定" (the "Provision") or the "通知" (the "Circulation")[509], and the lower courts de facto abide by these Provisions and Circulations.[510] Besides, the lower courts would request the Supreme Court to provide its opinion on cases in lower courts. The China Applied Law Institution, an affiliated institution to the Supreme Court, publishes several cases monthly and comments on these cases, which represent the leading cases in the respective fields. These rulings, opinions, judicial interpretations, and leading cases present the views of the people's courts.

The laws and regulations mentioned in the previous section show that China implements its international obligations within the domestic legal system in different ways. China directly applies rules of international agreements, transforms these rules, or both. The laws and regulations are not consistent. However, the judicial decisions appear to vary as well.

i. Interpretations and Rulings Recognizing Direct Effect of International Agreements

In 1987, the Supreme Court and the five administrative departments jointly issued Measures on Several Issues Concerning Treatments of Cases Involving Foreign Factors, which is a guideline for the lower courts and all the administrative departments concerned.[511] The Measure reveals a general position on the effect of international agreement in the early stages of the reforms of the Chinese legal system. Paragraph 1, subparagraph 3 of the Measure states the administrative departments and courts concerned must implement the international obliga-

---

terpretation Work), (promulgated by Standing Committee of NPC, June 10, 1981), para. 4, available at http://www.lexiscn.com/law/content.php?provider_id=1&isEnglish=N&origin_id=66730&eng=0&keyword=&t_kw=.

509 *E.g.* Provisions of the Supreme People's Court on Several Issues Concerning the Trial of Administrative Cases of International Trade, Circular of Supreme People's Court on Implementing Convention on the Recognition and Enforcement of Foreign Arbitral Awards Entered by China. The official translations seem to be confusing. Regulation is the ordinary meaning of the term "Gui ding" and the term "Tong zhi" normally means notice or circular. However, these regulations made by the Supreme Court are not really laws and these notices mean more than passing messages.

510 The status of these interpretations, see generally, Cao Shinbing, *The Legal Status of Decision and Judicial Interpretations of the Supreme Court of China*, 3 (1) FRONTIERS OF LAW OF CHINA 1 (2008).

511 Guan yu chu li sho wai an jian ruo gan wen ti de gui din (Provision on Several Issues concerning Treatments of Cases Involving Foreign Factors), Fa Fa [1987] No. 54, (promulgated by Supreme People's Court, Aug. 27, 1987), available at http://www.lexiscn.com/law/content.php?provider_id=1&isEnglish=N&origin_id=276261&eng=0&keyword=&t_kw=.

tions on the bases of reciprocity. Whenever laws and regulations conflict with international obligations undertaken in international agreements, the rules of international agreements will be applied (except for reservations declared in advance). The last sentence of this subparagraph further provides that no administrative departments can refuse to implement the international obligations undertaken due to the domestic laws or regulations.[512] The Supreme Court and five administrative departments did not explain the reasons for their joint decision. They simple restated the provisions of laws and regulations (e.g., Article 142, paragraph 2 of General Principles of Civil Law). As far as civil and commercial matters are concerned, the Supreme Court constantly holds the international agreements should be applied or even may prevail over domestic laws and regulations. The Notice of the Supreme People's Court on Several Noteworthy Issues Concerning Adjudication and Implementation of Civil and Commercial Matters Involving Foreign Factors contains provisions similar to that Measure issued jointly by the Supreme Court and the administrative departments.[513][514] In the Opinions of the Supreme People's Court on Several Issues Concerning the Implementation of the General Principles of the Civil Law of the People's Republic of China, the Supreme Court reiterated the priority of rules of international agreements in different terms. Paragraph 191 reads "Where a foreigner dies within the territory of China, his property left within the territory of China shall be handled according to the Chinese law if no one inherits it or accepts bequeath, unless there are provisions otherwise specified by the international conventions concluded or joined in by the two countries."[515]

---

512 Paragraph 1, subparagraph 3 of the Provision: "处理涉外案件，在对等互惠原则的基础上，严格履行我国所承担的国际条约义务。当国内法或者我内部规定同我国所承担的国际条约义务发生冲突时， 应当适用国际 条约的有关规定 (我国声明保留的条款除外)。各主管部门不应当以国内法或者内部规定为由拒绝履行我国所承担的国际条约规定的义务。"

513 See Zui gao ren ming fa yuan guan yu shen li han zhi xing sho wei ming shang shi an jian ying dang zhu yi de ji qe wen ti de tong zhi (Circulation of the Supreme People's Court on Several Noteworthy Issues concerning Adjudication and Implementation of Civil and Commercial Matters involving Foreign Factors), Paragraph 2, Fa [2000] No. 51, (promulgated by Supreme People's Court, Apr. 17, 2000), available at http://www.lexiscn.com/law/content.php?provider_id=1&isEnglish=N&origin_id=265156&eng=0&keyword=&t_kw=.

514 See also paragraph 1 of the Circular of Supreme People's Court on Implementing Convention on the Recognition and Enforcement of Foreign Arbitral Awards Entered by China, Fa Jing Fa [1987] No. 5, promulgated on Oct. 4, 1987, available at http://www.lexiscn.com/law/law-english-1-492246.html.

515 Opinions of the Supreme People's Court on Several Issues concerning the Implementation of the General Principles of the Civil Law of the People's Republic of China, Fa Ban Fa[1988] No. 6, promulgated on Jan. 26, 1988, available at http://www.lexiscn.com/law/law-english-1-234065.html.

Several leading cases show that the rules and the guidelines set by the Supreme Court are strictly followed. The lower courts similarly recognize rules of international agreements must be applied. The courts indicate the acceptance of the international agreement at issue is the prerequisite for applying such an international agreement.[516] In several cases, the Supreme Court mentioned, in light of Article 142, paragraph 2 of General Principle of Civil Law, two conditions should be met for applying international agreements. In *Italian Ferrero SPA v. Montresor Company and Zhengyuan Company*, the Ferrero SPA argued that features of the packaging and decoration of Montresor's Tresor Dore Chocolate product, distributed by Zhengyuan Company, are almost identical to those of Ferrero Rocher chocolates; therefore, the acts of these companies should constitute unfair competition. Montresor was dissatisfied with the judgment of second instance and appealed to the Supreme Court. The Supreme Court upheld the judgment of the High People's Court of Tianjin but disagreed with the High Court's reasoning that the Paris Convention for The Protection of Industrial Property should be applied. The Supreme Court held that the conflict between the domestic law at issue and rules of international agreements is the condition for their application within domestic legal system. The Supreme Court found the domestic law at issue (i.e., Law for Countering Unfair Competition)[517] in conformity with the Paris Convention; therefore, the Paris Convention was not applicable in this case.[518]

Another condition for applying international law was provided when the Supreme Court responded to the lower court's question. The High People's Court

516 E.g. Shanghai Zhenhua ji xie yiou xian gong si su Meiguo lian ho ba guo yun song fu wu gong si guo ji hiang kong huo wu yun shu he tong biao shu guai di yan wu pei chang jiu fen an (Shanghai Zhenhua Port Machinery Co., Ltd. Claim against United Parcel Services Company of United States for Compensation for Delivery Delay of Bid Documents) (Jing'an District People's Court, May 18, 1995); Lu Chenye ding su Zhang Suxia ding fan ge shou yi ren que ding de chu guo lao wu ren yuan zai guo wai huo de de si wang bao xian pei chang jian an (Lu Chenye et al claim against Zhang Shuxia et al for Distribution of the Death Benefits Acquired Overseas) (Nanjing Intermediate People's Court, Mar. 31,1997); (Meiguo) Pu luo ke te hang an bu er gong si su Shanghei Chenxuan zhi neng ke ji fa zhan you xian gong si bu dang jing zheng an ((US)Puluocter and Ganbool Companies Claim against the Unfair Competition of Shanghai Chenxuan Intellectual Science & Technology Developing Company, Ltd), Hu-Lu-Gao-Zhong-Zi No. 4, (Shanghai High People's Court, July 5,2001).

517 Law of the People's Republic of China for Countering Unfair Competition, (promulgated by Standing Committee National People's Congress, Sep. 2,1993, effectively Sep. 2, 1993), available at http://www.lexiscn.com/law/law-english-4-043A80047.00007B00.2A01.html.

518 Zui gao ren ming fa yuan shen li Yidali fei lie luo gong si su Mengtesa (Zhangjiagang), Tianjin jing ji ji su kai fa qu Zhengyuan xing xiao yiu xian gong si bu zheng dang jing zheng jiu fen ti shen an (Italian Ferrero SPA claim ageist Montresor Company and Zhengyuan Company for unfair competition), Ming-San-Ti-Zi No. 3 (2006), (Supreme People's Court, Mar. 24, 2008).

of Shandong raised the question of whether domestic vessels sailing within Chinese territorial waters may resort to the maximum liability provided for in Protocol of 1992 to amend the International Convention on Civil Liability for Oil Pollution Damage. In light of the wording of Article 142, paragraph 2 of General Principle of Civil Law, international agreements could be applied in civil and commercial matters such as this one. In other words, the Protocol should have direct effect. However, the Supreme Court indicated the rules of international agreements could be applied only if foreign parties are involved.[519] In other words, these rules are not applicable at all times.

In summary, the Supreme Court set two additional conditions for direct effect when the laws or the regulations have recognized international agreements directly effective. First, the domestic law at issue should conflict with an applicable international agreement. Second, the case should involve foreign parties or foreign factors.

ii. Interpretations and Rulings Implying Refusal of Direct Effect

The Supreme Court appears to avoid applying international agreements on several occasions. The Supreme Court did not explicitly refuse the direct effect of international agreements. Rather, they simply chose not to list the rule of international agreements under the laws binding on the courts and administrative departments. In the guideline for reviewing the administrative litigations concerning international trade (i.e., the Provisions of the Supreme People's Court on Several Issues Concerning the Trial of Administrative Cases of International Trade) the legal bases referred to are "laws and administrative statutes of the People's Republic of China," "departmental rules," and "local statutes."[520] International agreements are not deemed as law under which the courts may review the measures of administrative departments. The Supreme Court similarly did not take the international agreements as legal basis for the reviews of the antidumping and countervailing measures. The Provisions concerning the reviews of antidumping and countervailing measures state that the courts review the legality

519 Zui gao ren ming fa yue guan yu fei hang xing yu guo ji hang xian de wo guo chuan buo zai wo guo hai yu ziao qeng you wu sun hai de min shi pei chang zo ren shi yong fa lu wen ti de ching shi de da fu (The Supreme People's Court in respond to Legal Question concerning Civil Liability for Oil Pollution Damage Caused by National Vessels within Territorial Waters), Min-Si-Ta-Zi No.20 (2008), (Supreme People's Court , July 3,2008).

520 See Articles 7 and 8, the Provisions of the Supreme People's Court on Several Issues Concerning the Trial of Administrative Cases of International Trade, Fa Shi [2002] No. 27 (promulgated by Supreme People's Court, Aug. 27, 2002), available at http://www.lexiscn.com/law/law-english-1-229715.html.

of these measures pursuant to "laws, administrative statutes, and departmental rules."[521] The rules of international agreements are omitted. Such omission could be deliberate or unintentional. Considering Article 9 of Provisions of the Supreme People's Court on Several Issues Concerning the Trial of Administrative Cases of International Trade, the former is more likely. Pursuant to Article 9 of the Provision, the courts are required to interpret consistently with the rules of international agreements, if there is more than one reasonable interpretation of laws and the regulations at issue.[522] Rules of international agreements are required only to be mandatory guidelines for interpreting domestic laws. In other words, the indirect effect of international agreements is required. *Zhongqing Zenton Medicine Co. Ltd. v. State Administration for Industry & Commerce* concerned trademark registrations; the Supreme Court did not apply the Paris Convention. By resorting to Article 9 of the Provision, the Court took the Convention as an important reference to interpreting the Trademark Law. The parties argued about the definition of the "agent" in Article 15 of Trademark Law. The Supreme Court held the agent in the Trademark Law should be understood similarly as the definition and the interpretations of the term "agent" in the Paris Convention.[523] The Supreme Court implies the refusal of direct effect of international agreements, at least in the administrative litigations.

d) Preliminary Observations on the Practice of China

Both the laws and practices show that China's position on the effect of international agreements is not consistent. It would be legally acceptable either to rec-

521 See Article 6, Zui gao ren min fa yuan guan yu shen li fan bu tiei xing zheng an jian shi yong fa lu ruo gan wen ti de qui ding (Provision of the Supreme People's Court on Several Issues Concerning the Laws applicable for the Review of the Countervailing Measures), Fa Shi [2002] No. 36, (promulgated by the Supreme People's Court, Nov. 21, 2002), available at http://www.lexiscn.com/law/con tent.php?provider_id=1&isEnglish=N&origin_id=262873&eng=0&keyword=&t_kw=t7Q%3D; Article 6 of Zui gao ren min fa yuan guan yu shen li fan ching xiao xing zheng an jian shi yong fa lu ruo gan wen ti de qui ding (Provision of the Supreme People's Court on Several Issues Concerning the Laws applicable for the Review of the Anti-dumping Measures), Fa Shi [2002] No. 35, (promulgated by Supreme People's Court, Nov. 21, 2002, available at http://www.lexiscn.com/law/con tent.php?provider_id=2&isEnglish=N&origin_id=43818&eng=0&keyword=&t_kw=t7Q%3D.

522 See *supra* note 520.

523 Zhongqing Zenton yiao yei you xian gong si, Guo jia gong shang xing zheng zong qu shang biao ping shen wei yuan hei su Sichuan Huashu dong wu yiao ye you xian gong si shan biao xing zheng jiu fen zai shen an (Retrial for the Trademark Dispute between Zhongqing Zenton Medicine Co. Ltd. and State Administration for Industry & Commerce and Sichuan Huashu Animal Pharmacy C. Ltd.), [2007] Xing Ti Zi No. 2, (Beijing High People's Court, Aug. 31,2007), available at http://www.lexiscn.com/law/content_case_analysis.php?case_id=119102 &keyword=&t_kw=&eng=0.

ognize or to refuse the direct effect because the Constitution does not provide any decision. The dominant opinion holds that China actually has generally recognized direct effect.[524] Laws and regulations recognizing direct effect are much more common than those that do not.[525] Besides, the direct effect is not absolutely excluded, even if the implementation legislation is required. The implementation legislations still could contain provisions stating the supremacy of that international agreement. To exclude direct effect, the implementation legislations should have done it in an explicitly way. Moreover, China has expressed a preference for the direct effect in international forums. In the fifty-first meeting of the Committee against Torture, China made a diplomatic statement that "When China accedes to any convention it becomes binding as soon as it entered into force. China then fulfilled all its obligations, and it was not necessary to draft special laws to ensure conformity."[526] In this light, the international agreements should be directly effective. A few years later, China reiterated such an opinion in the report on implementation of The Convention against Torture and Other Cruel, Inhuman or Degrading Treatment or Punishment (hereafter the Convention against torture).[527] Although this report is not legally binding, it is the Chinese government's official observation on the effect of international agreements in general. China would hold an open attitude toward international agreements, probably because the procedure for concluding international agreements is no different from the legislation procedure. Such an attitude is also in line with China's willingness to fulfill its international obligations.[528]

Some suggest demonstrating caution about the conclusion that China might have generally accepted the direct effect only because of those provisions, which

---

524 See e.g. Guo ji fa (International law), (Wang Tieya ed., 1995); Wang Liyu, Guo ji tiao yue zai Zhongguo guo ne fa zhong de shi yong *(The Application of International Agreements within the Chinese Legal System),* 1993 CHINESE YEARBOOK OF INTERNATIONAL LAW 282 (1993); Li Shishi, *Zhongguo de li fa, tiao yue yu guo ji fa (*The Legislation of China, Treaties and International Law), 1993 CHINESE YEARBOOK OF INTERNATIONAL LAW 264 (1993); Jiang Guoqing, *Guo ji fa yu guo ji tiao yue de ji ge wen ti* (Few Issues Concerning International Law and International Treaties), 2000 (3) JOURNAL OF FOREIGN AFFAIRS COLLEGE 8 (2000); Zeng Lingliang, *WTO xie yi zai wo guo de shi yong gi wo guo fa zhi jian she de go ming (The Application of WTO Agreements in Our Country and the Revolution of Our Legal System)*, 2000 (6) CHINA LEGAL SCIENCE 38 (2000).

525 See Wang Yong, *supra* note 485, table 14, at 112, table 16, at 128.

526 See U.N. Committee Against Torture, 14 th Sess., 51 st mtg., at 2, U.N. Doc. CAT/C/SR. 51, (May 4, 1990); Chinese Version, see supra note 483, at 121.

527 U.N. Committee Against Torture, Consideration of Reports Submitted by States Parties Under Article 19 of The Convention: Initial Reports of States Parties Due in 1989: China, para. 61,CAT/C/7/Add.14 (Jan 18, 1993).

528 Jiang Guoqing, *supra* note 524, at 17.

explicitly or inexplicitly recognize the direct effect.[529] The direct effect issue involves constitutional considerations, such as distribution of powers. Although the laws or regulations may provide solutions for conflict of laws, they cannot provide legitimate grounds for general acceptance of direct effect, especially when the Constitution has remained silent.[530] Concerns also exist regarding the potential conflicts between relevant laws and regulations. In a given case, one provision at issue might require direct effect while another states the opposite. The conflicts might further lead to disorder and inconsistent application of domestic law as well as international agreements.[531] Furthermore, administrative institutions would also excessively intrude on the competence of legislative organs, if direct effect is generally recognized.[532] Also, direct effect of the international agreements might jeopardize the sovereignty of China. International agreements are formed jointly by the contracting parties. Acceptance of direct effect implies that foreign countries might share the domestic legislations and, to some extent, the administrative institutions would be bound by them. Moreover, the judges might not be familiar with the rules of international agreements and thus may not properly interpret and apply these rules. The misuses might cause inconsistent applications and might even breach the international obligations of China.[533]

In practice, international agreements are not always applicable in a given case, even if they could be directly effective. The laws and regulations might establish conditions of their application. For instance, international agreements are applicable only if the domestic laws do not fully address the matters concerned. Moreover, the Supreme Court has set two additional limitations on their application. First, a conflict should exist between domestic law and international agreements. Second, the case should involve foreign factors. Such limitations were based on the Supreme Court's readings of Article 142 of General Principle of Civil Law, which may be applicable to civil and commercial matters, provides for the pattern of "where an international agreement differs from domestic laws, the former shall apply."

Logically speaking, the international agreement superior to the domestic laws should be directly effective, whether or not a conflict exists. The rules of the provisions for the foreigners still could and should be applied in disputes purely

---

529 E.g. Liu Yongwei, *supra* note 474; Zhang Xiaodong, *Yei lun guo ji tiao yue zhi wo guo de shi yong (*Application of International Agreements in Our County), 2001 (6) LAW REVIEW 73 (2001); Li Ming, *Ying chong li fa shang kao lu tiao yue zai wo gui de xiao li wen ti* (The Effect of Treaties within China Should Be Subject to the Decisions of Legislative Organs), 2006 (3) PEKING UNIVERSITY JOURNAL 351 (2006).

530 See Li Ming *id*,357.

531 SeeLiu Yongwei, *supra* note 474, at 147.

532 See *id.*

533 See·Zhang Xiaodong, *supra* note 529, at 77-78.

among nationals, if the matters at issue are no different in nature. The Court reads the laws and regulations recognizing the direct effect so narrowly that the rules of international law are applicable only in a situation exactly the same as stated in the laws and regulation. The Supreme Court excludes any further inference from the laws and regulations, even a logical one. Since the Supreme Court strictly follows the literal meaning of the laws and regulations, the Court might not generally recognize the direct effect of international agreements, unless the laws have done so. For now, China appears to take a case-by-case approach. The effect of international agreements is determined by virtue of the particular domestic laws and regulations applicable in a given case.

2.1.1.2. Relationship to Domestic Law

The laws and practices rarely address the general relationship between directly effective international agreements and domestic laws. The only hint is the provisions stating the supremacy of international agreements.[534] The question is whether such provisions imply the supremacy of international agreement in general or they show only the tendency; the issue has yet to be settled. Several prominent scholars observe international agreements are inferior to the Constitution but have the same status as laws and regulations,[535] because the legislative organ and its permanent body (i.e., Standing Committee of the NPC) and administrative institutions both have authority to accept international agreements. Also, the procedures for accepting international agreements are similar to the procedures for adopting laws and regulations.[536] International agreements should have the

---

534 See Part I, section 2.1.1.1. b) *supra*.

535 See *e.g.* Che Pizhao, *Lun tiao yue zai wo guo de shi yong* (On the Application of Treaty in China), 2005 (3) LAW SCIENCE MAGAZINE 96 (2005); Chen Hanfong et al., Guo ji tia yue yu guo nei fa de guan xi ji zhong guo de shi jian (Relationship between treaties and domestic laws and the practices thereof in China), 2000 (2) TRIBUNE OF POLITICAL SCIENCE AND LAW 117 (2000); Dong Guolu, *Guo ji fa zai Zhongguo de shi yong* (the application of international law in China), 2002 (3) WUHAN UNIVERSITY JOURNAL (PHILOSOPHY & SOCIAL SCIENCES) 349 (2002); Mu Yapin &. Xi Yifan, *WTO xie yoi zai wo guo guo ne de shi yong wen ti* (On the Enforcement of the WTO Agreements in Mainland China), 2003 (1) JOURNAL OF JINAN UNIVERSITY 54 (2003); Wu Yarong, *Lun WTO xie yi de fa lu xiao li ji zai wo quo fa yuan de shi yong* (The Effect of the WTO agreements and its application in the Chinese courts),2001 (2) JOURNAL OF LAW APPLICATION 11 (2001); Li Xingxiang, *Wo guo shi shi WTO xie yi de ji ge zhu you wen ti tan xi (*Analysis of the Major questions of the Application of the WTO Agreements), 71 FUJIAN FA XUE 38 (2002).

536 See Articles 8,9and 11 of Law of the People's Republic of China on the Procedure of the Conclusion of Treaties, supra note 478; Articles 7 (2) and (3) and 40, The Law of the People's Republic of China on Legislation (promulgated by the Standing Committee of National People's

legal status the same as the domestic laws and regulations, which are adopted under similar procedures. The hierarchy of the norms in China is as follows: (1) Constitution, (2) basic laws, (3) laws and international agreements ratified by the Standing Committee of NPC, (4) administrative regulations and international agreements approved by the State Council, (5) departmental rules,[537] and international agreements without ratifications or approval.

Some view the relation between international agreements and domestic laws differently. Except for the Constitution, according to some observers, international agreements should be superior to all domestic laws.[538] Article 142 of the General Principle of Civil Law acknowledges all international agreements prevail, including those without ratification or approval. This provision clearly did not fit the thesis mentioned above.[539]

It is generally agreed that the hierarchy of domestic laws should be decided ultimately by the Constitution. The supremacy of international agreement is thus just a tendency, not a general rule.[540] In practice, there is no consistent position. The question appears unsettled.

2.1.2. The Legal Status of the WTO Agreements

China tends to recognize the direct effect of international agreements, but that tendency is not a firm rule. The effect of the WTO agreements depends on the intent of the legislative and executive branches on a case-by-case approach. In other words, it should be determined by virtue of the laws and regulations that might be applicable in WTO-related cases. The scope of the WTO agreements is so broad that it includes many matters, which the domestic laws and regulations also address. In this section, the author will mention only a few significant legal documents and make a general observation. China acceded to the WTO only 9 years ago; laws and practices have not been completely developed yet. The observation is only preliminary and partial.

Congress, Mar. 15, 2000, effectively July, 1, 2000) 2000 Standing Committee of National People's Congress Gazette 112 (P.R.C.).

537 The ministries, commissions and other competent departments (collectively referred to as "departments") of the State Council could issue departmental rules within the jurisdiction of their respective departments and in accordance with the laws and administrative regulations. See Article 71 of the Law of the People's Republic of China on Legislation (promulgated by the Standing Committee of National People's Congress, Mar. 15, 2000, effectively July, 1, 2000) 2000 Standing Committee of National People's Congress Gazette 112 (P.R.C.).

538 See Li Peihao, TIAO YUE FA GAI LUN (Introduction of Law of Treaties), 395 (1987).

539 See Wang Yong, *supra* note 485, at 98-99.

540 See Wang Tieya, GUO JI FA YIN LUN (Introduction of International Law), 210 (1998).

2.1.2.1. *Accession Documents of China*

China did not address the effect of WTO agreements in its Protocol of Accession. China has expressed its willingness to perform the WTO obligations in the Report of the Working Party on the Accession of China (hereafter the Working Party Report). Preamble of the Protocol of Accession states that the WTO and China would "take note" of the Working Party Report.[541] The Working Party Reports would not necessarily become an integral part of the WTO agreements unless the Report has been incorporated into the Protocol of Accession. However, the Report could always be considered in interpreting these obligations.[542] China ensured that all the laws and regulations pertinent to trade or to other trade-related issues would conform to WTO agreements and other commitments of China. To reach this end, China would systematically revise its domestic laws. China stated: "[T]he WTO Agreement would be implemented by China in an effective and uniform manner through revising its existing domestic laws and enacting new ones fully in compliance with the WTO Agreement."[543] China further confirmed the relevant administrative regulations and departmental rules would be issued within the time frames in which China promised to implement the WTO agreements. Even if these regulations and rules did not occur within the time frames, the authorities "would still honour China's obligations under the WTO Agreement and Draft Protocol."[544] In the same paragraph, China also promised to revise or annul the WTO-inconsistent administrative regulations and departmental rules. The Working Party noted these commitments.

According to paragraph 67 of the Working Party Report, China would implement the WTO agreements through domestic laws and regulations; the direct effect of WTO agreements is therefore clearly excluded. However, paragraph 68, which has been incorporated into the Protocol of Accession,[545] is somewhat ambiguous. On one hand, the administrative institutions should take more specific measures, *inter alia* promulgation, revision, nullification of administrative regulations and rules, to implement the WTO agreements. On the other hand,

541 Protocol of Accession of People's Republic of China, WT/L/43 (Dec. 11, 2001).

542 *E.g.* the Panel on *Argentina – Textiles and Apparel* made reference to the Report of the Working Party on Accession of the Democratic Republic of the Congo, when they interpret Article VIII of the GATT. See Panel Report on *Argentina – Measures Affecting Imports of Footwear, Textiles, Apparel and other Items* (*Argentina – Textiles and Apparel*), para 6.76,WT/DS56/R (Nov. 25, 1997)

543 Working Party on the Accession of China, *Report of the Working Party on the Accession of China*, para. 67, WT/ACC/CHN/49 (Oct. 1, 2001).

544 *Id*, para. 68

545 General Council, Decision on the Accession of People's Republic of China, p. 2, WT/L/432 (Nov.23, 2001).

authorities would "honor" the obligations of the WTO agreements if the implementing regulations and rules do not occur within the time frames. The term "honor" implies that the administrative institutions would follow or even apply the rules of WTO agreements. Some observed the WTO agreements might be directly effective on such an exceptional occasion.[546]

It should be noted that individuals are not necessarily granted the right to invoke the WTO agreements in such circumstances.[547] Administrative intuitions are not obliged to apply the WTO agreements directly. They are obligated merely to respect these agreements. Direct effect of the WTO agreements is only one option. For instance, the administrative institutions may take provisional measures to implement the WTO rules until the administrative regulations and rules have been issued. To some extent, the Working Party Report seems to deny the direct effect.

2.1.2.2. Laws, Regulations, and Courts' Interpretations Relevant to the Effect of the WTO Agreements: Divergent Views on the Direct Effect

As mentioned previously, China does not accept or refuse the direct effect of international agreements in general. Whether the WTO agreements are directly effective depends on all the domestic laws and regulations applied in a given case. The Working Party Report reveals China's preliminary attitude toward direct effect of WTO agreements. Still, the effect of these agreements is determined by domestic laws, regulations, and the courts' interpretations, which are relevant to trade in goods and services, intellectual property rights, as well as those rights subject to plurilateral agreements (e.g., government procurements).

Among all the pertinent laws and regulations, only a few address the effect of the international agreements. Besides the General Principle of Civil Law, Civil Procedure Law and Administrative Procedure Law, which are often applicable in the WTO-related cases, three laws and regulations might allow the rules of WTO agreements to be applied in a given case. These laws and regulations are as follows: Regulations for the Implementation of Copyright Treaties;[548] Patent Law;[549] Border

546 Kong Xiangqen, *WTO fa lu de quo ne shi yong (*Domestic Application of WTO Law), Legal Daily, Beijing, Dec. 16, 2001.

547 See Xin Zhang, Domestic Effect of WTO Agreement in China, 3 (5) JOURNAL OF WORLD INVESTMENT 913, 925-26 (2002).

548 See Article 19, the Regulations for the Implementation of Copyright Treaties, (promulgated by State Council, Sep. 25, 1992, effectively Sep. 25, 1992), available at http://www.lexiscn.com/law/content.php?lawid=136780.

549 See Article 20 (3), Patent Law of the People's Republic of China (promulgated by Standing Committee National People's Congress, Mar. 12, 1984, revised on Dec. 27, 2008), available at http://www.lexiscn.com/law/law-english-1-480068.html.

Health and Quarantine Law.[550] All these laws and regulations contain a provision declaring the supremacy of international agreements over domestic law. These provisions do not specify the international agreements applicable; instead, they generally refer to all relevant international agreements. WTO agreements are logically included.

Four other laws and regulations, however, indicate the rules of WTO agreements are not directly effective: Administrative Measures for Adopting the International Criteria;[551] Regulation for the Implementation of the Trademark Law;[552] Detailed Implementing Rules for the Patent Law;[553] Regulations of the Origin of Imported/Exported Goods.[554] These regulations either require transformation of international agreements or omit the rules of international agreements as part of the applicable legal basis. Besides such regulations, the State Council has clearly rejected the direct effect of international agreements in a Circular, which directs all the administrative institutions on reforming the administrative examination and approval system.[555] This Circular is highly relevant to implementing WTO agreements; many economic activities (including those provided in the WTO agreements) are subject to the administrative examinations and approvals.[556] Although the Circular is not legally binding on the institutions of central and local governments, it has significant influence over their measures. The State Council states the following: "International conventions, treaties or customs, which

550 See Article 24, Border Health and Quarantine Law of People's Republic of China (Promulgated by Standing Committee National People's Congress, Dec. 29, 2007, effectively Dec. 29, 2007), available at http://www.lexiscn.com/law/content.php?lawid=233127.

551 See Articles 1 and 4, Administrative Measures for Adopting the International Criteria (promulgated by General Administration of Quality Supervision, Inspection and Quarantine of the People's Republic of China, Jan. 5, 2002, effectively Jan. 5, 2002), available at http://www.lexiscn.com/law/content.php?provider_id=2&isEnglish=N&origin_id=38502&eng=0&keyword=&t_kw= (last visited on Apr. 15, 2010).

552 See Article 12, Regulation for the Implementation of the Trademark Law of the People's Republic of China (promulgated by the State Council, Aug. 3, 2002, effectively Sep. 15, 2003), available at http://www.lexiscn.com/law/law-english-1-228726.html.

553 See Article 101, Detailed Implementing Rules for the Patent Law of the People's Republic of China (promulgated by the State Council, Jan. 9, 2010, effectively Feb. 9,2010), available at http://www.lexiscn.com/law/law-english-1-530667.html.

554 See *supra* note 503.

555 Guan yu guan che xing zheng shen pi zhi du gai ge de wu xiang yuan ze xu yao ba wo de jig e wen ti (Issues Necessary for Implementing the Five Principles for the Reform of the Administrative Examination and Approval System), (2001) Guo-Shen-Gai-Fa No.1 (promulgated by the State Council, Dec.11, 2001), available at http://www.lexiscn.com/law/content.php?provider_id=1&isEnglish=N&origin_id=30034&eng=0&keyword=&t_kw=udjT2rnhs7nQ0NX%2ByfPF%2BtbGtsi4xLjvtcTO5c%2Fu1K3U8tDo0qqw0c7VtcS8uLj2zsrM4g%3D%3D.

556 See Part I, section 2.1.2.3 b) infra.

China has acceded to or recognized, could be applied under the domestic legal system, only if they are transformed via legislation into domestic laws, regulations, decrees, or other normative documents."[557] Without such transformation, they cannot serve as legal basis for administrative examination and approval.

The Judges of the Supreme Court also have conflicting ideas about the direct effect of WTO agreements. Judge Li Guoguang, the Deputy Chief of the Supreme Court, supports the direct effect and the supremacy of the WTO agreements.[558] Another Deputy Chief of the Supreme Court, Judge Zao Jianming, stated that China has committed only to transform the TRIPS agreement and other WTO agreements. These agreements thus should not have direct effect.[559] Just before China acceded to the WTO, the Supreme Court circulated an opinion on the courts' reactions to the impacts of the new political and economical situations (including the accession of the WTO). In this opinion, the Supreme Court requested the judges to learn about and apply the international trade law. The Supreme Court stated international agreements concluded by China are the "legal basis for the cases involving foreign factors," provided that a reservation has been made.[560]

In 2002, the Supreme Court gave more clues about the direct effect issue in three interpretations that are highly relevant to the WTO agreements. Article 1 of the Provisions of the Supreme People's Court on Several Issues Concerning the Trial of Administrative Cases of International Trade indicates the Provision was set to deal with administrative litigations in connection with trade in goods, trade in services, trade-related intellectual property rights, and other trade-related issues. In other words, this Provision might apply to all WTO-related cases, where the government is one of the parties. Articles 7 and 8 of this Provision[561] do not list the international agreements as the applicable legal basis. Although these provisions do not expressively reject the direct effect, they certainly mean to do

---

557 See *supra* note 555, Section 2, Subsection 1, para. 2.2.

558 Hu Qihua & Shao Zongwei, Laws Pave Way for WTO Entry, China Daily, Oct. 31, 2000.

559 Zui gao ren min fa yaun fu yuan zhang Cao Jianming zai quan guo fa yuan zhi shi cai chan qan shen pan gong zuo zuo tan hui de jiang hua (Speech of Deputy Chief of Supreme People's Court in the National Workshop on the Adjudication of the Intellectual Property Rights), (circulated Jan. 18, 2007), available at http://law1.chinalawinfo.com/newlaw2002/slc/slc.asp?db=chl&gid=110259.

560 See Guan yu chong fen fa hui shen pan zhi neng zuo yong wei jing ji fa zhan ti gong si fa bao zhang han fa lu fu wu de yi jian (Opinion on Making the Adjudicative Function Fully to Support and to Provide Legal Service for the Economic Development), Section 4, Subsection 2, Fa Fa [2000] No. 8, (promulgated by Supreme People's Court, Mar. 8, 2000) available at http://www.lexiscn.com/law/content.php?provider_id=3&isEnglish=N&origin_id=113503200001&eng=0&keyword=&t_kw=zqq%2BrbzDt6LVuczhuanLvreosaPVz7rNt6jCybf%2BzvG1xNLivPs%3D.

561 *Supra* note 520.

so.[562] If the administrative litigations concern anti-dumping or countervailing measures, the Provisions concerning the reviews of antidumping and countervailing measures are also applicable. Under these two Provisions, international agreements are not the legal basis provided for.[563] However, Article 11 of the Provision Concerning the Reviews of Countervailing Measures states the courts may refer to the provisions for civil actions involving foreign parties in Civil Procedure Law, which recognizes the direct effect of the international agreements. As a result, the rules of international agreements might still be applicable in cases under the Provision Concerning the Reviews of Countervailing Measures. The Supreme Court seems to rejects the direct effect of WTO agreements most of the time; however, it does not totally exclude such a possibility.

2.1.2.3. The Effect of WTO Agreements under the Current Legal Framework

According to the previously mentioned legal documents, China (in particular the Supreme Court) might reject the direct effect of the WTO agreements. Nonetheless, China failed to do this clearly. Whenever certain legal documents suggested the refusal of the direct effect, other documents showed otherwise. Several Judges of the Supreme Court and scholars contend the WTO agreements as a whole are by no means directly effective.[564] Their conclusion is not based on the domestic laws and regulations, or the judicial interpretations, which are actually in force. Instead, they resort to the policy considerations. In particular, the disadvantages lead by the unilateral acceptance of direct effect when the major trade partners of China (i.e., the United States and the EU) have explicitly rejected such effect. Besides, they argue the judges may not be capable of applying and interpreting the rule of WTO agreements. Furthermore, the transformation of WTO agreements provides the legislative organs the final determination on how

---

562 See *supra* not 547, at 933.

563 *Supra* note 521

564 See *supra* note 559; Liu Hanfu, *Shi jie mao yi zu zhi fa zai ne quo fa yuan zhi jie shi yong de wen ti (*The Issues Concerning the Direct Application of WTO Law in Chinese Courts) ,2000 (7) PEOPLES' JUDICATURE 49, 51 (2007); Zhao Daguang, *"ru shi" hou wo guo si f ashen cha gong zuo de ruo gan wen ti* (Problems of the Judicial Review after the Accession to the WTO), 2001 (S1) JOURNAL OF LAW APPLICATION 37,39 (2001); Wang Zhenqing, *Zuo hao ru shi hou zhi shi chan quan you quan de shen pan gong zuo* (The Judicial Review of Intellectual Property Right after the Accession to the WTO), 2001 (S1) JOURNAL OF LAW APPLICATION 52, 53 (2001); Cao Jianming, *WTO and the Rule of Law in China*, 16 TEMPLE INTERNATIONAL AND COMPARATIVE LAW JOURNAL 379,380 (2002); Yuan Quan, *You guan WTO gei ze zai wo guo shi yong de ruo gan fa lu wen ti (*Certain Legal Problems on Internal Application of the Rules of WTO), 22 (7) Hebei Law Science 57,61 (2004).

to implement these agreements.[565] These arguments might shed light on the development of laws and practices. However, they cannot explain why laws and regulations exist in favour of the direct effect of WTO agreements. A more accurate conclusion would be that China denies the direct effect of WTO agreements in part.

a) *Provisions Concerning the Relationship between Private Parties Tend to Be Directly Effective*

In light of the civil and commercial laws and regulations, the rules of WTO agreements could be directly effective, at least in cases between the private parties. Both General Principle of Civil Law and Civil Procedure Law recognize the supremacy of international agreements; moreover, no other civil and commercial laws and regulations concerned has stated otherwise. Opponents of the direct effect suggested the Supreme Court clarify that Article 142, paragraph 2 of General Principle of Civil Law is not applicable to the WTO-related cases.[566] Such suggestion precisely reveals the direct effect is possible or even required in civil matters. Provisions of the TRIPS provide specific protections for right holders, including terms of protections and compensations for the damages. They should be directly effective, if the Copyright Law, Patent Law, Trademark Law or the Unfair Competition Law do not exclude the application of international agreements. Such an observation was confirmed by several judgements. In *Kodak v. Koood Hydraulic Elevator*, the Kodak Company filed a claim against the Koood Company for infringing its trademark. The Suzhou Intermediate Court states "the domestic laws concerned, the Paris Convention and the TRIPS agreement shall apply to this case."[567] In *Lacoste v. Zhang-Sha Parkson*, the Chang-Sha Intermediate Court stated the obligations undertaken under the TRIPS should be embodied in the application of domestic laws. Although the parties did not resort to the TRIPS agreement, the Intermediate Court used the TRIPS to support its finding. The defendant argued that the consumers can distinguish the crocodile mark, the trademark of complainant, from the trademark of the applicant. The defendant

---

565 See Liu Hanfu, *id*, at 50-51.

566 See iu Hanfu, *Ru shi hou de li fa yu si fa jie shi gong zuo* (The Legislations and Judicial Interpretations after the Accession to the WTO), 2001 (S1) JOURNAL OF LAW APPLICATION 60, 63.

567 See Jiangsu sheng Suzhou shi zhong ji ren min fa yuan shen li yuan gao Yishiman Keda gong si su bei gao Suzhou Keda yie ya dian ti you xian gong si shang biao qin quan jiu fen (Ruling of Suzhou Intermediate People's Court on the Trademark Dispute between the Koda and the Koood Hydraulic Elevator Co. Ltd), (2005)Su-Zhong-Ming-San-Chu-Zi No. 0213 (Suzhou Intermediate People's Court, Apr. 6, 2006), available at http://www.lexiscn.com/law/content_case_analysis.php?case_id=12718&keyword=dHJpcHM%3D&t_kw=&eng=0.

also declared the distinctions while marketing and selling. They thus argued no confusion was created. The Intermediate Court noticed that the confusion of the consumers is deemed to be existent under the TRIPS, once the same mark is applied to the same products or services. The Intermediate Court found the distinctions insignificant and presumed the confusion of consumers necessarily exists by virtue of the TRIPS agreement.[568]

Except for the TRIPS, the connection between the disputes of private parties and the WTO agreements seems to be dim. In fact, they still might take part in the disputes between the private parties. The GATS was involved in *KLP v. Olympic Co. Ltd.* KLP, an American architectural firm, concluded a contract with the Olympic Co. Ltd to design buildings. The KLP finished the project but was not paid. The KLP filed the claim for the remuneration.[569] The defendant argued the KLP did not register in China and did not have the qualifications for architectural firms as required by administrative regulations. The contract was inconsistent with administrative regulations and thus invalid. The complainant resorted to Article 142 of General Principle of Civil Law and the Commitments of China under the GATS. In light of China's commitment, foreign architectural firms are allowed to provide cross-border service. The complainant therefore argued they did not have to obtain the qualifications required by the administrative regulations and the contract was valid.[570] The Quan-Zhou Intermediate Court considered the schedule of the commitments on the architectural sector, under which the market access was provided. According to the schedule of commitments, the national treatment would also be granted, if the service provider has been registered in its own country. The Court found the KLP, as a qualified architectural firm in United States, must be treated the same as qualified domestic architectural firm. Like domestic architectural firms, the KLP should be entitled to conclude the construal contract.[571] The Intermediate Court implied

568 See (Fa guo) Lakosite chen shan gu fen you xian gong si su Shanghai hong qiao bai sheng shang mao you xian gong si Changsha fen gong sis hang biao qin quan jiu fen an (French Lacoste Inc. Claim against Shanghai Hongqiao Parkson Trade Co. Ltd, Zhang-sha Branch, for Infringement of Trade Mark), (2004) Chang-Zhong-Ming-San-Chu-Zi No. 307, (Changsha Intermediate People's Court, Oct. 8, 2004), available at http://www.lexiscn.com/law/content_case_analysis.php?case_id=49154&keyword=dHJpcHM%3D&t_kw=&eng=0.

569 See Meiguo KLP jian zhu she ji gong si su Quanzhou shi ao lin pi ke zhi ye tou zi you xian gong si jian she gong cheng she ji he tong jiu fen an (Keller Limited Partnership v. Quan-Zhou Olympic Property Investment Co. Ltd., Disputes on the Contracture Contract), (2006) Quan-Zhou-Ming-Chu No.100, para 1 (Quanzhou Intermediate People's Court, Apr. 4, 2006), available at http://www.lexiscn.com/law/content_case_analysis.php?case_id=49830&keyword=d3Rv&t_kw=&eng=0.

570 See *id*, para. 6.

571 See *id*, para. 8.

that the KLP did not have to fulfil the qualification requirements under the administrative regulations. In this sense, these requirements for the national treatment in the schedule of commitments replace such administrative regulations.

In these cases, the courts apply the rules of WTO agreements on the ground that China, as a member of the WTO, should apply the rules of these agreements or undertake its obligations. Such reasoning is not theoretically persuasive; direct effect is not the only way to ensure compliance with international obligations. Their conclusions are nonetheless sustainable by the related civil laws.

b) *Provisions Governing the Measures of Governments Appear Not to Be Directly Effective*

The administrative laws and regulations show no consistency in terms of the effect of the WTO agreements. Unless a particular law or regulation specifically set forth general rules for the effect of WTO agreements, all of these administrative laws and regulations are effective and should be read in harmony as much as possible. The Administrative Litigation Law states the international agreement shall prevail in case of a discrepancy between international agreement and the Administrative Litigation law.[572] The WTO agreements do contain procedural requirements for the judicial reviews on administrative measures (e.g., Article 13 of the AD agreement and Article 23 of SCM agreements). Such provisions could be directly effective pursuant to the Administrative Litigation Law. The provisions concerning the subsidies in the Agriculture Agreement and the SPS Agreement might also be directly effective because the Agricultural Law and the Border Health and Quarantine Law similarly acknowledge the supremacy of international agreements.[573] On the contrary, the TBT agreement, the rules of origin, and the provisions concerning the registrations of trademark and the patent in the TRIPS could not have direct effect because the corresponding domestic laws and regulations imply otherwise.[574]

Contrary to the readings of these laws and regulations, the State Council and the Supreme Court tend to reject the direct effect of WTO agreements as a whole. They do not notice that the wordings of certain administrative laws and regulations do leave room for the direct effect of the WTO agreements. The State Council has stressed that international agreements are not laws, by which the adminis-

572 See *supra* note 490.

573 See *supra* note 550.

574 See Administrative Measures for Adopting the International Criteria, Regulation for the Implementation of the Trademark Law, Detailed Implementing Rules for the Patent Law, Regulations of the Origin of Imported/Exported Goods, *supra* notes 551-554.

trative institutions may impose administrative examinations and approvals.[575] The administrative examination and approval refer to the administrative reviews on "the applications for the approval for certain activities, the confirmation of the qualifications or certifications, the confirmation of certain civil relationships, and conformation of the capacity to have rights and obligations, or of the legal capacity."[576] The administrative institutions may impose such examinations and approvals on investment projects; production of goods; market access of bank, insurance, and securities sectors; and the certifications for certain professions.[577] They actually cover a large part of administrative measures, which are subject to the WTO agreements. In light of this Circular, the administrative institutions probably would not apply the rules of WTO agreements as they conduct the administrative examinations and approvals.[578] The room for direct effect would be fairly limited, if not totally eliminated.

The Provisions of the Supreme People's Court on Several Issues Concerning the Trial of Administrative Cases of International Trade implies the Supreme Court also tends to refuse the direct effect of the WTO agreements as whole, but acknowledges their indirect effect. The only exception appears to be the SCM agreements because the Provision Concerning the Reviews of Countervailing Measures does leave room for the direct effect.[579]

It is not clear whether the Supreme Court intended to make such a distinction. The State Council and the courts become cautious about the direct effect in cases in which the government is involved. Their positions are inconsistent with several administrative laws and regulations. However, they did not provide reasons for refusing direct effect. The Circular of the State Council cannot prevail over the administrative laws and regulations when a conflict exists. Neither can the interpretations of the Supreme Court.[580] Individuals might still resort to the administrative laws and regulations recognizing the direct effect with a view to applying the WTO rules. In fact, both the complainant and the defendant have done so. In *Pfize v. the Patent Reexamination Board of the State Intellectual Property Office (SIPO)*, the complainant, Pfize Ireland Pharmaceuticals, argued the patent rejection was inconsistent with TRIPS and thus invalid. The defendant, the reexamination board, did not argue the applicability of the TRIPS. Rather, they insisted

575 See *supra* note 555.

576 *Supra* note 555, section 1, para. 2.

577 See *id*, section 2, subsection 2.

578 See Xin Zhang, *supra* note 547, at 928.

579 See Part I, section 2.1.2.2 supra.

580 See Articles 87 and 88, the Law of the People's Republic of China on Legislation (promulgated by the Standing Committee of National People's Congress, Mar. 15, 2000, effectively July 1, 2000) 2000 Standing Committee of National People's Congress Gazette 112 (P.R.C.).

the rejection was fully compatible with the TRIPS.[581] However, the court ultimately did not address this argument. The courts have remained silent in several other cases in which the parties used WTO agreements as a legal basis for their arguments.[582] It has not yet been seen whether the courts would strictly follow the judicial interpretations of the Supreme Court and reject the direct effect of the WTO agreement as a whole.

2.1.2.4. Problems under the Current System and Possible Developments

The biggest problem with assessing the effect of the WTO agreements is the inconsistency in laws and in practices. No law or regulation has ever specifically addressed the issue or indicated a uniform and definite position. The assessment of the effect of the WTO agreement becomes more complicated if the relevant legal documents are not consistent. Although the Working Party Report reveals the intention of China in part, it is not a legally binding document under the WTO. Moreover, the relevant paragraphs in the Report are not completely clear. Also, there is no consistency in the provisions of the domestic laws and regulations pertinent to the implementation of WTO agreements. Some of these laws and regulations support the direct effect, whereas others imply otherwise. Through several judicial interpretations, the Supreme Court set forth a clear position (i.e., refusal of direct effect). Nonetheless, the direct effect issue remains unsettled because the judicial interpretations may not contradict the laws and regulations; moreover, the Supreme Court does not have the competence to solve the conflicts between the laws and regulations.[583] Under such circumstances, it would be hard to say whether China really has rejected direct effect of the WTO

---

581 Beijing shi di yi zhong ji ren min fa yaun shen li yuan gao Huirui Aierlan yiao pin gong si bu fu bei gao Zhonghua Renmin Gongheguo guo jia zhi shi chan quan ju zhan li fu shen wei yuan hui zuo chu de di 6228 hao wu xiao xuan gao qing qiu shen cha jue ding xing zheng pan jue shu (Judgment of The First Beijing Intermediate People's Court on the Claim for the Nullification of the Patent Reexamination Board Decision No. 6228), (2004)Yi-Zhung-Xin-Chu-Zi No. 884, (Beijing First Intermediate People's Court, June 2, 2006), available at http://www.lexiscn.com/law/content_case_analysis.php?case_id=9436&keyword=d3Rv&t_kw=&eng=0.

582 *E.g.* Li Junji su Zhuhai shi wei sheng ju chin quan an (Li Jun-Jie v. Zhuhai Department of Health), Xian-Xin-Chu-Zi No.19 (2003), (Zhuhai City, Xiangzhou District People's Court, Sep. 28, 2003); Shenjun shi Xianbang hua gong you xian gong si yu Haofuman Luoshi you xian gong si chin fan yao pin du zhan quan jou fen yi an (Xian-Bang Chemical Ltd. Shen Jun city v. F. Hoffmann-La Roche AG) Yue-Gao-Fa-Min-Zhong-San-Zi No. 429 (2006), (Guangdong High People's Court, Feb. 1, 2007); TMT mao yi you xian gong si chi su bei xin wu liu you xian gong sis hang biao qin quan jou fen yi an (TMT Trading Ltd. claim against CNBM Investment Co. Ltd. for trade mark) Sui-Zhong-Fa-Min-Zhi-Chu-Zi No.989 (2004), (Guangzhou Intermediate People's Court, Oct.17, 2005).

583 See Articles 85 and 90 of the Law on Legislation, *supra* note 537.

agreements. At most, such a tendency could be found in practice, especially in cases involving the measures of government. To some extent, China's position is uncertain. Its attitude toward the questions concerning the effect of WTO agreements is also uncertain (e.g., the relationship between the WTO agreements and domestic laws, the effect of the panel and Appellate Body report in the domestic legal system, as well as government liability to individuals for non-compliance with WTO agreements).

Under the current system, the effect of the WTO agreements should be decided by virtue of the laws and regulations applied in the given cases. In the meantime, the State Council and the Supreme Court suggest rejecting the direct effect of the WTO agreements as a whole. The practice of the courts would certainly clarify the situations wherein the WTO agreements might be in fact directly effective. However, the direct effect of WTO agreements was mentioned in only few cases. In these cases, the WTO provisions provide additional support for certain interpretation of the law or regulation at issue.[584] The courts have never supported a claim based solely on the WTO provisions. It is still unknown whether the courts would indeed embrace the direct effect, when the laws and regulations so require. A good example would be the claims challenging the administrative laws or regulations *per se*. According to Article 12, paragraph 2 of the Administrative Litigation Law, the admissibility of such claims is excluded and the courts may review only specific administrative acts.[585] This provision is believed to conflict the judicial reviews requirements, which is provided in GATT X: 1 and GATS VI.[586] While Article 72 of the Administrative Litigation Law explicitly states the supremacy of international law, the Supreme Court holds domestic norms as the only legal basis for the reviews of trade-related measures. It is not clear where the courts would stand.

China actually has not provided the reasons for accepting or denying the direct effect of the WTO agreements. The reasoning does not appear anywhere in the legal documents relevant to laws and regulations that regulate trade-related matters. The government's considerations have not been revealed to the public. It

---

584 *E.g.* Lacoste v. Zhang-Sha Parkson, *supra* note 568; KLP v. Olympic Co. Ltd, *supra* note 569.

585 See *supra* note 490.

586 See Kong Xianjun, *WTO dui si f ashen cha de yao chiu ji wo quo si f ashen cha mian li de ren wu han tiao zhan* (The Judicial Review Requirements of the WTO and the Tasks and the Challenges for the Judicial Review System of China), 2001 (10) JOURNAL OF LAW APPLICATION 17,19 (2001); Jiang Bixin, *WTO yu wo guo de si f ashen cha zhi du* (The WTO and the Judicial Review System of China), 2001 (3) JOURNAL OF LAW APPLICATION 10,12 (2001); Zeng Lingliang, *Zhongguo jia ru WTO ji chi si fa shen cha zhi du de wan shan* (Chinese Accession to the WTO & Chinese Judicial Review System Improvement), 54 (3) WUHAN UNIVERSITY JOURNAL (PHILOSOPHY & SOCIAL SCIENCES) 261, 266 (2001).

is hard to tell whether China has viewed the effect of WTO agreements as diverse as the laws and regulations indicated. To solve the inconsistency among laws, regulations, and practices, the legislative branch (the NPC or the Standing Committee of the NPC) should adopt the law or resolution on implementing the WTO agreements.[587] However, no actions have been taken.

The major Chinese scholars observe that the direct effect of WTO agreement should be rejected in part or in whole.[588] They seldom resort to domestic laws

---

587 See He Xiaoyong, *Lun WTO xie yi yu guo ne fa de fa lu guan xi wen ti* (Issues concerning the Relation between WTO agreements and the Domestic Law), 1 JOURNAL OF POLITICAL SCIENCE AND LAW 25,26 (2001); see also Qingjiang Kong, *Enforcement of WTO Agreements in China: Illusion or Reality?*, 35 (6) JOURNAL OF WORLD TRADE 1181, 1210 (2001); *Jiang wei & Wang Jingchi, WTO xie yi yu Zhongguo min shi si fa zhi du de wan shan* (The WTO Agreements and the Perfection of China's Civil Judicial System,2001 (1) CHINA LEGAL SCIENCE 25, 26 (2001).

588 Direct effect of WTO agreements should be rejected as a whole, se Che Pizhao, *Lun tiao yue zai wo guo de shi yong* (On the Application of Treaty in China), 2005 (3) LAW SCIENCE MAGAZINE 96 (2005); Wu Yarong, *Lun WTO xie yi de fa lu xiao li ji zai wo quo fa yuan de shi yong (*The Effect of the WTO agreements and its application in the Chinese courts),2001 (2) JOURNAL OF LAW APPLICATION 11 (2001); Liu Hanfu, *Shi jie mao yi zu zhi fa zai ne quo fa yuan zhi jie shi yong de wen ti (*The Issues Concerning the Direct Application of WTO Law in Chinese Courts) ,2000 (7) PEOPLES' JUDICATURE 49 (2000); Zhao Daguang, *"ru shi" hou wo guo si f ashen cha gong zuo de ruo gan wen ti* (Problems of the Judicial Review after the Accession to the WTO), 2001 (S1) JOURNAL OF LAW APPLICATION 37 (2001); Wang Zhenqing, *Zuo hao ru shi hou zhi shi chan quan you quan de shen pan gong zuo* (The Judicial Review of Intellectual Property Right after the Accession to the WTO), 2001 (S1) JOURNAL OF LAW APPLICATION 52; Xu Minyou & Chen Weidong, Ou gong ti wei rao WTO xie yi zhi jie xiao li de wen ti de zheng lun ji chi dui wo guo de chi shi (The Arguments of the Direct Effect of the WTO Agreements in the EU and the Lessons Learned by China),108 LAW REVIEW 90 (2001); *Lun WTO xie yi de fa lu xiao li ji zai wo quo fa yuan de shi yong (*The Effect of the WTO agreements and its application in the Chinese courts),2001 (2) JOURNAL OF LAW APPLICATION 11 (2001); Mu Yapin &. Xi Yifan, *WTO xie yoi zai wo guo guo ne de shi yong wen ti* (On the Enforcement of the WTO Agreements in Mainland China), 2003 (1) JOURNAL OF JINAN UNIVERSITY 54 (2003); Quan Yuan, You quan WTO gui ze zai wo guo shi yong de ruo gan fa lu wen ti (Certain Legal Problems on Internal Application of the Rules of WTO), 22 (7) HEBEI LAW SCIENCE 57 (2004); Tang Shumei, Lun WTO gui ze yu guo ne fa han guo ji tiao yui de guan xi (The Relationship among WTO Rules, Domestic Laws and International Agreements), 2004 (3) JOURNAL OF REMIN UNIVERSITY OF CHINA 79 (2004); Xiao Bing, WTO han yi, xiao li chong du yu chi shi (Reinterpretation and Enlightenment of Significance and Effectiveness of WTO) 41 (6) JOURNAL OF NAJIN UNIVERSITY 64 (2004). In principle direct effect should be rejected, but exceptions should be allowed, see Jiang Bixin, *WTO yu wo guo de si f ashen cha zhi du* (The WTO and the Judicial Review System of China), 2001 (3) JOURNAL OF LAW APPLICATION 10 (2001); Zeng Lingliang, *WTO xie yi zai wo guo de shi yong gi wo guo fa zhi jian she de go ming (The Application of WTO Agreements in Our Country and the Revolution of Our Legal System)*, 2000 (6) CHINA LEGAL SCIENCE 38 (2000); *Jiang wei & Wang Jingchi, WTO xie yi yu Zhongguo min shi si fa zhi du de wan shan* (The WTO Agreements and the Perfection of China's Civil Judicial System, 2001 (1) CHINA LEGAL SCIENCE 25; Kong Xiangqen, *WTO fa lu de quo ne shi yong (*Domestic

and regulations probably because these norms do not give a definite answer. Their observations are more like policy suggestions. The Chinese academic community is in favour of the direct effect of the international agreements, but they considered the WTO agreements as an exception. The WTO agreements are described as too abstract to be directly effective. It is also questionable if the judges are capable of applying the WTO rules.[589] These features are common to all of the other international agreements, which China has deemed as directly effective. Nonetheless, these features actually have not stopped the academia from supporting their direct effect. The positions of other members appear to be one of the keys for such a distinction. The US and the EU, the most significant trade partners of China, have rejected the direct effect of the WTO agreements. Scholars worry about the deficit China would suffer, if the direct effect were unilaterally granted.[590] They also emphasize that China is not obliged to accept the direct effect. Although China usually will recognize direct effect of international agreements, it is not a general rule set by the Constitution or laws. In addition, concerns exist about the protection of "national interest." If direct effect had been granted, the decision-making power of legislation on the economic affairs would have been constrained. The means for protecting the "national interests" are therefore limited. Ultimately, the "national interests" could have been jeopardized.[591] Some also criticize the excessive powers of the courts. Pursuant to the Constitution, the courts do not have the power to review the actions of legislative branch. Neither do they have full power to scrutinize all the administrative actions. The direct effect of the WTO agreements requires the courts to conduct the reviews, which exceed their powers provided by the Constitution.[592]

The Supreme Court, the State Council, and the academia suggest rejecting the direct effect of the WTO agreements. A few members have suggested China should accept the direct effect during the accession negotiations. China has rejected such a suggestion because its major trade partners (i.e., the US and the EU) did not do the same.[593] If that is the case, China will explicitly refuse the

---

Application of WTO Law),Legal Daily, Beijing, Dec. 16, 2001; Li Xingxiang, *Wo guo shi shi WTO xie yi de ji ge zhu you wen ti tan xi (*Analysis of the Major questions of the Application of the WTO Agreements), 71 FUJIAN FA XUE 38 (2002).

589 See Liu Hanfu, *id*, at 50-51; Yuan Quan, *id*, at 60.

590 See Liu Hanfu , *id*, at 50;Xin Zhang, *supra* note 547, at 935; Mu Yaping & Xi Yifan, *supra* note 588, at 59; Che Pizhao, *supra* note 588,at 99; Jiang Wei & Wang Jingchi, *supra* note 588, at 27; Kong Xiangqun, *supra* note 588.

591 SeeMu Yaping & Xi Yifan, *supra* note 588, at 59.

592 SeeWu Yarong *supra* note 588, at 14.

593 See Kong Xianqun, *supra* note 546. The author has talked with a former Chinese official, who participated in the negotiations. The anonymous official confirmed such saying.

direct effect of the WTO agreements eventually. Before that happens, the practitioners and scholars still must review all the documents that might be relevant and presume the position of China.

2.1.3. Conclusion

The Constitution remains silent on the effect of the international agreements in the domestic legal system. Several laws and regulations appear to acknowledge the direct effect of international agreements, whereas other laws or regulations suggest the opposite. Therefore, the issue remains highly controversial. The dominant opinion holds that the international agreement would spontaneously become part of domestic law by their acceptance and that China actually has generally recognized direct effect. Nonetheless, the general relationship between directly effective international agreements and domestic laws is not clear. Although several laws and regulations acknowledge the supremacy of international agreements, the hierarchy of domestic laws should be decided ultimately by the Constitution. The supremacy of international agreement is only a tendency – not a general rule; the Constitution does not give any instruction. In practice, laws and regulations are inconsistent on the issue. The question appears unsettled.

In light of the Working Party Report on the Accession of China, the direct effect seems to be totally rejected or limited. Nonetheless, several laws and regulations do accept the direct effect. The WTO agreements could be directly effective in cases between private parties; the civil and commercial laws and regulations consistently favor the direct effect. Such a tendency could not be found for the administrative laws and regulations. Unless a particular law or regulation specifically sets forth general rules for the effect of WTO agreements, all these administrative laws and regulations are all effective and should be read in harmony as much as possible. The effect of the WTO agreements depends upon that specific law or the regulation applicable in the given case. The effect of the WTO agreements in administrative litigation should depend on that specific administrative law or the regulation applicable in the given case. For instance, the TBT agreement, the rules of origin, the provisions concerning the registration of trademark and the patent in the TRIPS could not have direct effect because the corresponding domestic laws and regulations imply otherwise. Regardless of the laws and regulations recognizing the direct effect, the State Council and the Supreme Court totally deny the application of WTO agreement to administration litigations. Apparent inconsistency exists between practices and the laws and regulations. Although the judicial interpretation of the Supreme Court and the statement of the State Council cannot overturn the laws and regulations, they present a more recent attitude toward the direct effect, especially in the administrative litigations. China leans toward refusing direct effect; however, it has not totally abandoned such effect.

In comparison to the open attitude toward the international agreements in general, China is more conservative about the direct effect of the WTO agreements. Moreover, scholars stress China should reject the direct effect because the other members have done so. During the negotiation of accession, China reportedly rejected the suggestion of a few members that it should accept the direct effect. China eventually might move forward to reject the direct effect totally.

2.2. Laws and Practices in Taiwan

In 1971, the government of Republic of China (the ROC) lost the right to represent China and exercise its rights and obligations under the UN Charter. The United Nations General Assembly Resolution declared the representatives of the People's Republic of China (PRC) as "the only legitimate representative of China to the United Nations" and expelled the representatives of Chiang Kai-shek "from the place which they unlawfully occupy at the United Nations and in all organizations related to it."[594] The ROC (i.e., Taiwan) qualifies as a sovereignty state; however, in legal terms it is invisible to the United Nations and international society. Except for the WTO, Taiwan seldom has officially acceded to international organizations, international conventions, or multilateral agreements. Taiwan may be free from the obligations of many significant international agreements, but it cannot enjoy the rights or the benefits provided by them either. In other words, Taiwan's international relations are more subject to the rule of power and far less subject to the rules of international agreements. Facing such unique political circumstances, Taiwan manages to construct the legal relation between Taiwan and other states in an indirect and unofficial way. Its international agreements are rarely titled as agreements. Instead, they appear in the form of notes, letters, or even memorandum of meetings. For instance, Taiwan exchanged notes or letters with other states, which recognize specific international agreement as legal rules for their relationship.[595] The interactions between Taiwan

594 United Nations General Assembly, *Restoration of Lawful Rights of People's Republic of China in the United Nations*, G.A. Res. 2758 (XXVI), U.N. Doc. A/L.630 and Add. 1-2.

595 *E.g.* Exchange of Letters between The Coordination Council for North American Affairs And The American Institute in Taiwan Concerning Mutual Implementation of 1974 International Convention for The Safety of Life at Sea, Sep. 07, 1982, available at http://law.moj.gov.tw/LawClass/LawAll.aspx?PCode=Y0000035; Exchange of Notes between The Republic of China And The Republic of Korea Concerning Mutual Implementation of The International Conven-

and other states are disguised as activities of private parties.[596] In Taiwan's legal system, the term "international agreement" covers non-governmental agreements.

2.2.1. The General Domestic Legal Status of International Agreements

The Constitution of Republic of China has not provided a clear statement about the effect of international agreements. Further interpretation and clarification are required. The judgments of the courts indicate Taiwan's attitude about the effect of international agreements in the domestic legal system.

2.2.1.1. International Agreements as Part of Domestic Law

a) The Rules of the Constitution

At first glance, Article 141 of the Constitution, titled as foreign policy, seems to provide the legal status of the international agreement in the domestic legal system, which reads:

> The foreign policy of the Republic of China shall, in a spirit of independence and initiative and on the basis of the principles of equality and reciprocity, cultivate good-neighborliness with other nations, and *respect treaties* and the interests of Chinese citizens residing abroad, promote international cooperation, advance international justice and ensure world peace.[597] (emphasis added)

Some hold that Article 141 has clarified the legal status of the international agreements within the domestic legal system.[598] The term "respect" could be construed as "comply with."[599] In the Chinese version of treaties and the translations of the treaties or international agreements, the government often uses terms akin to "respect," which appear less binding on the contracting parties, to refer to

---

tion on Tonnage Measurement of Ships, 1969, Feb. 17, 1981, available at http://law.moj.gov.tw/LawClass/LawAll.aspx?PCode=Y0000030.

596 See generally Francoise Mengin, *A Pretence of Privatization: Taiwan's External Relations* in PRIVATING THE STATES, 147 (Beatrice Hibou &Jonathan Derrick eds, 2004).

597 Constitution of Republic of China (promulgated on Dec. 25, 1947), available at http://www.judicial.gov.tw/constitutionalcourt/en/p07_2.asp?lawno=36.

598 See 吳嘉生 (Wu, Chia-Sheng), 國際法與國內法關係之研析 (THE ANALYSIS OF THE RELATIONSHIPS BETWEEN INTERNATIONAL LAW AND DOMECTIC LAW), 105 (1998); 沈克勤 (Shen, Ko-chin), 國際法 (International Law), 87 (1991).

599 See Wu, Chia-Sheng, *id.*

strong willingness to fulfill international agreements. Since the government is obliged to implement the international obligation, the effect of international agreement within domestic legal system should be strengthened as well. The courts thus should be allowed to apply the treaties.[600] Moreover, the Congress, the Legislative Yuan, is entrusted with approving the treaty. The treaties are subject to the legislative scrutiny just as any domestic law must be scrutinized.[601]

Given the context of Article 141, such reading is not sustainable. Nothing in the text of the Constitution can prove that the term "respect" is a synonym for "comply with." Even if the Constitution had used the term "comply with treaties," the direct effect is not necessarily required. Besides, this provision appears in the chapter on Fundamental National Policies. It is generally agreed that a few provisions of the Fundamental National Policies impose obligations on the legislative Yuan to implement these policies. The other provisions are mere instructions for the policy or the objects of the state.[602] These provisions, including Article 141, do not establish any obligations. Based on only this provision, it would be hard to prove that the Constitution requires the direct effect of treaties.

The rulings of the Constitutional Court, Judicial Yuan interpretations (hereafter the J.Y. Interpretation),[603] give more clues on the effect of treaties. The J.Y. Interpretations are superior to the laws and regulations. They are also binding on the government as well as to individuals.[604] In J.Y. Interpretation No. 329, the Constitutional Court was requested to clarify the meanings of "treaties" and identify international agreements subject to the deliberation of Legislative Yuan. The Court held the term "treaty" refers to an international agreement concluded between the R.O.C. and other nations or international organizations. Its content involves important issues of the nation or rights and duties of the people.[605] Agreements may also qualify as the "treaties," if they are concluded between institutions and groups authorized by governmental agencies and those authorized by other states. The Constitutional Court briefly mentioned the effect of

600 *Id.*

601 *Id.*

602 See 林紀東 (Lin, Chi-Tung),中華民國憲法逐條釋義 (Commentary to Constitution of Republic of China), Vol.4 ,248-249 (1993); 陳新民 (Chen, Hsin-Min) , 中華民國憲法導論 (Introduction of the Constitution of Republic of China),431-433 (2005); 李惠宗 (Li Hui-Tsung), 憲法要義 (Principles of Constitution), 661-662 (5th ed., 2009); 法治斌 (Fa, Chih-Pin) &董保城 (Tung, Pao-Cheng),中華民國憲法 (Constitution of Republic of China),444 (2001); 許育典 (Hsu, Yu-Tien), 憲法 (The Constitution), 419-422 (2009).

603 Articles 78,79 and 173 of Constitution.

604 See Article 78 of Constitution and J.Y. Interpretation No. 185 (Jan. 27, 1984) , available at http://www.judicial.gov.tw/CONSTITUTIONALCOURT/en/p03_01.asp?expno=185.

605 J.Y. Interpretation No. 329 (Dec. 24, 1993), available at http://www.judicial.gov.tw/constitu tionalcourt/EN/p03_01_printpage.asp?expno=329.

international agreements. The Court stated the international agreements concluded under the procedures provided in the Constitution "hold the same status as laws."[606] This finding was not based on a specific provision of the Constitution. The Courts' finding seems to be based on the similarity between the procedures of treaties conclusion and the legislative procedures.[607] The Constitutional Court has accepted the direct effect of international agreements.[608]

In short, the Constitution actually does not explicitly address the effect of international agreements. Instead, the authoritative interpretation of the Constitution recognizes international agreements as part of domestic laws.

b) The Practices of the Legislative and Executive Branches

In practice, the legislation apparently favors the direct effect. The legislative history of the Civil Code has indicated that the drafters had long accepted the direct effect of international agreements, at least in cases regarding the recognition of foreign legal persons. Paragraph 10 of the Principles for Drafting the General Principle of Civil Code has touched the effect of international agreements, which reads: "International agreements are binding on the contracting parties, when they are ratified by the parties. Some contend they should be simultaneously binding on the nationals, while the others hold the implementation legislation necessary. The former is proposed to be taken."[609]

The Legislative Yuan also takes different approaches to implement the international obligations. It would transform the rules of international agreements into domestic laws.[610] Sometimes, the rules of international agreements may be incorporated into domestic law by general reference. Article 1 of the Law of Extradition, for instance, states the extradition "shall" abide by treaties. The rules of this law apply only if no treaty provision is applicable.[611] A similar provision

606 *Id.*

607 *Id.*

608 See 廖福特 (Liao, Fu-Te), 國際人權公約國內法化之方法與策略 *(The Method and Strategy of Internalizing the International Covenants on Human Rights)*, 109-110, (Research, Development and Evaluation Commission, Executive Yuan, Research Project Oct. 2002), available at http://grbsearch.stpi.org.tw/GRB/result.jsp?id=600734&plan_no=rdec-res-091-003&plan_year=91&projkey=PG9105-0023&target=plan&highStr=.

609 See民法總則篇立法原則(Legislative Principles for the Part of General Principles of the Civil), 1 LEGISLATIVE DIGEST15-16 (1929).

610 *E.g.* The Act of Capture of Ships and Cargos (promulgated on June 2, 1995), available at http://law.moj.gov.tw/LawClass/LawAll.aspx?PCode=F0120006; Nationality Act (promulgated on Jan. 27, 2006) http://law.moj.gov.tw/Eng/LawClass/LawContent.aspx?PCODE=D0030001.

611 See Law of Extradition (promulgated on July 14, 1980), available at http://law.moj.gov.tw/Eng/LawClass/LawAll.aspx?PCode=I0030001.

could also be found in the Law of the Enforcement of the Request for the International Judicial Assistance.[612] Besides, the legislation would also acknowledge that international agreements concluded by Taiwan could entitle foreigners to the certain rights reserved for the nationals. The Copyright Act[613]and Patent Act[614] contain such kind of provisions.

Furthermore, certain legislations incorporate the rules of international agreements so generally to include the international agreements, which Taiwan might not even accede to. Article 11 of the Law of Exclusive Economic Zone and Continental Shelf is one such legislation. According to paragraph 3 of Article 11, the vessels under judicial investigation or impoundment still may resume the navigation if "appropriate procedures have been taken in accordance with *international agreements*, whereby compliance with requirements for any bond or other appropriate financial surety has been assured"[615] (emphasis added). The Legislative Yuan did not specify the international agreements referred to. Considering Taiwan's unique status in international society, Taiwan would possibly not accede to all the relevant international agreements. The Legislative Yuan frequently adopted this type of provision.[616] The Legislative Yuan would also authorize the administrative departments to adopt the rules of international agreements not concluded by Taiwan while they draft administrative regulations. For instance, Article 64 of Shipping Law states the Ministry of Transport and Communications may reference or adopt the rules of international agreements while they issue the regulations supplementing the law.[617] The Civil Aviation Act and several other laws provide similar provisions.[618] The Legislative Yuan views the rules of interna-

---

612 See Article 1, Law of the Enforcement of the Request for the International Judicial Assistance (promulgated on Apr. 25, 1963), available at http://law.moj.gov.tw/LawClass/LawAll.aspx?PCode=B0010014.

613 See Article 4, Copyright Act, amended on Feb. 10, 2010, available at http://law.moj.gov.tw/Eng/LawClass/LawAll.aspx?PCode=J0070017 (last visited on May 1, 2010).

614 See Article 4, Patent Act (promulgated on Mar. 25, 1944, latest amendment on Aug. 25, 2010), available at http://law.moj.gov.tw/Eng/LawClass/LawAll.aspx?PCode=J0070007.

615 Law of Exclusive Economic Zone and Continental Shelf of Republic of China, (promulgated on Jan. 21, 1998), available at http://law.moj.gov.tw/Eng/LawClass/LawAll.aspx?PCode=A0000010.

616 *E.g.* Article 7, paragraph 2, Law on the Territorial Sea and the Contiguous Zone of the Republic of China (promulgated on Jan. 21, 1998), available at http://law.moj.gov.tw/Eng/LawClass/Law Content.aspx?PCODE=A0000009; Article 37, Fisheries Act (Promulgated on Nov. 11, 1929, latest amendment on Jan. 9, 2008), available at http://law.moj.gov.tw/Eng/LawClass/LawAll.aspx?PCode=M0050001.

617 See Shipping Law (promulgated on June 3, 1981, latest amendment on Jan. 30, 2002), available at http://law.moj.gov.tw/Eng/LawClass/LawContent.aspx?PCODE=K0070001.

618 Article 121, Civil Aviation Act (promulgated on May 30,1953, latest amendment on Jan. 23, 2009), available at http://law.moj.gov.tw/Eng/LawClass/LawContent.aspx?PCODE=K0090001; Article 50, The Commercial Port Law amended (promulgated on May 2,1980, latest amendment on

tional agreement as a part of domestic legal system, even if they are not concluded by Taiwan. Such an extraordinary position is criticized for inconformity with the Constitution. International agreements could become part of domestic law only through the procedures under the Constitution. [619] Otherwise, it would be meaningless for the Constitution to distribute powers on the conclusion of treaties. It is also criticized that the Legislative Yuan fails to deliberate each and every international agreement before accepting that agreement.[620] Nevertheless, the Legislative Yuan obviously does not intend to modify these provisions. According to these provisions, the courts and the administrative regulations still may directly resort to rules of international agreements.

The executive branch also holds an open attitude toward the international law. The Executive Yuan and the Ministry of Foreign Affairs have respectively requested the Ministry of Justice (hereafter the MOJ) to clarify the effect of the international agreements. The MOJ constantly recognizes the direct effect of international agreements. Nonetheless, the MOJ notices such effect is not explicitly provided by the Constitution. In response to the request from the Ministry of Foreign Affairs, the MOJ stated the international agreement should be considered as the statute law within the domestic legal system. The MOJ explained international agreements could have been directly involved in the rights and obligations of individuals; the conclusion of such agreement is considered legislative activity. Accordingly, Article 63 of the Constitution would empower the legislative Yuan to review the conclusion of international agreements.[621] Furthermore, the procedures for ratifying international agreements are identical to those for legislation. The international agreements are published in the Legislative Yuan Gazette (立法院公報) and Legislative Digest (立法專刊), which were founded to publish the domestic laws.[622]

To reply to the questions raised by the Executive Yuan, the MOJ submitted a report on the application of international agreements and their relation to other domestic laws.[623] The MOJ noticed the Constitution and the legislations did not

---

Feb, 5, 2005), available at http://law.moj.gov.tw/Eng/LawClass/LawAll.aspx?PCode=K0080001; telecommunications Act, Article 71, (promulgated on Dec. 23, 1958, latest amendment on July 11, 2007), available at http://law.moj.gov.tw/Eng/LawClass/LawAll.aspx ?PCode=K0060001.

619 See 黃異 (Huang, Yi), 國際條約及國際習慣法在我國內國領域之效力 (The Effect of International Agreements and Customary International Law within the Domestic Legal System of Taiwan), 27 輔仁法學雜誌 51,71-72 (2004).

620 *Id.*

621 72) 法律字第 1813 號, para.1 (promulgated by Ministry of Justice, Feb. 21, 1983), available at http://jirs.judicial.gov.tw/Index.htm .

622 *Id*, at paragraph 2.

623 77) 法參字第 20108 號 (promulgated by Ministry of Justice, Nov. 19, 1989), available at http://jirs.judicial.gov.tw/Index.htm.

establish the effect of international agreements. By the time the report was made, the Constitutional Court had not issued the interpretation No. 329. The MOJ refers to paragraph 3 of Article 58, paragraph 3 of Article 57, and Article 63 of the Constitution to conclude that international agreements should have the effect of domestic law and have the same status as statute law.[624] The MOJ also recognized the concept of self-executing treaties or provisions. The courts, administrative institutions, and individuals may not resort to the international agreements if an implementing legislation is necessary to apply the treaty or the provision of the treaty.[625] The opinions of the MOJ actually are not legally binding on administrative institutions, but these opinions certainly are important instruction for them.

c) Cases Addressing the Effect of International Agreements

The legal system of Taiwan is based on civil law. The rulings of the courts are binding only to the parties at issue, except for the J.Y interpretations (i.e., the rulings of the Constitutional Court). The judgements of the courts do not have the status of *stare decisis*. In practice, the Supreme Court would select the leading cases as *de facto* precedents for the lower courts. The lower courts in fact would follow these precedents so strictly that the Constitutional Court would have to deem the precedent as "laws and regulations concerning the finality of the judgements" and review the legality of the precedents.[626] Only a few cases or precedents are related to the effect of international agreements. These cases clearly indicate that the courts would tend to recognize the direct effect of international agreements.

In the instructions for the Ministry of Judicial Administration (the predecessor of the MOJ) issued in 1931, the Judicial Yuan[627], for the first time, inexplicitly accepted the direct effect. The Judicial Yuan stated in this instruction that the international agreements in principle should prevail over the laws and regulations.[628]

The Constitutional Court occasionally would use rules of international agreements, inter alia those pertinent to human rights, to support its reading of

---

624 *Id*, para. 2.

625 *Id*, para. 2.

626 J.Y. Interpretation No. 154, paragraph 2 of the reasoning (Sep. 29, 1978), available at http://www.judicial.gov.tw/constitutionalcourt/p03_01.asp?expno=154.

627 Judicial Yuan is the highest judicial organ of Taiwan. The Constitutional Court is affiliated with the Judicial Yuan. See Article 77 of Constitution and J.Y. Interpretation No. 185 (Jan. 27, 1984), available at http://www.judicial.gov.tw/CONSTITUTIONALCOURT/en/p03_01.asp?expno=185 (last visited on May 1, 2010).

628 訓字第 459 號訓令 (The Oder to Ministry of Judicial Administration No. 459) , July 27, 1931, 中華民國六法理由判解全編, Vol. 1, 8 (1964).

Constitution.[629] Furthermore, the Constitutional Court takes the international law as source of domestic law if the legislation generally refers to international agreements. In the J.Y. Interpretation No.428, the Postal Regulation was alleged to exceed the authorization under the Postal Act for establishing additional conditions for compensation for lost and damaged mail. Pursuant to Article 13 of the Postal Act, "international postal treaties or agreements shall govern where applicable."[630] Accordingly, the Constitutional Court reviewed the legality of the Regulation under the Universal Postal Convention. The Constitutional Court held the Regulation did not exceed the authorization because these conditions for compensation were in line with this Convention.[631]

The Supreme Court also appears to favour the direct effect. In the precedent 27 Shang No. 1074, the Supreme Court for the first time recognized the supremacy of international agreements.[632] In precedent 79 Tai-fei No. 277, the Supreme Court repealed the judgement of the Taiwan High Court. The High Court held the matter at issue occurred in a foreign aircraft, which is (by virtue of customary international law) part of the territory of that foreign state. The High Court dismissed the case for lack of jurisdiction.[633] However, the Supreme Court held the High Court wrongfully applied the international rules concerning the criminal jurisdiction. The Court found the aircraft landed in Taiwan. The domestic courts therefore should have jurisdiction according to the international agreements concluded.[634] Both the Supreme Court and the High Court made their ruling by virtue of international law.

The direct effect issue was intensively argued and directly addressed in Case 79 Shang-geng No.128. The Encyclopædia Britannica, Inc. (hereafter the Britannica) made a claim against Tanching Limited (hereafter the Tanching) for infringement of copyright. The case was appealed to the Supreme Court, which remanded the case back to the High Court. According to Article 17 of the Copyright Act, the work at issue, Britannica Concise Encyclopaedia, did not register

---

629 *E.g.* J.Y. Interpretation No. 372 (Feb. 24,1995), available at http://www.judicial.gov.tw/constitutionalcourt/en/p03_01.asp?expno=372; J.Y. Interpretation No. 392 (Feb. 22, 1995), available at http://www.judicial.gov.tw/constitutionalcourt/en/p03_01.asp?expno=392; J.Y. Interpretation No.587 (Dec. 30, 2004), available at http://www.judicial.gov.tw/constitutionalcourt/en/p03_01.asp?expno=587.

630 See Postal Act (promulgated July 5, 1935, latest amendment on July 10, 2002), available at http://law.moj.gov.tw/Eng/LawClass/LawAll.aspx?PCode=K0050001.

631 J.Y. Interpretation No. 428, paragraph 3 of the reasoning (May 23, 1997), available at http://www.judicial.gov.tw/constitutionalcourt/en/p03_01_printpage.asp?expno=428.

632 最高法院23上字第1074號判例 (Jan. 1, 1934).

633 最高法院79年台非字第277號判例, Dec. 28, 1980, 中國國際法與國際事務年報, Vol. 5, 402 (1989).

634 *Id.*

in Taiwan and therefore was not entitled to copyright.[635] Meanwhile, the nationals are entitled to copyright upon the complementation of the work.[636] To exclude the application of Article 17 of the Copyright Act, the Britannica turned to the national treatment, which was provided in the Treaty of Friendship, Commerce and Navigation between the United States of America and the Republic of China (hereafter the FCN Treaty).[637] Article 9 of the FCN Treaty established the national treatment regarding the copyright. The Tanching contended the sovereignty would have been in jeopardy, if FCN Treaty were self-executing and had prevailed over the domestic law. The Tanching observed the conditions for national treatment provided in the FCN Treaty were rather abstract and general. It would be quite easy to fulfil these conditions. In other words, the US citizens and corporations may enjoy the rights and benefits preserved for the nationals. The domestic laws may not limit their capacities to have rights and obligations; moreover, the domestic laws may not limit their legal capacities. If that is the case, the United States needs no longer conduct trade negotiations; instead, the United States could directly resort to the court for implementation of the FCN Treaty. Taiwan would totally lose control of the market access.[638] Moreover, the United States, as a matter of fact, does not consider the FCN Treaty self-executing.[639]

The Britannica rebutted that the concerns for sovereignty were absurd. The FCN Treaty did establish specific and rigid conditions for the rights and privileges. The provisions of the FCN Treaty contain provisos like "not forbidden by laws and regulations,"[640] "not reserved exclusively for the nationals,"[641] or "provided that the right to exercise such function…is otherwise consistent with the laws and regulations."[642] The Britannica contended FCN Treaty would by no means deprive the sovereignty.[643] Besides, Article 9 is clear and specific enough

---

635 See The Copyright Act (promulgated on May 14, 1928, amended on June 28, 1985, latest amendment on Feb. 10, 2010), available at http://lis.ly.gov.tw/lgcgi/lglaw?@89:1804289383:f:NO%3DE01176*%20OR%20NO%3DB01176$$11$$$PD%2BNO.

636 Article 10, Copyright Act, (promulgated on May 14, 1928, latest amendment on Feb. 10, 2010), available at http://law.moj.gov.tw/Eng/LawClass/LawAll.aspx?PCode=J0070017.

637 Treaty of Friendship, Commerce and Navigation between the United States of America and Republic of China,, Nov. 4, 1946, 63 Stat. 1299; TIAS 1871; 6 Bevans 761.

638 See 蕭雄淋 (Hsiao, Hsiung-Lin), 大英百科全書官司攻防戰：最高法院發回後有關中美條約適用的爭執 (上) (The Battle over the Britannica Encyclopedia Case: the Debates about the Application of the FCN Treaty (1)), 160律師通訊 50, 54 (1993).

639 *Id.*, at 56.

640 *Supra* note 637, Article II:2.

641 *Id.*

642 *Supra* note 637, Article III:2.

643 See Hsiao, Hsiung-Lin, *supra* note 638, at 56-57.

to be self-executing; such a reading is also consistent with the object of the Treaty as well as the intention of the parties. Moreover, the Britannica argued the practices of administrative institutions and the courts confirm its reading of Article 9 of the FCN Treaty. The Executive Yuan should know the object of the treaty and the intention of both parties fairly well; it played a part in negotiating and concluding the FCN Treaty. The Executive Yuan stated, "[T]he US right holders are entitled to the treatments identical to the nationals … The registration requirement imposed on foreign right holders is not applicable thereto."[644] The courts also frequently applied the FCN Treaty.[645]

The High Court was aware that the laws did not clearly establish the effect of international agreements. The High Court held international agreements should nonetheless have the same status as statute law. According to Articles 58, 63, and 57 of the Constitution, the international agreements will be reviewed by Legislative Yuan via procedures similar adopting domestic law. The courts should thus apply the rules of international agreements.[646] However, the High Court actually did not respond to the parties' arguments. The Court mentioned rules of copyrights would greatly influence the development of research and culture. Besides, the courts in most of the countries usually would not be bound by treaties concerning copyrights. The Court held these treaties should be implemented by the legislative organs via domestic legislation. Accordingly, Article 9 of the FCN Treaty was found non-self-executing.[647] The Court did not review the wordings and object of the FCN Treaty *per se*. It simply considered the copyright provisions are politically not suitable for self-executing. The High Court Then stressed the principle of reciprocity and respect for international agreements, which is embodied in Article 141 of the Constitution. Ultimately, the High Court held this provision should be applicable.[648] This finding is quite confusing. On one hand, the High Court acknowledged the concept of self-executing treaty provisions. On the other hand, the Court still applied the non–self-executing provisions. Did the Court intend to establish that the courts should perceive international agreements the same as domestic laws at all times? Or did the High Court hold that the courts should have discretion in applying non-self-executing provisions? If both of them are not the intentions of the High Court, its findings would be contradictory. The Court either did not notice such contradiction, or simply ignored it. It was observed that the High Court highly respected

644 74內字 24097號函 (promulgated by Executive Yuan, Dec. 30, 1985).

645 See Hsiao, Hsiung-Lin, *supra* note 638, at 57.

646 See 台灣高等法院79上更 (一) 128號, Jan. 28, 1992, 中國國際法與國際事務年報, Vol. 5, 427 (1989).

647 *Id.*

648 *Id.*

the opinions of the administrative departments on copyright protection for foreigners, which embodies the outcomes of US–Taiwan negotiations on intellectual property rights.[649] To cope with the policy made, the Court managed to find legal basis for the application of Article 9; however, the endeavour was not successful.

In summary, the executive, legislative, and judicial branches generally agree that the international agreements should be treated exactly as domestic law (i.e., the courts and individuals may resort to these agreements) if they are adopted by the Legislative Yuan via the procedures provided in the Constitution. Occasionally, the various branches of government mentioned the self-executing and non–self-executing provisions. However, they seldom set forth any requirement for self-executing provisions. In light of the practices in this regard, almost all the international agreements would be self-executing.[650]

2.2.1.2. Relationship to Domestic Laws

The legal documents mentioned previously indicate that international agreements are directly effective. The next question is the relationship between the international agreements, as part of domestic law, to other domestic laws and regulations. The MOJ has illuminated the status of international agreements in the hierarchy of domestic laws. The MOJ stated, "A treaty shall have the effects of domestic law. Moreover, the MOJ explained that by virtue of the spirit of Article 141 of the Constitution, the treaty should prevail when the treaty conflicts with domestic laws."[651] The "treaty" refers only to international agreements approved by the Legislative Yuan. The MOJ emphasized the executive agreements would not be superior to domestic laws. The supremacy of international agreements is based on the presumption that the Legislative Yuan would review them through procedures similar to adopting domestic legislation. Using this procedure could grant the international agreement the legitimacy of norms in the domestic legal system. The MOJ could not find a persuasive legal basis for supporting the supremacy of executive

649 蕭雄淋 (Hsiao, Hsiung-Lin), 大英百科全書官司攻防戰：最高法院發回後有關中美條約適用的爭執 (下) (The Battle over the Britannica Encyclopedia Case: the Debates about the Application of the FCN Treaty (2)), 161律師通訊 53, 55 (1993).

650 See 丘宏達 (Chiu, Hung-Ta),國際法在我國國內法上的地位 (The Status of International Law within Domestic Legal System, 19 (4) 憲政時代 81, 88 (1993); 陳純一 (Chen, Chun-Yi), 國際法在國內法的定位 (International Law in Municipal Law: Practices and Theories of Mainland China, Taiwan, Hong Kong, and Macao), (National Science Council, Research Project NSC90-2414-H034-009) 3, available at http://grbsearch.stpi.org.tw/GRB/advSearch.jsp (last visited Jan. 10, 2011).

651 See *supra* note 621, at paragraph 2.

agreements.[652] In short, the internal agreements have the status of statute laws. International agreements unquestionably prevail over laws issued before their ratification. However, the MOJ is unclear about the conflict between the international agreements and the laws issued after their ratification. The MOJ merely stated that "the issue is worth thinking about" and the legislative organs are presumed to be unwilling to pass laws infringing their international obligations.[653]

In its early days, the Judicial Yuan held international agreements unquestionably prevailed, if they conflicted with laws issued before their ratification. The Judicial Yuan stated that "[I]f the international agreements are adopted before the law was passed, the conflicts should be submitted and further deliberation is required."[654] The Judicial Yuan seemed yet to decide whether the international agreements prevail over legislation issued after their ratification. The Constitutional Court has not ruled on the issue either.

The Supreme Court indicated international agreements should prevail over domestic law in general.[655] In Case 72 Tai-fei No. 228, a US company initiated a private prosecution. The lower court dismissed the claim of the US Company because the company was not recognized as legal person under the Civil Code and therefore did not have rights provided in criminal procedure law. The Prosecutor General found the lower courts unduly disregarded the FCN Treaty, which granted the US company full access to the courts.[656] The Prosecutor General filed an "extraordinary appeal"[657] to the Supreme Court. The Court supported his view and found the international agreements as *lex specialis* and the FCN Treaty should prevail.[658] In Case 79 Shang-geng No.128 (i.e., the dispute between Britannica and Taching), the High Court held the international agreements always prevail pursuant to Article 141 of Constitution.[659] The High Court further stressed the *lex specialis derogat legi generali* should apply in this connection. In other words, the international law should prevail over the laws passed after their ratification.

Both the courts and the MOJ resort to Article 141 of the Constitution to support the supremacy of international agreements over domestic laws. Their inter-

---

652 See *id*, at paragraph 3.

653 *Supra* note 623.

654 See *supra* note 628.

655 *E.g.* 最高法院23上字第1074號判例, *supra* note 632; 最高法院73臺非字69號判決 (Apr. 4, 1984), 中國國際法年報, Vol. 1, 458 (1985).

656 See Paragraph 4 of Article 4 of the CFN Treaty, supra note 637, 6 Bevans 767.

657 Introduction of extraordinary appeals, see http://www.tps.moj.gov.tw/ct.asp?xItem=31768&CtNode=12112&mp=096 (last visited on Jan 10, 2011)

658 最高法院72年臺非字第228 (Dec. 9, 1983), available at http://jirs.judicial.gov.tw/Index.htm.

659 See *supra* note 646.

pretation of Article 141, however, is misconceived. Article 141 is merely a distribution or a general instruction on the foreign policy and does not establish any specific obligations. At most, the Constitution calls for respecting international agreements, which is significantly different from obligating to grant direct effect.[660] Given the procedures for ratifying international agreements, these agreements should be treated the same as statute law. The rules for the conflicts of domestic laws are provided in Article 16 of Central Regulation Standard Act.[661] Article 16 contains the doctrines of *Lex specialis derogat legi generali* and *Lex posterior derogat legi priori* and *Lex specialis derogat legi generali.* The outcome depends on the comparison of the laws at issue. Compared with the specific domestic law in a given case, international agreements would not always govern more specific matters or set forth more specific rules. No legal basis could be found for the priority of international agreements. Unless the international agreement at issue is *Lex specialis*, another doctrine for the conflicts of domestic laws (i.e., *Lex posterior derogat legi priori*) should be followed.[662]

2.2.2. The Legal Status of the WTO Agreements

Right after the accession to the WTO, the administrative departments wondered about legal status of the WTO agreements, *inter alia* the direct effect issue and the solutions for the conflicts with the domestic laws. The MOJ was requested to provide their opinion. The MOJ did not give any definite suggestion or instructions, as they did on the effect of international agreements. The MOJ noticed the Law Committee of Executive Yuan discussed similar issues in 1995 and no conclusion was reached.[663] The MOJ suggested the administrative departments make their own assessments. For their reference, the MOJ summarized the laws and the judgments concerned, which would be the starting point for assessing the legal status of the WTO agreements in Taiwan. The MOJ summarized the arguments against the direct effect as follows: (1) According to the Foreign Trade Act, a trade agreement could not be effective until the implementing legislation

---

660 See Part I, section 2.2.1.1.a) *supra*.

661 Central Regulation Standard Act amended on May 19, 2004, available at http://law.moj.gov.tw/Eng/LawClass/LawAll.aspx?PCode=A0030133 .

662 See Huang, Yi, supra note 620, at 69, also See 羅昌發 (Lo, Chang-Fa), 中美智慧財產權談判及其所涉及之法律問題之分析 *(The IPR Negotiations between Taiwan and the United States and the Legal Issues Pertinent thereto)* in 貿易關係之法律問題 (LEGAL ISSUES CONCERNING TRADE RELATIONS) 165, 212 (1998).

663 See 法律字0910005828 (promulgated by Ministry of Justice, Mar. 20), 2002, available at http://jirs.judicial.gov.tw/Index.htm.

is adopted. (2) Trade agreements usually set forth general, non-specific rules. They are not reviewed by the Legislative Yuan in procedures identical to the legislation procedures.[664] The MOJ also noted that the courts often recognize international agreements as directly effective. Their rulings could similarly support the direct effect of the WTO agreements.[665]

The answer to the issue would be quite clear, when the legislative history relating to the accession to the WTO and the new rulings of the courts are considered.

2.2.2.1. *Ratifying the WTO Agreements and Laws Pertinent to the Effect of the WTO Agreements*

a) *Accession Documents of the Separate Customs Territory of Taiwan, Penghu, Kinmen, and Matsu and the Ratification of the Protocol of Accession*

Taiwan is titled officially as the Separate Territory of Taiwan, Penghu, Kinmen, and Matsu (also known as TPKM or Chinese Taipei) under the WTO. Pursuant to the second sentence of Article 3 of the Protocol of Accession, several commitments provided in the Report of the Working Party on the Accession of the TPKM (hereafter the Working Party Report) are an integral part of the WTO obligations.[666] In paragraph 15 of the Working Party Report, which has been incorporated into the accession protocol, Taiwan committed to fully implement its obligations via eliminating the WTO-inconsistent measures and amending the laws. It appears that implementing legislations are required for applying WTO agreements. Some members of the Working Party did ask if the international agreements are self-executing under the law of Taiwan. The representative stated "[I]nternational treaties enter into force after being duly ratified and promulgated and have the same force and effect as domestic laws."[667] In other words, WTO agreements could be directly effective. Taiwan nonetheless committed to modify the laws or administrative measures incompatible with its WTO obligations.

After the General Council adopted the Protocol of the Accession of Taiwan, the Executive Yuan submitted the Protocol to the Legislative Yuan. The protocol was reviewed under procedure, which is more swift but similar to the legislative procedures. The proposals of the international agreements need not go through all three readings. They could be accepted in the second reading.[668] That is the

664 *Id*, paragraph 2.1.

665 *Id.*

666 General Council, *Decision on the Accession of the Separate Territory of Taiwan, Penghu, Kinmen and Matsu*, p. 2, WT/L/433, (Nov. 23, 2001).

667 *Id*, at para.14.

668 See Legislative Competence Exercise Act, Article 7, amended on May 28, 2008, available at http://law.moj.gov.tw/LawClass/LawAll.aspx?PCode=A0020058.

only distinction between the ratification procedure and the legislative procedure. Such a distinction would not be very significant. The major discussions and deliberations for both the legislation and international agreements would take place in the second reading. Except for polishing the wordings of the text, the results of the second reading generally remain unchanged in the third reading.[669] Whether to accept the protocol was not an issue in the discussion of the proposal for the Protocol of Accession during the second reading. The Legislators were concerned about the impacts on the domestic industries and the agriculture.[670] One Legislator criticized the administrative departments for trying to avoid the supervision of the Legislative Yuan. The administrative departments had not informed the Legislative Yuan about the trade negotiations, nor did they send the documents concerning the WTO agreements in time so that the Legislators could duly review them.[671] Although the executive branch apparently overlooked the supervision of the Legislative Yuan, the Legislators had never considered limiting the effect of the WTO agreements in the domestic legal system. Instead, they urged the administrative departments to take appropriate measures to deal with the side effects of the accession.[672] The Legislative Yuan ratified unanimously the Protocol of Accession.

The accession documents and the ratification of the Protocol of Accession indicated that executive and the legislative branches did not exclude the direct effect of the WTO agreements.

b) Foreign Trade Act and Regulation Governing the Implementation of the Imposition of Countervailing and Anti-Dumping Duties

The Foreign Trade Act provides general principles for government's trade-related activities (e.g., import and export resections, trade remedies, and trade negotiations). The opponents of direct effect believed Article 7 of the Foreign Trade Act excluded the direct effect of the WTO agreements.[673] Paragraph 4 of Article 7 reads: "A pact or an agreement with contents involving amendment of any existing law or enactment of a new law shall become effective only after completion of legislative procedures."[674] The provision is contrary to the practice that international agreements are generally directly effective and superior to

669 See *id*, paragraph 2 of Article 11.

670 Minutes of the 7 th Meeting, 6 th Session, the Fourth Legislative Yuan, Nov. 16, 2001, 90 (57) LEGISLATIVE YUAN GAZETTE 4, 15-28 (2001).

671 *Id*, at 16.

672 *Id*, at 18,21,22.

673 See *supra* note 663, paragraph 2.1.

674 See Foreign Trade Act, amended on Jan. 13, 2010, Article 7, available at http://law.moj.gov.tw/Eng/LawClass/LawAll.aspx?PCode=J0090004.

domestic laws. It seems that such general rules do not apply to the WTO agreements. According to the legislative history, the Legislators actually did not intend to exclude the direct effect of every trade agreement.

It is noteworthy that The Foreign Trade Act was drafted in light of the principles established in the GATT 1947.[675] The drafters hardly would undermine the rules of the GATT and WTO or support the domestic laws inconsistent with these rules. Besides, Article 7 originally was addressed only to the agreements not subject to the deliberation of the Legislative Yuan, which should not have the same effect as domestic laws. The drafters considered consultations and negotiations between the governments essential for diminishing the trade barriers (tariff and non-tariff) and resolving the trade frictions. The administrative departments should be authorized to conduct such negotiations constantly.[676] The first paragraph of the draft of Article 8, becoming paragraph 1 of Article 7, provides a general authorization for the administrative departments on the negotiations of trade agreements. Due to the diplomatic difficulties, the second paragraph of the draft Article 8 allows the administrative departments to entrust private entities with such tasks.[677] The effect of such trade agreements was set forth in the third paragraph of the draft Article 8. The first sentence reads: "[T]he trade agreements and the matters negotiated shall be implemented after the approval of the Executive Yuan." The second sentence states these agreements would not be effective immediately if their implementation requires modifying domestic laws. It was clarified in the explanatory note of the draft Article 8 that the scope of authorization is limited to matters consistent with domestic laws.[678] The original idea of the draft Article was that the Legislative Yuan generally authorized the administrative departments in advance of the trade negotiations. Such agreements would involve only technical matters or administrative arrangements; these agreements should be executive agreements, not the "treaties" in the Constitution and the J.Y. Interpretations.[679] Since these agreements are not subject to the deliberation of Legislative Yuan, they certainly would not have the same

675 See The Draft of Foreign Trade Act, 院總字1534號, 政府提案第3686號, p. 45, available at http://lis.ly.gov.tw/lgcgi/lgmeetimage?cfcec7cbcecccfcfc5c7cfd2c6c8 (last visited Jan. 10, 2011).

676 *Id*, at 52.

677 *Id.*

678 *Id.*, at 53.

679 See Testament of Chiang Ping-kun, Deputy Mister of Economic Affairs, *Hearing before the Economic Committee and Judiciary Committee on the proposal of Trade Law, Nov. 17, 1990*, 80 (46) LEGISLATIVE YUAN GAZETTE 276,277 (1990); Testament of Hu Ko-sheng, Director General of Bureau of Foreign Trade, *Hearing before the Economic Committee and Judiciary Committee on the proposal of Trade Law, Nov 21,1990*, 80 (48) LEGISLATIVE YUAN GAZETTE 246, 253 (1990).

effect as domestic laws. The second sentence of the third paragraph of the draft Article 8 became the fourth paragraph of Article 7; the first sentence was deleted during party caucus negotiation.[680] The intent of Article 7 would have been clear, if the first sentence had not been deleted.

The Legislators deleted the first sentence of the third paragraph of the draft Article 8 not because they sought to exclude the direct effect of all trade agreements. Instead, they want to confine the authorization to administrative departments. The Legislators stressed the trade agreements include both executive agreements and "treaties" in the Constitution.[681] Paragraph 1 of Article 7 covers both the executive agreements and the treaties. In other words, the administrative departments have general authorizations to negotiate the trade agreements. However, they would not have general authorizations to conclude all the trade agreements without the approval of the legislature. Trade treaties, agreements, and pacts might substantially affect the rights and the benefits of individuals. Such agreements, regardless of their names, should not always be considered as executive agreements and thus free from the supervision of the Congress.[682] The Legislators modified the clauses, which give the impression that all the trade agreements are executive agreements. Paragraph 3 of the draft of Article 8, the first sentence appeared to be one of these clauses.[683] Nonetheless, paragraph 4 of Article 7 still could be construed to be applied only to the executive agreements. The WTO agreements are the treaties ratified by the Legislative Yuan – not the trade agreements, which paragraph 4 of Article 7 was intended to cover.

The provision to support the direct effect of the WTO agreements could also be found in the Regulation Governing the Implementation of the Imposition of Countervailing and Anti-dumping Duties. Article 48 of the Regulation clearly states the authorities "may refer to relevant international agreement or customary practices, provided that there are no specific provisions prescribed in the Act or in the Regulations."[684] Clearly, the SCM agreement and the SG agreement are the relevant international agreements.

---

680 Introduction of the party caucus negotiations, see generally 胡文棟 (Wu, Wen-Tung), 我國立法院黨團協商制度之探討 *(A Study of the Party Caucus Negotiation System in the Legislative Yuan)*,14 社會科學學報 112 (2006).

681 Second Reading of Foreign Trade Act, Jan. 12,1993,82 (3) LEGISLATIVE YUAN GAZETTE 33,57 (1993).

682 See statement of Legislator Chen Shui-pien, *supra* note 679 at 279; statement of Legislator Peng Pai-hsien, *supra* note 679, at 283.

683 See paragraph 3 of Article 7, *supra* note 674.

684 Regulation Governing the Implementation of the Imposition of Countervailing and Anti-dumping Duties (promulgated on Nov. 7, 1984, latest amendment on Feb. 23, 2005) , available at http://law.moj.gov.tw/Eng/LawClass/LawAll.aspx?PCode=G0350034.

2.2.2.2. Cases Addressing the Effect of the WTO Agreements

Taiwan acceded to the WTO in 2002. As of June 2010, 491 cases have involved the effect of the WTO agreements; either the parties resorted to the WTO rules or the courts applied them.[685] These cases concern mainly intellectual property rights. The government procurement and anti-dumping measures are occasionally brought before the courts. Some cases have been appealed to the Supreme Court and the Supreme Administrative Court. Although the courts do not always directly address the request for applying the WTO agreements, the courts do tend to support the direct effect of the WTO agreements.

a) The TRIPS Agreement

Several courts have deemed the provisions of the TRIPS as part of the legal bases for protecting foreign intellectual property rights.[686] For instance, in Case 93 Shang-su No. 2940, the Taiwan High Court found the work of the Sony Corp., Japanese Company, was entitled to Copyright Act protections. The Court explained: "The computer programs listed in the annex two was published after Jan. 1, 2002, when our country has acceded to the WTO. In accordance with Article 9.1 of the TRIPS and Article 3 of the Bern Convention, our country shall protect the work of the nationals of the members of the WTO. Japan is the member of the WTO. In the light of the proviso of Article 4 of the Copyright Act, the works in the annex two therefore shall be protected under the Act."[687] In Case 94 Tai-shang No. 7039, the Supreme Court also referred to the TRIPS as legal basis for copyright protection for foreigners. The Supreme Court ruled as follows: "After accession to the WTO, our country, according to the TRIPS agreement, shall protect the works of the nationals of other members. Besides, the works of the nationals of all the WTO members also would be protected by virtue of subsection of Article 4 of the Copyright Act, because the reciprocal copyright pro-

685 474 cases concerning intellectual property rights; 8 cases relate to the government procurements; 9 cases involve anti-dumping measures. The data is based on the judgments available at http://www.rootlaw.com.tw/ (last visited on Jan 10, 2011)

686 *E.g.* 台灣高等法院, 93年度上訴字第2940號判決, Dec. 28, 2004; 臺灣臺北地方法院93年度易字第1747號判決,Jan. 31,2005;台灣台北地方法院 96 年 訴 字第 456 號, Dec. 13, 2007;智慧財產權法院97年民專上字第20號, Mar. 19, 2009; 智慧財產權法院98 年刑智上更(一) 字第6號, May 21, 2009; 智慧財產權法院98年民著上字第13號, Nov. 12, 2009, all available at http://jirs.judicial.gov.tw/Index.htm.

687 台灣高等法院, 93年度上訴字第2940號判決, Reasoning para.4, Dec. 28, 2004, available at http://jirs.judicial.gov.tw/Index.htm. (last visited on May 1, 2010).

tection was established between our country and all the WTO members."[688] The courts refer to the criteria of eligibility for protection under the TRIPS agreement (i.e., Article 9.1 of the TRIPS and Article 3 of the Bern Convention) because it could be incorporated through Article 4 into the Copyrights Act. In these cases, the courts do not recognize the TRIPS *per se* as directly effective.

By applying the rules of the TRIPS not incorporated into the domestic laws, the courts clearly have favored their direct effect. In Case 92 Pan No. 1649, Rolex Corp. appealed to the Administrative Supreme Court that the Fair Trade Commission failed to find the Surich Co. Ltd. misleading the place of origin. The appellant, Rolex Corp., contended the prohibition on such misleading and deceiving conduct in Article 21 of the Fair Trade Act[689] actually involved the protection of geographical indication provided in Article 22.2 of the TRIPS agreement. The appellant noted that Taiwan has not yet joined the WTO. Nevertheless, the appellant argued that the interpretation of Article 21 of the Fair Trade Act should be in line with the TRIPS due to Article 141 of Constitution, which requires respect for the international agreements.[690] By the time the judgment was made, Taiwan had acceded to the WTO; the Court did apply and interpret Article 22.2 of the TRIPS (i.e., the protection for geographic indication). The Court held this provision applicable only to the products, whose qualities depend highly on the geographical elements of their origins. In other words, the provision was set mainly for the agricultural products – not for the industrial products. Therefore, the products at issue (i.e., the watches) should not be subject to Article 22.2 of the TRIPS.[691]

The Administrative Supreme Court also constantly applied the TRIPS agreement. A Dutch company, ASML Mask Tools B.V., has filed 44 appeals to the Administrative Supreme Court based on Article 70.2 of the TRIPS.[692] Al-

---

688 最高法院94臺上字第7039七號判決, Reasoning para. 2, Dec.15, 2005, available at http://jirs.judicial.gov.tw/Index.htm.

689 See 公平交易法 (Fair Trade Act), amended Feb. 6, 2002, available at http://law.moj.gov.tw/Eng/LawClass/LawAll.aspx?PCode=J0150002.

690 See 最高行政法院 92判1649號判決, Fact para.5, Nov. 27, 2003, available at http://jirs.judicial.gov.tw/Index.htm.

691 *Id*, Reasoning para. 3.

692 最高行政法院 95判字第597號判決, (Apr. 4, 2006); 最高行政法院 95 判字第458號判決, (Apr. 7, 2006); 最高行政法院 95判字第460號判決 (Apr. 7, 2006); 最高行政法院 95. 判字第493號判決, (Apr.13, 2006); 最高行政法院 95判字第485號判決 (Apr. 13, 2006); 最高行政法院年度判字第493號判決 (Apr. 13, 2006); 最高行政法院 95判字第503號判決 (Apr. 13, 2006); 最高行政法院 95 判字第544號判決 (Apr. 20, 2006); 最高行政法院 95 判字第545號判決 (Apr. 20, 2006); 最高行政法院 95 判字第549號判決 (Apr. 20, 2006); 最高行政法院 95 判字第570號判決 (Apr. 27, 2006); 最高行政法院 95 判字第579號判決 (Apr. 27, 2006); 最高行政法院 95 判字第597號判決 (Apr. 27, 2006); 最高行政法院 95

though the Court dismissed the appeals, it has not even once rejected the application of the TRIPS. All 30 cases concern the identical issue, but different subject matters for patent applications. The Appellant, ASML, has filed patent applications in the United States, the EU, and Holland. It asserted the priority right of Article 27 of the Patent Act should be granted on the date of the patent application abroad. Pursuant to Article 27 of the Paten Act, the priority right would be granted if the nationals of Taiwan can be entitled to such priority in the states where the patent applications were filed.[693] Both ASML and the Intellectual Property Office agreed the patent applications filed in the members of the WTO certainly qualified for the priority right. However, the Intellectual Property Office further clarified in a Regulation that the priority date for such application would be January 1, 2002, the date of accession of Taiwan – not the effective date of filing. The appellant filed the application before 2002 and argued the priority date should be the date of filing by virtue of Article 70.2 of the TRIPS. According to appellant's reading of the Article 70.2, Taiwan is obligated to protect priority rights existing on the date of the application of the TRIPS. Such obligation should arise retroactively from the date of filing (i.e., the time the priority rights exist). The appellant held the measure refusing the priority rights invalid for imposing additional limitations not provided in Article 70.2 of the TRIPS.[694] The appellant argued the lower court did not correctly apply all the laws concerned, including the TRIPS agreements. The Administrative Supreme

判字第602號判決 (May 4, 2006); 最高行政法院 95 判字第616號判決 (May 4, 2006); 最高行政法院 95 判字第617號判決 (May 4, 2006); 最高行政法院 95 判字第621號判決, (May 4, 2006); 最高行政法院 9 判字第624號判決, (May 4, 2006); 最高行政法院 95 判字第639號判決 (May 4, 2006); 最高行政法院 95判字第648號判決 (May 4, 2006); 最高行政法院 95裁字第639號判決 (May 4, 2006); 最高行政法院 95判字第679號判決 (May 11, 2006); 最高行政法院 95 判字第688號判決 (May 11, 2006); 最高行政法院 95判字第689號判決 (May 11, 2006); 最高行政法院 95判字第728號判決 (May 18, 2006); 最高行政法院 95判字第740號判決 (May 18, 2006); 最高行政法院 95判字第835號判決 (June 8, 2006); 最高行政法院 95判字第836號判決 (June 8, 2006); 最高行政法院 95判字第837號判決 (June 8, 2006); 最高行政法院 95 判字第838號判決 (June 8, 2006); 最高行政法院 95判字第839號判決 (June 8, 2006); 最高行政法院 95判字第840號判決 (June 8, 2006); 最高行政法院 95 判字第933號判決 (June 22, 2006); 最高行政法院 95判字第1181號判決 (July 31, 2006); 最高行政法院95判字第1277號判決 (Aug. 10, 2006); 最高行政法院 95判字第1278號判決 (Aug. 10, 2006); 最高行政法院 95判字第1279號判決 (Aug. 10, 2006); 最高行政法院 95判字第1280號判決 (Aug.10, 2006); 最高行政法院 95判字第1281號判決 (Aug.10, 2006); 最高行政法院95判字第1545號判決 (Sep. 21, 2006); 最高行政法院 95判字第1775號判決 (Oct. 31, 2006), available at http://jirs.judicial.gov.tw/Index.htm.

693 See Patent Act (promulgated on May 29, 1944, latest amendment on Aug. 25, 2010), available at http://law.moj.gov.tw/Eng/LawClass/LawAll.aspx?PCode=J0070007.

694 See *e.g.* 最高行政法院95判字1775判決, Reasoning, appellant's arguments, (Oct. 31, 2006), available at http://jirs.judicial.gov.tw/Index.htm.

Court sustained the rulings of the lower courts. However, the lower court did not refuse the applicability of the TRIPS. Moreover, the lower court did not refuse to refer to the Appellate Body report and even sought the opinion of the Intellectual Property Division of the WTO on the issue. The lower court ultimately held Article 70.2 and the Appellate Body report would not support the appellant's arguments.[695] The Administrative Supreme Court confirmed its interpretation of the TRIPS.

In Case 93 Pan No. 281, the Administrative Supreme Court mentioned the conditions for the direct effect. In Case 93 Pan No. 281, the appellant, an American Company, claimed the Articles 86 and 73 of the Patent Act did not fully protect the patent rights of the American citizens and companies. These provisions are not consistent with the FCN Treaty and the Article 62.4 of the TRIPS.[696] The Court recognized the domestic law and international law as sources of administrative laws. However, the Administrative Supreme Court held the international law could become such source of law when certain conditions were met. International agreements are directly effective if "the agreement *per se* has specified the rules or the obligations, or the contents of the agreement have via legislation been provided in the domestic laws and the judicial entities have adopted them as precedent."[697] If the international agreements were directly effective, they would prevail over the inconsistent domestic law. The Court found Article 62.4 of the TRIPS provides specific rules, but the provision did not support the appellant's argument.[698]

In short, the direct effect of the TRIPS agreement is generally accepted. In all these cases, the courts never questioned the direct effect of the TRIPS. At most, the court only set conditions for such effect. The courts did not explain the grounds for the direct effect either. They seem to follow the practice concerning the effect of international agreements.

b) *The Anti-Dumping Agreement and the Agreement on Government Procurement*

In a few cases, the parties have based their argument on the Anti-dumping and the Agreement on Government Procurement. However, the Administrative Supreme Court has yet to explicitly apply the rules of these agreements. For instance, in Case 96 Pan No.1063, the appellant challenged the determination of the Ministry

695 See *id*, Reasoning, section of the rulings of the lower court.

696 最高行政法院93判字281, Reasoning, appellant's argument, (Mar. 18, 2004), available at http://jirs.judicial.gov.tw/Index.htm.

697 *Id*, Reasoning, the opinion of the Court.

698 *Id*.

of Economic Affairs on the dumping margins by virtue of Articles 6.10 and 9.4 of the Anti-dumping agreement.[699] In defending the case, the Ministry of Economic Affairs submitted its reading of these provisions and argued the investigation complied with the AD agreement.[700] The Administrative Supreme Court did not address the arguments about the interpretations of the AD agreements, but the Court agreed with the methodology taken by the Ministry.

In a recent case, Case 95 Su No. 2790, the Taipei High Administrative Court interpreted the laws at issue by virtue of the provisions of the GPA, although neither party requested the application of the GPA. The Administrative High Court explained the Government Procurement Act was drafted in line with the GPA. The Court used the provision of the GPA to clarify the terms of the Government Procurement Act.[701] The case was referred to the Administrative Supreme Court; the Court did not reverse the High Court's interpretation.[702]

The Administrative Supreme Court actually did not reject the arguments and the interpretation of the domestic laws based on the AD agreement and the GPA. The administrative departments and the lower courts hold these agreements have the same effect as the domestic laws.

2.2.2.3. The Grounds for the Direct Effect of the WTO Agreements

The direct effect of the WTO agreements has been widely accepted in the domestic legal system, according to the legal documents concerning the accession of Taiwan, the relevant domestic legislations, as well as the judgments of the courts.The discretions of the political branches on the trade policies might be confined. Consequently, concerns might exist for the sovereignty and the lack of reciprocity in this regard. However, none of these concerns was raised in the legal documents concerning the effect of the WTO agreements in Taiwan.

Taiwan holds an open attitude toward the legal status of the WTO agreements in the domestic legal system. The WTO laws are seen more as protections for trade opportunities than as constraints on sovereignty. Since the UN Resolution 2758, Restoration of Lawful Rights of People's Republic of China in the United Nations, Taiwan has been blocked from most multilateral agreements or international organizations. Accession to an international agreement would be taken as

---

699 See 最高行政法院96判字1603號判決, Reasoning, section 2, (Sep. 6, 2007), available at http://jirs.judicial.gov.tw/Index.htm.

700 See *id*, Reasoning, section 3.

701 See 台北高等行政法院95訴2790號判決, Reasoning, Part 2, section 1, May 29, 2008, available at http://jirs.judicial.gov.tw/Index.htm.

702 See 最高行政法院97判字976號判決, Reasoning, section 7, (Nov. 6, 2008), available at http://jirs.judicial.gov.tw/Index.htm.

the breakthrough of the blockade to international society, an achievement that draws more attention to the contents of the international agreements.[703] The government would tend to respect the international agreement, to which they have endeavored to accede. Besides, in comparison with the bilateral negotiations, the WTO apparently would be the better forum for trade negotiations. The economy of Taiwan depends on international trade, particularly exports to the major economies. The internal market is relatively small and less appealing to Taiwan's trade partners. In other words, the trade retaliation might not even hurt its trade partners, most of which are large or mega economies. Therefore, bargain chips might be quite limited. The obligations under the WTO agreements seem to be fair; Taiwan might not have better offers from its trade partners in the bilateral negotiations. The unpleasant bilateral negotiations with the United States also give such an impression. A series of negotiations on intellectual property rights was conducted from 1983 to 1992. Under the threat of unilateral trade retaliations (i.e., section 301 of Trade Act 1974) Taiwan had to accept the request of the United States, even if these requests might infringe the autonomy of the legislative and judicial branches.[704] On one hand, Taiwan must undertake, as requested by the United States, obligations similar to or stricter than the multilateral agreements, such as the Bern Convention or the draft of the TRIPS agreement. On the other hand, Taiwan cannot be entitled to the protections under the multilateral agreements.[705] Taiwan would rather be directly subject to the WTO agreements, if the entrance fees for the WTO must be paid one way or another. In the WTO forum, Taiwan also may join with states that have similar interests and negotiate with other larger states. All these advantages would make Taiwan friendly to the rules of WTO agreements. Also, Taiwan might not prefer the scope of manoeuvre for the alleged non-compliance, which might lead to bilateral negotiations and trade retaliations.

In fact, the political branches do not intend to confine how WTO agreements are applied in Taiwan. A thorough discussion on the accession to the WTO agreements was held in the hearing before Foreign and National Defence Com-

---

703 See the coverage about the accession to the WTO, *e.g.* 我重返GATT大會據理爭權益 *(Endeavors for the Return to the GATT)*, 經濟日報, Taipei, Apr. 14, 1994; 蕭萬長：台灣應定位自由貿易區 *(Hsiao Wan-chang: "Taiwan Should be A Free Trade Area")*, 經濟日報, Taipei, Nov. 15, 2001; 入世條約案立院周五審議 (Legislative Yuan Deliberates the Accession Protocol on Friday), 經濟日報, Taipei, Nov. 12, 2001.

704 See 羅昌發, *supra* note 662, at 208-210.

705 See 羅昌發,由雙邊架構通往多邊體系的中美智慧財產權保護關係 (From the Bilateral to the Multilateral Framework: The Protection of Intellectual Property Right between Taiwan and the United States) in 貿易關係之法律問題 (LEGAL ISSUES CONCERNING TRADE RELATIONS) 217, 260-261 (1998).

mittee and Economics Committee. The Deputy Ministers of Foreign Affairs, Economic Affairs, Finance, Agriculture, and Economic Planning and Development jointly described the issues concerning the accession to the WTO. The officials illustrated the efforts on the accession and the measures that would be taken to comply with the WTO obligations.[706] Their attitudes toward the effect of the WTO agreements can be found in the matters concerning the sanitary and phytosanitary measures and the regulations for the service sector. These measures and regulations, which are crucial for public health and customer protection respectively, belonged to the domain of the legislative and executive branches. After the accession, these measures and regulations also would have to be subject to the control of the WTO. The standards of protection for public health and consumers might be incompatible with WTO rules, if the standards are so high as to form the trade barriers. In such circumstances, some states (e.g., the United States) would choose to confine the application of the WTO rules in the domestic legal system.[707] The Deputy Minister of Agriculture, however, stated the government would modify the sanitary and phytosanitary measures in light of the international rules.[708] The official of the Minister Economic Planning and Development bluntly admitted that consumer protection would no longer be considered in the policy making concerning the service sector. He stressed consumers should not always expect the government will shield them from inadequate service suppliers through restrictive measures on market access. Instead, consumers should be careful when choosing service suppliers, especially when the service is provided overseas.[709] Also, he emphasized compliance with the international economic laws (in particular the WTO) is inevitable because the Taiwanese economy depends on the international trade and closely connects with the framework of the global market.[710]

The governments did not show any intention not to follow the WTO agreements in the domestic legal system. In other words, the government did not pay attention to the flexibility or the "scope for manoeuvre" for implementing the obligations under the WTO, which is a practical reason against the direct effect. In the hearing, the legislators raised 24 questions. The discussion focused mainly on the relationship between Taiwan and China under the WTO framework. The Legislators worried whether Taiwan can accede to the WTO simultaneously, or

706 See Hearing before the Foreign and National Defence Committee and Economics Committee, the 4 th Legislative Yuan, 2nd Session, Nov. 22, 1999, 88 (54) LEGISLATIVE YUAN GAZETTE 39, 39-58.

707 See Part I, section 1.1.3.1. b) *Supra.*

708 See *supra* note 706, at 54.

709 See *supra* note 706, at 58.

710 *Id.*

shortly after China's accession.[711] They were also concerned about the name of the membership. The Legislators also urged the government to diminish the impact on agriculture.[712] No question was raised about the effect of the WTO agreements in the domestic legal system. It seems that legislators would not treat the WTO agreements other than those concluded by Taiwan.

If the legislative and executive branches do not apparently oppose the direct effect of the WTO agreements, the court has no reason to change their practice on this issue. Besides, several legislations allow or request the application of international agreements.[713] Accordingly, the international agreements would not be totally alien to the courts. The courts get used to turn to the rules beyond the domestic legal system.

2.2.3. Conclusion

The Constitution did not mention the effect of international agreements. The authoritative interpretation of the Constitution recognizes international agreements as part of domestic laws. The similarity between the ratification procedure and the legislation procedure is the major reason for recognizing the direct effect of international agreements. Both the courts and the Ministry of Justice resort to Article 141 of the Constitution to support the supremacy of international agreements over domestic laws. Their interpretation of Article 141, however, is flawed. The international agreement should have exactly the same status as domestic law. In other words, *Lex posterior derogat legi priori* and *Lex specialis derogat legi generali* should apply.

The Ministry of Justice did not give any definite suggestion or the instructions on the effect of the WTO agreements. Given the legislative history relating to the accession to the WTO and the recent rulings of the courts, the direct effect of the WTO agreements is recognized. Taiwan has an open attitude toward the WTO law. Taiwan felt disadvantaged in the bilateral negations with its trade partners because of the less appealing internal market and its unique political situation. WTO law is deemed more as protections for trade opportunities than as constraints on sovereignty. Neither the legislative nor the executive branches show any intention to exclude the direct effect of the WTO agreements. The courts thus would not find it necessary to reconsider their general practice on the effect of international agreements.

---

711 See *supra* note 706, at 59.

712 See *supra* note 706, at 60.

713 See Part I, section 2.2.1.1. b) *supra*.

2.3. Conclusion: Considerations for the Status of the WTO Agreements in the Domestic Legal System

The Constitutions of China and Taiwan did not specify the effect of international agreements on domestic legal systems. The Constitutional Court of Taiwan gave a general instruction on the legal status of international agreements, whereas the competent authorities have the final say on such matters. Nevertheless, quite a number of laws recognize the direct effect of international agreement both in China and Taiwan. They have different views on the direct effect of the WTO agreements.

In practice, the direct effect of international agreements is generally recognized. However, China is ambiguous about the effect of the WTO agreements. The laws, regulations, and the interpretations of the courts show no unified position on this issue. Reading all these laws, regulations, and the courts' interpretations in harmony, several rules are still created. The WTO agreements could be directly effective at least in cases between the private parties. In the administrative litigation, the effect of the WTO agreements depends on that specific law or the regulation applicable in the given case. Although the laws and regulations might have recognized the direct effect, the recent practices of the State Council and the Supreme Court denied applying WTO agreement to administration litigations. The concerns for direct effect were not revealed to the public. The reciprocal consideration might play an important role because the major trade partners (i.e., the United States and the EU) have refused the direct effect of the WTO agreements.

On the contrary, Taiwan pays far less attention to lack of reciprocity in the enforcement. Moreover, Taiwan does not have preference for the scope of manoeuvre for the alleged non-compliance. In terms of the effect within the domestic legal system, no distinction was made between the WTO agreements and all other international agreements concluded. The WTO agreements, as international agreements concluded by Taiwan, may have the same status of domestic law. In terms of the political and economical situations, the major trade partners of Taiwan (e.g., the US, the EU, and China) have more bargaining chips in bilateral trade negotiations, which are ruled more by power. Taiwan would rather abide by the WTO agreements, which are a much more rule-based system.

In summary, China and Taiwan consider not only that the laws and regulations address the effect of international agreements, but also the substantial trade interests. China and Taiwan should and could have recognized the direct effect of the WTO agreements in light of their respective domestic laws and regulations. The different interests lead to the different decisions on the direct effect.

Part II:
An Analysis of the Grounds For and Against

Chapter 1: Major Arguments For and Against the Direct Effect of the WTO Agreements

The practices of the members illustrated previously show various appraisals on the WTO's intervention in implementing the WTO agreements. The smaller member states (e.g., Taiwan) believe they would not have much control over the international trade politics. Thus, the rule-oriented international agreements would be more of a source of protection than constraint. The larger or more developed member states, on the contrary, would like to maintain the greater flexibility in international economic relations and claim "sovereignty" or the "scope for manoeuvre" against the interference of international organizations, which they seldom experienced in the past.[714] Their decisions are based more on political considerations than on pure legal reasoning. The academic community, on the contrary, analyzes the issues of the direct effect from normative perspectives. Many authors have written profound articles arguing for and against as well as suggesting an intermediate position of direct effect. In this chapter, the arguments will be explored.

1.1. Arguments for the Direct Effect of the WTO Agreements

The direct effect of the WTO agreements requires the courts to intervene in the implementation of the WTO obligations, which are used under the full discretion of the government; in particular, the administrative institutions. Tumlir and Petersmann are the most notable proponents of direct effect for their full-fledged theories, which argue for the involvement of the courts by emphasizing the protections for individuals. There are many other advocates of direct effect who present arguments from different perspectives. However, in order to show a clear and focused view of the rationale for direct effect, only the major arguments will be briefly addressed.

714 Similar observation, see John Jackson & Alan O. Skys, *Questions and Comparisons* in IMPLEMENTING THE URUGUAY ROUND 457, 466 (John Jackson & Alan O. Skys ed., 1997).

1.1.1. Constitutionalization of International Economic Law

Tumlir and Petersmann based arguments for direct effect on the idea of the constitutionalization of international economic law, which holds international economic law as the constitutional norm limiting the powers of the states and offering protections for individuals.[715]

The late Tumlir tried to incorporate the international economic rules into the domestic constitutional system and to find the grounds for confining the governments' discretion on foreign trade. International economic rules, in his view, are set to protect the world market against the governments. These rules are drafted in negative mode and they seek to restrain certain kinds of policy.[716] In Tumlir's time, no international authority with effective power existed to make rules, to adjudicate under these rules, and to enforce the decisions of this authority. The sovereign states have ultimate political authority. Accordingly, he considered the international economic order essentially as a "reflection of national constitutional control."[717] However, national constitutional control over trade policy seemed to be loose. He noted an excessive transfer of decision-making powers concerning trade policy from the legislatures to the executive. In addition, according to Tumlir, the courts had abandoned their task of quality control over such policy.[718]

Tumlir also argued that the governments, through international economic rules, provide a stable framework for international transactions, which maintain their citizens' freedom of international transactions and the non-discrimination treatments for all the participants in the transactions. Such rules can reinforce the constitutional protection of private property rights and serve as "the second line of national constitutional entrenchment."[719] He believed that the international economic order and the national constitution should support each other more effectively by strengthening the status of governments' international commitments within the national legal system. In this way, Tumlir emphasized, "the foreign trade policy would become an explicit and systematic concern of constitutional jurisprudence. This would also imply a gradual restoration of constitutional over-

715 See Johann Ludwig Duvigneau, Die Konstitutionalisierung des WTO-Rechts: Zur juristische Diskussion über Verfassungsstrukturen im Bereich des Handelsvölkerrechts, 56 (3) Außenwirtschaft 293, 298 (2001); Lukas Engelberger, DIE UNMITTELBARE ANWENDBARKEIT DES WTO-RECHTS IN DER SCHWEIZ 202. (2004).

716 Jan Tumlir, *International Economic Order and Democratic Constitutionalism*, 34 ORDO: JAHRBUCH FÜR DIE ORDNUNG VON WIRTSCHAFT UND GESELLSCHAFT 71, 72 (1983).

717 *Id*, at 80.

718 See *e.g.* Jan Tumlir, Protectionism: Trade Policy in Democratic Societies 14 (1985).

719 See *supra* note 716, at 80.

sight in domestic economic matters."[720] To this end, he suggested a rigid commitment to the Most Favored Nation (the MFN) obligation that could be enforceable in domestic law (i.e., a MFN commitment with direct effect).[721]

Generally speaking, Tumlir considered the freedom of international transaction and non-discrimination as grounds allowing the court to intervene in implementing trade commitments.[722] Another advocate for the direct effect, Petersmann, followed this approach and further elaborated on this thesis.

1.1.1.1. The Need for the Restraint on Discretion in Trade Policy

The foreign policy, including trade policy, used to be entrusted exclusively to the political branches. The courts should respect their discretion. At the outset, it should be established why the political branches, *inter alia* the administrative institutions, should not maintain broad discretion in trade policy.

Petersmann argued that rights of the individuals are deeply involved in the trade policy area. Trade transactions reflect the exercise of individual freedoms and property rights. To be more specific, the import restrictions, tax or non-tariff barriers, would confine individuals' "freedom to choose" and reduce the real income of consumers. These restrictions would disturb non-discriminatory competitions between domestic importers and producers, both of whom are citizens of the importing country. The import restrictions would essentially tax the domestic consumers and allow the domestic producers to raise the price and collect the "protection rents."[723] The restriction of free trade is actually the restriction of the exercise of individual freedom and property right at transnational level. These rights are no less subject to constitutional guarantees of non-discrimination, proportionality, and judicial review than the restriction of the exercise of individual freedom and property rights at a purely national level.[724]

Petersmann contends "protectionist biases" exist in domestic decision-making regarding trade policy. In his view, the periodically-elected trade politicians and the trade bureaucrats promote their self-interests by exchanging trade protection for political support by protectionist interest groups, mostly by big incorporations.[725]

---

720 *Id.*

721 See Tumlir, *supra* note 718, at 61-70.

722 Critical analysis of Tumlir's theory, see Rebort E. Hudec, *The Role of Judicial Review in Preserving Liberal Foreign Policies* in NATIONAL CONSTITUTIONS AND INTERNATIONAL ECONOMIC LAW 503,508 ff. (Meinhard Hilf & Ernst-Ulrich Petersmann eds., 1993).

723 See Ernst-Ulrich Petersmann, Constitutional Functions and Constitutional Problems of International Economic Law, 112 (1991).

724 See *id*, at 391.

725 See *supra* note 723, at175-204.

Although economists have proven free trade benefits the general public, such general public interest is not equally represented. Petersmann described such phenomena as a "government failure," which denotes policy institutions and democratic decision-making process failing to have political decisions, and legal rules that can maximize the equal rights and individual and social rights of the citizens.[726] The constitutional rules, such rules of law, and judicial protection of individual freedom of foreign trade can correct these government failures.[727]

1.1.1.2. The Liberal International Trade Rules As Constitutional Constraints on the Discretion in Trade Policy

Petersmann suggested that liberal international trade rules should be incorporated into the domestic constitutional systems and serve as the criteria by which the court reviews the discretion of the government. He implied that liberal international trade rules may function similarly to the domestic constitutions and may supplement their deficiency in constraining the discretion of governments in trade-related matters.

a) Liberal International Trade Rules Can Have Constitutional Features

The concept of a constitution, by which Petersmann started his arguments, is based on economic and legal liberalism; individual fundamental rights should play the central role. The individuals are believed to be the best judges for their own welfare. Also, they should be granted the widest possible freedom of choice and of corresponding responsibility. The tasks of the governments are to maintain the equal freedoms and "markets", through which individuals may exercise their freedom and property rights, and also to supply "public goods" (e.g., the agreed standard of income distribution and social justice). However, the government does not often act like an efficient, impartial, omniscient servant of the public goods. Constitutional law is set to restrain the abuse of government powers and prevent the government from deviating from their tasks.[728] All forms of government interventions should conform to the "rule of law", which means all legislative, executive, and judicial organs should follow a set of transparent, general, non-discriminatory rules and procedures.[729] All of these constitutional

726 See *supra* note 723, at 205.
727 See *supra* note 723, at 392.
728 See *supra* note 723, at 365.
729 See *supra* note 723, at 364.

requirements and principles have been recognized as applicable to the exercise of the governmental powers of trade policy.[730]

The purpose of the liberal international trade rules, such as the GATT/WTO, is to maintain and extend equal freedoms so that individual citizens may have maximum freedom of choice. Petersmann held that the international trade rules and the national constitutions actually rest on the same value premise: individuals are the best judge of their own welfare.[731] He emphasized non-discriminatory market competition and liberal trade would not only tend to maximize the individual freedom of choice and property rights, but also may maximize the social welfare, such as ensuring real income and property rights of all members of the society. In the meantime, they may also contribute to the principles of national constitutions, *inter alia* democracy and limitation of abuse of powers. Moreover, they also promote other goals of national constitutions, such as non-inflationary economic growth or public choices of more proportionate internal policy instruments for the given economic or social policy objectives.[732]

In short, liberal principles are the very ideas of democratic constitutions and the liberal international trade rules. The democratic constitutions guarantee the political and economic liberalization and thereby simultaneously protect the freedoms and property rights of individuals. The liberal trade rules, which advocate for the economic liberalization at an international level, certainly also would contribute to the freedoms and property rights of individuals. In this regard, the liberal international trade rules have the same premise of values and pursue the same objectives as do democratic constitutions. To some extent, such trade rules have constitutional features.

b) *Integrating Liberal International Trade Rules into Domestic Constitutional Systems*

Liberal international trade rules are not only designed by virtue of liberal principles, upon which most of the democratic constitutions rest. Additionally, Petersmann found liberal international trade rules contain provisions protecting individual rights, *inter alia* the "freedom of trade", and limiting the abuse of discretionary government powers.[733] The GATT/WTO is typical of these liberal trade rules. Plenty of the GATT/WTO provisions embody the constitutional principles set

730 See *supra* note 723, at 401.

731 See *supra* note 723, at 364.

732 See *supra* note 723, at 366.

733 See *supra* note 723, at 274-275; see also Petersmann, *National Constitutions and International Economic Law* in NATIONAL CONSTITUTIONS AND INTERNATIONAL ECONOMIC LAW 3, 15, 22, 49. (Meinhard Hilf & Ernst-Ulrich Petersmann eds., 1993).

forth in domestic constitutions and they can protect the rights of individuals, especially with regard to the freedom to trade with foreigners.[734] Furthermore, Petersmann did not perceive that the GATT/WTO could reach individual citizens only through the intermediation of states, not only because the traditional perception of the characteristic differences between a "federal order" and an "international order" is not particularly obvious in the contemporary international agreements. This is also because the international obligations are voluntary and self-imposed obligations of the states and by nature is the result of government actions.[735] If democratic constitutions demand that governments protect the free exercise of individual rights under the rule of law, then the international obligation to protect individual freedom of trade in transnational transitions, as products of the government action, must be presumed to protect rights of the domestic citizens by the constitutions.[736]

Petersmann further noted that the legal limitations of government powers set by domestic constitutions and the GATT/WTO could supplement each other. The domestic constitutions can provide the citizens only with freedoms and the other constitutional guarantees within the domestic legal systems. The freedoms and the constitutional guarantees for the citizens engaging in transnational trades, such as access to the foreign markets, can be effectively protected by reciprocal obligations among the states. By such means, the constitutional guarantees of non-discriminatory treatment can be effectively enlarged.[737] He argued that the effectiveness of the international agreements depends on the domestic constitutions and *vice versa*. In an economically interdependent world, the constitutional guarantees of equal freedoms, non-discrimination, and welfare-increasing policymaking would not effectively occur without the complementary international trade, monetary, and investment rules. The domestic constitutions otherwise could become partial constitutions.[738] The interpretation, application, and the observance of international trade rules are subject to the discretions of the governments, which were exactly the trade rules set to be constrained. The appropriate application and interpretation of the international trade rules can be secured only if the safeguards guaranteed by parliamentary legislation, the limited delegation of powers, and the judicial protection of individual rights also apply to the governmental discretion in the application and interpretation of such rules.[739]

734 See *supra* note 723, at 222-235.

735 See *supra* note 723, at 402.

736 See *supra* note 723, at 424.

737 See *supra* note 723, at 370.

738 See Ernst-Ulrich Petersmann, *Multilevel Constitutionalism and Judicial Protection of Freedom and Justice on the International Economic Law of the EC*, in CONTINUITY AND CHANGE IN EU LAW: ESSAYS IN HONOUR OF SIR FRANCIS JACOBS 338, 341 (Anthony Arnull et al. eds, 2008).

739 See *supra* note 723, at 371.

Petersmann concluded that the domestic constitutional guarantees of equal freedoms and property rights should justify a presumption in favor of direct effect of the GATT/WTO. These self-imposed international legal restraints on the discretionary trade powers of the governments tend to maximize equal freedoms, property rights, and economic welfare of domestic citizens.[740] He urged the courts to notice the connection between the observance of the GATT/WTO rules and fundamental rights guarantees of domestic citizens. Petersmann also suggested the recognition of freedom of trade as basic individual rights.[741]

In short, Petersmann took several steps to establish the ground for accepting direct effect of the GATT/WTO. First, he paralleled the non-discriminatory liberal trade rules, such as the GATT/WTO, with legal protection of equal freedoms and property rights, which are provided in domestic constitutions. In his view, such trade rules have premises and objectives similar to the domestic constitutions and may undertake constitutional functions. Then, he clarified that the obligations under such trade rules are not actually derived from alien rules, but from the self-imposing commitments. The line between international rules and domestic rules is therefore blurred. Finally, he concluded that the GATT/WTO rules, as the non-discriminatory liberal trade rules, may supplement domestic constitutions, particularly the control over trade policy.

1.1.2. Arguments Based on the Political Economy and Ordnungspolitik (Economic Governance)

Tumlir and Petersmann champion the direct effect of the WTO agreements on the grounds of economic theories.[742] This approach is conceivable, given that the justification for free trade regime was built on economic concepts and theories.[743] Meng also used the political economy, or, to be more specific, the "public-choice" theory, to illustrate why the application of the direct effect of WTO agreements is wishful. Although the liberalization of trade, even unilateral, is proven to be beneficial for the states; in reality, the states are reluctant to open their markets and extremely cautious about implementing liberal measures. This is because the pro-protectionist interest groups could better contribute to the interests of political parties than the less-organized consumer groups and exporters. Furthermore, the advantages of free trade are not imminent and depend on the cooperation of

740 See *supra* note 723, at 424.

741 See *supra* note 723, at 463.

742 Tumlir and Petersmann take economy theory to support the constitutionalization of international law. See Tumlir, *supra* note 716; Petersmann *supra* note 723, at 96 ff.

743 See Jackson et al., *supra* note 7, at 4 ff; Lester, *supra* note 134, at 45 ff.

other states.[744] Then comes what the economists call the "prisoner's dilemma." The states have to decide independently whether to take liberal or protectionist measures, while the best solution for all of them could be found through their cooperation. The states would tend to take protectionist measures, eventually causing all of the states to suffer from the disadvantages, because of the fear that their trade partners would take protectionist measures in return for their unilateral liberalization of trade.[745] Meng held that the dilemma could be solved, if the actions of the states could be regulated and therefore become predictable. This requires an international agreement, which would set forth a definite obligation of liberalization as well as its enforcement.[746] He maintained the Dispute Settlement Procedures can significantly reduce the flexibility of the WTO rules, which the European Commission and the ECJ have taken as an obstacle for the direct effect. In his view, the direct effect could support a stable system of international trade and impede the member states from leaning toward protectionism.[747]

Drexl, another advocate for the direct effect, agreed with Petersmann's opinion, but developed the arguments on the basis of the *Ordnungspolitik* (economic governance), which claims the states should create the legal, political, and institutional conditions for a functional free market and should maintain these conditions. However, individual participants of the market, not the policy makers, have the right to make the economic decisions.[748] In the light of the *Ordnungspolitik*, the direct effect is concerned with the essential legal framework for the function of a global free market, where the individuals may exercise their economic decisions beyond the boundaries of the states.[749] Drexl observed that the direct effect of international economic agreements is preliminarily acceptable under the *Ordnungspolitik*, because it could provide legal certainty of the rules of the market, by which the individual participants could predict the situation of the world market and then make their decisions. On the contrary, the discretionary implementation of the agreements would deprive the individual participants of

---

744 See Wener Meng *Gedanken zur Frage unmittelbarer Anwendung von WTO-Recht in der EG*, in RECHT ZWISCHEN UMBRUCH UND BEWAHRUNG: FESTSCHRIFT FÜR RUDOLF BERNHARDT 1063, 1080 (Berlin et. al. 1995).

745 See *id*, at 1081.

746 See *supra* note 744, at 1082.

747 See *supra* note 744, at 1085.

748 See Walter Eucken, *Die Wettbewerbungsordnung und ihre Verwirklichung*, 2 ORDO: JAHRBUCH FÜR DIE ORDNUNG VON WIRTSCHAFT UND GESELLSCHAFT 1, 36 ff. (1949); see generally, Erich Hoppmann, *Walter Euckens Ordnungsökonomik: heute*, 46 ORDO: JAHRBUCH FÜR DIE ORDNUNG VON WIRTSCHAFT UND GESELLSCHAF 41 (1995).

749 Josef Drexl, *Unmittelbare Anwendbarkeit des WTO- Rechts in globalen Privatrechtsordnung*, in Festschrift für Wolfgang Fikentscher zum 70. Geburtstag 822, 841 (Bernhard Großfeld et al., 1998).

the right of the economic decisions.[750] He further set forth the conditions in terms of *Ordnungspolitik* for the direct effect of the WTO agreements. First, the rules of the WTO agreements could serve as a basis for the constitution of the world economy. The WTO agreements prohibit the infringement of the principles of liberalization, while permitting exceptions based on social considerations. This is sufficient for Drexl to conclude the WTO agreements as being the legal framework that the *Ordnungspolitik* requires.[751] Second, the direct effect could contribute to the establishment of a constitution of international economy, if the WTO rules are enforceable and could stop the infringement of the member states. Drexl believed the Dispute Settlement Procedure has increased the enforceability of the WTO agreements.[752]

1.2. Arguments Against The Direct Effect of The WTO Agreements

The arguments in favor of direct effect emphasis the need for legalizing the implementation of the WTO agreements. The opponent of the direct effect would rather support the political branches to dominate the implementation of the WTO rules.

1.2.1. Policy Analysis on the Direct Effect

Jackson, one of the most prominent opponents of direct effect, deliberated upon the policy grounds for and against direct effect on the basis of empirical and pragmatic considerations. He summarized polices favoring direct effect as the following: enhancement of the effectiveness of international law; better assurance of the rights of individuals when the international agreement contains norms designed to apply to those individuals.[753] In the meantime, he also listed several "functional arguments" opposing direct effect, in particular, the democratic participation in the treaty-making process and the wishes of legislatures to tailor-make the implementation of international agreements. The legislatures may have other policy in mind; for example, they might want to clarify the ambiguity in the provisions of international agreements, or translate the text into their own official language, or even preserve the opportunity to breach the international

750 See *id*, at 843.

751 See *supra* note 749, at 846-847.

752 See *supra* note 749, at 848-849.

753 Jackson *supra* note14, 322 (1992).

agreements in its method of application.[754] Moreover, the flexibility in application of the international agreements, even if it implies deviations from the obligations, is preferable to the alternative of refusing to join the international agreement altogether.[755] There are also concerns about the asymmetry in the application of international agreements and the inconsistent interpretations of the international agreements by international and national courts.[756]

Jackson stressed that policy analysis cannot provide a definite and generalized answer to the direct effect. All the foregoing policy considerations are true in certain ways. The answer to direct effect would vary, depending on the actual situations in each state and factual context of the international agreement at issue.[757] In other words, the only rule is "never say never." Jackson, nevertheless, indicated that the key is the level of confidence that the policymakers and the citizens have in international institutions, relative to their national institutions. If the citizens trust international institutions and international agreements more than their own government, direct effect would be preferred as a check on their government. This also explains why individuals in autocratic states might prefer international agreements of human rights.[758] In reality, the states, especially the democratic states, would have more confidence in their own laws and legal system. The democratic states might have struggled for compromises of interests, which are finally drafted in the domestic law, and therefore would avoid actions that might upset those compromises. Considering this reality, Jackson stood against direct effect. At least for now, international agreements without the rigidity of implementation could further international cooperation more effectively. Instead of direct effect, there are other better ways to increase the effectiveness of international agreements, such as ensuring the democratic participation of citizens or improving the international dispute settlement system.[759]

There are other authors opposed to direct effect of the WTO agreements out of policy considerations. Particularly in the European Union, the attention is on the trade policy consideration, which the statement of Kuijper has clearly presented:

> [T]he party whose constitutional and judicial system does not know the mechanism of direct effect of treaty provisions – or worse still, specifically exclude such direct effect – places itself in such favourable position that it

754 See *id*, at 325.

755 See *id*; see also Trachtman, *supra* note 35, at 678.

756 See Jackson *supra* note14, at 327.

757 See Jackson *supra* note14, at 329, 338.

758 See Jackson *supra* note14, at 332.

759 See Jackson *supra* note14, at 340.

> becomes fundamentally unfair to its trading partners. In this way it shields itself against what was called above the most powerful enforcement mechanism for treaties, and its negotiators, when discussing interpretation and application of the treaty, arrive with free hands at the table, contrary to their counterparts from countries with direct effect, whose hands are tied by the interpretation of their courts.[760]

The direct effect of the WTO agreements, in this view, is not by nature unacceptable. The argument is a reflection of political realism. The direct effect is treated as the trade accession that could be acquiesced only through negotiations.

Another consideration is what Eeckhout called "judicial policy," which emphasizes that domestic courts are not the proper forum for the disputes concerning the implementations of the WTO agreements. These disputes might entail complicated problems and legal issues better solved at the international level.[761] For instance, direct effect does not necessarily guarantee that the courts of member states would interpret and enforce the WTO agreements in a way that the penal or the Appellate Body would agree. It would be a big problem to solve the conflicts between the national courts and between national courts and international tribunals. Cases could flood the national courts, forcing the courts to become day-to-day interpreters or enforcers of the WTO agreements.[762] A similar concern is whether domestic courts have the competence to interpret the WTO rules.[763] It is the Ministerial Conference and the General Council that have the exclusive authority of the interpretation of the WTO agreements.[764]

1.2.2. Democratic Deficit of the WTO Agreements

The arguments in the previous subsection are based on realist or pragmatic considerations. There are also normative arguments against direct effect. However, the direct effect *per se* is not criticized. The opponents rebut the more general idea of the constitutionalization of the WTO law. Krajewski, for example, illustrated in detail the shortcomings and flaws of the constitutionalization theory pro-

760 Jan Peter Kuijper, The New WTO Dispute Settlement System – The Impact on the European Community, 29 (6) JOURNAL OF WORLD TRADE 49, 64 (1995).

761 See Piet Eeckhout, *The Domestic Legal Status of the WTO Agreements: Interconnecting Legal Systems*, 34 (1) COMMON MARKET LAW REVIEW 11, 58 (1997); see also WOLFGANG BENEDEK, DIE RECHTSORDNUNG DES GATT AUS VÖLKERRECHTLICHER SICHT 87 (1990).

762 See Eeckhout, *supra* note 467.

763 See Engelberger, *supra* note 715, at 197.

764 Marrakesh Agreement IX:2.

moted by Petersmann.[765] Krajewski argued that the WTO agreements do not have the constitutional function of international law. The constitutional function of international agreements, in his view, is to limit the governance and law-making by fundamental material values of the society, which legitimates the governance and law-making in general.[766] The democratic deficit of the WTO agreements makes it constitutionally inappropriate to replace democratically-enacted national law with WTO agreements in any event. The combination of binding force and the democratic deficit is even more harmful to constitutional principles. Instead of the "second line of constitutional entrenchment", as Tumlir described,[767] the WTO agreements should be called as the "first line of constitutional endangerment."[768]

As shown below, the WTO agreements are perceived to be deficient in democratic legitimacy. The WTO, as an international norm, takes a more indirect approach to meet the democratic principle by keeping people "in chains."[769] Although the negotiators usually are not directly responsible to the constituencies, they are appointed by those depending on the elections. The agreements also must be ratified through domestic procedures. Theoretically, the WTO agreements will fulfill the requirements of democratic decision-making, insofar as the governments of members are democratic.[770] In reality, there is no effective democratic control, at a national level, over the negotiation and the conclusion of the WTO agreements.

First, the chains of delegations are quite long and opaque. It is questionable that individuals can actually substantially influence the delegations. The WTO negotiations were confidential. The public usually did not know the actual positions taken by their governments and faced *faits accomplis*.[771] Besides, the chain could be longer than expected in practice. For instance, Article 3 of the SPS agreement urges that the members harmonize their sanitary or phytosanitary measures by adopting the international standards. If the member states want to take measures with standards higher than the international ones, they have to provide scientific justification or risk assessment. In *EC-Hormones*, the Appel-

765 See generally, Markus Krajewski, Verfassungsperspektiven und Legitimation des Rechts der Welthandelsorganisation (WTO) 202 ff. (2001).

766 Markus Krajewski, *Democratic Legitimacy and Constitutional Perspectives of WTO Law*, 35 (1) JOURNAL OF WORLD TRADE 167, 175 (2001).

767 Tumlier, *supra* note 716, at 80.

768 See Krajewski, *supra* note 766, at 183.

769 See Robert O. Keojane & Joseph S. Nye, *The Club Model of Multilateral Cooperation and Problems of Democratic Legitimacy*, in EFFICIENCY, EQUITY, AND LEGITIMACY: THE MULTILATERAL SYSTEM AT THE MILLENNIUM 264, 275 (ROGER B. PORTER ET AL. EDS, 2001).

770 See *id*; also James Bacchus, *A Few Thoughts on Legitimacy, Democracy, and the WTO*, in REFORMING THE WORLD TRADING SYSTEM: LEGITIMACY, EFFICIENCY AND DEMOCRATIC GOVERNANCE 429, 431 (Ernst Ulrich Petersmann ed., 2005).

771 See Keojane & Nye, *supra* note 769, at 266.

late Body further based its decision on the Codex Alimentarius Commission (hereafter the CAC), which was established jointly by the Food and Agriculture Organization of the United Nations and the World Health Organization.[772] The international standards, to some extent, will become the rules substantially governing the level of the sanitary or phytosanitary protections.[773] In this context, the democratic link between the rule maker (e.g., the CAC) and those affected by these rules is even weaker.[774]

Second, the parliaments have little chance to participate in the Uruguay Round negotiations and review the results of the negotiations. Unless the WTO agreements were ratified by referendum, the WTO rules could hardly have substantial democratic legitimacy at a national level. For instance, the parliaments in the European Union and the United States have faced the difficulties of supervising the results of the Uruguay Round negotiations. In the European Union, the legislative bodies, the Council, and the European Parliament did not play decisive roles in the decision-making procedures. The Council could have issued negotiating directives, which would restrict the margin of Commission's discretion on negotiation. Except for the negotiations on agriculture, the Council actually did not issue any formal negotiating directives.[775] The European Parliament has monitored the negotiations and made its view known to the Commission, whereas the European Parliament was kept from substantially intervening in the negotiations.[776] The legislative bodies, especially the European Parliament, minimized their involvement in the negotiations to avoid three-way negotiations among the Commission, the Council, and the European Parliament, which would have decreased the ability and flexibility of the Community in the negotiations.[777] In other words, the democratic participation was intentionally omitted in the negotiations of the WTO agreements. Moreover, the legislative bodies could not substantially review the results of the Uruguay Round negotiations. The European Parliament was given only two months to review the thousands of WTO provisions. The Council and the member states similarly had not much

---

772 See Appellate Body Report on *EC-Measures Affecting Meat and Meat Products (Hormones)*, para. 201 ff., WT/DS26/AB/R, WT/DS48/AB/R (Jan.16, 1998).

773 See Meinhard Hilf & Matthias Reuß, *Verfassungsfragen lebensmittelrechtlicher Normierung*, 1997 ZEITSCHRIFT FÜR DAS GESAMTE LEBENSMITTELRECHT 289, at 294-295 (1997).

774 See Meinhard Hilf & Matthias Reuß, *Verfassungsfragen lebensmittelrechtlicher Normierung*, 1997 ZEITSCHRIFT FÜR DAS GESAMTE LEBENSMITTELRECHt 289, at 297 (1997).

775 See Van den Bossche, *supra* note 362, at 56-59.

776 See *id*, at 69-72.

777 See Pieter Jan Kuijper, *The EC's Common Commercial Policy: Which Way the Swing of the Pendulum*, 88 AMERICAN SOCIETY OF INTERNATIONAL LAW PROCEEDINGS 294,297 (1994).

time to consider whether to accept the WTO agreements.[778] The legislative bodies deliberated on the content of the WTO agreements in a latter stage; that is, in the process of the legislation implementing the WTO agreements.[779] The democratic participation actually occurred after the WTO agreements were adopted. In the United States, the Congress could effectively oversee the trade policy.[780] However, the decision-making power of the WTO-relevant issues has significantly shifted from the legislative branch to the executive branch because of the fast-track procedure, under which the US Congress authorized the negotiations and implemented the WTO agreements.[781] Under this procedure, Congress can only approve or reject the implementations Bill of the WTO rules as a whole.[782] Furthermore, the fast-track process is ultimately less open to public debate than the normal legislative process. The fast-track process also allows for that the last-minute deals struck prior to the submission of the implementations Bill. These deals actually are not subject to Congressional and public discussion.[783] In short, the fast-track process was a way of insulating the WTO agreements from the direct political pressures of the normal legislative process. The anti-democratic features of the fast-track process are the deliberate efforts of the executive branch, and are meant to limit certain forms of political access to the decision-making process of trade policy.[784]

Third, the parliaments only have a spurious choice between accepting the WTO agreements as a whole and withdrawing from the multilateral legal system.[785] A rule-oriented system is more advantageous for medium and small members. For instance, the legislators of Taiwan ratified the WTO agreements, although they did not even have the chance to scrutinize these agreements and might not be contented with them.[786] Such a dilemma is common to the parliaments of the member states. Most of the parliaments do not really have the means to exert perceptible

---

778 See Van den Bossche, *supra* note 362, at 79 and 81.

779 History of the implementation of the WTO agreements by the EU, see *id*, at 84-92.

780 See Leebron, *supra* note 231, at 181-197.

781 See Slaughter *supra* note 233.

782 See Part I, Section 1.1.3.1. *supra*.

783 See Leebron, *supra* note 231, at 203-204.

784 See Robert E. Hudec, *Comment on "The Club Model of Multilateral Cooperation and Problems of Democratic Legitimacy"*, in Efficiency, Equity, and Legitimacy: The Multilateral System at the Millennium 295, 297 (Roger B. Porter et. al. eds., 2001).

785 See Gail E. Evans, Law Making under the Trade Constitution: A Study in Legislating by World Trade Organization 205 (2000).

786 See the second reading of the Protocol of Accession to the WTO, 90 (57) LEGISLATIVE YUAN GAZETTE 4, at 15-16.

influence on the WTO negotiations.[787] The parliaments will lose some of their function as legislators, if they are bound to accept the result of the negotiations.[788]

At the international level, the WTO does not take any measures to compensate for the democratic deficit at a national level. The parliaments do not have access to the ongoing negotiations under the WTO. The WTO rules cannot directly gain substantial democratic authorizations from the parliaments. Furthermore, the decision-making process of the WTO does not meet democratic principles. [789] First, The WTO does not have such a forum, where the necessary balancing of private and public interests of various kinds can take place in a way similar to the bargaining in the national parliaments.[790] In principle, the WTO focuses more on trade issues. The member states, not the WTO itself, would balance trade-related rights or interests with other economic and social rights and needs. The WTO will involve itself in the assessment on such a balance, only if it is brought up to the Panel or the Appellate Body. However, the Panel and the Appellate Body are not political forums; they are judicial institutions. Second, the WTO also fails to meet the requirement that the decision-making process should be transparent and based on deliberation and rational discourse.[791] Documents of negotiations, documents relating to working parties on accession, and minutes of meetings are confidential until the procedure at issue has completed.[792] The written submissions to the Panel and the deliberations of the Panel are also confidential, in principle.[793] The public has access to the information after the actions or the measures are actually adopted.[794] Besides, the negotiators reach the solution by

---

787 See Christophe Bellmann & Richard Gerster, *Accountability in the World Trade Organization*, 30 (6) JOURNAL OF WORLD TRADE 31, 51-53 (1996); Reports of different countries, see generally IMPLEMENTING THE URUGUAY ROUND (John H. Jackson & Alan O. Sykes ed., 1997).

788 Bellmann & Gerster, *id*, at 54.

789 Requirements of democracy at international level see Americo Beviglia Zampetti, *Democratic Legitimacy in the World trade Organization: The Justice Dimension*, 37 (1) JOURNAL OF WORLD TRADE 105, 109-118 (2003).

790 See Zampetti, *id*, at 122; see also Mavroidis, *supra* note 12, at 195.

791 See *id*; also Michael Zürn, *Democratic Governance beyond the Nation-State: The EU and Other International Institutions*, 6 (2) EUROPEAN JOURNAL OF INTERNATIONAL RELATION 183,186 (2000). See also Steve Charnoviz, *The WTO and Cosmopolitics*, in REFORMING THE WORLD TRADING SYSTEM, LEGITIMACY, EFFICIENCY AND DEMOCRATIC GOVERNANCE 437, 441 (Ernst Ulrich Petersmann ed., 2005).

792 General Council, *Procedures for the Circulation and Derestriction of WTO documents*, WT/L/160/Rev.1 (Jul. 18, 1996), revised version, WT/L/452 (May 14, 2002).

793 Paragraph 3 of the Appendix 3 to the DSU.

794 See Gabrielle Marceau & Peter N. Pedersen, Is the WTO Open and Transparent? A Discussion of the Relationship of the WTO with Non-governmental Organizations and Civil Society's Claim for More Transparency and Public Participation, 33 (1) JOURNAL OF WORLD TRADE 5.31 (1999).

bargaining, not by rational arguments. They must have something to trade for the concessions from their counterparts. Deliberation and rational discourse do not dominate in the decision-making process of the WTO.[795]

In sum, the democratic deficit of the WTO could be described from two aspects. At a national level, the WTO rules meet the democratic principles only in form. The parliaments of members have limited control over the content of the WTO rules. At an international level, the WTO does not provide sufficient means to secure democracy in the WTO decision-making process. Denial of direct effect should be viewed as a mechanism to reinforce the democratic legitimacy of the WTO rules.[796]

1.2.3. The Inconsistencies with the Constitutional Principles

Von Bogdandy maintains the direct effect of the international agreement is a purely domestic matter and should be reviewed under domestic constitutional principles.[797] However, his arguments are not based on dualism. He considered that, as the theory of legal pluralism[798] has correctly described, international and national legal systems are not strictly separated. Rather, there is an interaction between these two legal systems. While the international agreements address domestic issues, which often are dealt with by domestic laws, the internal effects of these agreements are mediated or, in von Bogdandy's term, "coupled" by the actions of political and judicial institutions. The direct effect of international agreement is one of the "couplings" between the two systems.[799] Out of legitimacy considerations, von Bogdandy argued that the doctrine of direct effect must be

795 See Krajewski, *supra* note 766, at 177.

796 See Joel P. Trachtman, *Bananas, Direct Effect and Compliance*, 10 (4) EUROPEAN JOURNAL OF INTERNATIONAL LAW 655, 677 (1999).

797 See Armin von Bogdandy, Pluralism, Direct Effect, and the Ultimate Say: on the Relationship between International and Domestic Constitutional Law, 6 (3-4) INTERNATIONAL JOURNAL OF CONSTITUTIONAL LAW 397, 398 (2008).

798 The legal pluralism see generally Franz von Benda-Beckmann, *Who's Afraid of Legal Pluralism?*, 47 JOURNAL OF LEGAL PLURALISM 37 (2002); Keebet von Benda-Beckmann, *Globalization and Legal Pluralism*, 4 INTERNATIONAL LAW FORUM DU DROIT INTERNATIONAL 19 (2002); Paul Schiff Berman, *Global Legal Pluralism*, 80 SOUTHERN CALIFORNIA REVIEW 1155 (2007); William Burke-White, *International Legal Pluralism*, 25 MICHIGAN JOURNAL OF INTERNATIONAL LAW 963 (2004).

799 Bogdandy, *supra* note 797, at 401.

construed as implementing a balance of constitutional principles such as international cooperation, democratic government, legal certainty, or subsidiarity.[800]

Von Bogdandy argued that granting direct effect to the WTO agreements would upset the constitutional principles. He acknowledged international cooperation as a constitutional principle supporting direct effect. Nevertheless, he considered that this principle can only serve the international agreements with goals of economic integration or harmonization, neither of which the WTO agreements have. Besides, direct effect also cannot provide legal certainty for the national producers, for the producers cannot be certain whether their foreign competitors would follow the WTO rules to the same extent as they do.[801] Furthermore, the direct effect of the WTO agreements could seriously compromise the principle of legal equality. There is no mechanism in the WTO to ensure the uniform application by the member states.[802] Reverse discrimination, which is usually found in the cases concerning the SPS agreement, infringes on the principle of legal certainty.[803] Moreover, the WTO agreements are not qualified as granting individual economic rights or human rights. Von Bogdandy argued that international agreements need particular justification for granting individual economic rights. The EU treaty has established such justification by emphasizing the normative aim of a common market. The WTO actually does not have the normative aim of a global market that should be realized through the WTO agreements. Thus, the justification for the individual economic rights in the EU context is not applicable in the WTO context, even if the WTO agreements contain market-oriented provisions that are highly similar to those in the EU treaty.[804] For the foregoing reasons, von Bogdandy objected to the direct effect of the WTO agreements.

1.3. An Intermediate Position for the Direct Effect of the WTO Agreements

In addition to the polar opposite positions, some authors have tried to find a third position for the direct effect of the WTO agreements. Eeckhout and Cottier have proposed two different solutions.

---

800 Bogdandy, *supra* note 797, at 403.

801 See Bogdandy, *supra* note 797, at 405.

802 See Bogdandy, *supra* note 797, at 406.

803 See Bogdandy, *supra* note 797, at 411.

804 See Bogdandy, *supra* note 797, at 408-409.

1.3.1. Intermediation through the Panel and Appellate Body Report

Eeckhout held, on one hand, that full direct effect of the WTO agreement is totally undesirable by recognizing the policy concerns against direct effect. On the other hand, for the following reasons, it would be just as inadequate that the courts of member states ignore the WTO rules.[805] First, the Dispute Settlement mechanism might not effectively enforce the WTO rules. Second, the WTO agreements cannot be completely separated from the rights of individuals, although the contracting parties were and are not intended to form any meaningful rights.[806] Third, the courts assume the role to ensure the enforcement, stability, coherence, and review of all political decisions, including those taking place at the international level.[807] The major problem is under what conditions WTO agreements should intrude into the domestic legal system.

Eeckhout proposed that the direct effect be granted to the adopted panel and Appellate Body reports. When panel or the Appellate Body finds an infringement of the WTO agreements, the obligation of the member state becomes rather specific and fixed. In such a circumstance, the discretions members have are also significantly restrained. Many arguments would no longer be sustainable; such arguments include, in particular, the argument of flexibility, the doubt of the precision of the firmness of the WTO law, the problem about the division of powers between legislature and judiciary, and the concerns with respect to the appropriate dispute settlement forum.[808] In the context of European Union law, this suggestion has been clearly turned down by the ECJ. Eeckhout then proposed the rulings of the panel and the Appellate Body not *per se* directly effective, but do constitute the "particular obligations," which the European Union intends to implement, and indirectly become the laws the ECJ would apply.[809] However, the ECJ recently has already excluded such possibility.[810]

---

805 See Eeckhout, *supra* note 467, at 102. The flaws of the Dispute Settlement Procedures see Introduction, section 0.3 *supra*.

806 See Eeckhout, *supra* note 467, at 103.

807 See *id.*

808 See Eeckhout, *supra* note 761, at 53-55.

809 See Eeckhout, *supra* note 467, at 107.

810 See Part I, section 1.2.2.2 (d) *supra*.

1.3.2. The Theory of Justiciabilty

Cottier has set forth a theory on whether the international agreements, in particular the WTO agreements, should have direct effect. He held that the issue should be considered purely in the context of domestic constitution.[811] The direct effect actually concerns a constitutional fundamental issue (i.e., the allocation of powers between different branches of government). The core question of the direct effect is whether the international norms are addressed to the legislature for further elaboration and implementation, or whether the courts may assert such tasks.[812] In other words, it is a decision regarding who should undertake and ensure the implementation of international agreements.

The answer lies in the constitutional status and the competence of courts in a constitutional system.[813] The competence of the courts is defined by what Cottier calls "the justiciabilty." The justiciabilty should be assessed on the basis of the rule of law; particularly, the principle of legality.[814] The principle of legality is a tool of the allocation of powers that is implemented in the law-making between legislative and executive branches.[815] This principle incorporates the principles of separation of powers and democratic rules. The criteria for the power distribution are based on suitability and the aptitude of different government branches by virtue of their respective authority, legitimacy, composition, and working procedures.[816] Cottier suggested applying the principle of legality, not only in defining the relationship between the executive and legislative branches, but also in defining the province of the courts in international economic law.[817] He observed that the principle of legality does not mean that the legislature makes all basic decisions. Rather, the principle of legality recognizes that other government branches may make important decisions in their respective provinces.[818] In this light, it would

---

811 See also Armin von Bogdandy, Pluralism, Direct Effect, and the Ultimate Say: On the Relationship between International and Domestic Constitutional Law, 6 (3-4) INTERNATIONAL JOURNAL OF CONSTITUTIONAL LAW 397, 403 (2008).

812 See Cottier, *supra* note 6, at 321; See also Daniel Thürer, *WTO- Teilordnung im System des Völker-und Europarechts* in GATT 94 UND DIE WELTHANDELSORGANISATION: HERAUSFORDERUNG FÜR DIE SCHWEIZ UND EUROPA 41,51 (Daniel Thürer & Stephan Kux eds, 1996).

813 See Cottier, *supra* note 6, at 323.

814 See Thomas Cottier, *The Judge in International Economic Relations*, in Economic Law and Justice in Times of Globalization. Festschrift für Carl Baudenbacher 99,111 (M. Monti, et al eds, 2007).

815 See Daniel Wüger, Anwendbarkeit und Justiziabilität völkerrechtlicher Normen im schweizerischen Recht: Grundlagen, Methoden und Kriterien 115 (2005).

816 See Cottier, *supra* note 6, at 325.

817 See Cottier, *supra* note 814, at 109.

818 See Cottier, *supra* note 6, at 327.

be crucial whether the provisions of an international agreement are so precise that no more political decision is required. Cottier emphasized that there would be no difference between the domestic and international law in terms of the boundary of judicial power. The courts would refrain from granting individuals rights based on highly programmatic constitutional norms. They would equally refuse the direct effect of international norms with similar features. If basic democratic decisions have been made, the court should accept the direct effect of international agreements as much as the court would give effect to domestic legislations.[819] Besides the principle of legality, the role of courts in terms of protecting rights of individuals or the interests weakly represented in political process is another criterion for assessing the province of the courts. This explains why the elaboration of open-textured norms of human rights is usually entrusted to courts.[820] The direct effect of international agreements depends on an overall assessment on whether the courts by virtue of their composition, procedures, and legitimacy should engage in implementing international agreements under the context and the facts of that particular case. In other words, it is determined on a case-by-case basis.[821]

According to the theory of justiciabilty, it cannot be concluded in general terms whether the principle and rules of the WTO as a whole may have direct effect.[822] The formal structure or the text of the norms could be considered, but would no longer be the decisive element. It should be taken into consideration that the involvement of the court could balance the disproportionate influences of certain groups in the political process. If the interests of the importers, consumers are poorly represented in the political process, the courts should play a more active role in implementing the international economic law.[823] Cottier suggested that at least two kinds of provisions could have direct effect. The first set is the administrative and judicial protections for the procedural rights (e.g., Article X of the GATT, Article III of the GATS, and Article 63 of the TRIPS). These provisions rarely entail policy choices; instead, they simply elaborate or repeat the principles of laws established in the national and international frameworks. They would rather belong to the realm of law-making by the judicial branch and thus by nature suitable for the direct effect. Another set contains provisions of the fundamental principles of non-discrimination and their exceptions. The non-discrimination principles, the MFN, and the national treatment, could be compa-

---

819 See Cottier, *supra* note 6, at 326.

820 *Id.*

821 *Id.*

822 See Cottier, *supra* note 6, at 327.

823 See Thomas Cottier, International Trade Law: The Impact of Justiciabilty and Separations of Powers in EC Law, 5 (2) EUROPEAN CONSTITUTIONAL LAW REVIEW 307, 326 (2009).

rable with the protection of equality and universal standards of human rights. However, acceptance of the direct effect of these provisions would reinforce the market access rights and a high level of global integration. Such implications concern policy choices; therefore, the involvement of the legislative branch appears significant.[824] In other words, these provisions should be subject both to the political and judicial branches. These provisions *per se* may belong to the province of the courts, while their implications make the consent of the legislature necessary. Cottier concluded that it is desirable to conduct international negotiations for the direct effect of these provisions.

In summary, Cottier held that the protection and the relief for the individual rights, which are the domain of courts, are significant elements for accepting the direct effect. The courts should intervene in implementing WTO rules, if these rules provide substantial or procedural protections for individual rights.

1.4. Summary and Preliminary Observations

The debates about the direct effect of the WTO agreements focus on the distribution of the competence regarding the implementation of the WTO agreements. Advocates of direct effect maintain the courts of the member states should be involved in the application and the interpretations of the WTO rules within their domestic legal systems. On the contrary, the opponents insist the political departments, i.e., the legislatures and the executive, should have exclusive competence of the implementation. Both sides have provided normative and pragmatic arguments.

From the normative perspective, direct effect issue is deliberated under constitutional principles and doctrines. Direct effect should be granted, because the constitutional guarantees of freedom of trade could serve as the ground for judicial control over trade policy. The GATT/WTO could supplement the function of the domestic constitutional system, particularly in terms of constraining the governments' discretion on foreign trade. The adversaries pointed out that the direct effect is an endangerment to constitutional principles.

The pragmatic arguments emphasize the economic and the policy considerations. The grounds for granting direct effect are summarized as following: a) avoiding protectionism by increasing the mutual trust between the member states; b) ensuring the rights of the market participants to make the economic decisions; c) the enhancement of the effectiveness of international law; and d) better assurance of the rights of individuals when the international agreement

824 See Cottier, *supra* note 6, at 329.

contains norms designed to apply to those individuals. The grounds denying direct effect are provided in particular: a) the wishes of legislatures to tailor-make the implementation of the WTO agreements; b) the disincentive to joint the WTO agreements; c) the asymmetric positions of the member states in trade negotiations; d) the inconsistent applications and interpretations of the WTO agreements; and e) the overburden for the domestic courts. The authors in the intermediate position acknowledge arguments of both sides. However, they are not really neutral on the issue, but favor the direct effect of the WTO agreements. They consider that only part of the WTO agreements should have the direct effect. What they care about are the conditions for the direct effect.

The arguments pro and con have revealed three questions, which are significant for the determination of the direct effect of the WTO agreements. The first one is whether the WTO agreements could be construed to grant individual rights to stand against the governmental power of trade affairs. Another is whether the WTO agreements are legitimate, in terms of democracy or constitutional principles, so as to be applied by domestic courts. The third question is whether the direct effect is practically possible or acceptable. The arguments mentioned previously actually do not fully solve these questions.

The arguments in favor the direct effect do not provide a satisfying ground for recognizing the individual rights. The theory of constitutionalization is built on the presumption that individuals have “freedom of trade,” which is a right limiting the abuse of the governmental power of foreign trade. However, the “freedom of trade” is not recognized as a right either in constitutions or the WTO agreements. There is the same problem with the “right to make economic decisions.” The theory of justiciabilty is rather ambiguous in this regard. It seems to me that individuals are recognized to have procedural rights or rights comparable with human rights under the WTO agreements. But the theory of justiciabilty, in my understanding, denies these rights alone could serve as a legal basis to defend against the governmental power of trade affairs. If a right of an individual cannot entitle him or her to certain protections, what is the point of recognizing it as a right?

The arguments criticizing the democratic legitimacy of the WTO agreements seem to forget that not all the domestic norms can satisfy these requirements for legitimacy. For instance, administrative regulations are not democratically more legitimate than the WTO agreements. The regulations are not subject to the approval of the legislatures and not necessarily drafted in the democratic decision-making procedures. This does not stop the national courts from applying the administrative regulations. The WTO agreements are even more democratically legitimate than the administrative regulations, since the agreements are ratified by the parliaments. The democratic deficit of the WTO agreements could not support the argument that the national courts should not apply the WTO agreements. In addition, the arguments based on legal certainty and principle of legal equality are rather questionable. The contents of the WTO agreements do not upset the principle of equality or legal certainty. The WTO agreements have never demanded more favorable treatments to the imported goods or services. The reverse discrimination is just an incidental consequence of the application of the WTO agreements. Also, the uncertainty of the domestic producers cannot be attributed exclusively to the direct effect of the WTO agreements. The producers are not uncertain about the content of the WTO rules, but about whether the other states would faithfully apply the WTO rules. The states unwilling to adhere to the WTO rules should take the blame.

Whether the direct effect is practically possible or acceptable is important for actually determining the direct effect of the WTO agreements. However, the practical difficulties should not be a decisive argument against direct effect. Just because the world is a certain way does not mean that it should be that way. For instance, lack of reciprocity in the implementation could be the exact reason for negotiating direct effect in a multilateral system.[825] The practical problems of direct effect might no longer exist, if the legal, political, or economic situations in the member states or in the international community have changed. The arguments focusing on the factual problems of the direct effect can only explain why direct effect could not be accepted at the present time. They cannot tell whether direct effect should be granted in the future.

In the next chapter, the author will analyze the key questions raised by the arguments presented thus far.

---

825 See Cottier, *supra* note 6, at 315.

Chapter 2: Assessments on the Grounds For and Against

Recognizing and refusing direct effect are both consistent with Article XVI: 4 of the Marrakesh Agreement.[826] It should be reiterated that the contracting parties did not express their wills about the direct effect issue.[827] The question explored in this chapter is whether further restraints on the discretion on implementation should be imposed on the members; in particular, through the intervention of domestic courts on the implementation of the WTO agreements. If the discretion of implementation should be confined, there should be further clarification for Article XVI: 4 of the Marrakesh Agreement or an additional obligation attached to the substantial obligations. Either method requires political consensus and negotiations. The panel and the Appellate Body do not have the mandate to give general and definite interpretation of the WTO agreements.

It should be noted that the WTO agreements actually contain quite a number of the specific and unconditional obligations.[828] They are well presented in prohibitive rules, rules of non-discrimination, and rules of establishing liberties, such as prohibition of quantitative restrictions (GATT XI), MFN and national treatment (GATT I & III), and the tariff bindings (GATT II). These provisions are capable of having direct effect.[829] The precision of the provisions of the

826 See Panel Report on China-Intellectual Property Right, supra note 4; Panel Report on US-Section 301 Trade Act, supra note 2.

827 See Rolf Schwartmann, Private im Wirtschaftsvölkerrecht 148 (2005).

828 See Cottier & Nadakavukaren *supra* note 19, at 92; Lukas Engelberger, DIE UNMITTELBARE ANWENDBARKEIT DES WTO-RECHTS IN DER SCHWEIZ, 183 ff. (2004); John H. Jackson, *U.S. Constitutional Principles and Foreign Trade Law and Policy* in NATIONAL CONSTITUTIONS AND INTERNATIONAL ECONOMIC LAW 65,81 (Meinhard Hilf & Ernst-Ulrich Petersmann eds, 1993); Ernst-Ulrich Petersmann, CONSTITUTIONAL FUNCTIONS AND CONSTITUTIONAL PROBLEMS OF INTERNATIONAL ECONOMIC LAW, 115-117 (1991); Ernst-Ulrich Petersmann, *National Constitutions and International Economic Law*, in NATIONAL CONSTITUTIONS AND INTERNATIONAL ECONOMIC LAW 3,49 (Meinhard Hilf & Ernst-Ulrich Petersmann eds,1993); Meng, *supra* note 426, at 1085; Roul Duggal,TRIPS-ÜBEREINKOMMEN UND INTERNATIONALES URHEBERRECHT, 110 (2001).

829 Pierre Pescatore, Free World Trade and the European Union-The Reconciliation of Interests and Revision of Dispute Resolution Procedures in the Framework of the WTO, in FREE WORLD TRADE AND THE EUROPEAN UNION 9,10 (Antonio Pérez van Kappel& Wolfgang Heusel eds., 2000).

WTO agreements would not be a major problem for the courts to apply them directly, particularly the provisions setting specific and unconditional obligations.[830]

In the previous chapters, the author has explored both the practices of the member states and the literature to find the key elements that touch upon the direct effect of WTO agreements. The discussions of direct effect of the WTO agreements did not use the well-accepted criteria for the direct effect of international agreements.[831] Rather, the focus of the discussions is the rationale behind these criteria. The practices of the given member states have shown several key considerations for the determination of the direct effect of the WTO agreements. The United States rejected direct effect out of concern for the insufficient participation of the Congress in the negotiations and the drafting of the WTO agreements, as well as the limits on the autonomy of the United States. The European Union and China refused to grant direct effect in order to maintain flexibility in the implementation of the WTO agreements *vis-à-vis* their trade partners. In other words, they worry about lack of reciprocity in the implementation of the WTO rules. Taiwan would support direct effect, hoping for a more effective legal system of world trade and de-politicalizing the international trade relations. In the literature, three questions are found to be particularly important. The first one is whether the WTO agreements could be construed to grant individual rights to stand against the governmental power of trade affairs. Another is whether the WTO agreements are legitimate, in terms of democracy or constitutional principles, so as to be applied by domestic courts. The third question is whether direct effect is practically possible or acceptable. There are some overlaps between the considerations of the given member states and the questions

---

830 Detail illustrations of these provisions, see ROLF SCHWARTMANN, PRIVATE IM WIRTSCHAFTSVÖLKERRECHT 471-500 (2005). Nonetheless, a number of provisions call for further negotiations or implementing measures. Such provisions obviously cannot be directly effective.

831 There are volumes of literature on the crtieria for the effect of international norms in domestic legal system, *e.g.* see generally ALBERT BLECKMANN, BEGRIFF UND KRITERIEN DER INNERSTAATLICHEN ANWENDBARKEIT VÖLKERRECHTLICHE VERTRÄGE (1970); ARNOLD KOLLER, DIE UNMITTELBARE ANWENDBARKEIT VOLKERRECHTLICHER VERTRAGE UND DES EWG-VERTRAGES IM INNERSTSATLICHEN BEREICH (1971); Charles H. III Dearborn, *The Domestic Legal Effect of Declarations That Treaty Provisions Are Not Self-Executing*, 57 (2) TEXAS LAW REVIEW, 233 (1979); Yuji Iwasawa, *The Doctrine of Self-Executing Treaties in the United States: A Critical Analysis*, 26 (3) VIRGINIA JOURNAL OF INTERNATIONAL LAW 627 (1985); Jordan Paust, *Self-Executing Treaties*, 82 (4) AMERICAN JOURNAL OF INTERNATIONAL LAW 760 (1998); Carlos Manuel Vizquez, *The Four Doctrines of Self-Executing Treaties*,89 (4) AMERICAN JOURNAL OF INTERNATIONAL LAW 695 (1995); GABY I. BUCHS, DAS PHÄNOMEN DER UNMITTELBARE ANWENDBARKEIT VÖLKERRECHTLICHER VERTRAGSBESTIMMUNGEN: AM BEISPIEL DER RECHTSPRECHUNG DER GERICHTE DEUTSCHLANDS, ÖSTERREICHS, DER SCHWEIZ UND DER VEREINIGTEN STAATEN, 31-41 (1993); PATRICK EDGAR HOLZER, DIE ERMITTLUNG DER INNERSTAATLICHEN ANWENDBARKEIT VÖLKERRECHTLICHER VERTRAGSBESTIMMUNGEN (1998).

raised in the literature. The concern for congressional participation in the negotiations and the drafting of the WTO agreements is the same as criticism about the democratic deficit of the WTO agreements. The request for reciprocity shows one of the practical difficulties for the direct effect. In this chapter, the author will appraise the considerations and the questions previously raised.

2.1. Ground for the Direct Effect I: Rights of Individuals under the WTO agreements

One of the requisites of the direct effect of an international agreement is that individuals are entitled to have rights under that agreement.[832] Quite a number of the provisions set forth specific and unconditional protections for individuals.[833] However, it is questionable whether these protections constitute rights for individuals. The rulings of the panel and Appellate Body are equivocal. In the case of *US-Section 301 Trade Act,* the panel carefully kept the question open.[834] It seems that there has to be justification for construing these provisions as creating rights for individuals.

2.1.1. Human Rights Dimension of the WTO Agreements

The advocates did not establish a convincing ground to read the provisions providing protections for individuals in that way.[835] Petersmann might have noticed the general "freedom of trade" lacks of textural support in the WTO agreements. He shifted to emphasize the analogy between human rights and the trade law. He argued that the rules ensuring free trade also have human rights implications.[836] By emphasizing the human rights implications, Petersmann claimed the protections for free trade as the rights of individuals.[837] He perceived the separation of human rights from the liberalization of trade was intended to avoid the political

---

832 See Jurisdiction of the Courts of Danzig, Advisory Opinion, paras 26, 37, 1928 P.C.I.J. (ser. B) No. 15 (Mar. 3). See also Case 26/62, *NV Algemene Transport-en Expeditie Onderneming van Gend & Loos v. Neth. Inland Revenue Admin.*, 1963 E.C.R. 1, 1963.

833 See Charnovitz, *supra* note 11, at 99; Rolf Schwartmann, *supra* note 827, Second Part, Ch. 2 (2005).

834 *Supra* note 2.

835 See Part II, section 1.4 *supra.*

836 See Ernst-Ulrich Petersmann, *Human Rights and International Economic Law in the Twenty First Century*, 4 JOURNAL OF INTERNATIONAL ECONOMIC LAW 3, 6-7 (2001).

837 See Deborah Z. Cass, The Constitutionalization of the World Trade Organization: Legitimacy, Democracy, and Community in the International Trading System 150-51 (2007).

debates on the meaning of human rights and facilitate functional intergovernmental cooperation.[838] Human rights have gradually become universally accepted, and fundamental principles of human rights form customary or general international law. Further, the national governments and international organizations are obligated to respect human rights.[839] Now it seems no longer necessary to disregard the human rights aspect of the affairs undertaken by organizations that do not aim at human rights protection.[840]

Additionally, the WTO rules as well as human rights, in Petersmann's view, have the same underlying values, such as individual freedoms, equal opportunities, and rule of law.[841] He argued the goal of the WTO agreements, namely maintaining the free market, can be justified in terms of human dignity – the very origin of human rights – if human dignity is understood from the perspective of Kant.[842] For Kant, the capacity of human beings to choose their own actions, or free will, in a manner respecting equal autonomy and maximizing equal freedoms of all others, was grounded in human dignity. Human dignity and human liberty are indivisible or two sides of one token. Human dignity reveals itself in the moral and rational acts of human choice.[843] Respecting human dignity requires treating a person as an end in him/herself, as well as respecting his/her free choices and legal protection for maximizing equal freedoms of individuals.[844] All participants in the free market are presumed reasonable and could make the best choice for themselves. The market is governed by "the invisible hand," which is driven by the various needs of the participants. No participant is supposed to unilaterally decide the conditions for exchanging the economic resources. In

838 See Ernst-Ulrich Petersmann, Human Rights, Markets and Economic Welfare: Constitutional Functions of the Emerging UN Human Rights Constitution, in INTERNATIONAL TRADE AND HUMAN 29, 46 (Federick M. Abbort et al. eds., 2006).

839 SeeErnst-Ulrich Petersmann, Time for Integrating Human Rights into the Law of Worldwide Organization 14-15, (Jean Monnet Working Paper 7/01,2001) http://centers.law.nyu.edu/jean monnet/papers/01/012301.html (last visited Apr. 12,2011); see also Brownlie, *supra* note 51,at 562.; U.N. Econ. & Soc. Council, Commission on Human Rights, Sub-commission on the Promotion and the Protection of Human rights, 53rd. Sess., 12th mtg., para. 24, E/CN.4/Sub.2/ 2001/SR.12 (Aug. 14, 2001).

840 *Supra* note 838.

841 Ernst-Ulrich Petersmann, *The WTO Constitution and Human Rights*, 3 (1) JOURNAL OF INTERNATIONAL ECONOMIC LAW 19, 22 (2000).

842 See Ernst-Ulrich Petersmann, Human Rights, Markets and Economic Welfare: Constitutional Functions of the Emerging UN Human Rights Constitution, in INTERNATIONAL TRADE AND HUMAN 29, 31 (Federick M. Abbort et al. eds., 2006).

843 Immanuel Kant, GRUNDLEGUNG ZUR METAPHYSIK DER SITTEN 37, 64 (Wilhelm Weischedel eds, BA ed.,1968)

844 Immanuel Kant, DIE METAPHYSIK DER SITTEN, EINLEITUNG IN DIE RECHTSLEHRE, § B, 33 (Wilhelm Weischedel eds, AB ed., 1968)

other words, the rule of the market is determined collectively by the persons participating in the market in a mutually beneficial way. In a well-functioning free market, a person may decide the person to trade with, the objects of trade (e.g., labor, goods, properties), and the value of the trade object. In this light, the core of the market is nothing more than respect for personal autonomy. Protecting the free market also protects the freedom of individuals in the economic arena.[845]

2.1.2. Assessment of the Relation between Human Rights and WTO Agreements

By discovering the human rights dimension of the WTO agreements, Petersmann has shown a ground for the domestic courts to protect precise and unconditional WTO rules.[846] The human rights dimension of the WTO agreements could be a strong argument for direct effect, for in the human rights regime, the states are in a position in which their citizens could check the implementation of their international obligation.[847] The states have progressed from the sole competent norm-setters to the enforcers of international standards.

At first blush, the human rights dimension of the WTO agreements is minimal. It is also true that the human rights and the GATT/WTO rules are considered under different policy frameworks. Human rights are basically assumed to derive from human dignity.[848] The GATT/WTO aimed at global welfare (i.e., increasing prosperity worldwide and reducing poverty). However, Petersmann has correctly described the relation between human rights and the WTO agreements.

A considerable number of legal instruments relate to human rights. The focus here will be on the International Bill of Rights because they are more relevant to the WTO agreements. The International Bill of Rights includes the Universal Declaration of Human Rights (hereafter referred to as UDHR)[849], the International

845 See Petersmann, *supra* note 842, at 31-32.

846 See Petersmann, *supra* note 842, at 33-34.

847 See Stephan Hobe, Der offene Verfassungsstaat zwischen Souveränität und Interdependenz: Eine Studie zur Wandlung des Staatsbegriffs der deutschsprachigen Staatslehre im Kontext internationaler institutionalisierter Kooperation 230 (1998).

848 See *e.g.* the Preamble of Universal Declaration of Human Rights,para.1,GA Res. 217A, UN GAOR, 3d Sess. Pt 1, Resolution, at 71, UN Doc A/810 (Dec. 12, 1948); World Conference on Human Rights, June 14-25, 1993, *Vienna Decoration and Programme of Action*, Preamble, para. 2 ,UN doc. A/CONF.157/23 (July, 12, 1993).

849 Universal Declaration of Human Rights, G.A. Res. 217A, UN GAOR, 3d Sess. Pt 1, Resolution, UN Doc A/810 (Dec. 12, 1948).

Covenant on Civil and Political Rights (hereafter referred to as ICCPR)[850], and the International Covenant on Economic, Social, and Cultural Rights (hereafter referred to as ICESCR).[851]

The WTO rules and human rights actually share same objective. Both the human rights regime and the GATT/WTO rules are part of the scheme of peace-keeping after World War II.[852] As clarified in Article 55 of the UN Charter, "peaceful and friendly relations among nations" depend on respect for human rights, better standards of living, full employment, as well as social and economic progress.[853] The Preamble of the UDHR implies the close connection between "friendly relationship" and human rights, and reaffirms the task of the states to "promote social progress and better standards of life in larger freedom."[854] The GATT/WTO rules do not explicitly refer to peace or human rights, but generally aim at better standards of living and full employment. As part of the Bretton Woods system, the GATT/WTO was set to maintain world peace via mutually advantageous trade and economic policies. It is often forgotten that peacekeeping is an important objective of the GATT/WTO.[855]

Besides the common goal of peacekeeping, the values of human rights and the GATT/WTO rules share underlying values, in particular individual freedom,[856] non-discrimination,[857] rule of law,[858] access to courts,[859] and promotion of social welfare through peaceful cooperation among citizens.[860] They both are responses to the profound history of the totalitarianism entirely absorbing the individual and prescribe the boundaries of state actions and regulations.[861] The power and legitimacy of the GATT/WTO essentially could be based on the same underlying values as human rights, although the GATT/WTO relied on economic

850 International Covenant on Civil and Political Rights, Dec. 16, 1966, 999 UNTS 171 (enter into force Mar. 23, 1976).

851 International Covenant on Economic, Social and Cultural Rights, Dec. 16, 1966, 993 UNTS 3m (enter into force Jan. 3, 1976).

852 See John Jackson, Reflections on the Possible Research Agenda for Exploring the Relationship between Human Rights Norms and International Trade, in INTERNATIONAL TRADE AND HUMAN RIGHTS 19, 23 (Federick M. Abbort et al. eds., 2006).

853 Charter of United Nations, U.N.C.I.O. XV, 335, June 26, 1945.

854 Supra note 852.

855 Supra note 852.

856 *E.g.* Articles 8, 9,12,18,19 of ICCPR, Dec.16, 1966, 999 UNTS 171 (enter into force on Mar. 23, 1976).

857 *E.g.* Articles 2 and 26 of ICCPR.

858 *E.g.* Articles 10, 11 of UDHR, Articles 14 and 19 of ICCPR.

859 *E.g.* Article 14 of ICCPR.

860 Provisions reflecting these principles, see subsection *c) infra.*

861 See Thomas Cottier, *Trade Law and Human Rights: A Relationship to Discover*, 5 (1) JOURNAL OF INTERNATIONAL ECONOMIC LAW 111, 115-116.

theory for its legitimacy.[862] Relying on economic theory for legitimacy does not mean that the central idea of the GATT/WTO (i.e., maintaining the free market) is removed from human rights. The basic idea of maintaining the free market is, as Jackson has pointed out, that "increasing the amount of resources of each individuals is the best way to allow that individual to follow his or her choices, lifestyle and goals in life."[863] The goal of the free market is to facilitate the fulfillment of human rights.

2.1.2.1. Conflicts as a Result of Different Perceptions of the Relationship among States, Individuals, and the Market

The common values shared by the human rights regime and the GATT/WTO are often disregarded.[864] Some even considered the WTO agreements as a threat to human rights and condemned them as a "nightmare for developing countries and women."[865] In the report of the High Commissioner for Human Rights, the water dispute in Bolivia is provided as an example of the negative impact of trade in services.[866] The water distribution system in Cochabamba, Bolivia was sold to a foreign service provider. The transaction led to significant price increase. Faced with mass demonstrations, the government eventually restored public ownership of the water supply. It was observed that: "Had Bolivia committed its water distribution system to liberalization under GATS, such a reversal would have been open to challenge from other WTO members, placing increased pressure on the government to resist a political solution and continue with the military option."[867] Ironically, the developing countries, which are believed to be suffering under the tyranny of the WTO, do not always agree with breaching the WTO agreements for the sake of human rights protection. Significant numbers of WTO member states have great concern that the protections of human rights would be

---

862 *Id*, at 115.

863 John H. Jackson, *The WTO 'Constitution' and Proposed Reforms: Seven 'Mantras' Revisited*, 4 (1) JOURNAL OF INTERNATIONAL ECONOMIC LAW 67, 68 (2001).

864 See *e.g.* Philip Alston, *Resisting the Merger and Acquisition of Human Rights by Trade Law: A Reply to Petersmann*, and 13 (4) EUROPEAN JOURNAL OF INTERNATIONAL LAW 815, 825-26 (2002).

865 See e.g. U.N. Econ. & Soc. Council, Sub-Commission on the Promotion and Protection of Human Rights, *The Realization of Economic, Social and Cultural Rights: Globalization and Its Impact on the Full Enjoyment of Human Rights* , U.N. Doc. E/CN.4/Sub.2/2000/13 (June 15, 2000) (prepared by J. Oloka-Onyango and Deepika Udagama).

866 See U.N. Econ. & Soc. Council, Sub-Commission on the Promotion and Protection of Human Rights, Report of High Commissioner, *Liberalization of Trade in Services and Human Rights*, UN Doc. E/CN.4/Sub.2/2002/9 (June 25, 2002).

867 John Hilary, The Wrong Model: GATS, Trade Liberalization and Children's Right to Health, 43 (2001).

abused as instruments to protect domestic producers from foreign competition, in particular from developing countries, and therefore aggravate their development problems.[868] The developing members insisted human rights considerations should be left exclusively to human rights institutions.[869]

The conflicts between human rights and the WTO agreements are superficial rather than fundamental. Analyzing the content of the WTO agreements, there is no convincing evidence for systemic conflicts.[870] The underlying values of human rights are also respected in the WTO framework. The conflicts actually derive from the different perceptions of the role of the market and the governmental interferences in a free market.[871] Human rights require governments to protect individuals from human rights infringements by themselves and other private persons. In addition, governments also should promote and fulfill human rights.[872] Governments are both the potential foe and guardian to human rights. In regard to trade and the free global market, it appears to the advocate for human rights that governments are more the guardians than the foes of human rights. Human rights advocates considered a free global market as implying mercantilism and the unfair competitions between the foreign multinational enterprises and domestic industries. Governments are supposed to provide individuals, smaller companies, and farmers protections against their foreign competitors, particularly the multinational corporations seeking the maximal profits at the expense of human rights. In this context, governments should protect the domestic market and producers to secure full enjoyment of human rights. The international agreements promoting free markets, *inter alia* the WTO agreements, are usually presumed harmful to human rights. The governmental interference in the market or even the protectionism is appropriate and admirable.[873] Such a view implies that a closed market is somehow more able to bring about protections for human rights.[874]

868 For detailed discussions on such disguised protectionism, see generally Thirukodikaval Nilakanta Srinivasan, *Trade and Human Rights*, in CONSTITUENT INTERESTS AND U.S. TRADE POLICIES (Alan Verne Deardorff & Robert Mitchell Stern eds, 1999).

869 See Krista Naddakavukaren Schefer, *Dancing with the Devil: A Heretic's View of Protectionism in the WTO Legal System*, 4 (2) ASIAN JOURNAL OF WTO & INTERNATIONAL HEALTHY LAW AND POLICY 423,438 (2009).

870 See Ernst-Ulrich Petersmann, The 'Human Rights Approach' Advocated by The UN High Commissioner for Human Rights and by The International Labour Organization: Is It Relevant for WTO Law and Policy?, 7 (3) JOURNAL OF INTERNATIONAL ECONOMIC LAW 605, 622 (2004).

871 See Hoe Lim, *Trade and Human Rights: What's at Issue?*, 35 (2) JOURNAL OF WORLD TRADE 275, 297-99 (2001).

872 See Manfred Nowak, Introduction to the International Human Rights Regime, 23 ff. (2003).

873 See *e.g.* human rights-based criticisms of the WTO, Anne-Christine Habbard & Marie Guiraud, *The World Trade Organization and Human Rights* (FIDH Position Paper, Nov. 1999), http://www.fidh.org/rapports/wto-fidh.htm (last visited Jan 10, 2011).

874 Hoe Lim, *supra* note 871, at 297.

In contrast, the WTO agreements recognized the value of the free market and criticized the protectionism and excessive governmental interference. A free market is believed to maximize benefits of all the participants in the market and efficiently distribute economic resources. Protectionism distorts the markets, causes prices to rise by limiting suppliers, and gives benefits to inefficient domestic producers.[875] Not only may the multinational corporations benefit from a global free market. Individuals and local companies also participate and prosper in such a market. Moreover, the protections for domestic producers in fact are not always taken for the purpose of human rights. On the contrary, the protections offer advantages for domestic producers capable of lobbying for protective policy (e.g., larger corporations) by exploiting consumers. In certain cases, the protective measures are proven harmful to human rights.[876] Protectionism usually benefits the "haves" at the expense of the "have nots" – as such, protectionism is contrary to the ideal of justice.[877] From the perspective of the WTO agreements, the observation in the water supply case in Bolivia is misconceived. In cases like the water supply conflict in Bolivia, the foreign suppliers, according to the ideal liberalization under the GATS, are supposed to provide additional water distribution systems and offer the citizen more choices. The GATS requires only the chance for foreign suppliers to compete with the original service providers. The GATS does not ever require privatization or replacement of the public service provider with foreign suppliers.

It should be noted that the WTO agreements do not support laissez-faire markets; neither do they require the supremacy of free trade over other non-trade considerations, including human rights. Instead, the WTO agreements explicitly recognize that non-trade considerations may play a role in the application and implementation of the agreements. The free trade requirements should yield if the member states decide to prioritize human rights obligations.[878] Although the

---

875 Adam Smith argued against protectionism, see generally ADAM SMITH, WEALTH OF NATIONS, 348 ff. (Charles Jesse Bullock ed., 2007). The contemporary economists also criticize protectionism. See *e.g.* Anne O. Krueger, *Trade Policy in Developing Countries*, in 1 HANDBOOK OF INTERNATIONAL ECONOMICS 519, 543-547 (Ronald W. Jones & Peter B. Kenen eds, 1988); CHARLES P. KINDLEBERGER, INTERNATIONAL ECONOMICS, 17-33 (5th Ed., 1973); Milton Friedman & Rose Friedman, The Case for Free Trade, 1997 (4) HOOVER DIGEST (Oct. 30, 1997), available at http://www.hoover.org/publications/hoover-digest/article/7125; Jagdish N. Bhagwati, PROTECTIONISM (1990).

876 For adverse effects of protectionism on right to food, see U.N. Econ. & Soc. Council, Commission on Human Rights, Report of the High Commissioner for Human Rights, *Globalization and Its Impact on the Full Enjoyment of Human Rights*, paras. 18-31, UN Doc. E/CN.4/2002/54 (Jan. 15, 2002).

877 Schefer, *supra* not 869, at 439.

878 See Ernst-Ulrich Petersmann, *Trade and Human Rights I*, in 1 THE WORLD TRADE ORGANIZATION: LEGAL, ECONOMIC AND POLITICAL ANALYSIS, 625,655 (Patrick F.J. Macrory et al. eds., 2005).

human rights considerations are not explicitly referred to in the WTO agreements, the objectives of the WTO (i.e., "raising standards of living, ensuring full employment and a large and steadily growing volume of real income") unmistakably contribute to the welfare of human beings. The free market is not an end in itself, but is presumed by the WTO agreements to be the best means to increase the welfare of human beings. While civil, political, social, economic, and cultural rights of individuals are directly protected in the human rights regime, the WTO agreements secure the means for these ends. The free market promoted in the WTO agreements recognizes multiple values, such as free and fair competition, public morals, human and animal lives, and national securities, as well as human rights considerations. In this light, the free market pursued by the WTO is different from the imagination of the critics of the WTO. Those who argue that the WTO agreements are inconsistent with human rights actually presume that human rights values are totally disregarded in the free market.

2.1.2.2. WTO Provisions Embodying the Protection for Human Rights

In analyzing the WTO agreements themselves, the guiding principles can be said to mirror the principles of the human rights regime.[879] To some extent, the WTO agreements, at least those provisions containing the principles of human rights, could be deemed as protections for individuals as well. Human rights issues are considered in the light of exception clauses, such as Article XX (b) of the GATT.[880] In addition, certain provisions of the WTO agreements directly reflect or elaborate on human rights, particularly, property rights, rights to remedy, non-discrimination treatment, and the rule of law.

First, the WTO agreements provide protection for property rights. The protection for property rights is presumed rather than explicitly addressed under the WTO framework, given that private right over goods and other material property is the precondition for participating in transactions in the market economy. In contrast, the protections for intellectual property are explicitly provided for in the TRIPS agreement.

The ICESCR focused less attention on protection for property rights and seemed to disconnect the property rights from the protections of economic activities and resources pertinent to standard of living, which are recognized as human rights. The omission of the protection for property rights derived from the ideo-

---

879 The Secretary General, *Globalization and Its Impact on Full Enjoyment of Human Rights*, para. 14, *delivered to the General Assembly*, para. 14, U.N. Doc. A 55/342 (Aug. 31, 2000).

880 For detailed illustration of GATT XX and human rights, see *e.g.* Gabrielle Marceau, *The WTO Dispute Settlement and Human Rights*, in INTERNATIONAL TRADE AND HUMAN RIGHTS 181, 217-225 (Federick M. Abbort et al. eds., 2006).

logical battles of the Cold War and should be reconsidered.[881] The protection for property rights is relatively clear in the UDHR and regional human rights instruments, such as the European Convention for the Protection of Human Rights and Fundamental Freedoms (hereafter referred as ECHR).[882] Article 17 of UDHR reads "Every one has the right to own property alone as well as in association with others. No one shall be arbitrarily deprived of his property."[883] Article 1 of the Protocol 1 to the ECHR confirmed natural as well as the legal person is entitled to the enjoyment of possessions, unless the deprivation of such possessions is for the purpose of the public interest and subject to the conditions set by law or general principles of international law.[884]

According Paragraph 2 of Article 27 of UDHR and Article 15, paragraph 1 (c) of ICESCR, protection of intellectual property should be a human right.[885] Nonetheless, intellectual property conceptualized as a universal human right differs in fundamental ways from its treatment as an economic interest under intellectual property law. From a human rights perspective, on one hand, intellectual property has intrinsic value as an expression of human rights and, on the other hand, involves the interests of wider society. The rights of the creator are not absolute, but conditional on contributing to the common good and welfare of the society. To be recognized as a universal human right, intellectual property rights should be implemented first and foremost consistently with the realization of other human rights.[886]

The question then, is whether the intellectual property rights in the TRIPS agreement may balance the public interests as required by human rights instruments, particularly by the ICESCR. Several provisions of the TRIPS reveal the consideration for the balance between the interests of the right holders and the wider objective of promoting social and economic welfare. Article 7 of the

---

881 Cottier, supra note 861, at 122.

882 European Convention on Human Rights, 213 UNTS 221, signed on Nov. 4 1950, entered into force on Sep. 3, 1953.

883 Universal Declaration of Human Rights, *supra* note 849, at 76.

884 Protocol to the Convention for the Protection of Human Rights and Fundamental Freedoms, as amended by Protocol No. 11, signed on Mar. 20, 1952, Headings of articles added and text amended according to the provisions of Protocol No. 11 (ETS No. 155), as of its entry into force, on 1 Nov. 1, 1998.

885 See Audrey R. Chapman *Approaching intellectual property as a human right: obligations related to Article 15 (1) (c)*, XXXV (3) COPYRIGHT BULLETIN 4, 13 (2001); Paul L.C. Torremans, *Copyright (and Other Intellectual Property Rights) as a Human Right in Intellectual Property and Human Rights*, in ENHANCED EDITION OF COPYRIGHT AND HUMAN RIGHTS 195, 199-206 (Paul L.C. Torremans ed., 2008); but see Robert L. Ostergard, *Intellectual Property: A Universal Human Right?*, 21 (1) HUMAN RIGHTS QUARTERLY 156, 175 (1999).

886 See Chapman, *id*, at 14.

TRIPS states its objective is to "contribute to the promotion of technological innovation and to the transfer and dissemination of technology, to the mutual advantage of producers and users of technological knowledge and in a manner conducive to social and economic welfare, and to a balance of rights and obligations." Members, pursuant to Article 8, may take measures to "protect public health and nutrition, and to promote the public interest." Besides, members can deny granting intellectual property rights for public considerations, such as protection for human, animal, or plant life or health, and the environment (e.g., TRIPS Article 27). Moreover, members may adopt measures to prevent the abuse of the intellectual property rights by the right holders (e.g., TRIPS Articles 31 and 40). Furthermore, the TRIPS agreement encourages the international cooperation and technology transfer (e.g., TRIPS Article 66, paragraph 2 and Article 67). Although the TRIPS agreement might not fully consider all the other human rights, it is also agreed that the TRIPS offers significant flexibility to cope with the other human rights considerations. [887] The intellectual property rights in the TRIPS actually do consider the balance required by human rights instruments and should thus have the quality of human rights.

Second, the WTO agreements set forth the right to remedy. Article 8 of the UDHR requests the right to effective remedy by the national tribunals for the infringement of fundamental rights granted by constitution or by law. Paragraph 1 of Article 14 of the ICCPR also sets forth the access to the courts for "determination of criminal charge" and "determination of rights and obligations in a suit at law."[888] In the WTO context, numerous provisions were set to secure the effective remedy at the national level, such as: judicial protections in matters relating to trade regulations (GATS Article VI: 2 (a)); the civil and the administrative proceedings for the enforcement of intellectual property rights (TRIPS Articles 42, 49, 59); the judicial or quasi-judicial reviews on imposition of countervailing duties and the anti-dumping duties (SCM Article 23, AD Article 13); right of appeal for the determination of custom values (CV Article 11); challenging procedures for the bidder for a government procurement (GPA Article XX); appeal procedures and review procedures for the grievance of the exporters about the preshipment entities (PSI Articles 2.21 and 4). In short, the WTO sets forth procedural protections for individuals engaging in trade. Members are obliged to

887 For the divergence between the TRIPS agreement and other human rights, see U.N. Econ. & Soc. Council, Sub-Commission on the Promotion and Protection of Human Rights, *The Impact of the Agreement on Trade-Related Aspects of Intellectual Property Rights on Human Rights*, paras. 21-27, UN Doc. E/CN.4/Sub.2/2001/13 (June 27, 2001).

888 International Covenant on Civil and Political Rights, Dec.16, 1966, 999 UNTS 171 (entered into force Mar. 23, 1976).

provide effective remedies, if certain rights or the interests of the individuals under the WTO agreements are affected.

Third, the WTO agreements guarantee the non-discrimination treatment on all trade-related matters. The non-discrimination requirements in the WTO not only can be justified by the economic theories, but can also be supported by the principle of non-discrimination in the human rights regime. The non-discrimination principle appears in several universal and regional human rights instruments, such as Article 2 of UDHR, Article 2 of ICESCR, and Article 14 of ECHR. However, the prohibition of discrimination under these instruments should be in conjunction with other human rights provisions.[889] Significantly, Article 26 of ICCPR recognizes the right to equality, which guarantees equality of all persons before the law and equal protection of the law. Article 26 states as follows:

> All persons are equal before the law and are entitled without any discrimination to the equal protection of the law. In this respect, the law shall prohibit any discrimination and guarantee to all persons equal and effective protection against discrimination on any ground such as race, color, sex, language, religion, political or other opinion, national or social origin, property, birth or other status.

In the General Comment No.18, the Human Rights Committee further elaborated that Article 26 by itself is an autonomous right to non-discrimination. It prohibits discrimination in law or in fact in any field regulated and protected by public authorities. In other words, rights not provided for in the ICCPR are also subject to the non-discrimination requirements.[890] Besides, the list of the prohibited grounds for discriminations is not exhaustive. Those not explicitly identified may fall within the category of "other status." The Human Rights Committee has declared allegations of discrimination on various grounds admissible under Article 26,

---

889 *E.g.* The European Court of Human Rights, for instance, has reiterated in several cases that the prohibition of discrimination complements other provisions or protocols of the ECHR. See Dudgeon v. the United Kingdom, App. No. 7525/76, para. 67 (Oct. 12, 1981), http://cmiskp.echr.coe.int/tkp197/view.asp?action=html&documentId=695350&portal=hbkm&source=externalbydocnumber&table=F69A27FD8FB86142BF01C1166DEA398649; Chassagnou and Others v. France, App. Nos. 25088/94, 28331/95 and 28443/95, para. 89 (Apr. 4, 1999), http://cmiskp.echr.coe.int/tkp197/view.asp?item=1&portal=hbkm&action=html&highlight=25088/94&sessionid=65046055&skin=hudoc-en; Burden v. the United Kingdom [GC], App. No. 13378/05, para. 58 (Apr. 29, 2008), http://cmiskp.echr.coe.int/tkp197/view.asp?item=1&portal=hbkm&action=html&highlight=13378/05&sessionid=65046055&skin=hudoc-en; Andrejeva v. Latvia, Application no. 55707/00, para. 74 (Feb. 18, 2009). http://cmiskp.echr.coe.int/tkp197/view.asp?item=1&portal=hbkm&action=html&highlight=55707/00&sessionid=65046055&skin=hudoc-en.

890 U.N. Human Rights Committee, *CCPR General Comment No. 18: Non-discrimination* (Nov. 10, 1989), available at , http://www.unhcr.org/refworld/docid/453883fa8.html.

such as discrimination based on nationality,[891]citizenship,[892] marital status,[893] educational background,[894] etc. Moreover, the General Comment also indicates that Article 26 not only covers the legislation, which explicitly set forth discriminative measures. But also, Article 26 prohibits the effect of nullifying or impairing the equal footing of all rights and freedoms.[895] Such understanding expands the protection for non-discrimination treatment and would further prevent disguised discrimination.

In terms of trade in service, the GATS protects the service suppliers from discrimination on the grounds of national origin or nationality. MFN and national treatment accord not only to the service, but more importantly to the service suppliers (GATS Articles II: 1 and XVII: 1). Moreover, like the ICCPR, the GATS also prohibits treatments, which are equal in appearance, but have discriminatory effect. Formally, identical treatment shall also be deemed as discriminatory, if it put alien service or service suppliers in less competitive conditions (GATS XVII:3). In regards to intellectual property, the members shall not differentiate between the protections for intellectual property rights according to the nationalities of the right holders (TRIPS Articles 3 and 4). In terms of trade in goods, non-discrimination treatments (i.e., the MFN and national treatment) are accorded directly to the product and indirectly to the importers and exporters (GATT Articles I and III). Nonetheless, the discrimination between the products actually is discrimination between the individuals on the ground of product origin. For instance, the seller and the buyer of foreign products are subject to higher taxes or charges than those of domestic products. To some extent, these provisions could be conceived as requiring the member states to apply the non-discrimination obligations under Article 26 of ICCPR to trade-related matters.

Fourth, the WTO agreements include a considerable number of provisions reflecting the rule of law. Certain human rights provisions, such as Article 14 of ICCPR, contain the principle of rule of law. Although rule of law *per se* has not yet been recognized as a human right, it is an integral part of the protections for

---

891 *E.g.* Human Rights Committee, *Gueye et al. v. France*, Communication No. 196/1985 (1989), U.N. Doc. CCPR/C/35/D/196/1985 (Apr.3, 1989); Human Rights Committee, *Griffin v. Spain*, Communication No. 493/1992, U.N. Doc. CCPR/C/49/D/493/1992 (Apr. 5, 1995)

892 *E.g.* Human Rights Committee, *Adam v. Czech Republic*, Communication No. 586/1994, U.N. Doc.CCPR/C/57/D/586/1994 (July 25, 1996).

893 *E.g.* Human Rights Committee, *Danning v. Netherlands*, Communication No. 180/1984, U.N. Doc. CCPR/C/29/D/180/1984 (Apr. 9, 1987); Human Rights Committee, *Hoofdman v. Netherlands*, Communication No. 602/1994, U.N. Doc. CCPR/C/64/D/602/1994 (Nov. 25,1998)

894 *E.g.* Human Rights Committee, *Gomez v. Spain*, Communication No. 856/1999, U.N. Doc. CCPR/C/78/D/856/1999 (Nov. 5, 2001).

895 See *Danning v. Netherlands*, *supra* note 893, at para.7.

human rights.[896] The rule of law does not focus on specific substantial rights. Rather, it concerns the way in which the governments reach their decisions. Individuals are protected, through procedural requirements, from capricious and arbitrary decisions of government. This principle involves every aspect of governmental activities, including the trade-related matters. Besides the access to judicial review for the given trade-related matters, numbers of the rules in the WTO agreements are set to avoid arbitrary decisions. For instance, the imposition and administration of anti-dumping and countervailing duties are subject to extensive procedural requirements (e.g., SCM Articles 10, 11, 12; AD Articles 1, 5, 6). Several procedural rules regulate the civil and administrative proceedings implementing the intellectual property rights (TRIPS Articles 42-61). All domestic regulations that affect trade in services shall be administrated in a reasonable, objective, and impartial manner (GATS Article VI). There are also extensive procedural principles and rules for determining or administrating the custom valuations and import licensing (e.g., CV Articles 2-8; the LIC Articles 1-3). Many other provisions also mirror the rule of law and ensure that the governments duly conduct trade-related affairs.

The convergence between the provisions of the WTO agreements and the human rights protection are not coincidence. The human rights obligations in the UN framework and the GATT/WTO agreements both aim at protecting liberty, non-discrimination, social and economic welfare as well as other human rights values. The convergence reveals the human rights aspect of the WTO agreements. The author does not suggest that the distinctions between the WTO agreements and human rights are no longer necessary, or that the WTO should extend the competence to include all human rights matters. Rather, the human rights dimension of the WTO agreements shows the individuals should no longer be considered as beneficiaries who are indirectly protected under the WTO agreements. The previously-mentioned provisions have set forth specific and unconditional rules; which according to the text could be construed as creating rights for individuals. The objective of the WTO agreements; namely, to maintain a free global market; could be further traced back to human rights protection. Since the contents of the WTO agreements virtually mimic the human rights protection as stated in the UNDHR, ICCPR, and ICESCR, it would be inappropriate to assume that member states intend to deny the rights of individuals.

---

896 For the relationship between human rights and rule of law, see generally *e.g.* Gary L. McDowell & Stephen B. Presser, *Forward: Human Rights, Rule of Law, and National Sovereignty*, 2 NORTHWESTERN JOURNAL OF INTERNATIONAL HUMAN RIGHTS Rts. 1 (Apr. 2004), http://www.law.northwestern.edu/journals/jihr/v2/1; Mary Ann Glendon, *The Rule of Law in The Universal Declaration of Human Rights*, 2 NORTHWESTERN JOURNAL OF INTERNATIONAL HUMAN RIGHTS Rts. 5 (Apr. 2004), http://www.law.northwestern.edu/journals/jihr/v2/5.

2.2. Ground for the Direct Effect II: the Effectiveness of the WTO Agreements

The national courts have been required to supervise and intervene in the implementation of the WTO rules, if the obligations cannot be properly enforced by the DSU.[897] The effectiveness of the WTO agreements would be a strong argument for direct effect. When provisions of the WTO agreements are construed to create the rights of individuals, the effectiveness of these provisions would be very questionable. The enforcement mechanism of the WTO, namely DSU procedures, cannot fully redress the damages caused by a WTO-inconsistent measure.[898] Furthermore, except for the amicus curiae, the individuals cannot participant in the procedures, even if they are directly involved in the disputes.[899] However, the panel and the Appellate Body are not obligated to accept the amicus curiae.[900]

For the small and medium member states, the enforcement mechanism also might not secure the compliance of the WTO agreements. The member states can still choose the means for the implementation of the WTO rules, even if domestic laws or measures have been found to be infringing upon the WTO agreements.[901] Except for consistently resorting to the compliance panel under Article 21.5 of the DSU, members cannot stop the WTO-inconsistent measures that appear in different facets.[902] The only disincentive to infringement of the WTO agreements is retaliation. However, retaliation could work only if the retaliating states are economically no less powerful than the states being retaliated upon. In the meantime, the retaliating states also have to also have to endure some overall efficiency losses.[903] The retaliations clearly would favor larger economies, for retaliations of larger economies could hurt the retaliated ones, and they have greater capacity

---

897 *E.g.* practices of the GPA, see Introduction, section 0.6 *supra.*

898 See Introduction, section 0.3. *supra.*

899 E.g. Panel Report, *Australia – Subsidies Provided to Producers and Exporters of Automotive Leather*, WT/DS126/R (May 25, 1999). The subject at issue is the loans contract between Australia and an individual (in this case a company).

900 See Appellate Body Report, European Communities-Trade Description of Sardines (EC-Sardines), para. 166, WT/DS231/AB/R (Sept. 22, 2002); also United States- Imposition of Countervailing Duties on Certain Hot-Rolled Lead and Bismuth Carbon Steel Products Originating in the United Kingdom (US- Lead and Bismuth II), at paras. 40-41 (May 10, 2000).

901 See Panel Report, United States – Anti-Dumping and Countervailing Measures on Steel Plate from India (US- Steel Plate),WT/DS206/R, para. 8.8 (Oct. 4, 2002).

902 See Panel Report, Guatemala-Antidumping Investigation Regarding Portland cement from Mexico (Guatemala – Cement I), paras 8.3, WT/DS60/R (June 19, 1998).

903 See Steve Charnovitz, *Should the Teeth Be Pulled? An Analysis of WTO Sanctions*, in THE POLITICAL ECONOMY OF INTERNATIONAL TRADE LAW: ESSAYS IN HONOR OF ROBERT E. HUDEC 602, 621 (Daniel L.M. Kennedy & James. D. Southwick eds., 2002).

to endure the backfire of the retaliations. It seems that the more economically powerful the member states are, the more they can ensure or compromise the effectiveness of the WTO agreements. On the contrary, the member states less economically influential might have no choice but to follow the WTO rules.[904] In other words, the effectiveness of the WTO agreements depends on the economic power of the member states, which is contrary to the idea of "reciprocal and mutually advantageous arrangement."[905] The medium or the small economies certainly have a good reason to call for a strictly rule-oriented system of enforcement, such as direct effect, which could compensate for the disadvantages in the negotiations with their trade partners.

2.3. Grounds Against Direct Effect I: Allocation of Competence Between the WTO and the Member States

The grounds for direct effect of the WTO agreements are provided in the previous sections. To solve the debates about direct effect, the grounds against direct effect should be deliberated.

The member states have the motive to deny direct effect because they want to secure certain liberties in their international relations.[906] The direct effect is rejected in the name of sovereignty or autonomy of member states.[907] The United States is obviously in this position. This argument presumes that the implementation of international agreements should be the exclusive competence of the states and should be free from external influences. Such argument against direct effect must be modified because its presumptions do not necessarily fit the current international legal framework. In the current context of international cooperation, a sovereign state actually does not have ultimate or absolute power within its territory.[908] For instance, the prohibition of intervention provided in Article 2.7 of the UN Charter would be lifted if a serious infringement of human rights occurs.[909]

---

904 See Busch & Reinhardt, supra note 44, at 473-474.

905 Preamble of Marrakesh Agreement.

906 See Bleckmann, *supra* note 831, at 266.

907 See Bleckmann, *supra* note 831, at 267; see also Melville Fuller Weston, *Political Question*, 38 (2) Harvard Law Review 296, 327-28 (1925).

908 See Stephan Hobe, Der offene Verfassungsstaat zwischen Souveränität und Interdependenz: Eine Studie zur Wandlung des Staatsbegriffs der deutschsprachigen Staatslehre im Kontext internationaler institutionalisierter Kooperation 384-87 (1998), for detail at Part III, sections 1 & 2; see also Jackson, *supra* note 863, at 72.

909 See Hobe, *supra* note 831, at 220.

In the context of international cooperation, the relationship between sovereign states and international organizations could be understood as allocation of tasks for solving the challenges all people might encounter.[910] It is also questionable that certain tasks *a priori* should be exclusively undertaken by the states. In fact, all the tasks and competence of states can be transferred to the international level under certain conditions.[911] The author will follow the principle of subsidiarity to analyze the allocation of competence between the member states and the WTO.

Although the principle of subsidiarity was established in the EU law, it may arguably have a more general application for international law.[912] In fact, several international rules also adopted the idea of subsidiarity.[913] Two criteria are set for the involvement of the international organization: first, the task is transnational by nature; and second, the international organization is more suitable for accomplishing the task. The direct effect implies depriving the member states of the flexibility of implementation. According to the principle of subsidiarity, WTO agreements cannot have direct effect, if the WTO does not have the competence to supervise the implementation of the WTO agreements as intensively as direct effect implies.

2.3.1. Transnational Nature of the Implementation of the WTO rules

The implementation of the WTO agreements is a task with a transnational feature. The political and social circumstances leading to the WTO rules similarly call for international cooperation in implementing these rules.

The WTO agreements were drafted to cope with the economical subjects that the states cannot effectively regulate by themselves. Unilateral measures, *inter alia* artificial barriers of trade, are not the solution to the inability of the states in this regard. The artificial trade barriers may even lead to a disastrous end: war.[914] Liberalization of trade and international cooperation are the better options to cope with the economical challenges of the states. However, protective measures, including trade barriers, are easier to sell at the national level. This is because the disadvantages caused by the foreign competition are imminent, while the advantages of trade liberalization have not been realized and these advantages seem to

910 See Hobe, *supra* note 831, at 391.

911 See Hobe, *supra* note 831, at 392, 422.

912 See Hobe, *supra* note 831, at 401.

913 See Hobe, *supra* note 831, at 399, 402.

914 See Jackson, *supra* note 852, at 23.

depend on the cooperation of foreign governments.[915] There is always speculation that a state will seek advantages at the expense of others. The distrust further leads to what economists call the "prisoner's dilemma": when one state takes protective measures, another is likely to do the same, and in the end, all the states will be hurt.[916] The WTO regime, a rule-oriented cooperative mechanism at the international level, was set to resist the temptation of protectionism and bail the states out of the prisoner's dilemma.[917] It should be noted that the political and social circumstances are unchanged. There is still a tendency for protectionism at the national level and distrust among the states. For example, the US Department of Commerce insists the method for assessing the dumping margin, even after this method was found inconsistent with the anti-dumping agreement.[918] The member states might still be inclined to deviate from their obligations, while implementing the WTO rules. They also might not comply with certain rules, unless the other members have done the same. In other words, the overall implementation of WTO rules also depends on international arrangements for supervising and reviewing the implementation. The implementation of the WTO rules therefore should not be seen as a task exclusively addressed at a national level.

2.3.2. Inadequate Intervention on the Implementation of the WTO rules

The implementation of the WTO rules should not be left exclusively to the discretion of the member states. There should be arrangements at the international level for supervising and reviewing the implementation. The WTO has provided two arrangements: the Dispute Settlement Body (the DSB), which may review specific domestic measures implementing the obligations of the member states, and the Trade Policy Review Body (the TPRB), which periodically generally appraises the trade policies and practices of member states.[919] Direct effect, however, may not serve as the third one, because it would bring problems that cannot be properly handled under the current WTO framework.

The first problem is the asymmetries of applications of the WTO rules, if the WTO rules are interpreted divergently in different national legal systems.[920] The

---

915 See Meng, *supra* note 426, at 1080.

916 See Jackson, *supra* note 863, at 69.

917 See *id*, at 70.

918 See Part I, section 1.1.3.2. b) *supra*.

919 See *e.g.* DSB Articles 1, 3, 21; Agreement on Trade Policy Review Mechanism, paragraph C.

920 See Steven P. Croley and John H. Jackson, *WTO Dispute Procedures, Standard of Review, and Deference to National Governments*, 90 (2) AMERICAN JOURNAL OF INTERNATIONAL LAW 193, 209 (1996).

divergent interpretations at a national level would not be a big problem as long as the matter eventually gets to the WTO and there is a final and definite ruling. In reality, the WTO does not have mechanism to guarantee uniform application and interpretation of the WTO rules.[921] The national courts have no access to the WTO for advice on the application and interpretation of the WTO rules. Divergent interpretations at a national level are inevitable. Even if the matter eventually goes to the WTO, the WTO still may not give interpretations that are definite and legally binding on all the member states. The panels, as *ad hoc* bodies, cannot really give advice on the interpretations of specific provisions on a regular basis.[922] Moreover, neither the Panels nor the Appellate Body can give definite interpretations that are generally binding on all the member states.[923] The Ministerial Conference and General Council can adopt authoritative interpretation by a three-fourths majority of the Member states.[924] However, they cannot contribute much to the uniform interpretations and application, because it is difficult to reach the threshold for adopting authoritative interpretations.

Another problem is the WTO does not pay attention to the domestic considerations about the implementations of the international rules. The URAA confirmed Jackson's view that the legislatures may want to reword the international rules to match the domestic circumstances.[925] The United States has refused the direct effect because the Congress wants to maintain the power to resolve the conflicts between the implementation of WTO rules and other policy goals.[926] Furthermore, the WTO rarely clarifies the ambiguous provisions, let alone to consider translating the agreements, both of which would make implementing legislation inevitable.[927] Moreover, direct effect infers depriving the member states of the flexibility of implementation. The member states might need a forum to discuss and coordinate means of implementation which can match their

921 See Mavroidis et al., *supra* note 12, at 160; see also Bogdandy, *supra* note 797, at 406; MAKUS. KRAJEWSKI, VERFASSUNGSPERSPEKTIVEN UND LEGITIMATION DES RECHTS DER WELTHANDELSORGANISATION (WTO), 63-67 (2001).

922 *Id.*

923 See Appellate Body Report, *Japan – Taxes on Alcoholic Beverages*, p.13, WT/DS8/AB/R, WT/DS10/AB/R, WT/DS11/AB/R, (Oct.4,1996); Appellate Body Report, *United States – Measure Affecting Imports of Woven Wool Shirts and Blouses from India*, p. 19, WT/DS33/AB/R, (Apr. 25, 1997).

924 See Article IX: 2 of the Marrakesh Agreement.

925 See Jackson, *supra* note 14, at 324.

926 See Part I, section 1.1.3.1. b) i. *supra*.

927 The Ministerial Conference has only once interpreted the TRIPS agreement in regard to its relationship with public health. See Doha Declaration of TRIPS Agreement and Public Health, WT/MIN (01)/DEC/W2, para. 5 (Nov. 14, 2001).

domestic circumstances. If direct effect will be granted, the WTO should address the domestic considerations about the implementation of the WTO rules.

In short, implementation of WTO rules is a task of transnational nature and therefore should not be seen as a task exclusively addressed at the national level. But the WTO cannot cope with the problems of divergent interpretations and applications of the WTO rules. Neither can the WTO properly coordinate the domestic needs of member states regarding the implementation of the WTO agreements. Therefore, the WTO does not have the competence to supervise the implementation of the WTO agreements as intensively as direct effect implies.

2.4. Grounds Against Direct Effect II: Lack of Legitimacy in Terms of Democracy and Constitutional Principles

The opponents of direct effect argue that the WTO agreements lack of the legitimacy of being applied by the national courts.[928] Denial of direct effect is considered as a mechanism to reinforce the democratic legitimacy. The author would agree that the WTO agreements are deficient in terms of democracy. The parliaments of members have limited control over the content of the WTO rules. Furthermore, the WTO does not provide sufficient means to secure democracy in the WTO decision-making. However, the author would doubt that the democratic deficit could totally exclude the WTO agreements from laws applied by the national courts. The national courts would apply domestic norms less democratically legitimate than the WTO agreements, such as administrative regulations. The democratic argument, at best, only supports the contention that the WTO agreements cannot overturn the laws passed by the legislature.

The author would not agree with the criticism that the WTO agreements are inconsistent with constitutional principles, in particular the principle of legal certainty and the principle of legal equality. Indeed, several provisions of the WTO agreements call for further negotiations and implementation measures.[929] There are even more provisions with specific and unconditional stipulations,[930] which certainly do not upset the principle of legal certainty. It is also unconceivable for the author to find the WTO agreements inconsistent with the principle of legal equality. Reverse discrimination, which von Bogdandy takes as an example showing the inconsistency between the WTO agreements and the principle of

928 See Part II, sections 1.2.2 and 1.2.3 *supra*.

929 *E.g.* Articles 15 and 20 of Agreement on Agriculture, Articles IV and XIX of the GATS.

930 *Supra* note 830.

legal equality, is just an incidental consequence of the application of the WTO agreements. The reverse discrimination would rather result from the conflicts between the WTO rules and the laws of the member states. The WTO rules *per se* do not require preferential treatment for imported goods or services. The WTO agreements only ask the member states not to discriminate against foreign importers, service suppliers, and their nationals who purchase foreign products and services. The WTO agreements maintain the legal equality between the foreigners and the nationals, which constitutions of the member states often are less interested in. Furthermore, in the era of globalization, non-discrimination of the imported products and services infers the equal treatment of the nationals. The imported goods or services are not only for consumption, but also for the use of production. Providing protections for certain domestic producers might, at the same time, hurt other domestic producers. Contrary to the criticisms, the WTO agreements actually embody the principle of equality. It is not convincing to deny direct effect on the grounds of constitutional principles.

2.5. Grounds Against the Direct Effect III: Practical Problems of Direct Effect

Direct effect is criticized as practically impossible or unacceptable. As shown in chapter 3, the practical difficulties of granting direct effect are summarized as follows: a) the wishes of legislatures to tailor-make the implementation of the WTO agreements; b) the disincentive to join the WTO agreements; c) the asymmetry of the member states in trade negotiations; d) the inconsistent applications and interpretations of the WTO agreements; and e) the overburden for the domestic courts.

There are some overlaps between the practical considerations against direct effect and the considerations of competence allocation. In the previous section, the author elaborated that the WTO cannot coordinate the domestic needs of member states regarding implementation and addressed the divergent applications and interpretations of the WTO rules. In other words, a) and d) would be the obstacles for direct effect. However, the author does not hold the rest of the practical problems as sustainable or invincible. First, it is only an allegation that the member states would either refuse or join the WTO agreements just because of direct effect. The practices of the Government Procurement Agreement (the GPA) have shown that the challenging procedure, which is akin to direct effect,[931]

931 The challenging procedure is a general obligation of national courts to implement the GPA. Direct effect is one of the options to fulfill this obligation. See Introduction, section 0.6 *supra.*

would not stop the member states to join it.[932] The material contents of the agreement appear to be more important for the member states. Second, the asymmetry of member states in trade negotiations derives from the unilateral acceptance of direct effect. That could be easily solved by a multilateral arrangement. Third, the national courts would not be overburdened for directly applying the WTO agreements. The national courts have already undertaken the cases concerning the WTO agreements. The member states have adopted implementing legislation parallel to the WTO agreements. Before the disputes about the WTO agreements reach the DSB, the cases pertinent thereto have been brought before the national courts.[933] Besides, the practices of Taiwan also could ease the concern that the cases would flood to the national courts or that the national courts ought to be the day-to-day interpreters and enforcers of the WTO agreements. The number of the cases per year is insignificant, around fifty, in comparison to the normal case load of the courts in Taiwan.[934]

2.6. Conclusion

In the previous sections, the author has provided the grounds for and against. The protection for rights of individuals and the effectiveness of the WTO agreements supports direct effect, while the competence problem and the democratic deficit stand in the way. However, as explained below, the grounds in favor of direct effect cannot completely rebut the opposite grounds and *vice versa.* The author will take an intermediate position in the end.

At least, in the author's view, the provisions embedding the principles of human rights could be construed to create rights for individuals and could have direct effect. These provisions actually set a minimum standard of treatment to foreigners in their economic lives and to nationals trading with foreigners, in which the constitutions of the member states often are less interested. Should direct effect not be granted, these people might be fully subject to the discretions of the member states without constraints. Furthermore, the provisions embodying the principle of human rights are consistent with, or even copy, the constitutional principles of member states. It would be absurd to deny the applications of these provisions merely because international trade affairs are involved. Moreover, the human rights dimension of these provisions could compensate for the democratic deficit

932 The major economies have or prepare to sign the GPA. The European Union, the United States and Japan have signed the GPA in 1996 and China has initiated the negotiations for accession. See http://www.wto.org/english/tratop_e/gproc_e/memobs_e.htm (last visited on Jan. 10, 2011).

933 See cases in Part I, sections 2.1.3.2. and 2.2.2.2. *supra.*

934 See *supra* note 685.

of the WTO rules. A requirement for democracy is not an end in itself. Its justification lies in the promotion of the principle of autonomy that "persons … should be free and equal in the determination of the conditions of their own lives, so long as they do not deploy this framework to negate the rights of others."[935] The provisions with human rights dimensions promote freedom and equality in the economic lives of individuals.[936] By virtue of these provisions individuals can decide who and in what conditions to trade with by virtue of these provisions; while the exception clauses, which are provided in GATT and GATS as well as TRIPS, could avoid the choices of the individual to impinge upon the rights of others. In this sense, the provisions reflecting human rights do not contradict the very objective of democracy. In addition, the enforcement mechanism of the WTO could not fully secure the compliance of the member states with the WTO rules.

The only problem is, for now, that the WTO appears not to have the competence to supervise the implementation of the WTO agreements as intensively as direct effect implies. Granting direct effect only to the provisions creating rights of individuals could partially ease the problem of lack of competence. These provisions set forth specific and unambiguous obligations, which decrease the need for the involvement of the legislations. Also, the national courts are entrusted with balancing the individual rights and public interests in the cases before them.[937] The national courts could resolve the conflicts between the implementation of WTO rules and other policy goals by applying the exception clauses. In the foregoing case, the WTO does not have to coordinate the domestic considerations of implementation. However, given the lack of an ultimate say on the interpretations of the WTO rules, the member states might have to negotiate for a mutually-agreed solution for the WTO-inconsistent interpretations made by national courts. That means the economical power of the member state, not necessarily the rules provided, would be decisive for the enforcement of the WTO agreements. In this sense, no rights of individuals would actually be guaranteed, even if the direct effect were granted.

It should nonetheless be noted that the competence issue only reveals why the WTO now cannot become deeply involved in supervising the implementation measures of the member states. The implementation of the WTO agreements does not fall exclusively into the competence of the member states.[938] If the mechanism ensuring the uniform interpretations could be established, the obstacle to

935 See David Held, Democracy and Global Order: From the Modern State to Cosmopolitan Governance, 146-147 (1995).

936 See Part II, section 2.1.2.2. *supra*.

937 See Louis Henkin, Constitutionalism, Democracy, and Foreign Affairs 102 (1990).

938 See Part II, section 2.3.1. *supra*.

direct effect would be solved. In sum, the provisions construed as creating rights for individuals are capable of being directly effective, in particular: (1) non-discrimination treatments: such as GATS Articles II: 1 and XVII: 1, GATS XVII: 3, TRIPS Articles 3 and 4, GATT Articles I and III; (2) Right to remedy: such as GATS Article VI: 2 (a), TRIPS Articles 42, 49, 59, SCM Article 23, AD Article 13, CV Article 11, PSI Articles 2.21 and 4; (3) provisions reflecting the rule of law: such as SCM Articles 10, 11, 12; AD Articles 1, 5, 6, GATS Article VI, CV Articles 2-8; LIC Articles 1-3; and (4) protection for intellectual property rights: a substantial part of the TRIPS agreement. These provisions should be granted direct effect, but not until the WTO could properly solve the problem of divergent interpretations of national courts.

Summary

Paragraph 4 of the Article XVI of the Marrakesh Agreement Establishing the World Trade Organization (the Marrakesh Agreement) requires members to fulfill their obligations under the WTO agreements. It provides, "Each Member shall ensure the conformity of its laws, regulations and administrative procedures with its obligations as provided in the annexed Agreements." Paragraph 4 does not mention whether to grant the WTO agreements direct effect. The panel consistently leaves the door open for the direct effect of WTO agreements at the international level. The issue still might surface anytime in the future. This research primarily aims to give an answer to the debate of whether the direct effect of the WTO agreements should be granted.

The first question is what do the four members (i.e., US, EU, China, and Taiwan) think about the direct effect of the WTO agreements, and what are the reasons for such choices? In the United States, an international agreement could greatly influence the domestic legal system, if the Congress so wishes. In the GATT period, the Congress did not clearly address the effect of the GATT 1947 in the domestic legal system. In absence of Congress' expressive statement, it became complicated to determine the effect of the GATT. The courts should fill the gap the Congress left behind. Although the courts did not provide sufficient reasoning, few things are certain: The provisions of the GATT 1947 and its subsequent agreements are not directly effective. State law should yield to the obligations under these agreements, although the GATT 1947 and its subsequent agreements do not have direct effect. The URAA is consistent with practices of the GATT 1947, except that the URAA and SAA further limited the effect of the provisions of the WTO agreements. The provisions of the WTO agreements are not self-executing. Furthermore, the URAA itself would yield, whenever it conflicts with other statutes. Also, the WTO agreements would not prevail over state laws in cases of conflict. Congress intended to block the provisions of the WTO agreements from the US legal system for sovereignty concerns.

In particular, the WTO might excessively constrain domestic decision-making power. Also, states' autonomy might be degraded. Besides, accepting the WTO agreements in a fast-track procedure cannot meet the democracy legitimacy required by the Constitution. The courts also deny the indirect effect of the WTO agreements because the Congress has clearly entrusted the executive branch with implementing the WTO agreement. The courts are inclined not to interfere in the administrative authorities in this regard.

In the European Union, the ECJ plays a significant role in determining the effect of international agreements. Paragraph 7 of Article 300 of the EC (TFEU Article 216, paragraph 2) did not provide a clear answer to the legal status of the international agreements concluded by the Community. The ECJ by virtue of "the interpretation and application of the Treaties", which is provided in paragraph 1 of Article 220 of the EC (TEU Article 19), may have filled the gap and developed principles. The ECJ found the GATT 1947 and the WTO agreements not directly effective in the light of their spirit, structure, and terms. The ECJ would apply the GATT/WTO rules in exceptional cases, wherein the obligations under the GATT/WTO have been transposed to Community law or the Community intends to implement these obligations. In such cases, the WTO rules to some extent are incorporated into Community law and are not actually directly effective.

The ECJ's major rationale against direct effect of the GATT/WTO agreements is to maintain the "scope for manoeuvre" because these agreements are flexible and reciprocal by nature. The GATT/WTO agreements do leave some room in response to difficulties of the members in implementation. However, this scope for manoeuvre is limited. Also, it does not mean that the obligation of implementation is negotiable. The ECJ grants the political organs of the Community more space than they should have under the GATT/WTO agreements. The findings reflect the concerns over the good faith of Community's trade partners on the application of the WTO rules. Unilateral direct effect might put the EU at a disadvantage in the trade relations and negotiations. The ECJ awaits the political organs making the final determination.

China tends to recognize the direct effect of international agreements, but that tendency is not a firm rule. No law or regulation has ever specifically addressed the issue or indicated a uniform and definite position. The effect of the WTO agreements depends on the domestic laws and regulations applied in WTO-related cases. The WTO agreements could be directly effective in cases between private parties; the civil and commercial laws and regulations consistently favor the direct effect. Regarding the administrative laws and regulations, such a tendency could not be found. The WTO agreements could be directly effective in that specific case, if the administrative law or the regulation applicable in the given case so implies. In the meantime, the State Council and the Supreme Court totally deny the application of WTO agreement to administration litigations. The reasons for accepting or denying the direct effect of the WTO agreements did not appear anywhere in the legal documents relevant to laws and regulations, which regulate trade-related matters. The government's considerations are not revealed to the public. It is hard to tell whether China has viewed the effect of WTO agreements as diverse as the laws and regulations indicated. It was reported that a few members have suggested China should accept the direct effect during the accession negotiations. China has rejected such a suggestion because its major trade partners (i.e., the US and the EU) did not do the same. If that is the case, China will explicitly refuse the direct effect of the WTO agreements eventually.

Taiwan is quite open to direct effect of international agreements. Although the Constitution did not mention the effect of international agreements, the Constitutional Court recognizes international agreements as part of domestic laws and directly effective. As a treaty ratified by the Legislative Yuan, the WTO agreements will have direct effect. Unlike the political branches in the other member states, the legislative and executive branches did not ask for broad discretion on the implementation of the obligations under the WTO agreements. The WTO laws are seen more as protections for trade opportunities than as constraints on sovereignty. Accession to an international agreement would be taken as the breakthrough of the blockade to international society – an achievement that draws more attention to the contents of the international agreements. The internal market is relatively small and less appealing to Taiwan's trade partners, most of which are large or mega economies. Taiwan will not have advantages in a bilateral framework.

In the WTO forum, Taiwan also may join with states that have similar interests and negotiate with other larger states. Also, Taiwan might not prefer the scope of manoeuvre for the alleged non-compliance, which might lead to bilateral negotiations and trade retaliations. If the legislative and executive branches do not apparently oppose the direct effect of the WTO agreements, the court has no reason to change their practice on this issue. Besides, several legislations had allowed or requested the application of international agreements. The international agreements would not be totally alien to the courts. The courts become accustomed to turn to the rules beyond the domestic legal system.

In short, the policy considerations play a central role in the direct effect of the WTO agreements. The concerns against the direct effect are the excessive constraints on domestic decision-making power and lack of reciprocity in implementation of the obligations under the WTO agreements. The larger member especially would have such concerns. The smaller members (e.g., Taiwan) believe they would not have much control over the international trade politics. The rule-oriented international agreements would be more of a source of protection than constraint.

The second question is about the grounds for granting the direct effect of WTO agreements. Advocates of direct effect maintain the courts of the member states should be involved in the application and the interpretations of the WTO rules within their domestic legal systems. On the contrary, the opponents insist the political departments, i.e., the legislatures and the executive, should have exclusive competence of the implementation. Both sides have provided normative and pragmatic arguments.

From the normative perspective, the direct effect issue is deliberated under constitutional principles and doctrines. The direct effect should be granted, for the constitutional guarantees of freedom of trade could serve as ground for judicial control over trade policy. The GATT/WTO could supplement the function of the domestic constitutional system, particularly in terms of constraining the governments' discretion on foreign trade. The adversaries pointed out that the direct effect is an endangerment to constitutional principles.

The pragmatic arguments emphasize the economic and the policy considerations. The grounds for granting direct effect are summarized as following: a) avoiding protectionism by increasing the mutual trust between the member states; b) ensuring the rights of the market participants to make the economic decisions; c) the enhancement of the effectiveness of international law; and d) better assurance of the rights of individuals when the international agreement contains norms designed to apply to those individuals. The grounds denying direct effect are provided in particular: a) the wishes of legislatures to tailor-make the implementation of the WTO agreements; b) the disincentive to joint the WTO agreements; c) the asymmetric positions of the member states in trade negotiations; d) the inconsistent applications and interpretations of the WTO agreements; and e) the overburden for the domestic courts.

The last question is whether the direct effect of the WTO agreements should be granted. In author's view, the provisions embedding the principles of human rights could be construed to create rights for individuals and could have direct effect. These provisions actually set a minimum standard of treatment to foreigners in their economic lives and to nationals trading with foreigners, in which the constitutions of the member states often are less interested. The provisions embodying the principle of human rights are consistent with, or even copy, the constitutional principles of member states. It would be absurd to deny the applications of these provisions merely because international trade affairs are involved. Moreover, the provisions reflecting human rights do not contradict the very objective of democracy. In addition, the enforcement mechanism of the WTO could not fully secure the compliance of the member states with the WTO rules. The only problem is, for now, that the WTO appears not to have the competence to supervise the implementation of the WTO agreements as intensively as direct effect implies. Granting direct effect only to the provisions creating rights of individuals could partially ease the problem of lack of competence. However, given the lack of an ultimate say on the interpretations of the WTO rules, the member states might have to negotiate for a mutually-agreed solution for the WTO-inconsistent interpretations made by national courts. That means the economical power of the member state, not necessarily the rules provided, would be decisive for the enforcement of the WTO agreements. In this sense, no rights of individuals would actually be guaranteed, even if the direct effect were granted.

It should nonetheless be noted that the competence issue only reveals why the WTO now cannot become deeply involved in supervising the implementation measures of the member states. If the mechanism ensuring the uniform interpretations could be established, the obstacle to direct effect would be solved. In sum, the provisions construed as creating rights for individuals are capable of being directly effective, in particular: (1) non-discrimination treatments: such as GATS Articles II: 1 and XVII: 1, GATS XVII: 3, TRIPS Articles 3 and 4, GATT Articles I and III; (2) Right to remedy: such as GATS Article VI: 2 (a), TRIPS Articles 42, 49, 59, SCM Article 23, AD Article 13, CV Article 11, PSI Articles 2.21 and 4; (3) provisions reflecting the rule of law: such as SCM Articles 10, 11, 12; AD Articles 1, 5, 6, GATS Article VI, CV Articles 2-8; LIC Articles 1-3; and (4) protection for intellectual property rights: a substantial part of the TRIPS agreement. These provisions should be granted direct effect, but not until the WTO could properly solve the problem of divergent interpretations of national courts.

References

Literature

Abbott, Frederick M. et al. (eds.), International Trade and Human Rights: Foundations and Conceptual Issues (University of Michigan Press, Michigan, 2006).

Alber, Siegbert, *Opinion of Advocate General, Case C 93/02P, Établissements Biret et Cie SA v Council of the European Union*, 2003 ECR 10497.

Alter, Karen J., Establishing the Supremacy of European Law: The Making of Rule of Law in Europe (Oxford University Press, Oxford [et al.] 2001).

Alston, Philip, *Resisting the Merger and Acquisition of Human Rights by Trade Law: A Reply to Petersmann*, (2002) 13(4) European Journal of International Law 815.

American Law Institute, Restatement of Law, Third, The Foreign Relations of The United States (American Law Inst. Publ., St. Paul, Minn., 1987).

Anderson, Robert. D, *Renewing the WTO Agreement on Government Procurement: Progress to Date and Ongoing Negotiations*, (2007)16(4) Public Procurement Law Review 255.

Antoniadis, Antonis, *The European Union and WTO Law: a Nexus of Reactive, Coactive, and Proactive Approaches*, (2007) 6(1) World Trade Review 45.

Aust, Anthony, Modern Treaty Law and Practice, (Cambridge University Press, Cambridge [et al.], 2002).

Bacchus, James, *A Few Thoughts on Legitimacy, Democracy, and the WTO*, in Petersmann (ed.), Reforming The World Trading System: Legitimacy, Efficiency and Democratic Governance, (Oxford University Press, Oxford [et al.], 2005), 429.

– *Inside the World Trade Organization*, (2002) Discussion Paper No.18 (Columbia Business School), <http://www2.gsb.columbia.edu/apec/APECStudy Center, ColumbiaUniversity/Discussion_Papers.html>.

Barceló, John J., *Status of the WTO Rules in the US Law*, 25 (Cornell Legal Studies Research Paper No. 06-004, Mar.03, 2006), <http://ssrn.com/ab stract=887757>.

– *The Paradox of Excluding WTO Direct and Indirect Effect in the U.S. Law*, (2006) 21 Tulane European & Civil Law Forum 147.

Bebr, Gehard, *Agreements Concluded by the Community and Their Possible Direct Effect: from International Fruit Company to Kupferberg*, (1983) 20 Common Market Law Review 35.

Beise, Marc, Die Welthandelsorganisation (WTO): Funktion, Status, Organisation (Nomos, Baden-Baden, 2000).

Benedek, Wolfgang, Die Rechtsordnung des GATT aus völkerrechtlicher Sicht (Springer, Berlin, 1990).

Bellmann, Christophe & Gerster, Richard, *Accountability in the World Trade Organization*, (1996) 30(6) Journal of World Trade 31.

Bello, Judith H., *The WTO Dispute Settlement Understanding: Less is More*, (1996) 90 (3) American Journal of International Law 416.

Berkey, Judson Osterhoudt, *The European Court of Justice and Direct Effect for the GATT: A Question Worth Revisiting*, (1998) 9 European Journal of International Law 626.

Berman, Paul Schiff, *Global Legal Pluralism*, (2007) 80 Southern California Review 1155.

Bermann, George A. & Mavroidis, Petros C. (eds.), Trade and Human Health and Safety (Cambridge University Press, Cambridge [et al.], 2006)

Bhawati, Jadish, Protectionism (MIT Press, Cambridge, Mass. [et al.], 1990).

Bleckmann, Albert, Begriff und Kriterien der innerstaatlichen Anwendbarkeit völkerrechtliche Verträge: Versuch einer allgemeinen Theorie des self-executing treaty auf rechtsvergleichender Grundlage (Duncker & Humblot, Berlin,1970).

Bourgois, Jacques H., *Effects of International Agreements in European Community Law: Are Dice Cast?*, (1984) 82 Michigan Law Review 1250.

– *The European Court of Justice and the WTO: Problems and Challenges*, in Joseph H.H. Weiler (ed), The EU, the WTO and the NAFTA (Oxford University Press, Oxford [et al.], 2000), 71.

Brand, Ronald A., *The Status of General Agreement on Tariff and Trade in the United States Domestic Law*, (1990) 26 Stanford Journal of International Law 479.

– *Direct Effect for International Economic Law in the United States and the European Union*, 17 Northwestern Journal of International Law and Business 556 (1997).

Bronckers, Marco & van den Broek, Naboth, *Financial Compensations in the WTO: Improving Remedies in WTO Dispute Settlement*, in Dencho Georgiev & Kim van der Borght (eds.) Reform and Development of The WTO Dispute Settlement System (Cameron May, London, 2006), 43.

Brownlie, Ian, Principles of Public international Law (7th ed., Oxford University Press, Oxford [et al.], 2008).

Burke-White, William, International *Legal Pluralism*, (2004) 25 Michigan Journal of International Law 963.

Buchs, Gaby I., Das Phänomen der unmittelbare Anwendbarkeit völkerrechtlicher Vertragsbestimmungen: am Beispiel der Rechtsprechung der Gerichte Deutschlands, Österreichs, der Schweiz und der Vereinigten Staaten (Nomos, Baden-Baden, 1993).

Buergenthal, Thomas, *Self-Executing and Non-Self-Executing Treaties in National and International Law*, (1992) 235 Recueil Des Cours 303.

Busch, Marc L. & Reinhardt, Eric, *Testing International Trade Law: Empirical Studies of GATT/WTO Dispute Settlement*, in Daniel L.M. Kennedy & James D. Southwick (eds.), the Political Economy of International Trade Law: Essays in Honor of Robert E. Hudec (Cambridge University Press, Cambridge [et al.], 2002),457.

Cao, Jianming, *WTO and the Rule of Law in China*, (2002) 16 Temple International and Comparative Law Journal 379.

Cao, Shinbing, *The Legal Status of Decision and Judicial Interpretations of the Supreme Court of China*, 3(1) Frontiers of Law of China 1(2008).

Cass, Deborah Z., The Constitutionalization of the World Trade Organization: Legitimacy, Democracy, and Community in the International Trading System (Oxford University Press, Oxford [et al.] 2007).

Cassese, Sabino, *Shrimps, Turtles and Procedure: Global Standards for National Administrations* (Institute for International Law and Justice Working Paper No. 2004/4, New York University), <http://ssrn.com/abstract=692761>.

Chapman, Audrey R., *Approaching intellectual property as a human right: obligations related to Article 15 (1) (c)*, (2001) XXXV (3) Copyright Bulletin 4.

Che, Pizhao, *Lun tiao yue zai wo guo de shi yong* (On the Application of Treaty in China), (2005) 2005(3) Law Science Magazine 96.

陳純一(Chen, Chun-Yi), 國際法在國內法的定位*(International Law in Municipal Law: Practices and Theories of Mainland China, Taiwan, Hong Kong, and Macao)*, (National Science Council, Research Project NSC90-2414-H034-009) 3, available at <http://grbsearch.stpi.org.tw/GRB/advSearch.jsp> (last visited Jan.10, 2011).

Chen, Hanfong et al., Guo ji tia yue yu guo nei fa de guan xi ji zhong guo de shi jian (Relationship between treaties and domestic laws and the practices thereof in China), (2000) 2000(2) Tribune of Political Science and Law 117.

陳新民 (Chen, Hsin-Min), 中華民國憲法導論(Introduction of the Constitution of Republic of China), (4th ed., Published by the author, Taipei, 2001).

丘宏達 (Chiu, Hung-Ta), 國際法在我國國內法上的地位 *(The Status of International Law within Domestic Legal System)*, (1993) 19(4) 憲政時代 81.

Charnovitz, Steve, *The WTO and the Rights of the individual*, (2001) March/April Intereconomics 98.

– *Should the Teeth Be Pulled? an Analysis of WTO Sanctions*, in Daniel L.M. Kennedy & James. D. Southwick (eds.), The Political Economy of International Trade Law: Essays in Honor of Robert E. Hudec (Cambridge University Press, Cambridge [et al.], 2002), 602.– *The WTO and Cosmopolitics*, in Petersmann (ed.), Reforming The World Trading System: Legitimacy, Efficiency and Democratic Governance (Oxford University Press, Oxford [et al.], 2005) 437.

Cottier, Thomas, *Dispute Settlement in the World Trade Organization: Characteristics and Structural Implications for the European Union*, (1998) 38 Common Market Law Review 325.

– The Challenge of The WTO Law: Collected Essays (Cameron May, London, 2006).

– The *Judge in International Economic Relations*, in M. Monti, et al. (eds.), Economic Law and Justice in Times of Globalization: Festschrift for Carl Baudenbacher (Berlin, Nomos Verlag, 2007) 99.

– *Trade Law and Human Rights: A Relationship to Discover*, (2002) 5(1) Journal of International Economic Law 111.

Cottier, Thomas & Schefer, Krista Nadakavukaren, *The Relationship Between World Trade Organization Law, National and Regional Law*, (1991) 1 Journal of International Economy law 83.

Craig, Paul P., Once upon a Time in the West: Direct Effect and the Federation of the EEC Law, (1992) 12 Oxford Journal of Legal Studies 454.

Craig, Paul & De Búrca, Gráinne, EU Law: Text, Cases, and Materials (4th ed, Oxford University Press, Oxford [et al,], 2008).

Croley, Steven P. & Jackson, John H. J,*WTO Dispute Procedures, Standard of Review, and Deference to National Governments*, (1996) 90(2) American Journal of International Law 193.

Damrosch, Lori Filser et al. (eds.), International Law: Cases and Materials, (4th ed., West Group, St. Paul, Minn., 2001).

Dashwood, Alan & Hillion, Christophe (eds), The General Law of EC External Relations (Sweet & Maxwell, London, 2000).

Davies, Arwel, *Reviewing Dispute Settlement at the World Trade Organization: a Time to Reconsider the Roles of Compensation*, (2006) 5(1) World Trade Review 31.

– *Connecting or Compartmentalizing the WTO and United States Legal Systems? The Role of the Charming Betsy Canon*, (2007) 10(1) Journal of International Economic Law 117.

Dearborn, Charles H. III, *The Domestic Legal Effect of Declarations That Treaty Provisions Are Not Self-Executing*, (1979)57(2) Texas Law Review 233.

Dendauw, Isabel, *New WTO Agreement on Government Procurement: Analysis of the Framework for* Bid Challenge Procedure*s and the Question of Direct Effect*, (2000) 18(3) Journal of Energy &Natural Resources Law 254.

Di Gianni, Fabrizio & Antonini, Renato, *DSB Decisions and Direct Effect of WTO Law; Should the EC Courts Be More Flexible When the Flexibility of the WTO System Has Come to an End?*, (2006) 40(4) Journal of World Trade 777.

Dingel, Dorthe Dahlgaard, *Direct Effect of the Government Procurement Agreement*, (1996) Public Procurement Law Review 5, 245.

Dong, Guolu, *Guo ji fa zai Zhongguo de shi yong* (the application of international law in China), (2002) 2002(3) Wuhan University Journal (Philosophy & Social Sciences) 349.

Drexl, Josef, *Unmittelbare Anwendbarkeit des WTO- Recht* in globalen Privatrechtsordnung, in *s*, Bernhard Großfeld et al. (eds.), *Festschrift für Wolfgang Fikentscher zum 70. Geburtstag* (Mohr Siebeck, Tübingen,1998).

Duggal, Roul, TRIPs-Übereinkommen und internationales Urheberrecht, 110 (Heymann , Cologne [et al.], 2001).

Duvigneau, Johann Ludwig, Die Konstitutionalisierung des WTO-Rechts: Zur juristische Diskussion über Verfassungsstrukturen im Bereich des Handelsvölkerrechts, (2001) 56(3) Außenwirtschaft 293.

Eeckhout, Piet, External relations of the European Union: legal and constitutional foundations (Oxford University Press, Oxford [et al.], 2004).

– *Judicial Enforcement of WTO Law in the European Union-Some Further Reflections*, (2002) 5(1) Journal of International Economic Law 91.

– *The Domestic Legal Status of the WTO Agreements: Interconnecting Legal Systems*, (1997) 34(1) Common Market Law Review 11.

Engelberger, Lukas, Die Unmittelbare Anwendbarkeit des WTO-Rechts in der Schweiz: Grundlagen und Perspektiven im Kontext internationaler Rechtsentwicklungen (Peter Lang, Bern [et al.], 2004).

Epiney, Astrid, *Zur Stellung des Völkerrechts in der EU*, (1999) 1999 Europäische Zeitschrift für Wirtschaftsrecht 5.

Eucken, Walter, *Die Wettbewerbungsordnung und ihre Verwirklichung*, (1949) 2 Ordo: Jahrbuch für die Ordnung von Wirtschaft und Gesellschaft 1.

Evans, Gail E., Law Making under the Trade Constitution: A Study in Legislating by World Trade Organization (Kluwer Law International, Hague, 2000).

Everling, Ulrich, *Will Europe Slip on Bananas? The Bananas Judgment of the Court of Justice and National Courts*, (1996) 33 Common Market Law review 401.

法治斌 (Fa, Chih-Pin) & 董保城 (Tung, Pao-Cheng), 中華民國憲法 (Constitution of Republic of China), (National Open University Press, Taipei, 2001).

Friedman, Milton & Friedman, Rose, *The Case for Free Trade*, 1997(4) Hoover Digest (Oct.30, 1997), available at <http://www.hoover.org/publications/hoover-digest/article/7125>.

Fukunaga, Yuka, *Securing Compliance through the WTO Dispute Settlement System: Implementation of DSB Recommendations*, (2006) 9(2) Journal of International Economic Law 383.

Glendon, Mary Ann, *The Rule of Law in The Universal Declaration of Human Rights*, 2 Northwestern Journal of International Human Rights Rts. 5 (Apr. 2004), <http://www.law.northwestern.edu/journals/jihr/v2/5>.

General Agreement on Tariff and Trade(GATT), Contracting Parties, Decision on Differential and More Favourable Treatment Reciprocity and Fuller Participation of Developing Countries, L/4903(Nov. 28,1979).

– Contracting Parties, Signatures of the Torquay Final Act and Annexed Documents, GATT/CP/112/ADD.3 (June 22, 1951).

– Contracting Parties, Signature of various protocols, GATT/CP/40/ADD.14 (May 2 1950).

– Contracting Parties, Summary Record of the Nineteenth Meeting, SR. 13/19, 202 (Dec. 2, 1958).

– Report of Working Party 4 on the European Coal and Steel Community, G/35, 8 (Nov. 7, 1952).

Göttsche, Götz J. *Die WTO als Rechtordnung und Institution*, in Meinhard Hilf & Stefan Oeter (eds), WTO-Recht,103 (2nd ed., Nomos, Baden-Baden, 2010) 101.

Griller, Stefan, *Judicial Enforcement of WTO Law in The European Union Annotation to Case C-149/96, Portugal v. Council*, (2000) 3(3) Journal of International Economic Law 441.

Gulmann, Claus Christian, *Opinion of the Advocate General, Case C-280/93, Federal Republic of Germany v Council of the European Union*, 1994 ECR 4973.

Habbard, Anne-Christine & Guiraud, Marie, *The World Trade Organization and Human Rights* (FIDH Position Paper, Nov. 1999), <http://www.fidh.org/rap ports/wto-fidh.htm> .

Hackworth, Green H., Digest of International Law Vol. 5 (Government Printing Office, Washington, 1944).

Held, David, Democracy and Global Order: From the Modern State to Cosmopolitan Governance (Polity Press, Cambridge, 1995).

He, Xiaoyong, *Lun WTO xie yi yu guo ne fa de fa lu guan xi wen ti* (Issues concerning the Relation between WTO agreements and the Domestic Law), (2001) 1 Journal for Political Science and Law 25.

Henkin, Louis, Constitutionalism, Democracy, and Foreign Affairs (Columbia University Press, New York, 1990).

– Foreign Affairs and the United States Constitution (2nd ed., Clarendon Press, Oxford[et al.], 1996).

Henkin, Louis et al. (eds.), International Law: Cases and Materials (3rd ed., West Publ. St. Paul, Minn, 1993).

Hilary, John, The Wrong Model: GATS, Trade Liberalization and Children's Right to Health, (Save the Children UK, London, 2001).

Hilf, Meinhard, *How Can Parliamentary Participation in WTO Rule-Making and Democratic Control Be More Effective? The European Context*, in Petersmann (ed.), Reforming The World Trading System: Legitimacy, Efficiency and Democratic Governance, (Oxford University Press, Oxford [et al.], 2005), 413.

Hilf, Meinhard & Reuß, Matthias, *Verfassungsfragen lebensmittelrechtlicher Normierung*, (1997) 1997 Zeitschrift für das gesamte Lebensmittelrecht 289.

Hobe, Stephan, Einführung in das Völkerrecht (9thed., Francke, Tübingen,2008).

– Europarecht (5th ed, Heymann, Cologne, 2010).

– Der offene Verfassungsstaat zwischen Souveränität und Interdependenz: Eine Studie zur Wandlung des Staatsbegriffs der deutschsprachigen Staatslehre im Kontext internationaler institutionalisierter Kooperation (Duncker & Humblot, Berlin, 1998).

Hobe, Stephan & Müller-Sartori, Patrick, Rechtsfragen der Einbindung der EG/EU in das Völkerrecht, 2002 Juristische Schulung 2002, 8.

Holzer, Patrick Edgar, Die Ermittlung der innerstaatlichen Anwendbarkeit völkerrechtlicher Vertragsbestimmungen (Polygraph, Zürich, 1998).

Hoppmann, Erich, *Walter Euckens Ordnungsökonomik: heute,* (1995) 46 Ordo: Jahrbuch für die Ordnung von Wirtschaft und Gesellschaf 41.

蕭雄淋 (Hsiao, Hsiung-Lin), 大英百科全書官司攻防戰：最高法院發回後有關中美條約適用的爭執（上）*(The Battle over the Britannica Encyclopedia Case: the Debates about the Application of the FCN Treaty* (1)), (1993). 160律師通訊 50.

– 大英百科全書官司攻防戰：最高法院發回後有關中美條約適用的爭執（下）*(The Battle over the Britannica Encyclopedia Case: the Debates about the Application of the FCN Treaty (2))*, (1993). 161律師通訊 53.

許育典(Hsu, Yu-Tien), 憲法(The Constitution), (3th ed., Angle, Taipei, 2009).

Hu, Qihua & Shao, Zongwei, *Laws Pave Way for WTO Entry*, China Daily, Oct. 31, 2000.

黃異 (Huang, Yi), 國際條約及國際習慣法在我國內國領域之效力 *(The Effect of International Agreements and Customary International Law within the Domestic Legal System of Taiwan)*, 27 輔仁法學雜誌 51, 71-72 (2004).

Hudec, Robert E., T*he Legal Status of GATT in the Domestic Law of the United States*, in Meinhard. Hilf et.al. (eds.), The European Community and the GATT (Kluwer, Deventer [et al.], 1986), 187.

– *Comment on "The Club Model of Multilateral Cooperation and Problems of Democratic Legitimacy"*, in Roger B. Porter et.al. (eds.), Efficiency, Equity, and Legitimacy: The Multilateral System at the Millennium (Brookings Inst. Press, Washington DC, 2001), 295.

– *The Role of Judicial Review in Preserving Liberal Foreign Policies*, in Meinhard Hilf & Ernst-Ulrich Petersmann (eds), National Constitutions and International Economic Law (Kluwer, Deventer[et al.], 1993), 503.

Iwasawa, Yuji, *The Doctrine of Self-Executing Treaties in the United States: A Critical Analysis*, (1985) 26(3) Virginia Journal of International Law 627.

Jackson, John Howard, T*he General Agreement on Tariffs and Trade in the United States Domestic Law*, (1967) 66 Michigan law review 249.

– *Reflections on the Possible Research Agenda for Exploring the Relationship between Human Rights Norms and International Trade*, in Federick M. Abbort et.al. (eds.), International Trade and Human Rights (University of Michigan Press, Ann Arbor, Mich., 2006), 19.

– *Implementing the Tokyo Round: Legal Aspects of Changing International Economic Rules*, (1982) 80(2) Michigan Law Review 267.

– *Status of Treaties in Domestic Legal Systems: A policy Analysis*, (1992) 86 American Journal of International Law 310.

– Sovereignty, the WTO and Changing Foundations of International Law (Cambridge University Press, Cambridge [et al.], 2006).

– *The General Agreement on Tariffs and Trade in the United States Domestic Law*, (1967) 66 Michigan law review 249.

– *The Great 1994 Sovereignty Debate: United States Acceptance and Implementation of the Uruguay Round Results*, (1997) 36 Columbia Journal of Transnational Law 157.

– The Jurisprudence of GATT and the WTO (Cambridge University Press, Cambridge et al. 2000).

– *The WTO 'Constitution' and Proposed Reforms: Seven 'Mantras' Revisited*, (2001) 4(1) Journal of International Economic Law 67.

– *The WTO Dispute Settlement Understanding-Misunderstandings on the nature of Legal Obligation*, (1997) 91(1) American Journal of International Law 60.

– *U.S. Constitutional Principles and Foreign Trade Law and Policy*, in Meinhard Hilf & Ernst-Ulrich Petersmann (eds), National Constitutions and International Economic Law (Kluwer, Deventer[et al.], 1993), 65.

Jackson, John Howard et al., Legal Problems of International Economic Relations: Cases, Materials and Text on the National and International Regulation of Transnational Economic Relations (4th ed., West Publ., St. Paul, Minn., 2002).

Jiang Bixin, *WTO yu wo guo de si f ashen cha zhi du* (The WTO and the Judicial Review System of China), (2001) 2001(3) Journal of Law Application 10.

Jiang, Guoqing, *Guo ji fa yu guo ji tiao yue de ji ge wen ti (Few Issues Concerning International Law and International Treaties)*, (2000) 2000(3) Journal of Foreign Affairs College 8.

Jiang, Wei, & Wang, Jingchi, *WTO xie yi yu Zhongguo min shi si fa zhi du de wan shan* (The WTO Agreements and the Perfection of China's Civil Judicial System, (2001) 2001(1) China Legal Science 25.

Kaddous, Christine, *Effects of International Agreements in the EU Legal Order*, in Marise_Cremona & Bruno de Witte (eds.) EU Foreign Relations Law: Constitutional Fundamentals (Hart Publ., Oxford [et al.], 2008), 291.

Kant, Immanuel: Grundlegung zur Metaphysik der Sitten, reprinted in Wilhelm Weischedel (ed.), Schriften zur Ethik und Religionsphilosophie, Vol. 6 Part I (Wissenschaftliche Buchgesellschaft, Darmstadt, 1968).

Kant, Immanuel: Die Metaphysik der Sitten, reprinted in Wilhelm Weischedel (ed.), Schriften zur Ethik und Religionsphilosophie, Vol. 7 Part II (Wissenschaftliche Buchgesellschaft, Darmstadt, 1968).

Kelsen, Hans. Principles of International Law (Rinehart & Company, Inc. New York, 1952).

Keojane, Robert O. & Nye, Joseph S., *The Club Model of Multilateral Cooperation and Problems of Democratic Legitimacy*, in Roger B. Porter et al. (eds.), Efficiency, Equity, and Legitimacy: The Multilateral System at the Millennium (Brookings Inst. Press, Washington DC, 2001), 264.

Kindleberger, Charles P., International Economics, 17-33(5th ed., Irwin, Homewood, 1973).

Koller, Arnold, Die unmittelbare Anwendbarkeit völkerrechtliche Vertrage und des EWG-Vertrages im innerstaatlichen Bereich (Stämpfli , Bern,1971).

Kong, Qingjiang, *Enforcement of WTO Agreements in China: Illusion or Reality?*, (2001) 35(6) Journal of World Trade 1181.

Kong, Xianjun, *WTO fa lu de quo ne shi yong* (Domestic Application of WTO Law), Legal Daily, Beijing, Dec. 16, 2001.

Kong Xianjun, *WTO dui si f ashen cha de yao chiu ji wo quo si f ashen cha mian li de ren wu han tiao zhan* (The Judicial Review Requirements of the WTO and the Tasks and the Challenges for the Judicial Review System of China), (2001) 2001(10) Journal of Law Application 17.

Krajewski, Markus, *Democratic Legitimacy and Constitutional Perspectives of WTO Law*, (2001) 35(1) Journal of World Trade 167.

– Verfassungsperspektiven und Legitimation des Rechts der Welthandelsorganisation (WTO) (Duncker & Humblot , Berlin, 2001).

Krueger, Anne O., *Trading Phobias: Governments, NGOs and Multilateral System*, (2000) the Australian Financial Review, Oct.11, 2000.

– *Trade Policy in Developing Countries*, in Ronald W. Jones & Peter B. Kenen (eds.), Handbook of International Economics (Vol. 1, North-Holland, Amsterdam [et al.],1988), 519.

Kuijper, Pieter Jan, *The EC's Common Commercial Policy: Which Way the Swing of the Pendulum*, (1994) 88 American Society of International Law Proceedings 294.

Kuijper, Pieter Jan, T*he New WTO Dispute Settlement System – The Impact on the European Community*, (1995) 29(6) Journal of World Trade 49.

Kuilwick, Kees Jan, The European Court of justice and the GATT Dilemma: Public versus Individual Rights (Nexed Ed. Acad. Publ., Beuningen, 1996).

Kunig, Philip, *Völkerrecht und staatliches Recht* , in Wolfgang Graf Vitzthum (ed.) Völkerrecht (5th ed., De Gruyter, Berlin 2007),75.

Lamy, Pascal, *The Place of The WTO and Its Law in The International Legal Order*, (2007) 17(5) European Journal of International Law 969.

Leebron, David W., *Implementation of the Uruguay Round Results in the United States*, in John H. Jackson & Alan O. Skyes (eds.), Implementing the Uruguay Round (Clarendon Press, Oxford, 1997), 175.

Lester, Simon et al., World Trade Law, Text, Materials and Commentary (Hart, Oxford and Portland, 2008).

Li, Ming, *Ying chong li fa shang kao lu tiao yue zai wo gui de xiao li wen ti* (The Effect of Treaties within China Should Be Subject to the Decisions of Legislative Organs), (2006) 2006(3) Peking University Journal 351.

Li, Peihao, Tiao yue fa gai lun (Introduction of Law of Treaties), (Law Press, China, Beijing, 1987).

Li, Shishi, *Zhongguo de li fa, tiao yue yu guo ji fa (The Legislation of China, Treaties and International Law)*, (1993) 1993 Chinese Yearbook of International Law 264.

Li, Xingxiang, *Wo guo shi shi WTO xie yi de ji ge zhu you wen ti tan xi* (Analysis of the Major questions of the Application of the WTO Agreements), (2002) 71 Fujian Fa Xue 38.

李惠宗 (Li Hui-Tsung), **憲法要義** (Principles of Constitution) , (5th ed., Angel, Taipei, 2009).

廖福特 (Liao, Fu-Te), 國際人權公約國內法化之方法與策略 *(The Method and Strategy of Internalizing the International Covenants on Human Rights)*, 109-110, (Research, Development and Evaluation Commission, Executive Yuan, Research Project Oct., 2002), available at <http://grbsearch.stpi.org.tw/GRB/result.jsp?id=600734&plan_no=rdec-res-091-003&plan_year=91&projkey=PG9105-0023&target=plan&highStr=>.

Liavero, Maria Victoria, *The Possible Direct Effect of the Provision s on Competition in the EEC Free Trade Agreements in the Light of the Kupferberg Decision*, (1983)11 Legal Issues of European Integration 83.

林紀東 (Lin, Chi-Tung), 中華民國憲法逐條釋義 (Commentary to Constitution of Republic of China),(Vol.4 , 4th ed., Sanmin, 1993).

Lim, Hoe, *Trade and Human Rights: What's at Issue?*, (2001) 35(2) Journal of World Trade 275.

Liu, Hanfu, *Shi jie mao yi zu zhi fa zai ne quo fa yuan zhi jie shi yong de wen ti* (The Issues Concerning the Direct Application of WTO Law in Chinese Courts), (2000) 2000(7) Peoples' Judicature 49.

Liu, Hanfu, *Ru shi hou de li fa yu si fa jie shi gong zuo* (The Legislations and Judicial Interpretations after the Accession to the WTO), (2001) 2001(S1) Journal of Law Application 60.

Liu, Hanfu, *Shi jie mao yi zu zhi fa zai ne quo fa yuan zhi jie shi yong de wen ti* (The Issues Concerning the Direct Application of WTO Law in Chinese Courts), (2007) 2000(7) Peoples' Judicature 49.

Liu, Yuewei, Guo ji tiao yue zai zhong guo shi yong xi lun (Some New Thoughts on Application of Treaties), 2007(2) Jurists Review 144 (2007).

羅昌發 (Lo, Chang-Fa), 貿易關係之法律問題 (LEGAL ISSUES CONCERNING TRADE RELATIONS) (Angle, Taipei, 1998).

Ian Loveland, Constitution Law, Administrative Law and Human Rights: A Critical Introduction 428 (4th ed., Oxford University Press, Oxford [et al.], 2006).

Lukas, Marin, *The Role of Private Parties in the Enforcement of the Uruguay Round Agreements*, (1995) 29(5) Journal of World Trade 181.

Matsushita, Mitsuo, *Major WTO Dispute Cases Concerning Government Procurement*, (2006) 1 Asian Journal of WTO & International Health Law and Policy 299.

Marceau, Gabrielle, *The WTO Dispute Settlement and Human Rights*, in Federick M. Abbort et.al. (eds.), International Trade and Human Rights (University of Michigan Press, Ann Arbor, Mich., 2006), 181.

Marceau, Gabrielle & Pedersen, Peter N., *Is the WTO Open and Transparent? A Discussion of the Relationship of the WTO with Non-governmental Organizations and Civil Society's Claim for More Transparency and Public Participation*, (1999) 33(1) Journal of World Trade.

Maresceau, Marc, *The GATT in the Case Law of the European Court of Justice*, in Meinhard. Hilf et al. (eds.), The European Community and the GATT (Kluwer, Deventer [et al.], 1986).

Marvroidis, Petro C., *Remedies in the WTO Legal System: Between a Rock and a Hard Place*, (2000) 11(4) European Journal of International Economic Law 763.

Matsushita, Mitsuo et al., The World Trade Organization: Law, Practice, and Policy (Oxford University Press, Oxford [et al.], 2006).

Mavroidis, Petros C. et al., *Is the WTO Dispute Settlement Mechanism Responsive to the Needs of the Traders? Would a System of Direct Action by Private Parties Yield Better Results*, (1998) 32(2) Journal of World Trade 147.

Mavoidis, Petros C. & Zdouc,Werner, *Legal Means to Protect Private Parties' Interest in the WTO*,(1998)Journal of International Economic Law 1, 407.

Mayer, Franz C., Van Gend en Loos: The Foundation of a Community of Law, in Miguel Poiares Maduro & Loïc Azoulai (eds), The Past and Future of EU Law: The Classics of EU Law Revisited on the 50th Anniversary of the Rome Treaty (Hart Publishing, Oxford[et al.] 2010) 16.

McDowell, Gary L. & Presser, Stephen B., *Forward: Human Rights, Rule of Law, and National Sovereignty, 2 Northwestern Journal of International Human Rights* Rts. 1 (Apr. 2004), <http://www.law.northwestern.edu/journals/jihr/v2/1>.

Mcgivern, Brendan, *Implementation of Panel and Appellate Body Rulings: An overview*, in Rufus Yerxa & Bruce Wilson (eds.), Key Issues in WTO Dispute Settlement: the First Ten Years (Cambridge University Press, Cambridge [et al.], 2005), 98.

McRae, Donald M., *The WTO in International Law: Tradition Continued or New Frontier?* , (2000) 3(1) Journal of International Economic Law 27.

– *Measuring the Effectiveness of the WTO Dispute Settlement System*, (2008) 3 (1) Asian Journal of WTO & International Health Law and Policy 1.

Meesen, Karl, *The Application of Rules of Public International Law within Community Law*, (1976)13 Common Market Law review 485.

Meng, Werner, *Gedanken zur Frage unmittelbarer Anwendung von WTO-Recht in der EG*, in Ulrich Beyerlin et al. (eds), Recht zwischen Umbruch und Bewahrung (Springer, Berlin, 1995), 1063.

– *Das Vertragssystem der Welthandelsorganisation*, in Peter-Christian Müller-Graff (ed.), Die Europäische Gemeinschaft in der Welthandelsorganisation (Nomos, Baden-Baden, 1999) 63.

Mengin, Francoise, *A Pretence of Privatization: Taiwan's External Relations*, in (Beatrice Hibou & Jonathan Derrick (eds), Privatizing the States (Hurst, London, 2004), 147.

Mengozzi, Paolo, Opinion of the Advocate General, Case C-335/05, Řízení Letového Provozu ČR, s. p. v Bundesamt für Finanzen, 2007 ECR 4307.
– *Private International Law and the WTO Law*, 292 Recueil des Cours 253, 263 (2001).
Mora, Montana I, Equilibrium: A Rediscovered Basis for the Court of Justice of the European Communities to Refuse Direct Effect to the Uruguay Round Agreements, (1996) 30 Journal of World Trade 43.
Morrison, Wayne M., *Taiwan's Accession to the WTO and Its Economic Relations with the United States and China*, (Congress Research Service Report for Congress, 2003), <http://fpc.state.gov/documents/organization/23370.pdf>.
Mu, Yapin &. Xi Yifan, *WTO xie yoi zai wo guo guo ne de shi yong wen ti* (On the Enforcement of the WTO Agreements in Mainland China), (2003) 2003(1) Journal of Jinan University 54.
Nader, Ralph, *Prepared Statement of Ralph Nader, GATT Implementing Legislation: Hearings on S. 2467 Before the Senate Committee on Commerce, Science and Transportation*, 103d Cong., 2d Sess., 350 (1994).
Nowak, Manfred, Introduction to the International Human Rights Regime (Nijhoff, Leiden [et al.], 2003).
Oppenheim, Lassa, International Law: A Treatise 25 (Ronald F. Roxburgh ed., 3rd ed., Longmans, Green and Co. , 1920).
Ostergard, Robert L., *Intellectual Property: A Universal Human Right?*, (1999) 21(1) Human Rights Quarterly 156.
Paust, Jordan, *Self- Executing Treaties*, (1998) 82(4) American Journal of International Law 760.
Pauwelyn, Joost, *Enforcement and Countermeasures in the WTO: Rules Are Rules– Toward a More Collective Approach*, (2000) 94(2) American Journal of International Law Journal 335.
Peers, Steve, *Fundamental Right or Political Whim? WTO Law and the European Court of Justice*, in Gráinne de Búrca & Joanne Scott (eds.), The EU and the WTO, Legal and Constitutional Issues (Hart Publ., Oxford [et al.], 2001) 112.
Pescatore, Pierre, *Die Rechtsprechung des Europäischen Gerichtshofs zur innergemeinschaftlichen Wirkung völkerrechtlicher Abkommen*, in Rudolf Bernhardt et al. (eds), Völkerrecht als Rechtsordnung internationale Gerichtsbarkeit Menschenrechte – Festschrift für Hermann Mosler (Springer, Berlin, 1983), 661.
– *Free World Trade and the European Union – The Reconciliation of Interests and Revision of Dispute Resolution Procedures the Framework of the WTO*, in Antonio Pérez van Kappel & Wolfgang Heusel (eds.), Free World Trade and the European Union 9, 10 (Bundesanzeiger, Cologne, 2000), 9.

– The *Doctrine of Direct Effect: An Infant Disease of Community,* (1983) *8* EUROPEAN LAW REVIEW 155.
– *Treaty-Making by European Communities* in Francis G. Jacobs & Shelley Roberts (eds.),The Effect of Treaties in Domestic Law(Sweet & Maxwell, London, 1987), 171.
Petersmann, Ernst-Ulrich, *Application of GATT by the Court of Justice of the EC*, (1983) 20 Common Market Law Review 397.
– Constitutional Functions and Constitutional Problems of International Economic Law (University Press Fribourg, Fribourg, Switzerland, 1991).
– *Darf die EG das Völkerrecht ignorieren?*, (1997) 1997 Europäische Zeitschrift für Wirtschaftsrecht 325.
– *From the Hobbesian International Law of Coexistence to Modern Integration Law: The WTO Dispute Settlement System*, (1998) 1 Journal of International Economic Law 175.
– *Human Rights and International Economic Law in the Twenty First Century*, (2001) 4 Journal of International Economic Law 3.
– *Human Rights and the Law of the World Trade Organization*, (2003) 37 Journal of World Trade 241.
– *Human Rights, Markets and Economic Welfare: Constitutional Functions of the Emerging UN Human Rights Constitution*, in Federick M. Abbort et al. (eds.), International Trade and Human Rights (University of Michigan Press, Ann Arbor, Mich., 2006), 29.
– International and European Trade and Environmental Law after the Uruguay Round (Kluwer Law international, London, 1995).
– *Limited Government and Unlimited Trade Policy Powers? Why Effective Judicial Review of Foreign Trade Restrictions Depends on Individual Rights*, in Meinhard Hilf & Ernst-Ulrich Petersmann (eds.), National Constitutions and International Economic Law (Kluwer, Deventer [et al.], 1993), 537.
– *Multilevel Constitutionalism and Judicial Protection of Freedom and Justice on the International Economic Law of the EC*, in Anthony Arnull et al. (eds.), Continuity and Change in EU Law: Essays in Honour of Sir Francis Jacobs(Oxford University Press, Oxford [et al.], 2008), 338.
– *National Constitutions and International Economic Law*, in Meinhard Hilf & Ernst-Ulrich Petersmann (eds.), National Constitutions and International Economic Law (Kluwer, Deventer [et al.], 1993), 3.
– *Rights and Duties of States and Rights and Duties of Their Citizens*, in Ulrich Beyerlin et al. (eds), Recht zwischen Umbruch und Bewahrung (Springer, Berlin, 1995).

– *The EEC as a GATT Member-Legal Conflict between GATT Law and European Community Law*, in Meinhard. Hilf et al. (eds.), The European Community and the GATT (Kluwer, Deventer [et al.], 1986), 23.
– *The 'Human Rights Approach' Advocated by The UN High Commissioner for Human Rights and by The International Labour Organization: Is It Relevant for WTO Law and Policy?*, (2004) 7(3) Journal of International Economic Law.
– *Trade and Human Rights I*, in Patrick F.J. Macrory et al. (eds.), The World Trade Organization: Legal, Economic and Political Analysis (Vol. 1, Springer Science Business Media, Inc., Boston MA., 2005), 625.

Pühs, Wolfgang, Der Vollzug von Gemeinschaftsrecht: Formen und Grenzen eines effektiven Gemeinschaftsrechtsvollzugs und Überlegungen zu seiner Effektuierung (Duncker & Humblot, Berlin, 1997).

Ragosta, John A., *Unmasking the WTO-Access to the DSB System: Can the WTO DSB Live up to the Moniker "World Trade Court"*, (2000) 31 Law & Policy in International Business 739.

Reams, Bernard D. Jr. & Schultz, John S. (eds.), Uruguay Round Agreements: A Legislative History of Public Law Number 103-465 (Heins, Buffalo N.Y., 1995).

Römer, Karl, *Opinion of the Advocate General, Case 26/62, NV Algemene Transport-en Expeditie Onderneming van Gend & Loos v. Neth. Inland Revenue Admin.*, 1963 E.C.R. 19.

Rozès,Simone, *Opinion of Advocate General, Case 104/81, Hauptzollamt (Chief Tax Office) Mainz v. C. A. Kupferberg & Cie KG A.A.*, 1982 ECR 3641.

Schede, Christian, "*Trondheim Provision" in the WTO Agreement on Government Procurement: Dose This "Major Revision" Live up to the Needs of the Private Sector?*,(1995) 5 Public Procurement Law Review 161.

Schefer, Krista Naddakavukaren, *Dancing with the Devil: A Heretic's View of Protectionism in the WTO Legal System*, (2009) 4(2) Asian Journal of WTO & International Healthy Law and Policy 423.

Schlüter, Bernhard, *The Domestic Status of Human Rights Clauses of the United Nations Charter*, (1973) 61 California Law Review 110.

Seyr, Sibylle, *Der "effet utile" in der Rechtsprechung des* EuGH (Duncker & Humblot, Berlin, 2008).

Shaw, Malcolm N., International Law (6th ed., Cambridge University Press, Cambridge, 2010).

Silva, Guimaraes De Lima e, The Revision of the WTO Agreement on Government Procurement: to what extent might it contribute to the expansion of current membership, (2008) 17(2) Public Procurement Law Review 61.

Sir Ian Sinclair, The Vienna Convention on the Law of Treaties (2nd ed., Manchester University Press, Manchester, 1984).

沈克勤 (Shen, Ko-chin), 國際法 (International Law), (Student Book, Taipei, 1991).

Slaughter, Anne-Marie, Letter from Anne-Marie Slaughter, Professor of Law, Harvard Law School, S.2467, GATT Implementing Legislation Hearings before the Committee on Commerce, Science, and Transportation in the Senate, 103d Cong., 2d Sess., (Oct. 18, 1994).

Smith, Adam, Wealth of Nations (Charles Jesse Bullock ed., Cosimo Inc., New York, 2007).

Srinivasan, Thirukodikaval Nilakanta, *Trade and Human Rights*, in Alan Verne Deardorff & Robert Mitchell Stern (eds.), Constituent Interests and U.S. Trade Policies (University of Michigan Press, Ann Arbor, Mich., 1999).

Stotter, Charles W., *Self-Executing Treaties and Human Rights Provisions of United Nations Charter: a Separation of Powers Problem*, (1976) 25 Buffalo Law Review 773.

Streinz, Rudolf, *Der "effet utile" in der Rechtsprechung des Gerichtshofs der Europäischen Gemeinschaft*, in Ole Due et al. (eds), Festschrift für Ulrich Everling (Nomos, Baden-Baden, 1995), 1491.

Suzuki, Yoki, *Sequencing and Compliance*, in Dencho Georgiev & Kim van der Borght (eds.) Reform and Development of The WTO Dispute Settlement System (Cameron May, London, 2006), 367.

Tancredi, Antonello, *EC Practice in the WTO: How Wide is the "Scope for Manoeuvre"?*, (2004) European Journal of International Law 933.

Tang, Shumei, Lun WTO gui ze yu guo ne fa han guo ji tiao yui de guan xi (The Relationship among WTO Rules, Domestic Laws and International Agreements), (2004) 2004(3) Journal of Remin University of China 79.

Tesauro, Giuseppe, *Opinion of Advocate General,* Case C-53/96, Hermès International (a partnership limited by shares) v. FHT Marketing Choice BV, 1998 ECR 3603.

The Congressional Research Service, Library of Congress, Constitution of United States of America: Analysis and Interpretation, S. Doc. No. 108-17 (U.S. Government Printing Office, Washington, 2004).

The European Community/Union, Communication from the Commission to the Council: *Overall Approach*: *New Round of Trade Negotiations in Defence of Open Multilateral Trade*, EEC Doc. No. 7748/86, SEC (86) 840 final.

– Council Decision 94/800/EC, *concerning the conclusion on behalf of the European Community, as regards matters within its competence, of the agreements reached in the Uruguay Round multilateral negotiations (1986-1994)*, 1994 O.J. (L 336) 1.

Tomuschat, Christian, in Hans von der Groeben & Jürgen Schwarze (eds.), Kommentar zum Vertrag über die Europäische Union und zur Gründung der Europäischen Gemeinschaft, Article 281EC (Vol. 4, 6th ed., Nomos, Baden-Baden, 2003).

Torremans, Paul L.C., *Copyright (and Other Intellectual Property Rights) as a Human Right*, in Paul L.C. Torremans (ed.), Intellectual Property and Human Rights: enhanced Edition of Copyright and Human Rights (Wolters Kluwer Law & Business, Austin [et al.], 2008), 195.

Trachtman, Joel P., *Bananas, Direct Effect and Compliance*, (1999) 10(4) European Journal of International Law 655.

Tribe, Laurence, *Prepared Statement of Laurence Tribe, GATT Implementing Legislation: Hearings on S. 2467 Before the Senate Committee on Commerce, Science and Transportation*, 103d Cong., 2d Sess., 296.

Triepel, Heinrich, Völkerrecht und Landrecht (C.L. Hirschfeld, Leipzig, 1899).

Tumlir, Jan, *International Economic Order and Democratic Constitutionalism*, (1983) 34 Ordo: Jahrbuch für die Ordnung von Wirtschaft und Gesellschaft 71.

– Protectionism: Trade Policy in Democratic Societies (American Enterprise Institute for Public Policy Research, Washington DC, 1985).

Thürer, Daniel, *WTO- Teilordnung im System des Völker- und Europarecht*s, in Daniel Thürer & Stephan Kux (eds), GATT 94 und die Welthandelsorganisation: Herausforderung für die Schweiz und Europa (Nomos, Baden-Baden, 1996), 41.

Uerpmann, Robert, *International Law as an Element of European Constitutional Law: International Supplementary Constitutions* 32, (Jean Monnet Working Paper 9/03, 2003) <http://centers.law.nyu.edu/jeanmonnet/papers/03/030901.html>.

United Nations (UN), Committee against Torture, 14 th Sess., 51 st mtg. , at 2, U.N. Doc. CAT/C/SR. 51, (May 4, 1990).

– U.N. Committee against Torture, *Consideration of Reports Submitted by States Parties Under Article 19 of The Convention: Initial Reports of States Parties Due in 1989: China*,CAT/C/7/Add.14 (Jan 18, 1993).

– U.N. Econ. & Soc. Council, Commission on Human Rights, *Analytical study of the High Commissioner for Human Rights on the fundamental principle of non-discrimination in the context of globalization*, para. 26, U.N. Doc. E/CN.4/2004/40 (Jan 15, 2004).

– U.N. Econ. & Soc. Council, Commission on Human Rights, *Globalization and Its Impact on the Full Enjoyment of Human Rights*, UN Doc. E/CN.4/2002/54 (Jan. 15, 2002).

– U.N. Econ & Soc. Council, *Protocol of Provisional Application of the General Agreement on Tariffs and Trade*, E/PC/T/214.Add.2 Rev.1 (Jan 1, 1940).

- U.N. Econ. & Soc. Council, Commission on Human Rights, Open-ended Working Group on the Right of Development, *Study on the Current State of Progress in the Implementation of the Right to Development*, independent expert, para. 37, U.N. Doc. E/CN.4/1999/WG.18/2(1999) (prepared by Mr. Arjun K. Sengupta).
- U.N. Econ. & Soc. Council, Commission on Human Rights, Sub-commission on the Promotion and the Protection of Human rights, 53rd. Sess., 12th mtg., para. 24, E/CN.4/Sub.2/2001/SR.12 (Aug. 14, 2001).
- U.N. Econ. & Soc. Council, Sub-Commission on the Promotion and Protection of Human Rights, *Liberalization of Trade in Services and Human Rights*, UN Doc. E/CN.4/Sub.2/2002/9 (June 25, 2002).
- U.N. Econ. & Soc. Council, Sub-Commission on the Promotion and Protection of Human Rights, *The Impact of the Agreement on Trade-Related Aspects of Intellectual Property Rights on Human Rights*, UN Doc. E/CN.4/Sub.2/2001/13 (June 27, 2001).
- U.N. Econ. & Soc. Council, Sub-Commission on the Promotion and Protection of Human Rights, *The Realization of Economic, Social and Cultural Rights: Globalization and Its Impact on the Full Enjoyment of Human Rights*, U.N. Doc. E/CN.4/Sub.2/2000/13(June 15, 2000) (prepared by J. Oloka-Onyango and Deepika Udagama).
- U.N. General Assembly, *Restoration of Lawful Rights of People's Republic of China in the United Nations*, G.A. Res. 2758 (XXVI), U.N. Doc. A/L.630 and Add. 1-2.
- U.N. Human Rights Committee, *CCPR General Comment No. 18: Non-discrimination* (Nov. 10, 1989), <http://www.unhcr.org/refworld/docid/453883fa8.html>.
- U.N. Human Right Committee, *Adam v. Czech Republic*, Communication No. 586/1994, U.N. Doc.CCPR/C/57/D/586/1994 (July 25, 1996).
- U.N. Human Right Committee, *Danning v. Netherlands*, Communication No. 180/1984, U.N. Doc. CCPR/C/29/D/180/1984(Apr. 9, 1987).
- U.N. Human Right Committee, *Gomez v. Spain*, Communication No. 865/1999, U.N. Doc. CCPR/C/78/D/895/1999 (Nov. 5, 2001).
- U.N. Human Right Committee, *Gueye et.al. v. France*, Communication No. 196/1985(1989), U.N. Doc. CCPR/C/35/D/196/1985 (Apr. 3, 1989).
- U.N. Human Right Committee, *Griffin v. Spain*, Communication No. 493/1992, U.N. Doc. CCPR/C/49/D/493/1992 (Apr. 5, 1995).
- U.N. Human Right Committee, *Hoofdman v. Netherlands*, Communication No. 602/1994, U.N. Doc. CCPR/C/64/D/602/1994 (Nov. 25, 1998).
- Universal Declaration of Human Rights, G.A. Res. 217A, UN GAOR, 3d Sess. Pt 1, Resolution, UN Doc A/810(Dec.12, 1948).

– Responsibility of States for Internationally Wrongful Acts, G.A. Res. 56/83, UN. Doc. A/RES/56/83 (Dec. 12, 2001).
– The Preparatory Committee of the United Nations Conference on Trade and Employment, *ITO Preparatory Committee Final Meeting and Signing of Final Act and of Protocol of Provisional Application*, Press Release No. 479 (Oct.30, 1947).
– The Secretary General, *Globalization and Its Impact on Full Enjoyment of Human Rights*, para. 14, *delivered to the General Assembly*, U.N. Doc. A 55/342 (Aug. 31, 2000).
– World Conference on Human Rights, June 14-25, 1993, *Vienna Decoration and Programme of Action*, UN doc. A/CONF.157/23 (July 12, 1993).

U.S. House of Representatives, Trade Agreements Act of 1979: Statements of Administrative Action, H.R. Doc. No. 153 pt. 2, 96th Cong., 1st Sess. (1979).

Van den Bossche, Peter L.H., *The European Community and the Uruguay Round*, in John H. Jackson & Alan O. Skyes (eds).Implementing the Uruguay Round (Clarendon Press, Oxford, 1997), 23.

Van den Broek, Naboth, Legal Persuasion, *Political Realism, and Legitimacy: The European Court's Recent Treatment of The Effect of WTO Agreements in The EC Legal Order*, (2001) 4(2) Journal of International Economic Law 411.

Vazquez, Carlos Manuel, The *Four Doctrines of Self-Executing Treaties*, (1995) 89 American Journal of International Law 695.

Verdrross, Alfred & Simma, Bruno, Universelles Völkerrecht: Theorie und Praxis (3rd ed., Duncker & Humblot, Berlin, 1984).

Von Benda-Beckmann, Franz, *Who's Afraid of Legal Pluralism?*, (2002) 47 Journal of Legal Pluralism 37.

Von Benda-Beckmann, Keebet *Globalization and Legal Pluralism*, (2002) 4 International Law FORUM du droit international 19.

Von Bogdandy, Armin, *Constitutionalism in International Law: Comment on a Proposal from Germany*, (2006) Harvard International Law Journal 223.
– *Pluralism, Direct Effect, and the Ultimate Say: On the Relationship between International and Domestic Constitutional Law*, (2008) 6 (3-4) International Journal of Constitutional Law 397.

Wallach, Lori, *Prepared Statement of Lori Wallach, Implications of General Agreement on Tariff and Trade: Hearing before the Committee on Labor and Human Resources in the Senate*, 103d Cong., 2nd Sess. 65 (1994).

Wang, Liyu, *Guo ji tiao yue zai Zhongguo guo ne fa zhong de shi yong (The Application of International Agreements within the Chinese Legal System),* (1993) 1993 Chinese Yearbook of International Law 282.

Wang, Tieya, Guo ji fa yin lun (Introduction of International Law), (Peking University Press, Beijing, 1998).
Wang, Tieya (ed.), Guo ji fa (International law), (Law Press China, Beijing, 1995).
Wang, Yong, Tiao yue zia zhong guo shi yong zh ji ben li lun wen ti yan jiu (Studies on the Basic Theory of Treaty Application in China), 112-118 (Apr. 2006) (unpublished Ph. D. dissertation, East China University of Political Science and Law, (an file with China Knowledge Integrated Database, <http://eng.cnki.net/grid2008/index.htm>.
Wang, Zhenqing, *Zuo hao ru shi hou zhi shi chan quan you quan de shen pan gong zuo* (The Judicial Review of Intellectual Property Right after the Accession to the WTO), (2001) 2001(S1) Journal of Law Application 52.
Wengler, Wilhelm, *Europäischer Gerichtshof, 5.2.1963 – Rechtssache 26/62: Unmittelbare, individuelle Rechte begründende Wirkung des Art. 12; Auslegung des Art. 177; neue Rechtsordnung des Völkerrecht*, (1963) Neue juristische Wochenschrift 1751.
Weston, Melville Fuller, *Political Question*, (1925) 38(2) Harvard Law Review 296.
Wilson, Bruce, *Compliance by WTO Members with Adverse WTO Dispute Settlement Rulings*, the Record to Date, (2007) 10(2) Journal of International Economic Law 397.
Wils, Geert, *The Concept of Reciprocity of EEC Law: An Explanation into These Realms*, (1991) 28 Common Market Law Review 245.
Winter, Gerd (ed.), Multilevel Governance of Global Environmental Change: Perspectives from Science, Sociology and the Law (Cambridge University Press, Cambridge [et al.], 2006).
Winter, Jan A., Direct Applicability and Direct Effect: Two Distinct and Different Concepts in Community Law, (1972) 9 Common Market Law Review 433.
World Trade Organization (WTO), Committee on Trade and Development, Implementation of Special and Differential Treatment Provisions in WTO Agreements and Decisions, WT/COMTD/W/77(Oct. 25, 2000).
– Committee on Trade and Development, *Implementation of Special and Differential Treatment Provisions in WTO Agreements and Decisions*, 3, WT/COMTD/W/77(Oct. 25, 2000).
– Doha Declaration of TRIPS Agreement and Public Health, WT/MIN (01)/DEC/W2 (Nov. 14, 2001).
– General Council, *Decision on the Accession of People's Republic of China*, WT/L/432(Nov.23, 2001).
– General Council, *Decision on the Accession of the Separate Territory of Taiwan, Penghu, Kinmen and Matsu*, p.2, WT/L/433, (Nov.23, 2001).

– General Council, Procedures for the Circulation and Derestriction of WTO Documents,WT/L/160/Rev.1 (Jul. 18, 1996), revised version, WT/L/452 (May 14, 2002).
– Secretariat, Developing Countries and the Multilateral Trading System: Past and Present – Background Note by the Secretariat, Prepared for the High Level Symposium on Trade and Development, Geneva, 17-18 March 1999, Annexes I and II, <http://www.wto.org/english/tratop_e/devel_e/hlmdev_e.htm > (last visited Jan 10,2011).
– Understanding the WTO (4th ed., WTO, Geneva, 2008).
– Working Party on the Accession of China, *Report of the Working Party on the Accession of China*, WT/ACC/CHN/49 (Oct. 1, 2001).

吳嘉生 (Wu, Chia-Sheng), 國際法與國內法關係之研析 (The Analysis of the Relationships between International Law and Domestic Law), (Wunan, Taipei, 1998).

胡文棟 (Wu, Wen-Tung), 我國立法院黨團協商制度之探討 *(A Study of the Party Caucus Negotiation System in the Legislative Yuan*), (2006) 14 社會科學學報 112.

Wu, Yarong, *Lun WTO xie yi de fa lu xiao li ji zai wo quo fa yuan de shi yong* (The Effect of the WTO agreements and its application in the Chinese courts), (2001) 2001(2) Journal of Law Application 11.

Wüger, Daniel, Anwendbarkeit und Justiziabilität völkerrechtlicher Normen im schweizerischen Recht: Grundlagen, Methoden und Kriterien (Bern, Stämpfli Verlag 2005).

Xiao, Bing, WTO han yi, xiao li chong du yu chi shi (Reinterpretation and Enlightenment of Significance and Effectiveness of WTO) 41(6) Journal of Najin University 64 (2004).

Xu, Minyou & Chen, Weidong, Ou gong ti wei rao WTO xie yi zhi jie xiao li de wen ti de zheng lun ji chi dui wo guo de chi shi (The Arguments of the Direct Effect of the WTO Agreements in the EU and the Lessons Learned by China), (2001) 108 Law Review 90.

Yuan, Quan, You quan WTO gui ze zai wo guo shi yong de ruo gan fa lu wen ti (Certain Legal Problems on Internal Application of the Rules of WTO), (2004) 22(7) Hebei Law Science 57.

Zampetti, Americo Beviglia, *Democratic Legitimacy in the World trade Organization: The Justice Dimension*, (2003) 37(1) Journal of World Trade 105.

Zhang, Xiaodong, *Yei lun guo ji tiao yue zhi wo guo de shi yong* (Application of International Agreements in Our County), (2001) 2001(6) Law Review 73.

Zhang, Xin, Domestic Effect of WTO Agreement in China, (2002) 3(5) Journal of World Investment 913.

Zhao, Daguang, *"ru shi" hou wo guo si f ashen cha gong zuo de ruo gan wen ti* (Problems of the Judicial Review after the Accession to the WTO), (2001) 2001(S1) Journal of Law Application 37.

Zeng, Lingliang, *WTO xie yi zai wo guo de shi yong gi wo guo fa zhi jian she de go ming (The Application of WTO Agreements in Our Country and the Revolution of Our Legal System)*, (2000) 2000(6) China Legal Science 38.

Zonnekyn, Geert A., *EC Liability for Non-Compliance of WTO Dispute Settlement Decisions – Are the Dice Cast?*, (2004) 7(2) Journal of International Economic Law 483.

Cases

China, People's Republic of China (Alphabetical)

Beijing shi di yi zhong ji ren min fa yaun shen li yuan gao Huirui Aierlan yiao pin gong si bu fu bei gao Zhonghua Renmin Gongheguo guo jia zhi shi chan quan ju zhan li fu shen wei yuan hui zuo chu de di 6228 hao wu xiao xuan gao qing qiu shen cha jue ding xing zheng pan jue shu (Judgment of The First Beijing Intermediate People's Court on the Claim for the Nullification of the Patent Reexamination Board Decision No. 6228), (2004) Yi-Zhung-Xin-Chu-Zi No. 884, (Beijing First Intermediate People's Court, June 2, 2006), available at <http://www.lexiscn.com/law/content_case_analysis.php?case_id=9436&keyword=d3Rv&t_kw=&eng=0>.

(Fa guo) Lakosite chen shan gu fen you xian gong si su Shanghai hong qiao bai sheng shang mao you xian gong si Changsha fen gong sis hang biao qin quan jiu fen an (French Lacoste Inc. Claim against Shanghai Hongqiao Parkson Trade Co. Ltd, Zhang-sha Branch, for Infringement of Trade Mark), (2004) Chang-Zhong-Ming- San-Chu-Zi No. 307, (Changsha Intermediate People's Court, Oct. 8, 2004), available at <http://www.lexiscn.com/law/content_case _analysis.php?case_id=49154&keyword=dHJpcHM%3D&t_kw=&eng=0>.

Jiangsu sheng Suzhou shi zhong ji ren min fa yuan shen li yuan gao Yishiman Keda gong si su bei gao Suzhou Keda yie ya dian ti you xian gong si shang biao qin quan jiu fen (Ruling of Suzhou Intermediate People's Court on the Trademark Dispute between the Koda and the Koood Hydraulic Elevator Co. Ltd), (2005) Su-Zhong-Ming-San-Chu-Zi No. 0213 (Suzhou Intermediate People's Court, Apr. 6, 2006), available at <http://www.lexiscn.com/law/content_case_analy sis.php?case_id=12718&keyword=dHJpcHM%3D&t_kw=&eng=0>.

Li Junji su Zhuhai shi wei sheng ju chin quan an (Li Jun-Jie v. Zhuhai Department of Health), Xian-Xin-Chu-Zi No. 19 (2003), (Zhuhai City, Xiangzhou

District People's Court, Sep. 28, 2003); Shenjun shi Xianbang hua gong you xian gong si yu Haofuman Luoshi you xian gong si chin fan yao pin du zhan quan jou fen yi an (Xian-Bang Chemical Ltd. Shen Jun city v. F. Hoffmann-La Roche AG) Yue-Gao-Fa-Min-Zhong-San-Zi No. 429 (2006), (Guangdong High People's Court, Feb. 1, 2007).

Lu Chenye ding su Zhang Suxia ding fan ge shou yi ren que ding de chu guo lao wu ren yuan zai guo wai huo de de si wang bao xian pei chang jian an (Lu Chenye et al claim against Zhang Shuxia et al for Distribution of the Death Benefits Acquired Overseas) (Nanjing Intermediate People's Court, Mar. 31, 1997).

Meiguo KLP jian zhu she ji gong si su Quanzhou shi ao lin pi ke zhi ye tou zi you xian gong si jian she gong cheng she ji he tong jiu fen an (Keller Limited Partnership v. Quan-Zhou Olympic Property Investment Co. Ltd., Disputes on the Contracture Contract), （2006） Quan-Zhou-Ming-Chu No. 100, para 1 (Quanzhou Intermediate People's Court, Apr. 4, 2006), available at <http://www.lexiscn.com/law/content_case_analysis.php?case_id=49830&keyword=d3Rv&t_kw=&eng=0>.

(Meiguo) Pu luo ke te hang an bu er gong si su Shanghei Chenxuan zhi neng ke ji fa zhan you xian gong si bu dang jing zheng an ((US)Puluocter and Gan-bool Companies Claim against the Unfair Competition of Shanghai Chenxuan Intellectual Science & Technology Developing Company, Ltd), Hu-Lu-Gao-Zhong-Zi No. 4, (Shanghai High People's Court, July 5, 2001).

Shanghai Zhenhua ji xie yiou xian gong si su Meiguo lian ho ba guo yun song fu wu gong si guo ji hiang kong huo wu yun shu he tong biao shu guai di yan wu pei chang jiu fen an (Shanghai Zhenhua Port Machinery Co., Ltd. Claim against United Parcel Services Company of United States for Compensation for Delivery Delay of Bid Documents) (Jing'an District People's Court, May 18, 1995).

TMT mao yi you xian gong si chi su bei xin wu liu you xian gong sis hang biao qin quan jou fen yi an (TMT Trading Ltd. claim against CNBM Investment Co. Ltd. for trade mark) Sui-Zhong-Fa-Min-Zhi-Chu-Zi No.989 (2004), (Guangzhou Intermediate People's Court, Oct. 17, 2005).

Zhongqing Zenton yiao yei you xian gong si, Guo jia gong shang xing zheng zong qu shang biao ping shen wei yuan hei su Sichuan Huashu dong wu yiao ye you xian gong si shan biao xing zheng jiu fen zai shen an (Retrial for the Trademark Dispute between Zhongqing Zenton Medicine Co. Ltd. and State Administration for Industry & Commerce and Sichuan Huashu Animal Pharmacy C. Ltd.), [2007] Xing Ti Zi No. 2 (Beijing High People's Court, Aug. 31, 2007), available at <http://www.lexiscn.com/law/content_case_analysis.php?case_id=119102&keyword=&t_kw=&eng=0>.

Zui gao ren ming fa yuan shen li Yidali fei lie luo gong si su Mengtesa (Zhangjiagang), Tianjin jing ji ji su kai fa qu Zhengyuan xing xiao yiu xian gong si bu zheng dang jing zheng jiu fen ti shen an (Italian Ferrero SPA claim agist Montresor Company and Zhengyuan Company for unfair competition), Ming-San-Ti-Zi No. 3(2006), (Supreme People's Court, Mar. 24, 2008).

Zui gao ren ming fa yue guan yu fei hang xing yu guo ji hang xian de wo guo chuan buo zai wo guo hai yu ziao qeng you wu sun hai de min shi pei chang zo ren shi yong fa lu wen ti de ching shi de da fu (The Supreme People's Court in respond to Legal Question concerning Civil Liability for Oil Pollution Damage Caused by National Vessels within Territorial Waters), Min-Si-Ta-Zi No. 20 (2008), (Supreme People's Court, July 3, 2008).

European Court of Human Rights (Alphabetical)

Andrejeva v. Latvia, Application no. 55707/00, para. 74 (Feb. 18, 2009). <http://cmiskp.echr.coe.int/tkp197/view.asp?item=1&portal=hbkm&action=html&highlight=55707/00&sessionid=65046055&skin=hudoc-en>.

Burden v. the United Kingdom [GC], App. No. 13378/05, (Apr. 29, 2008), <http://cmiskp.echr.coe.int/tkp197/view.asp?item=1&portal=hbkm&action=html&highlight=13378/05&sessionid=65046055&skin=hudoc-en>

Chassagnou and Others v. France, App. Nos. 25088/94, 28331/95 and 28443/95, (Apr. 4, 1999), <http://cmiskp.echr.coe.int/tkp197/view.asp?item=1&portal= hb km&action=html&highlight=25088/94&sessionid=65046055&skin=hudoc-en>.

Dudgeon v. the United Kingdom, App. No. 7525/76, (Oct.12, 1981), <http://cmiskp.echr.coe.int/tkp197/view.asp?action=html&documentId=695350&portal=hbkm&source=externalbydocnumber&table=F69A27FD8FB86142BF01C1166DEA398649>.

European Union (Alphabetical)

C 106/77, Amministrazione delle Finanze dello Stato v Simmenthal SpA., 1978 E.C.R. 629.

Case C-268/99 Aldona Malgorzata Jany and Others v Staatssecretaris van Justitie, 2001 ECR 8615.

Case C-311/04, Algemene Scheeps Agentuur Dordrecht BV v. Inspecteur der Belastingdienst -Douanedistrict Rotterdam, 2006 ECR 609.

Case C-245/02, Anheuser-Busch Inc. V Budějovický Budvar, národní podnik, 2004 ECR 10989.

Case C-260/08, Bundesfinanzdirektion West v. HEKO Industrieerzeugnisse GmbH, 2009 ECR I-0000

Case 9/73, Carl Schlüter v Hauptzollamt Lörrach, 1973 ECR 1135.
Case C-61/94, Commission v. Federal Republic of Germany, 1996 ECR 3989.
Case 10/61, Commission of the European Economic Community v. Italian Republic, 1962 ECR 1.
Case 87/75, Conceria Daniele Bresciani v Amministrazione Italiana delle Finanze. 1976 ECR 129.
Case 70/87, Federation de l'industrie de l'huilerie de la CEE (Fediol) v Commission of the European Communities. Common commercial policy, 1989 ECR 1781.
Case C-280/93, Federal Republic of Germany v Council of the European Union, 1994 ECR 4973.
Case 6/64, Flaminio Costa v E.N.E.L., 1964 E.C.R. *585*.
Case 112/80, Firma Anton Dürbeck v Commission of the European Communities, 1982 ECR 1251.
Case 28/67, Firma Molkerei-Zentrale Westfalen/Lippe GmbH v. Hauptzollamt Paderborn, 1968 ECR. 143.
Case 104/81, Hauptzollamt (Chief Tax Office) Mainz v. C. A. Kupferberg & Cie KG A.A., 1982 ECR 3641.
Case C-53/96, Hermès International (a partnership limited by shares) v FHT Marketing Choice BV, 1998 ECR 3603.
Case C-377/02, Léon Van Parys NV v. Belgisch Interventie-en Restitutiebureau (BIRB), 2005 ECR 1465.
Case 218/83, Les Rapides Savoyards Sàrl and others v Directeur Général des Douanes et Droits Indirects, 1984 ECR 3105.
Case C-265/03, Igor Simutenkov v Ministerio de Educación y Cultura and Real Federación Española de Fútbol, 2005 ECR 2579.
Case C-69/89, Nakajima All Precision Co. Ltd v Council of the European Communities, 1991 ECR 2069.
Case 4/73, J. Nold, Kohlen- und Baustoffgroßhandlung v Commission of the European Communities, 1974 ECR. 491.
Case 26/62, NV Algemene Transport-en Expeditie Onderneming van Gend & Loos v. Neth. Inland Revenue Admin., 1963 ECR 1.
Case C-307/99, OGT Fruchthandelsgesellschaft mbH v. Hauptzollamt Hamburg, 2001 ECR 3159.
Case 181/73, R. & V. Haegeman v Belgian State, 1974 E.C.R. 449.
Case 7/81, Pabst & Richarz KG v Hauptzollamt Oldenburg. Pabst & Richarz KG v Hauptzollamt Oldenburg, 1982 E.C.R. 1331.
Case C-93/02 P, Biret International SA v. Council of the European Union, 2003 ECR 10497.

Case C-300/98, Parfums Christian Dior SA v TUK Consultancy BV and Assco Gerüste GmbH and Rob van Dijk v Wilhelm Layher GmbH & Co. KG and Layher BV, 2000 ECR 11307.

Case C-76/00 P, Petrotub SA and Republica SA v. Council and Commission, 2003 ECR 79.

Case C-149/96, Portuguese Republic v Council of the European Union, 1999 ECR 8395.

Case C-335/05, Řízení Letového Provozu ČR, s. p. v Bundesamt für Finanzen, 2007 ECR 4307

Case C-89/99, Schieving-Nijstad vof and Others v Robert Groeneveld, 2001 ECR 5851.

Case 266/81, Società Italiana per l'Oleodotto Transalpino (SIOT) v Ministero delle finanze, Ministero della marina mercantile, Circoscrizione doganale di Trieste and Ente autonomo del porto di Trieste, 1983 ECR 731.

Case 126/83, STS Consorzio per Sistemi di Telecomunicazione via Satellite SpA v Commission of the European Communities, 1984 ECR 2769.

Case C-257/99, The Queen v Secretary of State for the Home Department, ex parte Julius Barkoci and Marcel Malik, 2001 ECR 6557.

Case C-63/99; Case C-253/99, The Queen v Secretary of State for the Home Department, ex parte Eleanora Ivanova Kondova, 2001 ECR 6427.

Case C-308/06, The Queen on the application of International Association of Independent Tanker Owners (Intertanko) and others v. Secretary of State for Transport, 2008 ECR I-4057.

Joined Cases 267/81, 268/81 and 269/81, Amministrazione delle Finanze dello Stato v Società Petrolifera Italiana SpA (SPI) and SpA Michelin Italiana (SAMI), 1983 E.C.R. 801.

Jointed Cases 290/81 and 291/81, Compagnia Singer SpA and Geigy SpA v Amministrazione delle finanze dello Stato, 1983 ECR 847.

Jointed Cases C-120/06 P and C-121/06 P, Fabbrica italiana accumulatori motocarri Montecchio SpA (FIAMM) and Fabbrica italiana accumulatori motocarri Montecchio Technologies LLC (C-120/06 P), Giorgio Fedon & Figli SpA and Fedon America, Inc. (C-121/06 P) v Council of the European Union and Commission of the European Communities, 2008 ECR 6513.

Jointed Cases 21-24/72, International Fruit Company N.V. and Others v. Produktschap voor Groenten en Fruit, 1972 ECR 121.

Joined Cases 27/00 and C-122/00, The Queen v Secretary of State for the Environment, Transport and the Regions, ex parte Omega Air Ltd (C-27/00) and Omega Air Ltd , Aero Engines Ireland Ltd and Omega Aviation Services Ltd v Irish Aviation Authority (C-122/00), 2002 ECR 2569.

Jointed Case C-477/05 and 488/05, Thomson Multimedia Sales Europe and Vestel France v Administration des douanes et droits indirects, 2007 ECR 2049.

Jointed Cases C-402 & 415/05, Yassin Abdullah Kadi and Al Barakaat International Foundation v. Council of the European Union and Commission of the European Communities, 2008 ECR 6351.

Opinion 1/94, Competence of the Community to conclude international agreements concerning services and the protection of intellectual property, 1994 ECR 5267.

GATT/WTO (Alphabetical)

Appellate Body Report, European Communities – Regime for the Importation, Sale and Distribution of Bananas, WT/DS27/AB/R (Sep. 9, 1997).

– European Communities-Antidumping Duties on Imports of Cotton-Type Bed Linen from India (EC-Bed Linen), WT/DS141/AB/R (Mar. 1, 2001).

– European Communities- Measures Affecting Meat and Meat Products (Hormones), WT/DS26/AB/R, WT/DS48/AB/R (Jan.16, 1998).

– European Communities-Trade Description of Sardines (EC-Sardines), WT/DS231/AB/R (Sep. 22, 2002) – Japan – Taxes on Alcoholic Beverages, WT/DS8/AB/R, WT/DS10/AB/R, WT/DS11/AB/R, (Oct. 4, 1996).

– United States-Definite Safeguard Measures on Certain Steel Products (US-Steel Safeguards), WT/DS248/AB/R, WT/DS249/AB/R, WT/DS251/AB/R, WT/DS252/AB/R, WT/DS253/AB/R, WT/DS254/AB/R, WT/DS258/AB/R, WT/DS259/AB/R (Nov. 11, 2003).

– United States-Laws, Regulations and Methodology for Calculating Dumping Margins (US-Zeroing (EC)), WT/DS294/AB/R (Apr. 18, 2006).

– United States- Imposition of Countervailing Duties on Certain Hot-Rolled Lead and Bismuth Carbon Steel Products Originating in the United Kingdom (US- Lead and Bismuth II), WT/DS138/AB/R (May 10, 2000).

– United States - Measure Affecting Imports of Woven Wool Shirts and Blouses from India, p.19, WT/DS33/AB/R (Apr. 25, 1997).

– United States-Measures Relating to Zeroing and Sunset Reviews (US-Zeroing (Japan)), WT/DS322/AB/R (Jan. 9, 2007).

Article 21.5 Panel Report, Australia – Subsidies Provided to Producers and Exporters of Automotive Leather (Australia – Automotive Leather II), WT/DS 126/RW (Jan. 21, 2000).

Article 22.6 Arbitration Report, European Communities – Measures Concerning Meat and Meat Products (Hormones), WT/DS26/ARB (July 12, 1999).

Panel Report, Argentina – Measures Affecting Imports of Footwear, Textiles, Apparel and other *Items* (*Argentina – Textiles and Apparel*), WT/DS56/R (Nov. 25, 1997).

- Australia – Subsidies Provided to Producers and Exporters of Automotive Leather, WT/DS126/R (May 25, 1999).
- China – Measures Affecting the Protection and Enforcement of Intellectual Property Rights (China-Intellectual Property Right), WT/DS362/R (Mar. 20, 2009).
- Guatemala – Anti-Dumping Investigation Regarding Portland Cement from Mexico, WT/DS60/R (June 19, 1998).
- Norway-Procurement of Toll Collection Equipment for the City of Trondheim, BSID 40S/319 (May 13, 1992).
- United States – Anti-Dumping and Countervailing Measures on Steel Plate from India (US-Steel Plate), WT/DS206/R (Oct.4, 2002).
- United States – Sections 301-310 of the Trade Act of 1974 (US-Section 301 Trade Act), WT/DS152/R (January 27, 2000).

Decision by the Arbitrators, European Communities – Regime for the Importation, Sale and Distribution of Bananas – Recourse to Arbitration by the European Communities, WT/DS27/ARB/ECU (Mar. 24, 2000).

International Court of Justice and Permanent Court of International Justice (Alphabetical)

Corfic Channel case, 1949 I.C.J. 4, 23(Apr. 9).

Free Zones of Upper Savoy and District of Gex, 1929 P.C.I.J. (ser. A) No. 22, at 13 (Aug. 19).

Interpretation of Peace Treaties, 1950 I.C.J. 65, 77 (Mar. 30).

Interpretation of Peace Treaties (second phase), 1950 I.C.J.221, 229(July 18).

The United States (Alphabetical)

American Express Co. v. United States, 332 F. Supp.191 (Cust. Ct. 1971), affirmed, 472 F. 2d 1050 (C.C.P.A. 1973).

American Insurance Association v. Garamendi, 539 U.S. 396 (2003).

Arizona v. California, 373 U.S. 546 (1963).

Allegheny Ludlum Corp. v. United States, 367 F. 3d 1339 (Fed. Cir. 2004).

Bethlem Steel Corporation v. Board of Commissioners, 276 Cal. App. 2d. 80 (1969).

Bethlehem Steel Corporation v. Board of Commissioners, 276 Cal. App. 2d 221, 80 Cal. Rptr. 800 (1969).

Calnetics Corp. v. Volkswagen of America Inc., 532 F. 2d 674 (9th Cir.), cert. denied, 429 U.S. 940 (1976).

Caterpillar, Inc. v. United States, 941 F. Supp. 1241 (Ct. Int'l Trade 1996).

Chevron U.S.A. Inc. v. Natural Res. Def. Council Inc., 467U.S. 837 (1984).
Chicago & South Airlines Inc. v. Waterman S.S. Corp., 333 U.S. 103 (1948).
Crosby v. National Foreign Council, 530 U.S. 363 (2000).
Cook v. United States, 288 U.S.102 (1933).
Corus Staal BV v. Dep't of Commerce (Corus I), 259 F. Supp. 2d. 1253 (Ct. Int'l Trade 2003).
Corus Staal BV v. Department of Commerce, 395 F.3d 1343 (Fed. Cir. 2005).
Corus Staal BV v. United States, 502 F.3d 1370 (Fed. Cir. 2007).
Factor v. Laubenheimer, 290 U.S. 276(1932).
Foster v. Neilson, 27 U.S.253 (1829).
Footwear Distributors and Retailers of America v. United States, 18 C.I.T. 391, 410; 852 F. Supp 1078 (Ct. Int'l Trade 1994).
Fuji v. States, 38 Cal. 2d. 718 (1952).
Fujian Lianfu Forestry Co., Ltd. v. United States, 638 F. Supp. 2d 1325 (Ct. Int'l Trade, 2009).
George E. Warren Corp. v. Environmental Protection. Agency, 159 F.3d 616, 624 (D.C. Cir. 1998).
Head Money Cases (Edye and Another v. Robertson, Collector – Cunard Steamship Company v. Robertson), 112 U.S. 580 (1884).
Hines v. Davidowitz, 312 U.S. 52(1941).
Holm & Co. v. Hardin, 449 F. 2d 1009 (D.C. Cir. 1971).
Hyundai Elecs. Co. v. United States, 53 F. Supp. 2d 1334 (Ct. Int'l Trade 1999).
Japan Lines Ltd v. County of Los Angeles , 441 U.S. 434 (1979).
JTEKT Corp. v. United States, SLIP OP. 2009-147(Ct. Int'l Trade, 2009).
Koyo Seiko Co. v. United States, 551 F.3d 1286 (Fed. Cir. 2008).
Kolovrat v. Oregon, 366 U.S. 187, 194 (1961).
K.S.B. Technical Sales Corp. v. North Jersey Water Supply Comm'n, 75 N.J. 272,279, 381 A. 2d 774 (1977), appeal dismissed, 435 U.S. 982 (1978).
Maple Leaf Fish Co. v. United States,762 F. 2d 86, 89 (Fed. Cir.1985).
Murray v. Schooner Charming Betsy, 6 U.S. (2 Cranch) 64 (1804).
National Foreign Council v. Nations,181 F.3d 38 (1st Cir. 1999).
NSK Ltd. v. United States, 510 F.3d 1375 (Fed. Cir. 2007).
Public Citizen v. Office of United States Trade Representative, 804 F. Supp. 385, 388 (1992).
Reid v. Covert, 354 U.S. 1, 16 (1957).
Roca v. Thompson, 23 U.S. 332 (1912).
Sanchez-Llamas v. Oregon, 548 U.S. 331 (2006).
Schroder v. Bissell, 5 F 2d. 838, 845 (D. Conn.1925).
Searing Indus. v. United States, SLIP OP. 2009-129 (Ct. Int'l Trade, 2009).
Select Tier Salvage Co. v. United States, 386 F.2d 1008 (Ct. Claims, 1967).

SKF USA Inc. v. United States, 611 F. Supp. 2d 1351 (Ct. Int'l Trade, 2009).
Spector v. Norwegian Cruise Line Ltd., 545 U.S. 119 (2005).
Suramericana de Aleaciones Laminadas v. United States, 966 F.2d 660 (1992).
Timken Co. v. U.S., 354 F. 3d 1334 (Fed. Cir. 2004).
Territory of Hawaii v. Ho, 41 Haw. 565, 568 (1957).
United States v. Belmont, 301 U.S. 324 (1937).
United States v. Guy W. Capps Inc., 240 F. 2d 655 (4th Cir. 1953).
United States v. Hammond Legal Products Inc., 440 F. 2d. 1024,1031 (C.C.P.A), cert. denied, 404 U.S. 1005 (1971).
United States v. Pink, 315 U.S. 203 (1942).
United States v. one Bag of Paradise Feathers, 256 F. 301, 306 (2d Cir. 26, 1919).
United States v. Star Industries, Inc., 59 C.C.P.A. 159; 462 F.2d 557(1972).
United States v. Yoshida International Inc., 526 F. 2d 560 (C.C.P.A. 1975).
United States v. Yoshida International, Inc, 526 F. 2d 560 (C.C.P.A. 1975); Select Tire Salvage Co. v. United States, 386 F.2d 1008 (Ct. Claims, 1967).
Zenith Radio Corp. v. United States, 437 U.S. 443(1978).

Statutes, Decrees and other official documents of China and Taiwan

China, People's Republic of China (Chronological)

Resolution of the Standing Committee of NPC on the Strengthening of Legal Interpretation Work, (promulgated by Standing Committee of NPC, June 10, 1981), available at <http://www.lexiscn.com/law/content.php?provider_id=1&isEnglish=N&origin_id=66730&eng=0&keyword=&t_kw=>.
Constitution of Peoples' Republic of China (promulgated by National People's Congress, Dec. 4, 1982, latest amendment Mar. 14, 2004), available at <http://www.npc.gov.cn/englishnpc/Constitution/node_2825.htm>.
Patent Law of the People's Republic of China (promulgated by Standing Committee National People's Congress, Mar. 12, 1984, revised on Dec. 27, 2008), available at <http://law.npc.gov.cn:87/page/browseotherlaw.cbs?rid=en&bs=98139&anchor=0#go0>.
Law of Succession of the People's Republic of China (promulgated by Standing Committee National People's Congress, April 10, 1985, effectively Oct. 1, 1985), available at <http://law.npc.gov.cn:87/page/browseotherlaw.cbs?rid=en&bs=97364&anchor=0#go0>.
Regulations of the People's Republic of China concerning Diplomatic Privileges and Immunities (promulgated by Standing Committee National People's Con-

gress Sep. 5, 1986, effectively Sep. 5, 1986), available at <http://www.lexiscn.com/law/content.php?lawid=146191>.

Frontier Health and Quarantine Law of the People's Republic of China (promulgated by the Standing Committee National People's Congress, Dec. 2, 1986; revised Dec. 29, 2007), available at <http://law.npc.gov.cn:87/page/browseotherlaw.cbs?rid=en&bs=97400&anchor=0#go0>.

Circular of Supreme People's Court on Implementing Convention on the Recognition and Enforcement of Foreign Arbitral Awards Entered by China, Fa Jing Fa [1987] No. 5, (promulgated on Oct. 4, 1987), available at <http://www.lexiscn. com/law/law-english-1-492246.html>.

Provision on Several Issues concerning Treatments of Cases Involving Foreign Factors, Fa Fa [1987] No. 54, (promulgated by Supreme People's Court, Aug. 27, 1987), available at <http://www.lexiscn.com/law/content.php?provider_id=1&isEnglish=N&origin_id=276261&eng=0&keyword=&t_kw=>.

Opinions of the Supreme People's Court on Several Issues concerning the Implementation of the General Principles of the Civil Law of the People's Republic of China, Fa Ban Fa[1988] No. 6 (promulgated on Jan. 26, 1988), available at <http://www.lexiscn.com/law/law-english-1-234065.html>.

Administrative Litigation Law of the People's Republic of China (promulgated by the Standing Committee National People's Congress, Apr. 4, 1989, effectively Oct.1, 1990), available at <http://www.lexiscn.com/law/content.php?lawid=535696>.

Law of the People's Republic of China on the Procedure of the Conclusion of Treaties , (promulgated by the Standing Committee National People's Congress, Dec. 28, 1990, effective Dec. 28, 1990) available at <http://law.npc.gov.cn:87/page/browseotherlaw.cbs?rid=en&bs=97568&anchor=0#go0>.

Civil Procedure Law of the People's Republic of China (promulgated by the Standing Committee National People's Congress, Apr. 9, 1991; revised on Oct. 28, 2007), available at <http://law.npc.gov.cn:87/page/browseotherlaw.cbs?rid=en&bs=97585&anchor=0#go0>.

Foreign Trade Law of the People's Republic of China (promulgated by Standing Committee National People's Congress, May 12, 1994, revised on April 6, 2004), available at <http://law.npc.gov.cn:87/page/browseotherlaw.cbs?rid=en&bs=194917&anchor=0#go0>.

Individual Income Tax Law of the People's Republic of China (promulgated by the Standing Committee National People's Congress, Dec 25, 1995, revised on Dec., 27, 2007), available at <http://law.npc.gov.cn:87/page/browseotherlaw.cbs?rid=en&bs=271230&anchor=0#go0>.

Provisions of the People's Republic of China on the Use of Red Cross Signs (promulgated by The State Council, Jan. 29, 1996, effectively Jan. 29, 1996), available at <http://www.asianlii.org/cn/legis/cen/laws/potuorcs420/>.
Law of the People's Republic of China for Countering Unfair Competition, (promulgated by Standing Committee National People's Congress, Sep. 2, 1993, effectively Sep. 2,1993), available at <http://www.lexiscn.com/law/law-english-4-043A80047.00007B00.2A01.html>.
Custom Law of the Republic of China (promulgated by the Standing Committee National People's Congress, Sep. 10, 1998, revised on July 8, 2000), available at <http://law.npc.gov.cn:87/page/browseotherlaw.cbs?rid=en&bs=271230&anchor=0#go0>.
Patent Law of the People's Republic of China (promulgated by Standing Committee National People's Congress, Mar. 12, 1984, revised on Dec. 27, 2008), available at <http://www.lexiscn.com/law/law-english-1-480068.html>.
Regulations for the Implementation of Copyright Treaties, (promulgated by State Council, Sep. 25, 1992, effectively Sep. 25, 1992), available at <http://www.lexiscn.com/law/content.php?lawid=136780>.
Opinion on Making the Adjudicative Function Fully to Support and to Provide Legal Service for the Economic Development), Section 4, Subsection 2, Fa Fa [2000] No. 8, (promulgated by Supreme People's Court, Mar. 8, 2000) available at <http://www.lexiscn.com/law/content.php?provider_id=3&isEnglish=N&origin_id=113503200001&eng=0&keyword=&t_kw=zqq%2BrbzDt6LVuczhuanLvreosaPVz7rNt6jCybf%2BzvG1xNLivPs%3D>.
The Law of the People's Republic of China on Legislation (promulgated by the Standing Committee of National People's Congress, Mar. 15, 2000, effectively July, 1, 2000) 2000 Standing Committee of National People's Congress Gazette 112 (P.R.C.).
Circulation of the Supreme People's Court on Several Noteworthy Issues concerning Adjudication and Implementation of Civil and Commercial Matters involving Foreign Factors), Paragraph 2, Fa [2000] No. 51, (promulgated by Supreme People's Court, Apr. 17, 2000), available at <http://www.lexiscn.com/law/content.php?provider_id=1&isEnglish=N&origin_id=265156&eng=0&keyword=&t_kw=>.
Issues Necessary for Implementing the Five Principles for the Reform of the Administrative Examination and Approval System, (2001) Guo-Shen-Gai-Fa No. 1 (promulgated by the State Council, Dec. 11, 2001), available at <http://www.lexiscn.com/law/content.php?provider_id=1&isEnglish=N&origin_id=30034&eng=0&keyword=&t_kw=udjT2rnhs7nQ0NX%2ByfPF%2BtbGtsi4xLjvtcTO5c%2Fu1K3U8tDo0qqw0c7VtcS8uLj2zsrM4g%3D%3D>.

Administrative Measures for Adopting the International Criteria (promulgated by General Administration of Quality Supervision, Inspection and Quarantine of the People's Republic of China, Jan. 5, 2002, effectively Jan. 5, 2002), available at <http://www.lexiscn.com/law/content.php?provider_id=2&isEnglish=N&origin_id=38502&eng=0&keyword=&t_kw=>.

Regulation for the Implementation of the Trademark Law of the People's Republic of China (promulgated by the State Council, Aug. 3, 2002, effectively Sep. 15, 2003), available at <http://www.lexiscn.com/law/law-english-1-228726.html>.

Provisions of the Supreme People's Court on Several Issues Concerning the Trial of Administrative Cases of International Trade, Fa Shi [2002] No. 27 (promulgated by Supreme People's Court, Aug. 27, 2002), available at <http://www.lexiscn.com/law/law-english-1-229715.html>.

Provision of the Supreme People's Court on Several Issues Concerning the Laws applicable for the Review of the Countervailing Measures, Fa Shi [2002] No. 36, (promulgated by the Supreme People's Court, Nov. 21, 2002), available at <http://www.lexiscn.com/law/content.php?provider_id=1&isEnglish=N&origin_id=262873&eng=0&keyword=&t_kw=t7Q%3D>.

Provision of the Supreme People's Court on Several Issues Concerning the Laws applicable for the Review of the Anti-dumping Measures, Fa Shi [2002] No. 35, (promulgated by Supreme People's Court, Nov. 21, 2002, available at <http://www.lexiscn.com/law/content.php?provider_id=2&isEnglish=N&origin_id=43818&eng=0&keyword=&t_kw=t7Q%3D>.

Regulations of the Origin of Imported/Exported Goods of the People's Republic of China (promulgated by The State Council on September 3, 2004, effectively Jan. 1, 2005), available at <http://www.lexiscn.com/law/content.php?lawid=228136>

Zui gao ren min fa yaun fu yuan zhang Cao Jianming zai quan guo fa yuan zhi shi cai chan qan shen pan gong zuo zuo tan hui de jiang hua (Speech of Deputy Chief of Supreme People's Court in the National Workshop on the Adjudication of the Intellectual Property Rights), (circulated Jan. 18, 2007), available at <http://law1.chinalawinfo.com/newlaw2002/slc/slc.asp?db=chl&gid=110259>.

Crew Regulation of the People's Republic of China (promulgated by the State Council, Apr. 14, 2007, effectively Sep. 1, 2007), available at <http://www.gov.cn/flfg/2007-04/29/content_602810.htm>.

Border Health and Quarantine Law of People's Republic of China (Promulgated by Standing Committee National People's Congress, Dec. 29, 2007, effectively Dec. 29, 2007), available at <http://www.lexiscn.com/law/content.php?lawid=233127>.

Detailed Implementing Rules for the Patent Law of the People's Republic of China (promulgated by the State Council, Jan. 9, 2010, effectively Feb. 9, 2010), available at <http://www.lexiscn.com/law/law-english-1-530667.html>.

Taiwan, Republic of China (Chronological)

Copyright Act, (promulgated on May 14, 1928, latest amendment on Feb. 10, 2010), available at <http://law.moj.gov.tw/Eng/LawClass/LawAll.aspx?PCode=J0070017>.

Fisheries Act (Promulgated on Nov. 11, 1929, latest amendment on Jan. 9, 2008), available at <http://law.moj.gov.tw/Eng/LawClass/LawAll.aspx?PCode=M0050001>.

民法總則篇立法原則 (Legislative Principles for the Part of General Principles of the Civil), 1 Legislative Digest15-16 (1929).

訓字第459 號訓令 (The Oder to Ministry of Judicial Administration No. 459), July 27, 1931, 中華民國六法理由判解全編, Vol. 1, 8(1964).

Postal Act (promulgated July 5, 1935, latest amendment on July 10, 2002), available at <http://law.moj.gov.tw/Eng/LawClass/LawAll.aspx?PCode=K0050001>.

Patent Act (promulgated on Mar. 25, 1944, latest amendment on Aug. 25, 2010), available at <http://law.moj.gov.tw/Eng/LawClass/LawAll.aspx?PCode=J0070007>.

Constitution of Republic of China (promulgated on Dec. 25, 1947), available at <http://www.judicial.gov.tw/constitutionalcourt/en/p07_2.asp?lawno=36>.

Civil Aviation Act (promulgated on May 30, 1953, latest amendment on Jan. 23, 2009), available at <http://law.moj.gov.tw/Eng/LawClass/LawContent.aspx?PCODE=K0090001>.

Law of the Enforcement of the Request for the International Judicial Assistance (promulgated on Apr. 25, 1963), available at <http://law.moj.gov.tw/LawClass/LawAll.aspx?PCode=B0010014>.

Central Regulation Standard Act (promulgated on Aug. 31, 1970, latest amendment on May 19, 2004), available at <http://law.moj.gov.tw/Eng/LawClass/LawAll.aspx?PCode=A0030133>.

J.Y. Interpretation No.154, paragraph 2 of the reasoning (Sep. 29, 1978), available at <http://www.judicial.gov.tw/constitutionalcourt/p03_01.asp?expno=154>.

Law of Extradition (promulgated on July 14, 1980), available at <http://law.moj.gov.tw/Eng/LawClass/LawAll.aspx?PCode=I0030001>.

Shipping Law (promulgated on June 3, 1981, latest amendment on Jan. 30, 2002), available at <http://law.moj.gov.tw/Eng/LawClass/LawContent.aspx?PCODE=K0070001>.

法律字第 1813 號, (promulgated by Ministry of Justice, Feb. 21, 1983), available at <http://jirs.judicial.gov.tw/Index.htm>.

Regulation Governing the Implementation of the Imposition of Countervailing and Anti-dumping Duties (promulgated on Nov. 7, 1984, latest amendment on Feb. 23, 2005), available at <http://law.moj.gov.tw/Eng/LawClass/ LawAll.aspx?PCode=G0350034>.

74內字 24097號函 (promulgated by Executive Yuan, Dec. 30, 1985).

77法參字第 20108 號 (promulgated by Ministry of Justice, Nov. 19, 1989), available at <http://jirs.judicial.gov.tw/Index.htm>.

The Draft of Trade Act, 院總字1534號, 45, 1 st Legislative Yuan, 84 th Sess., 17th mtg., (Nov. 29, 1989), available at <http://lis.ly.gov.tw/lgcgi/lgmeetimage?cfcec7cbcecccfcfc5c7cfd2c6c8>.

Hearing before the Economic Committee and Judiciary Committee on the proposal of Trade Law, 1st Legislative Yuan, 86 Sess., Nov. 17,1990 (statement of Chiang, Ping-kun, Deputy Mister of Economic Affairs), 80(46) LEGISLATIVE YUAN GAZETTE 276,277(1990);

Hearing before the Economic Committee and Judiciary Committee on the proposal of Trade Law, 1 st Legislative Yuan, 86 Sess., Nov 21,1990 (statement of Hu, Ko-sheng, Director General of Bureau of Foreign Trade), 80(48) LEGISLATIVE YUAN GAZETTE 246,253(1990).

Foreign Trade Act, (promulgated on Feb. 5, 1993, latest amendment on Jan. 13, 2010), available at <http://law.moj.gov.tw/Eng/LawClass/LawAll.aspx?PCode=J0090004>.

Second Reading of Foreign Trade Act, Jan. 12, 1993, 82(3) Legislative Yuan Gazette 33, 57(1993).

J.Y. Interpretation No. 329 (Dec.24, 1993), available at <http://www.judicial.gov.tw/constitutionalcourt/EN/p03_01_printpage.asp?expno=329>.

J.Y. Interpretation No. 392 (Feb. 22, 1995), available at <http://www.judicial.gov.tw/constitutionalcourt/en/p03_01.asp?expno=392>.

J.Y. Interpretation No. 372 (Feb. 24, 1995), available at <http://www.judicial.gov.tw/constitutionalcourt/en/p03_01.asp?expno=372>.

The Act of Capture of Ships and Cargos (promulgated on June 2, 1995), available at <http://law.moj.gov.tw/LawClass/LawAll.aspx?PCode=F0120006>.

J.Y. Interpretation No. 428, paragraph 3 of the reasoning (May 23, 1997), available at <http://www.judicial.gov.tw/constitutionalcourt/en/p03_01_printpage.asp?expno=428>.

Law of Exclusive Economic Zone and Continental Shelf of Republic of China, (promulgated on Jan. 21, 1998), available at <http://law.moj.gov.tw/Eng/LawClass/LawAll.aspx?PCode=A0000010>.

Law on the Territorial Sea and the Contiguous Zone of the Republic of China (promulgated on Jan. 21, 1998), available at <http://law.moj.gov.tw/Eng/Law Class/LawContent.aspx?PCODE=A0000009>.

Legislative Competence Exercise Act, (promulgated on Jan. 25, 1999, latest amendment on June 15, 2010), available at <http://law.moj.gov.tw/LawClass/LawAll.aspx?PCode=A0020058>.

Hearing before the Foreign and National Defence Committee and Economics Committee, the 4 th Legislative Yuan, 2nd Session, Nov. 22, 1999, 88(54) Legislative Yuan Gazette 39.

Minutes of the 7 th Meeting, 6 th Session, the Fourth Legislative Yuan, Nov. 16, 2001, 90 (57) Legislative Yuan Gazette 4, 15-28 (2001).

Fair Trade Act (promulgated on Feb. 4, 2002, latest amendment on June 9, 2010), available at <http://law.moj.gov.tw/Eng/LawClass/LawAll.aspx?PCode=J0150002>.

法律字 0910005828 (promulgated by Ministry of Justice, Mar. 20), 2002, available at <http://jirs.judicial.gov.tw/Index.htm>.

J.Y. Interpretation No. 587 (Dec. 30, 2004), available at <http://www.judicial.gov.tw/constitutionalcourt/en/p03_01.asp?expno=587>.

The Commercial Port Law (promulgated on May 2, 1980, latest amendment on Feb. 5, 2005), available at <http://law.moj.gov.tw/Eng/LawClass/LawAll.aspx?PCode=K0080001>.

Nationality Act (promulgated on Jan. 27, 2006) <http://law.moj.gov.tw/Eng/LawClass/LawContent.aspx?PCODE=D0030001>.

Telecommunications Act, (promulgated on Dec. 23, 1958, latest amendment on July 11, 2007), available at <http://law.moj.gov.tw/Eng/LawClass/LawAll.aspx?PCode=K006000>.

Kolibri 360 GmbH
Ferdinand-Jühlke-Straße 7
99095 Erfurt, Deutschland
produktsicherheit@kolibri360.de